Crime Scene Investigator (CSI) Field Guide

Crime Scene Investigator (CSI) Field Guide is a convenient and handy reference guide ideally suited for use in the field by crime scene investigators (CSIs), both sworn and civilian. In addition to the field, it can also be used in the classroom as a comprehensive refresher as part of formal training.

A shift in personnel has occurred in forensic science over the past few years, and the "old school" detectives, older sworn personnel, are retiring—leaving it to newer, younger, but more inexperienced civilian personnel to take their place. As a result, and as new technologies are developed and training advances, this book will help bridge the gap between the "new" and the "old," the classroom and the field. CSI training is broadly extensive, though it can often vary in depth. In addition, it is not possible for a CSI to retain absolutely everything that they have been taught while mentally processing the scene they are involved in. This book seeks to address this by covering information for troubleshooting photographs; evidence collection, including what evidence to look for and process; and checklists for several types of scenes to ensure all necessary actions are taken.

A reliable reference to confirm steps, reference a chemical field test, or verify the necessary equipment required, the Crime Scene Investigator (CSI) Field Guide serves as an invaluable on-scene tool to any new or seasoned CSI professional.

Sarah Lambert holds a master's degree in forensic science from Nebraska Wesleyan University and worked as a crime scene investigator for over 12 years running all types of scenes. Sarah worked in Stockton, California, and Houston, Texas for the Crime Scene Unit responding to all evidence-related calls, including burglary, robbery, domestic violence, homicide, officer-involved shootings, as well as processing crime scene vehicles. Sarah is a certified senior crime scene analyst and member through the International Association for Identification (IAI) and a certified forensic manager 1 from the National Forensic Science Academy.

Crime Scene Investigator (CSI) Field Guide

Sarah Lambert

CRC Press
Taylor & Francis Group
Boca Raton London New York

CRC Press is an imprint of the
Taylor & Francis Group, an **informa** business

Designed cover image: Getty Images

First edition published 2026
by CRC Press
2385 NW Executive Center Drive, Suite 320, Boca Raton FL 33431

and by CRC Press
4 Park Square, Milton Park, Abingdon, Oxon, OX14 4RN

CRC Press is an imprint of Taylor & Francis Group, LLC

ISBN: 978-1-032-82293-8 (hbk)
ISBN: 978-1-032-82289-1 (pbk)
ISBN: 978-1-003-50389-7 (ebk)

DOI: 10.4324/9781003503897

Typeset in Times New Roman
by Apex CoVantage, LLC

This book is dedicated to all the CSIs out there trying to forge their way, but here are 2 you should know about.

Scottie Lambert (my grandfather, 1923–2015) who was an exemplary CSI well before my time. Although I did not learn his forensic methods (as he never brought work home), I learned his work ethic, perseverance, and motivation to pursue my interests. He retired from Buena Park Police Department in California with a strong respect for fingerprints, valuable friendships, and pride in his accomplishments.

Duane S., a valued Crime Scene Investigator from Houston, Texas who left behind a void after serving as an officer for 18 years while diligently working crime scenes and serving his community.

Contents

Acknowledgments

A special thank you to Chelsea Carpenter for reviewing the information and providing timely and highly valuable feedback. I would also like to thank Katie Busack, West Ryan, Alison Hutchens, and Chelsea Wills for the hours invested and all the wisdom they shared.

I am indebted to my family, who was graciously patient while I stayed in front of the computer weekend after weekend. You are gracious enough to support me with whatever I choose to do, and I hope I can do the same for you. Special thanks to my mom and sister for their tremendous help and support.

I would also like to thank Mark Listewnik and Ella Halstead at Taylor & Francis for making this collection possible and helping me share this mass of information, as well as the staff at Apex CoVantage.

Peer Reviewers

Having read this information in part or in full, each of these individuals contributed meaningfully to the completion of this work, and to them I extend my deepest gratitude.

Erin Bauer—Entomology Lecturer, University of Lincoln, Nebraska, Bauer brings a welcoming and educational connection to the field of entomology.

Jason Best—Chief of the Fremont Fire Department with 28 years of experience as a firefighter after starting his career in Grand Haven and has been generous with his vast knowledge and experience.

Katie Busack—CSCSA, Busack brings 14 years' experience as a CSI in Utah and Texas, bringing with her a great deal of experience and wisdom to all of the scenes she works and cases she impacts, sharing her knowledge, tools, or snacks with anyone who needs it.

Hannah Cervenka—Cervenka has spent 9 years in forensic anthropology, spending her time bringing education to the scientific community and assisting research to further knowledge in forensic anthropology and the decomposition process.

Deputy Michaila Duncan—CSCSA, Duncan has spent 9 years in the field as a CSI in Texas, becoming a genius in all things, and brings a kind face to a dark world.

Alison Hutchens—CCSA, Alison is currently an Identification Section Superintendent in Arizona with 28 years' experience with crime scenes. Alison brings a tremendous amount of experience and knowledge to this field and is currently the editor of the newsletter for the Arizona Division of the IAI.

Steve Flores—Flores spent 18 years conducting investigations and processing crime scenes in California, providing advice and support to any co-worker who needed it.

Jose Matos—CSI with 21 years' experience processing crime scenes in Puerto Rico and Texas, Matos brings a vast background and wealth of information he is happy to share with anyone who needs it.

Danielle O'Neill aka Dani—MSFS, worked as a criminalist for 4 years, served on the DC Science Advisory Board, and has published multiple articles as well as *The Criminal Investigation Handbook* and has lectured throughout the United States.

Frank Pierce—Pierce brings 30 years of experience in law enforcement, conducting investigations, collecting evidence, and assisting his peers while continuing to serve Houston, Texas.

Sandy Ramsey—MA, LPC, LMFT—30+ years in the mental health field, during which time she provided mental health services at disaster sites and mass fatalities, focusing on PTSD and vicarious trauma experienced by first responders.

Marisa Randall—MS, Randall spent 6 years in criminal justice and forensics, bringing a wealth of education to the field with a great eye for fine details.

David Reeder—With 25 years at Stockton PD, Reeder spent 11 as a homicide detective and has spent the last 6 as an Investigator for the District Attorney's Office. He was consistently professional and significantly contributed to each case.

Celia Rhodes—BS, MS, Rhodes has spent the last 6 years in forensics, working crime scenes as a CSI and for the medical examiner's office, continuing to this day to ensure the field is well educated and trained.

West Ryan—CCSA, Ryan has 4 years of experience in Houston, Texas, as a CSI and demonstrates attention to detail and organization in scene processing, and Ryan is the team member everyone needs.

Cassandra Trunk—Trunk has 18 years in the field, having begun as a CSI, always bringing a tremendous amount of experience and knowledge that she has obtained over the years while helping continue the education and training of the current generation of CSIs.

Chelsea Wills—BSc, CSI with 10 years' experience in law enforcement in jurisdictions in California, South Carolina, and North Carolina, bringing her vast knowledge base and love of helping others.

Introduction

Crime Scene Investigation is a demanding discipline—one in which mistakes can mean justice delayed or denied. In the United States alone, over 50% of murders in 2020 went unsolved.[1] Homicide clearance rates have steadily declined since the 1960s, leaving nearly *346,000* cases of homicide and non-negligent manslaughter unresolved between 1965 and 2023.[2] With more and more advanced technologies at our disposal, it is expected that we are able to leverage those tools to improve these numbers. Yet, technology alone is not enough—the integrity and precision of every Crime Scene Investigator (CSI) remains irreplaceable.

This field guide is designed to support CSIs in the complex and high-stakes process of scene investigation. Your role is critical. Once a scene is processed and released, it cannot be "revisited." Every detail matters. Every piece of evidence must be collected, documented, and preserved with the utmost care and integrity. The families impacted by these crimes deserve no less.

This guide is meant to be practical—a working tool for you in the field. It is designed to allow you to jot down notes, reminders, contact information, even doodles if they help you think. It does not replace formal training, written protocols, or agency-specific procedures.

This guide consolidates insights from a diverse group of investigators, researchers, CSIs, and educators. It encompasses methods ranging from advanced technological approaches to cost-effective solutions, recognizing the varied resources available to different agencies. I hope this guide serves as a valuable tool in the field, makes a significant contribution to ongoing investigations, and helps shape future investigative practices through the experiences of those who have preceded us.

Notes

1 Schilke, Rachel. "Half of US Homicides Go Unsolved, Ranking Last among Western Nations." *Washington Examiner*, 6 Mar. 2023, https://www.washingtonexaminer.com/news/2576215/half-of-us-homicides-go-unsolved-ranking-last-among-western-nations/.

2 Murder Accountability Project. "Murder Accountability Project." *Murder Data*, www.murderdata.org.

DOI: 10.4324/9781003503897-1

Equipment Options

1

There are various types of equipment that may be needed on the scene, included is a partial list of items that might be necessary. Understanding that each agency and CSI department work with different budgets, options for various budget levels are provided below to suit different agencies' policies and financial constraints. Regular cleaning and maintenance of equipment is essential to prevent cross-contamination and ensure high-quality processing; this includes all equipment including cameras. Having supplies ready in advance is important, although there may be situations where resources are limited, and improvisation is required. Whether collecting casings manually or using containing equipment such as an IBIS Clear Case,[1] it is crucial to understand available options beforehand to reduce mental fatigue and ensure adequate supplies. Some companies, such as Lynn Peavey Company[2] in the United States, help in customizing equipment to meet individual needs for your department. If you are unable to find suitable equipment for your agency, it is essential to continue searching. Maintaining an efficient workflow on scene is crucial, and the right equipment ensures this continuity.

Camera Equipment

- ☐ SLR or interchangeable lens camera
- ☐ Specialty camera (Crime Lite Auto,[3] UV/IR camera, etc.)
- ☐ Video camera
- ☐ Cleaning cloth/brush for internal and external wiping of moisture
- ☐ Sync cord/remote control
- ☐ Hot shoe level/bubble level
- ☐ Rubbing alcohol wipes/lens cleaning wipes
- ☐ Rain cover for camera, home-made or pre-made
- ☐ Compass for camera strap
- ☐ Reflective camera strap or tape on camera to find camera on scene
- ☐ Silicone/rubber bracelet on lens for easy adjustment—glow in dark or reflective helpful
- ☐ Detachable flashes
- ☐ Flash diffuser—diffuser, filter paper, white paper, white handkerchief
- ☐ Gray card for color metering
- ☐ Color chart or color card used for injury photographs

 DOI: 10.4324/9781003503897-2

Data Storage Cards

- ☐ + 2 for camera
- ☐ + 1 for video camera
- ☐ + 1 for digital scanner (Leica, Faro etc.)

Stabilizing Equipment, Standing Height, and Table Height

- ☐ Tripod/monopod/gimbal/beanbag/sandbags for weight

Lens

- ☐ Macro
- ☐ Extension tube—supplement lens to add macro capabilities
- ☐ Normal
- ☐ Wide angle
- ☐ Polarizing
- ☐ Macro/micro lens cell phone attachment (if using cell phone)

Filters

- ☐ Polarizing filter (reduces glare from light or water)
- ☐ UV filter—UV transmitting bandpass filter
- ☐ UV filter—clear filter, can be left on permanently for lens protection
- ☐ Macrophotography filter (place on ordinary lens for macro lens abilities)
- ☐ ALS filter (appropriate colors)

ALS Equipment Options

- ☐ Barrier filters—goggles, lens covers, sheets of colored plastic
- ☐ Equipment controls on cards or paper, laminated or in bags to prevent contamination
- ☐ Flashlights (single wavelength) or light unit (multi-wavelength)
- ☐ Orange, red, yellow, clear (UV), CSS filter (390–520nm)

Portable Lighting—*Do Not Forget to Wipe Off Screen for Brightest Output*

- ☐ Flashlights
  - ☐ High intensity for searches/night scenes
  - ☐ Lower intensity for fingerprinting
- ☐ LED handheld lights—good for viewing blood in grass, soil, water
- ☐ Blacklight for searching
- ☐ Extra scene lights/flood lights/pelican lights/portable lights for night scenes

- ☐ Headlamp (motion activated is a must have)
- ☐ Extension cords
- ☐ Car charger attachment for cords

Scales/Rulers—*Regularly Verify with NIST Traceable Ruler or Calibrate Equipment*

- ☐ ABFO #2 L scale—good for trace evidence, bite marks, bullet defects
- ☐ 300 mm L scale—good for damage, footwear, tire mark
- ☐ 6 inch scale of various colors, with circle on end—gray good for color metering, color chart good for injury photographs[4]
- ☐ Handheld measuring tape, retractable 50 and 100 feet
- ☐ Tape with printed measuring tape/ruler
- ☐ Pre-printed scales/labeled stickers/label book
- ☐ Walking measuring wheel (rolling wheel)[5]
- ☐ Laser measuring tool that works in sun/dark and for a good distance[6]
- ☐ Handheld compass
- ☐ Attach a small scale to the side of your detachable flash with Velcro for use
- ☐ Templates with sketch designs or bullet hole sizes
- ☐ Wax/dental wax to hold scales/spatter sticks in place on wall

Evidence Markers/Placards *Multiple Styles Recommended for Varying Scenes*

- ☐ Cardboard, disposable
- ☐ Plastic or metal tents with or without scale come in letters and numbers
- ☐ Stickers, fillable or pre-printed
- ☐ Scale stickers/scale tape—bullet holes, fingerprints, tool marks, blood spots, hair/fiber, curved surfaces, and so on.
- ☐ Small orange arrows for small areas and vehicles
- ☐ Reflective markers for night scene use, can be unmarked, letters or numbers[7]
- ☐ Flags for tall grass, fields, debris piles
- ☐ Driveway markers for use in fields, tall grass, large parks

PPE Equipment—*Ensure Equipment Is Not Expired. It Begins to Disintegrate Over Time*

Mask

- ☐ N95—good for decomposition, fingerprint powder
- ☐ R95—fire scene, volatile gas/fumes
- ☐ P95—keeps out biological fluids, particulates, microorganisms, smog in air

☐ Respirators, multiple types dependent upon needs—P100 filter recommended for basic crime scene

Disposable Laboratory Coats/Aprons

☐ Hair cover/shoe covers
☐ Sleeve covers—helpful for trace collection and black powder use
☐ Tyvek suits

Gloves and Gloves Liners

☐ Fingerless gloves or thin gloves for liners
☐ Thick gloves for searching through sharps
☐ Glove dispenser for belt or pocket liner recommended (sweat can transfer on to gloves in your pocket)

Disposal Receptacles

☐ Biohazard/sharps/trash/chemical

Decontaminate Equipment

☐ Bleach sprays/wipes
☐ Soap/water
☐ Waterless handwashing station

Disinfectant/Cleaning Solution for Equipment

☐ Dawn dish soap
☐ Distilled water for cleaning/rinsing
☐ Bleach source or solution

Hand Tools

☐ Bolt cutters
☐ Drywall saw
☐ Goggles/face cover
☐ Hammer
☐ Pliers
☐ Pry bars for metal and trim
☐ Rope/twine
☐ Sand scoops
☐ Screwdrivers
☐ Shovels—curved/flat/hand shovels
☐ Socket wrench set (including a universal socket is recommended)
☐ Wood chisel

Paper

- ☐ Cover sheets for photographs/video
- ☐ Fingerprint cards
- ☐ Forms, agency-specific
- ☐ Glossy backed 3 × 5 cards
- ☐ Grid paper/lined paper/blank paper
- ☐ Preprinted agency forms

Evidence Packaging/Collection

- ☐ Arson cans/bags
- ☐ Bags, paper—lunch bag, grocery sack, and lawn/leaf size recommended
  - ☐ Consider using thicker paper bags[8] that are reinforced and don't tear as easily
- ☐ Bags, rifle—(secured edge for rifles, shotguns, baseball bats, machetes, golf clubs, fire pokers, etc.[9])
- ☐ Biohazard stickers
- ☐ Boxes—gun/knife—store clean, pre-fold wearing gloves
- ☐ Cartridge case collectors of varying levels from collection to collection and storage such as Ibis Clear case,[10] Case Grabber,[11] and glassine envelopes
- ☐ Envelopes—glassine envelopes, paper envelopes (coin, 6 × 9, 10 × 13)
- ☐ Evidence tape to seal items
- ☐ Normal pens/pencils/Sharpie markers (retractable instead of lids, even Sharpie)
- ☐ Waterproof markers/pens/papers
- ☐ Paint marker for writing on tires/rubber
- ☐ Packing tape to help seal large items and large bags, to reinforce the bottom of items, and to cover corners of small items to prevent tearing
- ☐ Paper clips/rubber bands (*no staples*)
- ☐ Plastic disc containers/lid
- ☐ Test tubes/corks
- ☐ Scissors
- ☐ Paper towels

Bags

- ☐ Body bags/ID tags (single use recommended)
- ☐ Drawstring hand/foot bags or paper bags with tape (single use recommended)

Trace Evidence/DNA Collection Kit

- ☐ Evidence vacuums and new filters
- ☐ Known blood card for presumptive testing controls
- ☐ Liquid syringe
- ☐ Magnifying glass
- ☐ Pipettes—single use or cleaned
- ☐ Ruler/protractor
- ☐ Static lift/mylar/scissors
- ☐ Tweezers, angled/flat or forceps (reuseable or cleaned)
- ☐ Water for cotton (single-use ampules or refillable bottle)

Collection Medium *(DNA Free, Pick From Options Below)*

- ☐ Acrilan cloth
- ☐ Cotton tipped swabs/cotton fingernail swabs (pointed tip)
- ☐ Cotton balls
- ☐ Cotton pads
- ☐ Cotton thread #8
- ☐ Coffee filters
- ☐ Filter paper
- ☐ Gauze pads
- ☐ Nylon flocked swabs (less degradation of swab than cotton)[12]
- ☐ Polyurethane foam swabs (less degradation of swab than cotton)
- ☐ Toothpicks/nail picks

Packaging

- ☐ Butcher paper (clean, size of a bed)
- ☐ Glassine paper/craft paper
- ☐ Paper bindle (druggist fold, paper folded into envelope, can fold own or buy pre-folded bindles[13])
- ☐ Plastic bag/sheet protectors for tape lifts/narcotics

Adhesives *(Clean or Wrapped/Single Use)*

- ☐ Clean/wrapped fingerprint tape
- ☐ GSR stubs
- ☐ Gel lifters
- ☐ Lint roller
- ☐ Post-it notes

Blades

☐ Clean knife
☐ Single-use razor/scalpel blades and handles

Transient Evidence Collection Mechanism

☐ Ambient temperature/humidity gauge (recommended for all scenes)
☐ Ammonia reader (for neglect/hoarding scenes)
☐ Digital meat thermometer (for soil/liquid/maggot readings)
☐ Laser thermometer (for body/item readings)

Casting Equipment

☐ Casting frames
☐ Dental stone
☐ Distilled water
☐ Small cardboard box for transportation
☐ Zip lock bags (large) or mixing bowls/spoons

Fingerprint Kit

☐ Cards (pre-printed or 3 × 5 cards, black or white)
☐ Magnifying glass

Adhesives

☐ Fingerprint tape—1, 2, 3, or 4 inch tape, clear/frosted, hinged/rolls
☐ Gel lifters hand/finger size cut

Brushes

☐ Feather brush
☐ Fiberglass brush for regular use
☐ Horsehair brush/camelhair brush
☐ Magnetic brush

Powder

☐ Bi-chromatic powder
☐ Black powder/black magnetic powder
☐ Other powders of choice

Clean Supplies

☐ DNA-free powder (clean unused container/powder, with tape seal)
☐ DNA-free brush (new/wrapped)

- ☐ If you cannot afford treated powder/brushes, take small amount of powder from brand new container, using clean scoop/folded fingerprint card, place some powder in small disc container for single use only

Scene Re-creation Equipment

- ☐ Single-use re-creation dolls/markers
- ☐ Video camera, small LED light for soft lighting, small microphone optional

Trajectory Kit

- ☐ Angle finder/angle locator/digital angle finder
- ☐ Centering cones, rod connectors, rings
- ☐ Lasers/stand
- ☐ Leica Disto or another laser measuring device
- ☐ Level (not hot shoe level)
- ☐ Tape, masking/painters' tape
- ☐ Plumb bob on string
- ☐ String (colored, not white)/string hooks/string clips
- ☐ Protractor/half protractor, laser mount optional (forensic protractor has "zero edge" for accuracy[14])
- ☐ Rods—wooden/plastic/metal/fiberglass dowel rods, multiple of diameter options or cones to accommodate size change (can be forensic rods or home-made from hardware store)
- ☐ Scale labels/ruler tape
- ☐ Sharpie markers
- ☐ Spray fog
- ☐ Template sheet for hole size/angle
- ☐ Tips (pointed and for string attachment)
- ☐ Tripod or monopod with laser/camera mounts

Phone App Options for Scene Use

- ☐ Angle finder
- ☐ Calipers
- ☐ Compass
- ☐ Level
- ☐ Plumb bob

Search Equipment

- ☐ Endoscope camera for hard-to-see areas

- ☐ Ladder/step ladder
- ☐ Metal detector for land and water, with an arm and handheld

Magnets

- ☐ Magnet wand for small hard-to-reach areas
- ☐ Magnet on string for shallow water/silt
- ☐ Rolling magnet bars can be used in tall grass/fields to ensure no casings are missed

CANINE—*Can Search Air/Water/Land for*

- ☐ Bodies/missing persons—trees hold decomp odors so dogs will often hit on trees
- ☐ Drugs
- ☐ Electronics/SD cards
- ☐ Fire accelerant
- ☐ Firearms/cartridge cases

Sifting Equipment

- ☐ Buckets/paper bags
- ☐ Handheld metal detector
- ☐ Screen trays—1/4 inch mesh recommended on wooden/PVC frame
- ☐ Trowels/shovels

Underwater Search Tools

- ☐ Canine
- ☐ Sonar
- ☐ Underwater paper/pens/pencils
- ☐ Underwater flashlights
- ☐ Waterproof metal detector—can be used in shallow water, wet sand/mud

Entomology Tool Kit Supply Options

- ☐ Agency SOP (laminated or inside zip lock bag) and all note paperwork/forms
- ☐ Bleach wipes
- ☐ Boxes for item transportation
- ☐ Butterfly net/fish net—suggest 18 inch diameter with 3-foot handle
- ☐ Cooler packs (refreeze able or gel) and Styrofoam cooler for sample transport
- ☐ Cotton balls

- ☐ Dawn dish soap/wash tub/water supply
- ☐ Disposable spoons (for maggot collection)
- ☐ Ethanol/ethyl alcohol (70%–95%)
- ☐ Fine paint brush/camel-hair brush (for egg collection)
- ☐ Flashlight
- ☐ Forceps/tweezers
- ☐ Graphite pencil or waterproof pen and regular retractable ink pens and Sharpie markers
- ☐ Hand shovel/trowel
- ☐ Headlamp (for hands-free light)
- ☐ Labels for exterior packaging (adhesive labels) and heavy cotton paper labels for interior packaging
- ☐ Paper towels/tissue paper
- ☐ Pipette for aquatic sample
- ☐ Plastic freezer bags/zip lock bags/paper bags
- ☐ PPE
- ☐ Vials, containers, and sealant materials (neoprene stoppers or screw top closure)
- ☐ Ruler or scale
- ☐ Shovel (large and hand shovel)
- ☐ Solutions—premade—consider KAA for quick maggot kill on scene solution
- ☐ Thermometers (ambient air, probe, and laser or IR) and humidity gauge
- ☐ Thermos/hot water container
- ☐ Sticky paper strips/tape/pads

Personal Equipment

- ☐ Baby wipes/body wipes—for your hands, your face, your sweat, your arms, and so on
- ☐ Boots—steel shank *and* steel toe
- ☐ Charger for phone, flashlight, equipment
- ☐ Clipboard/posse box—recommend one with storage and lights
- ☐ Clipboard—board with clip on top to hold paper from moving for flat writing
- ☐ Posse box—clipboard with storage room below for forms/pens/scales/and so on
- ☐ Easy snacking foods such as granola bars and dry fruit
- ☐ First aid kit and supplies
- ☐ Hardhat/sun hat/rain hat/fly net hat/extra hair ties
- ☐ Hot/cold packs
- ☐ Hydration and electrolyte source

- ☐ Insect/sunscreen spray
- ☐ List of phone numbers you might need
- ☐ Pain reliever
- ☐ Pocket knife
- ☐ Pocket liners or pocket protectors to store gloves or envelopes DNA free
- ☐ Raincoat/umbrella
- ☐ Red dome lights for use in vehicles and for taking notes (helps reduce night blindness)
- ☐ Reflective vest for accident and rainy scenes
- ☐ Watch or time source
- ☐ Temperature-controlling equipment
  - ☐ Neck cooler cloth, neck fan
  - ☐ Hand warmers, neck warmer
  - ☐ Rain boots/mud boots

Notes

1. https://leadsonline.com/clearcase.
2. https://lynnpeavey.com/.
3. https://fosterfreeman.com/crime-lite-auto/.
4. https://arrowheadforensics.com/.
5. https://www.calculated.com/mobile/prd31/DigiRoller-Plus-III.html.
6. https://shop.leica-geosystems.com/measurement-tools/disto/disto-laser-distance-meters.
7. https://www.geteasymark.com/.
8. https://www.uline.com/BL_5502/Hardware-Bags.
9. https://www.sirchie.com.
10. https://leadsonline.com/clearcase.
11. https://casegrabber.com/.
12. Maloney, Michael S., and Donald G. Housman. *Crime Scene Investigation Procedural Guide*. CRC Press, 2014.
13. https://lynnpeavey.com/product/trace-evidence-wrap/.
14. https://www.shopevident.com/category/blood-trajectory/zero-edge-protractors.

2 Arrival

The initial actions taken at a crime scene can significantly impact the investigation's outcome and evidence value. Although extensive instructions at this stage are not required, it is essential to have a mental checklist for each step. This chapter begins with a checklist of tasks to complete upon arrival, including documentation and notes to take before the first set of overall photographs. While the list may vary depending on the crime scene type, this outlines necessary actions to take before photographing most scenes.

Establishing your perimeter is completed upon initial arrival and is crucial for maintaining the integrity of the scene as well as ensuring public safety. It helps maintain your boundaries while processing the scene which can be vital to the evidence. You have several options to choose from so set up your scene with the necessary boundaries to do your best work. If the crowd is unruly on one side, create a larger buffer zone. If severe weather is approaching, cover yourself and your equipment with a tarp. Move vehicles if they obscure evidence like tire marks or vehicles that belong to onlookers. Use a body screen if the victim's family is present. Always ensure the public's safety if there is a health hazard. Use your resources to ensure the scene is adequately protected.

Checklist—Initial Arrival Actions—*First*

Initial Arrival

- ☐ Arrive SLOWLY, look down, use flashlight—park outside tape until you can evaluate
- ☐ Add entry to crime scene log at perimeter (log maintained by perimeter staff, not CSI staff)

Meet with on-Scene Detective or First Responding Officer

- ☐ Determine CSI roles if others are coming to help
- ☐ Determine scene detective contact
- ☐ Gather initial case information (see documentation checklist)
- ☐ Ensure perimeter is being controlled by sworn personnel only
- ☐ Confirm all areas for processing have been cleared (by sworn personnel) for subjects/animals to include crawl spaces, porches, rooms, attics, and garages

DOI: 10.4324/9781003503897-3

- ☐ Determine north (interior and exterior scene, you will need it)
- ☐ Collect and secure any evidence collected from bystanders or first responders that is urgent
- ☐ Assess PPE needs and PUT ON—are booties required? Breathing requirements?
- ☐ Document all calls out and information from each phone call to include time, name, outcome

Initial Actions

- ☐ Determine appropriate path of travel through scene—look for dirt/dew/damaged grass/plants to determine suspect entry path
- ☐ Cover/secure any footwear prints located at entry/exit points
- ☐ Night scene—check ground for water/condensation/dew trails
- ☐ Conduct initial walk-through—only observation *no touching/searching*
- ☐ Ensure gloves are worn at all times if opening doors/windows; retain for booking if policy
- ☐ Check all entrances/exits
- ☐ Establish and adjust perimeter—keep patrol vehicles out of tape unless directly involved or needed for security/safety purposes in which case simply document in your notes the vehicle/reason
- ☐ Check the bottom of everyone's shoes on scene for any pieces of glass, small casings, pieces of jewelry, blood, and so on and all first responders before they leave (paramedics, coroner, etc.)
- ☐ Photograph first responder vehicles in place so they can leave
- ☐ Photograph crowd if fire scene, riot-related scene, or explosive scene
- ☐ Establish staging area—search ground prior to setting up. Ensure trash, gloves, mask, and booties are readily available for all parties during processing. Paper bags can be used for trash, write on exterior, and fold top.
- ☐ Establish storage area for items of evidence to be packaged and stored
- ☐ Watch any video recordings if available—firsthand viewing is beneficial to scene processing rather than relaying information to scene CSI/scene detective
- ☐ Assess safety needs—any spills or leaks found? Unknown substances? Puddles of liquids?
- ☐ Assign roles to be retained through entire scene processing and sections/zones
- ☐ If submersion burning is suspected (hot water), collect temperature of water source immediately and photograph/document position of water heater thermostat

Identify/Address Animals on Scene

- ☐ Arrange safe/appropriate removal/containment
- ☐ Photograph animals prior to/during removal

Identify Time-Sensitive Issues

- ☐ Transient evidence collection plan—hair/fiber blowing away? Getting wet in rain? Washing away?
- ☐ Move crowd away ONLY after crowd and perimeter are photographed[1]
- ☐ Completed photographs for subject on scene/off scene/GSR
- ☐ Weather/lighting/timing of local events—do you need to move/take cover/block body?
- ☐ Check supplies, identify needed supplies/reconstructive tools
- ☐ Do you need assistance? DOJ, FBI, Sheriff, DEA, HAZMAT, CSI, Entomology, M.E., Fire department
- ☐ Formulate plan of action
- ☐ Complete initial documentation BELOW—*if you did not write it down, you did not do it*

Checklist—Initial Documentation—*Second*

Case Information

- ☐ Case number/date/time of crime/address
- ☐ Note time received/time enroute/time arrived on scene
- ☐ Initial call information
- ☐ Legal authority—none, consent, warrant, pending, and so on

Actions Taken

- ☐ Immediate actions taken by first responders before your arrival
- ☐ Removed children, transported victims
- ☐ Collected items from witnesses
- ☐ Drove through tire marks or other evidence (drive over cartridge cases, shoeprints, etc.)
- ☐ Turned off a vehicle in the scene
- ☐ Turned on house lights or opened doors/windows
- ☐ Opened a window to ventilate or turned on AC system
- ☐ Moved a firearm/cleared a firearm
- ☐ Moved any other item of possible evidentiary value

Location Information

- ☐ Arrival conditions—weather/crowd/smells/sounds
- ☐ Doors/windows—open/closed/locked/damaged

- ☐ Description—house/complex/business/field/vehicle
- ☐ Entrance/exit—reported/identified—yard/gate/roof/floor/wall—open/damaged?
- ☐ Vehicles present—emergency/non-emergency vehicles of interest
- ☐ Vehicles leaving close to your arrival
- ☐ Lighting/visibility of scene—night/day—dark/light
- ☐ Streetlights/porchlights—on/off, are lightbulbs present? Check for missing lightbulbs in yard
- ☐ Room lights/vehicle lights—on/off
- ☐ Collect temperature/humidity upon arrival—exterior/interior temperature
- ☐ Record thermostat settings if visible

Ease of Access to Victim and Location

- ☐ Proximity to roadway/public access
- ☐ Foot travel/vehicle travel
- ☐ Doors/windows locked/unlocked/jammed/damaged
- ☐ Keys present
- ☐ Climbing/digging equipment
- ☐ Ventilation/duct system
- ☐ Alarm settings
- ☐ Video recordings available—scene/neighbors/government placed/business placed

Recent Movement in the Scene

- ☐ Furniture overturned/broken/moved
- ☐ Food left out is hot/cold, steam?
- ☐ Blood/paint is wet
- ☐ Beverage still has ice cubes/condensation
- ☐ Any strong smells—recent cigar smoke, urine
- ☐ Items left on? Stove, radio, faucet, lights, AC system, sink, shower, hose
- ☐ Vehicles at location—hot/cold/dusty/clean
- ☐ Fireplace/ashtrays warm/smoking—hover hand over to feel heat
- ☐ Items on the top of the trash can/bag, inside trash can/bag
- ☐ Lack of recent activity? Mail still in mailbox? Papers on porch? Bins still at curb?
- ☐ Items out of place/of concern
- ☐ Dust voids/movement scratches
- ☐ Purses/wallets/valuables present? Notepad by telephone?

Subjects Involved

- ☐ Name, DOB if known
- ☐ Signs of decomposition/lividity and/or lack of
- ☐ Blood activity/visible injuries
- ☐ Bug/animal activity/markings
- ☐ Clothing descriptions/jewelry/accessories/shoes/barefoot
- ☐ Transported where/when?
- ☐ Anything on-scene needing immediate photographs/GSR/clothing collection

Staffing

- ☐ Who you met with upon arrival
- ☐ Who is on scene before you/with you/to help you—what roles are they filling?
- ☐ Notification needs to be made to others, start call-outs?
- ☐ ME/coroner staff and case number
- ☐ Body removal staff and ID if applicable
- ☐ Escorts of body/vehicles if applicable

Setting the Perimeter

Useful on Scene Resource (Must Be Obtained in Advance)

- WMD Response Guidebook, LSU, 2024[2]

Material Options for Barrier Creation

- Natural barriers such as roadways, sidewalks, driveways, walls, gates, and fences
- Crime scene tape—red or yellow
- Police vehicles, tow trucks, fire engines, your vehicle
- Rope
- Cones
- Scene screens
- Shrubs
- People
- Garage doors
- Residence doors

Option: Use red tape instead of yellow for *inner perimeter* line—serves as a visual reminder to use PPE or area is limited to specific personnel

Inner Perimeter, Hot Zone *for All Scenes*

- Initial no entry zone, primary scene area—only CSI/detective/ME should be in area
- Highest level PPE required
- Huddles occur outside tape
- Place trash/PPE station at TAPE
- Crime scene log maintained at hot zone perimeter

Outer Perimeter, Warm Zone, Buffer Zone *for Large Scenes/ Media Presence*

- Lower level of PPE required in this zone
- Huddles, equipment staging occur in this zone
- Media not allowed in this zone

Scene-Specific Perimeter Considerations

All Scenes

- Start large—reduce/expand as needed
- Always remain uphill, upwind, upstream
- Considerations
  - Suspect exit route from scene
  - Staging area locations
  - Use natural entry/exit points
- If additional evidence is located outside of tape
  - If nearby, expand tape
  - If not nearby, create another scene perimeter

In any of the following scenarios, a specific chain of command will be deployed with the necessary personnel. Follow their instructions for safety.

Accident

- Ensure perimeter reaches from the start of tire marks to end of damages and debris field
- Consider outer perimeter if hazards are present

Biological Hazard

- Isolate minimum 75 feet/23 m in all directions
- Remain uphill/upstream/upwind
- Isolate the spill/hazard
- Decontaminate people/animals with soap/water
- Notify—Hazmat, Health department, Law Enforcement, Public Works, or Water department

Chemical Hazard

- Remain uphill/upwind/upstream
- Hot zone/exclusion zone
  - Area with highest exposure potential
- Transition between hot zone and warm zone
  - Decontamination takes place at this location
  - Change of uniform if needed
- Warm zone/contamination reduction zone
  - Responders enter/exit
  - Decontamination takes place
- Cold zone/support zone
  - Free from contamination
  - No PPE needed
  - Planning/staging area

Explosive Material, General Response

- Remain upwind/uphill/upstream
- Isolate area 1650 feet/503 m all directions (consider 2500 feet/762 m)
- Do no operate radio, cell phone, or MDC within that area

Explosive Material, Vehicle Bomb Response

- Bureau of Alcohol, Tobacco, Firearms (ATF)—1-888-ATF-BOMB
- Compact sedan—evacuate minimum 1,500 feet/457 m
- Passenger van—evacuate minimum 2,750 feet/838 m
- Semi-truck—evacuate minimum 7,000 feet/1,982 m

Fire

- Established by the fire department with safety considerations—follow their lead and ensure appropriate distance from structure/vehicle to crowd

Incendiary Material (Weapons Designed to Start Fires)

- Remain upwind/uphill/upstream
- Isolate 330–660 feet/100–201 m (consider 1000 feet/305 m)

Nuclear Material

- Remain upwind/uphill/upstream
- Isolate 75 feet/23 m of spill/1000 feet/305 m of fire all directions

Cases to Consider Regarding Initial Arrival

The JonBenet Ramsey, OJ Simpson, and Murdaugh crime scenes were compromised from the beginning for a variety of reasons:

- Friends/family were allowed to roam the home unattended
- Friends/family were documented to have put items away/cleaned areas
- Multiple initial observations were not documented nor relayed to CSI staff
- Initial communications that were relayed were not followed up by CSI staff

2011: When Ellen Greenberg's body was found stabbed over 20 times (including 10 from behind), the scene was permitted to be cleaned professionally as well as have personal items removed from the scene by family of Ellen's boyfriend, prior to CSI processing. The determination was suicide which remains today.

Notes

1 Organization of Scientific Area Committees for Forensic Science (OSAC) (2021) *N-0016—Standard for Initial Response at Scenes by Law Enforcement—Proposed Standard.*

2 https://www.ncbrt.lsu.edu/courses/guidebookrequest.php from LSU NCBRT/ACE—Louisiana State University National Center for Biomedical Research and Training/Academy of Counter-Terrorism Education.

Working the Camera 3

Photography is an essential but demanding aspect of documenting a crime scene. Under stress or time constraints, it can be easy to overlook settings; however, minor adjustments can greatly enhance the quality of results. Therefore, it really helps to have reminders about preferred settings on-site or camera suggestions when you are stuck and alone on scene. Possessing the appropriate equipment is equally important, as inadequate gear, such as a depleted camera battery or insufficient lighting, can hinder the processing significantly. Following a section on equipment options and recommendations, you will find guidance on camera operation, setting adjustments, and best practices. The first section provides concise tips for photographing in various lighting conditions, while the remaining chapter offers comprehensive information on camera functions and settings to improve your images.

Camera Equipment List Options

Regularly Clean/Maintain Equipment to Prevent Cross-contamination

- ☐ SLR or interchangeable lens camera
- ☐ UV/IR camera
- ☐ Video camera
- ☐ Cleaning cloth/brush
- ☐ Hot shoe level/bubble level
- ☐ Rubbing alcohol wipes/lens-cleaning wipes
- ☐ Reflective camera strap or tape on camera to find camera on scene
- ☐ Rubber bracelet for lens adjustment—glow in dark or reflective material helpful
- ☐ Detachable flashes
- ☐ Flash diffuser—diffuser, filter paper, white paper, white handkerchief
- ☐ Sync cord/remote control

Data Storage Cards

- ☐ + 2 for camera
- ☐ + 1 for video camera
- ☐ + 1 for digital scanner

DOI: 10.4324/9781003503897-4

Stabilizing Equipment, Standing Height/Table Height

- ☐ Tripod/gimbal/beanbag/sandbags

Lens

- ☐ Macro
- ☐ Normal
- ☐ Wide angle
- ☐ Polarizing
- ☐ Telephoto lens
- ☐ Macro/micro lens or telephoto lens cell phone attachment (if using cell phone)

Filters

- ☐ Polarizing filter
- ☐ UV filters—UV transmitting bandpass filter
- ☐ UV filter—clear filter, can be left on permanently for lens protection
- ☐ Macrophotography filter
- ☐ ALS filter
- ☐ IR filter

Scales/Rulers/Stickers—Regularly Verify with Nist Traceable Ruler or Calibrate Equipment

- ☐ *When scale with circle in corner ensure is visible, used for angle correction*
- ☐ ABFO #2 L scale—good for trace evidence, bite marks, bullet defects
- ☐ 300 mm L scale
- ☐ 6 inch scale of various colors
- ☐ Handheld measuring tape
- ☐ Tape with printed measuring tape/ruler
- ☐ Pre-printed scales/labeled stickers/label book
- ☐ Measuring tapes, retractable 50 and 100 feet
- ☐ Walking wheel (rolling wheel)
- ☐ Laser measurer

Alternative Ruler Options for Photographs: Everyday Standard Size Items for Emergencies (Don't Use If DNA Is Needed)

- ☐ Ink pen, standard
- ☐ Coin of minted currency (quarter, peso, etc.)
- ☐ FLAT currency bill (from wallet, not your back pocket)

Camera Setting Suggestions/Troubleshooting

As You Move through the Scene, Look Each Picture

- If you think you can take a better one, do so before you move on
- IT'S WORTH THE TIME IT TAKES

Bloody Item on Dark Background

- Blood will absorb light, making it harder to photograph

Option: Side lighting—30°–45° lighting can reduce glare and brighten area

Option: Overexpose Picture to Help Visualize Blood

- Take proper setting photograph first, then increase brightness by one or more of the following:
  - Turn exposure dial up—often up to +1
  - Increase flash output
  - Increase ISO
  - Lower F-stop setting

Option: ALS

- 395–435 nm range for search, most absorption for background distinction
- 415 nm with yellow filter recommended

Option: (IR) Infrared

- Very long wavelength—700–1100 nm

Option: Bluestar Enhancement

- Bulb setting, 800 ISO, F/2.8, 15, 30, 45 seconds—check at each time interval, adjust if needed

Option: Bluestar Enhancement

- 45 second shutter release, ISO 400, F/8

Blurry Pictures

- Make sure you have adjusted your diopter, if not do it now (if you look through your viewfinder and it is NOT sharp and in focus, adjust it now until you see clearly through viewfinder)

- Add light to help camera see
- Focus on edge of clothing/furniture/area with contrasting color
- Use shutter speed closest to lens length
- Secure tripod if in wind or hang sandbags from tripod
- Focus camera with your eye to the camera instead of using viewfinder
- Increase ISO slightly to brighten area/assist autofocus

Camera Shake Suggestions

- Stand feet facing perpendicular to subject of photograph, turning your body to face the camera 90°, tuck elbows
- Hold upper arms against body to stabilize camera
- Hold elbow out from body, press against a wall or someone's back for stability
- Exhale prior to pressing shutter release button
- Lower your own blood pressure/heart rate

Cell Phone/iPhone to Take Scene Video/Photographs

1. Create new files in phone
2. Use cover sheet always
3. Ensure stabilization is set
4. Hold elbows against body like video camera to reduce shake
5. Can use camera attachments for the phone such as lighting, lens, and filters

IR/UV Camera

- Manual focus instead of automatic focus
- 200–900 nm with green filter

Natural Color Metering (Point on These Items When Focusing)

- Asphalt
- Gray-colored scale
- Green grass
- Palm of hand

Night Scenes

- Live view not recommended for use in the dark—does not focus as well
- Consider taking another set once the sun comes up to show the following:

- entrances/exits
- lighting at time of crime if known (day/night)
- lighting at time of arrival to process (day/night)
- enhanced lighting for proper search and documentation

No Tripod

- Set camera on ladder step
- Set camera on tabletop
- Set camera on stack of toolboxes
- Use beanbag stand
- Turn body and stabilize against your own body
- Squat over item, place elbows on knees forming tripod

Picture of a Screen—Phone, Tablet, Monitor

- 1/60, F/8–11, ISO 100–250, flash off

Photographs Too Bright

- Turn F-Stop setting to higher number, try F/13
- Increase shutter speed
- Turn off flash
- Turn ISO to a lower number
- Paper/documents—ISO 100–250
- White vehicle interior—ISO 250

Photographs Too Dark

- Turn ISO to a higher number
- Decrease shutter speed
- Turn F-Stop setting to lower number, try F/8
- Black vehicle interior, clothing, backpack—ISO 500, F/8, increase flash exposure as needed

Reflection—Mirror

- Non-macrophotography
  - Stand at 70°–80° instead of 90° to eliminate you seeing your reflection in photo and reduce flash
- Macrophotography
  - Option: Cut hole in cardboard/paper plate/paper/CD—Take photographs through hole eliminating your reflection
  - Option: Scrape silver backing off back of mirror in area of interest

    - Option: Collect the mirror and take to the laboratory for photographs
    - Option: Place dark colored cloth behind you to reduce reflection

Reflection—Window/Windshield/Display Case

- Polarizing filters can reduce reflection
- Manual focus/flashlight can help with focus issues
- Place paper bag/butcher paper/posse box on other side of window to remove background
- Place paper bag/paper/posse box above item being photographed to remove reflection on glass

Unfriendly/Dangerous Scene Environment—Quick Set

1. Take 2–6 overall/mid-range photographs
2. Placard placement if safe to do so
3. Take 2–6 overall/mid-range photographs
4. Take individual close-ups as you are picking up items

Weather Related

Bright Sunny Day

- Use lens hood
- Turn body so that you photograph toward the sun to reduce shadows
- Hold hand up to block sun from lens
- Don't use flash
- Polarizer filter/lens to reduce glare
- Create shade to control lighting
    - Umbrella, body, tarp, screen, tent
    - Keep your back to the sun to control shadows
- Camera setting options
    - ISO 100, F/22, 1/60
    - ISO 100, F/16, 1/125

Bright Hazy Day

- Remove detachable flash
- ISO 100, F/16, 1/125
- ISO 200, F/11, 1/125

Bright Cloudy Day

- ISO 100, F/11, 1/60
- ISO 100, F/8, 1/125

Dark Overcast Day

- ISO 400, F/11, 1/60
- Light in shaded area with fill flash

Light Overcast Day

- ISO 100–300, F/8, 1/60
- ISO 100, F/5.6, 1/125

Deep Shade

- ISO 400, F/8, 1/60
- Use fill flash, or paint with light

Fog/High Humidity/Fire Scenes

- Timed exposures—ISO 300, F/8–11, 2 seconds, reduce flash output
- Don't use paint with light/bounced light—light will reflect off water droplets in air
- Clean lens/internal mirror on camera to remove condensation—can use rubbing alcohol, saliva, cloth

Indoor Settings

- ISO 400, F/11, 1/60,
- ISO 300, F/8, 1/60,
- Built-in flash recommended

Outdoor Nighttime Scene

- 2 second timer to reduce camera shake if on tripod
- Use detached flash or remote control for flash
- ISO 400, F/5.6, 5 seconds
- ISO 600, F/5.6, 8 seconds
- ISO 400, F/11, 10 seconds
- ISO 400–800, F/8–11, 2 seconds

Rainy Weather

- Camera cover—prefabricated or handmade with plastic sheets/bags
- Umbrella
- Scene tarp
- Evidence cones over top of cartridge cases to stop rain/wind contact

Snowy Weather

- Wear sunglasses to reduce glare and snow blindness
- Polarizing filter can reduce glare and reflection

- Camera lens hood
- Reduce exposure to −0.5 or −1
- Shutter speed 1/100 or 1/60
- Lower ISO setting
- Focus on areas with color contrast on autofocus or use manual focus

Strong Wind on Scene

- Hang weight or sandbag from bottom of tripod
- Remove detachable flash if not in use
- Brace arms against body frame
- Block tripod from wind with an umbrella extended out to the side of wind origin

Working the Camera

Focus

- Safety—when focusing with your eye to the camera, keep both eyes open (takes practice but valuable)
- Adjust diopter to ensure the camera matches your eyesight (generally upper right corner by eyepiece)
- Always be sure the correct content is in focus; camera will often default to the nearest object

Autofocus Function

- Depress shutter-release button halfway and hold until you receive set indicator (beep, green square)
- Camera will focus, then complete depression of button to take photo
- Autofocus is not as sharp when looking through live view (screen on back of camera)
- Can set camera to indicate when viewfinder is in focus with sound/visual

Modes of Autofocus

- AF-S Single autofocus mode—will not take photograph if it is not in focus, even when pressing shutter release button
- AF-C Continuous autofocus—will continue to refocus as the subject or camera moves if continuing to hold down the shutter release button
- AF-C Hybrid of the above 2 modes

Suggestions for Low Light Focusing

- Use center "focus point" to focus with
- Focus on contrasting areas in immediate background if subject of picture is not of contrasting colors
- Use back button focus and readjust frame
- Use AF-Assist
- "Auto slow sync" in flash modes, helps focus in low light
- Bounced lighting to add lighting while the camera is focusing, if indoors
- Switch to manual focus

Back Button Focus

- Continual focus while autofocus is engaged
- Good for photographing children/uncooperative subjects/animals/crowds
- Bad for cold weather/gloves, heavy lens equipment/tired shift/long day, multi-tasking

Canon—Setting up Back Button Focus

- Menu—Custom Functions—Custom Controls—Shutter button—select Metering Start—set AF-ON button to Metering and AF start

Nikon—Setting up Back Button Focus

- Menu—Custom Settings—Autofocus—AF Activation—AF-ON Only

Focal Points

- Focal point should be: 2/3 between your foreground/background
- Infinite focus ranges
  - With the right settings and focal point, all items in photo will be in focus
  - F/16 setting, focus 16 feet away, area in focus starts at 8 feet
  - F/11 setting, focus 24 feet away, area in focus starts at 12 feet

Settings

Reciprocal Exposure (For Same Lighting, Different Depth of Field)

- Inverse relationship between ISO, aperture, and shutter speed. Different combinations of settings are used to create the same exposure. For example, opening the aperture by one stop is equivalent to lowering the shutter speed by the same amount.

- ISO, F-stop, shutter speed may all be modified to create an ideal photograph
- Use RAW or TIFF settings if you think your pictures will be compared/altered/cropped later (recommend +JPEG as some government storage programs do not upload RAW and TIFF settings)
- Adjust for one, adjust for all to keep exposure

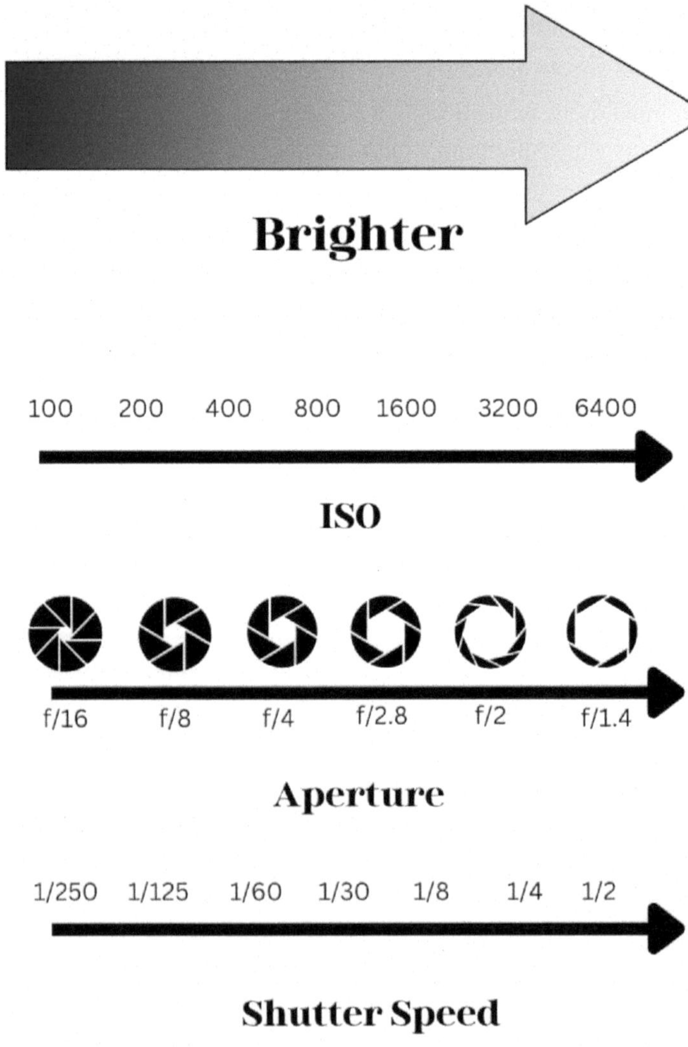

Figure 3.1 Reciprocal exposure chart.

Fstop—Aperture

Controls

- Intensity of captured light
- Depth of field (foreground to background)
- Higher F-stop number = smaller aperture = better depth of field = less background blur = lets in less light
- Lower F-stop number = larger aperture = less depth of field = more background blur = lets in more light
- F16+ will show dust specs on camera sensor—clean regularly

Diffraction

- Blurring of sharp lines due to light diffraction when using F/22+ is possible; consider staying F/11–22 for forensic work if able

Normal Depth of Field Ranges

- F/22–6 feet and on
- F/16–7–30 feet
- F/11–8–25 feet
- F/8–9–20 feet

Shutter Speed

- Controls how long lens is exposed to captured light
- Slower shutter speeds can cause blurriness but let in more light—you will need tripod or stabilizer if set below 1/30 seconds
- Faster shutter speeds stop movement but let in less light

Common Shutter Speed Settings

- 1/60 good for handheld pictures and photos of phone screens/computer screens
- 1/125 will freeze walking person in motion
- 1/500 will freeze bicyclists in motion
- 1/1000 will freeze vehicle in motion

Shutter Release

- Can use shutter release button on camera, cable button, remote control

Nikon

CL—often 3 frames captured with 1 press of shutter release

CH—often used with action scenarios, continuous shutter release (consider using if taking pictures of an altercation, someone fleeing, evidence collection, body movement, etc.)
Timer—gives you a 2- to 3-second timer, to help with camera stabilization (use when on tripod)

ISO *(Formerly "Film Speed")*

Controls

- Sensitivity to the captured light
- Higher ISO number = more sensitive to light, but more digital noise/graininess
- Lower ISO number = less sensitive to light, but less digital noise/graininess
- Higher ISO suffers from graininess with enlarged pixels

Common Settings

- ISO 300 and below provides highest quality photograph[1]
- Many CSIs stay at/below ISO 400–800 for highest quality photographs on scene
- ISO below 100 is now an option on some digital cameras
- Low ISO may require shutter speed of 3–4 seconds

Approximate Range Limits for ISO/Lighting

ISO 400

- F/22 can light up to 10 feet
- F/16 can light up to 15 feet
- F/11 can light up to 20 feet
- F/8 can light up to 30 feet

ISO 800

- F/22 can light up to 15 feet
- F/16 can light up to 20 feet
- F/11 can light up to 30 feet
- F/8 can light up to 40 feet

White Balance

- Responds to lighting type
- Lower white balance: Warmer tone—yellow/brown
- Higher white balance: Cooler tone—blue

Color Metering

Natural Color Metering—Focus on the Following (1/2 Press of Shutter Release Button)

- Gray colored 6 inch scale
- Green grass
- Asphalt
- Palm of hand

Camera Color Metering—Focus on Edge of Item (1/2 Press of Shutter Release Button)

- Camera will show meter in viewfinder of under/over exposure
- Adjust accordingly

Color Chart

- Consider using a color chart for injuries; it provides a color reference for exposure as well as color reference for injury comparison

Lens/Filter

50 mm Lens *(Natural View)*

- "Normal" lens
- No distortion

35 mm–50 mm Lens

- Recommended by most forensic photographers

28 mm Lens *(Wide Angle)*

- Greater depth of field than 50 mm
- Greater distance—camera to focal point
- Will have distortion

Possible Distortions

- Telephoto lens—compresses the scene, pincushion distortion
- Wide angle lens—elongates the scene, barrel distortion

Suggestions

- Keep rubber/silicone bracelet around lens for easy adjustment
- Adjust lens with arm/wrist/back of hand to keep hands clean
- Can keep a clear UV filter on lens for protection

- Polarizer filter and polarizer lens
  - Reduces reflections and light
  - Great for taking photographs through glass or water
  - Reduces glare on skin
  - Increases contrast
  - Reduces appearance of haze
  - Can be used together for stronger results called cross polarization
  - Rotate polarizing filter while on the lens, as lens position will impact the results in some cases

Batteries

Battery Drained Quicker by the Following Activities

- RAW/TIFF settings
- Detached flash
- Timed exposures
- Live view display being illuminated for extended time periods
- Age, change regularly according to policy
- Leaving on charger for extended time periods, remove battery once fully charged
- Adverse weather (extreme hot and cold, store them in pants pocket rather than car door pocket)

Recommended

- Extra batteries for all equipment
- Car chargers for all batteries

Light Reduction—Snow/Sun

Option: Polarizing Filter/Lens

- Reduces sun glare overall
- Reduces glare on water, helps see below surface

Option: Use Soft Light/Diffused Light

- Use diffuser of choice to reduce direct light

Option: Camera Settings Change

- Raise F-stop setting, F/16+
- Lower ISO setting, ISO 100–200

Option: Use Timed Exposures

- Shortened shutter speed

Option: Create Shadows to Control the Light

- Move body/item to create shadow covering area
- Control flash for even light distribution
- Good for mid-range/close-up photographs

Types of Added Lighting

Oblique

- Light held low to ground, 0°–45°
- Good for
  - 3D items
  - side lighting
  - Creates "fill flash" for shadows

Direct

- Light held at approximately 90°
- Considered normal lighting
- Good for
  - adding light to area
  - viewing prints on glass windows
  - considered normal lighting

Transmitted

- Light held below/behind item
- Good for
  - clear items
  - searching for fibers/hairs
  - fingerprinting plastic/glass

Diffused

- Softens direct flash
- Direct lighting with diffuser in front of light source—diffuser, filter paper, white paper, white handkerchief

Sources of Added Lighting

- Camera flash
- Handheld flashlight
- Handheld LED lighting
- Flood lighting/pelican lights/media lights
- Fire/EMS lighting equipment

Flash/Flash Equipment

On Camera Flash (Built in, Pop-up)

- Range 2–5 feet
- Less than 2 feet can leave shadow on bottom of frame
- Good for
  - subject photographs
  - mid-range/close-up photographs

Detachable Flash (Off Camera, Overhead)

- Range 5–15 feet
- Battery power will affect flash output
- Use with flash cord or remote control
- Good for
  - blue/red light reduction on night shift scenes
  - timed exposure for night scenes
  - bounced lighting on indoor scenes

Flash Syncing

- Telling detachable flash to communicate with camera when not directly attached
- Can be done with direct (flash cord) or Bluetooth communication

Transmitter Flash—(Formerly "Master")

- Flash fired directly from camera, built-in flash, also directs other remote flashes, and tells them when to flash

Receiver Flash—(Formerly "Slave")

- Flash fired off camera, told what to do by the transmitter flash or camera

Option: Detachable flash can be placed on camera (transmitter) to send transmissions to receiving flash units

Option: Camera transmits to detachable flash while placed off camera

Nikon

- On camera menu—flash control section
  - Set flash to "TTL auto" or "manual" (transmitter flash)
  - "Group flash options"—use for multiple flash units
  - "Radio remote flash"—remote control
- Set receiver flash(s) to "non-TTL auto" or "manual"

Canon

- Select shooting mode
- Control the screen
- Choose flash mode

Bounced Lighting

Good for

- adding indirect light to entire room
- reducing hotspots and glare on pictures, mirrors, wet surfaces
- inside use only, normal size room best
- securing light on tripod can reduce arm fatigue in large or detailed areas

Items to Bounce Light Off

- Butcher paper
- Ceiling
- Handheld mirror
- Light colored lamp shade
- Opposite wall of room
- White plastic binder
- White posse box

Option: Hold Steady Light (Flashlight) on Item Chosen

- Point light away from camera toward LIGHT colored item
- +/− as needed
- Helps illuminate room
- Can use with handheld photographs

Option: Added Lighting during Timed Exposures

- Used with tripod or camera stabilizing device
- While shutter is open, add small amount of light
- Helps fill dark voids
- Start with 10–20 seconds shutter speed, +/− as needed

Paint with Light

Good for

- outside in large areas
- filling dark voids in closets, under beds, and so on

Movement

- Can fill small shadows or large field
- Move light in linear fashion "painting" area with light
  - Move quickly and with intention
  - Avoid getting in view of camera, avoid pointing light directly at camera

Equipment

- Flags, cones, markers to mark boundary
- Flashlight
- Detached flash
- Floodlights
- Hot shoe lights
- Tripod

Filling Smaller Shadows

- Try with flash at full power first, adjust as needed

Option to Start: F/8–11, 2–4 seconds, ISO 400

- Add light while shutters are open
- Adjust settings for optimal results

Large Outdoor Area

Determine Boundary Area of Picture

- Place camera on tripod, frame area of interest
- Walking along boundary area in frame
  - Add light while looking through viewfinder
  - Determine placement to add light and eliminate subject holding light
  - Place markers on ground to identify boundaries to stand

Camera Settings

Option: F/5.6, 10 seconds, ISO 400, +/− as needed
Option: F/8, 20 seconds, ISO 500, +/− as needed
Option: BULB setting, +/− as needed

- Set flash to full power
- Control shutter with remote control, shutter release cable

Option: 1-Person Team

- Can use remote and move or add light from behind camera

Option: 2-Person Team

- 1 partner will move around lighting up dark areas
- Move in quickly and orderly

Flash Settings

- Consider using "repeating flash" setting or "manual flash" setting if large outdoor area
- Consider using a remote control for multiple flash units

Note

1 George, Chris. "Photography Cheat Sheet: Color Temperature & the Kelvin Scale." *Digital Camera World*, 2 Aug. 2024, www.digitalcameraworld.com.

Scene Photograph Types 4

With your camera prepared and your skills honed for capturing optimal images, it is essential to identify the key photographs required for thorough documentation. This chapter commences with a checklist for scene photographs, ensuring that no critical details are missed. These initial photographs are vital as they lay the groundwork for the entire investigation and support any evidence found later during the search. These images will validate that the items collected as evidence were originally present at the scene. The importance of photographs taken prior to any manipulation at a crime scene has been reiterated in many formats and court hearings.

Following this, you will find guidance on the fundamentals of comprehensive scene documentation, including coversheet options, overall photograph strategies, and viewpoints to consider. While certain universal rules of photography always apply, such as never deleting any photographs, even accidental ones, and ensuring the frame is filled with meaningful content, adhering to a clear list of best practices can simplify the process.

Don't Forget

- Photography will take place during ALL stages of processing
- Fill the frame—maximize depth of field—keep film plane parallel (try for 90°, 80–100° acceptable)
- Pan down as well as up, don't forget the floor, under the bed and low items
- Use a scale if size is a factor. Scale use is recommended when possible for evidence, stains, damages, and close-up photography. If used, it is required the area be photographed as-is prior to scale use.
- When using a scale with an angle adjusting circle, keep the circle visible for later adjustment

Checklist—Scene Photographs *before Searching*

☐ Camera settings—date/time/new file/flash/adjust settings needed for size of scene
☐ Cover sheet

 DOI: 10.4324/9781003503897-5

Exterior Scene Photographs

- ☐ Street signs/apartment complex signs
- ☐ Address of scene neighboring yards/address if related
- ☐ Streetlights and traffic, nearby vehicles, parked vehicles, moving vehicles
- ☐ Landmarks of importance
- ☐ Yard/area surrounding building
- ☐ Fencing
- ☐ Point of entry/exit
- ☐ Unused points of entry/exit
- ☐ Doors/windows/thresholds
- ☐ Defects/pry marks/holes
- ☐ Mobility barriers/stuff blocking movement (boards, piles of boxes)
- ☐ Locks engaged/broken/keys present/missing (close-up of all entryway locks even if no damage visible)
- ☐ Cameras/wiring

Vehicles of Interest

- ☐ Emergency vehicles/other vehicles—parking location, light activation, license plate
- ☐ Identifying information
- ☐ Picture through window showing keys/damage/glass, items on seat, and so on

Interior Scene Photographs

Overall Photographs of Each Room As-Is, before Searching and Marking[1]

- ☐ Doorway/door/thresholds—damages, tool marks, missing, and so on
- ☐ All corners/sides
- ☐ Floor/ceiling
- ☐ Windows—broken, locked
- ☐ Hallways/transitions between rooms

Mid-range of Each Room Before Searching

- ☐ Items on counters/dressers/flat surfaces
- ☐ Space beneath beds/dressers/chairs
- ☐ Contents on walls and ceilings
- ☐ Security pad/alarm and screen if applicable
- ☐ Thermostat and screen if applicable
- ☐ Items out of place and of interest

Room(s) with Decedent/Crime If Applicable

- ☐ Entrance/exit
- ☐ Inside/outside room
- ☐ Good view of body in relation to other items in room

Evidence of Movement

- ☐ Overturned furniture/dishes
- ☐ Broken windows/doors
- ☐ Kitchen activity
- ☐ Water on floor or inside shower
- ☐ Used toilet/sink

Search

- ☐ Search scene and mark items of evidence at this time

Checklist—Scene Photographs *after Searching* and *Markers Down*

Additional Overall/Mid-range/Close-up of Scene

- ☐ All rooms/bodies searched/marked
- ☐ Consider marking due north in photographs
- ☐ Defects with and without scale
- ☐ Items of evidence/impression evidence/defects/tool marks/patent prints with and without scale
- ☐ Blood/blood trails/debris trails
- ☐ Graffiti or handwriting/painting at scene
- ☐ New CCTV found—cameras/recording systems
- ☐ Items of interest that are not being collected

Furniture Previously Closed/Obstructed

- ☐ Underneath cushions/pillows
- ☐ Underneath chairs/couches
- ☐ Underneath beds/mattresses
- ☐ Inside drawers
- ☐ Inside trash cans
- ☐ Inside closets
- ☐ Inside refrigerator/freezer
- ☐ Behind doors/furniture

Other Photographs

- ☐ Overhead view if possible

- ☐ Witness perspective photographs—their view and location in scene
- ☐ Suspect entrance and damages caused
- ☐ Peephole of door if residence, damaged/working
- ☐ Path of suspect travel if known
- ☐ Trajectory and blood enhancement
- ☐ Macrophotography
- ☐ Trajectory and/or blood spatter
- ☐ Subject/decedent photography if applicable
- ☐ Exit photographs—search warrant return and/or overall of each room as leaving showing damages/lack of damages

Types of Scene Photographs Needed

1. Cover page
2. Overalls
3. Mid-ranges/relational
4. Close-ups

Cover Page *(For Each New Place, Person, Date)*

Camera Settings

- F11, ISO 250, 1/60 on camera flash
- Lens 35–50 mm focal length, hold at arm's length
- View picture, adjust, repeat until optimal

Cover Page Content[2]

- Case number
- Date
- Location
- Photographer/organization
- Subject name if applicable

Option: Pre-printed page (ANY SIZE) with sections filled out
Option: Piece of paper with Sharpie handwriting
Option: Photo ID
Option: Back of business card with ink pen
Option: Sharpie pen writing on gloved hand

Overall Photographs

- You need to depict the scene the way it was found[3]—you will depict what is important later
- Can start outside tape and show tape placement in photographs

- Should have 360° coverage—panning encouraged—30% overlap of frames
  - All locations/spaces with multiple angles to ensure showing the relationships of all nearby items
- Try to get 2 points of view for scenes
  - Realistic documentation and shows depth
  - South and east sides of the scene
  - Width and length of room
  - Overhead and natural view

Overall Photograph Options

Exterior Scene Panning

Option: L-Shape Scene Panning

- Panning, taking photographs in linear fashion along the width of scene
- Take photographs in linear fashion along the length of scene

Option: Circle Shape Scene Panning

- Stand in center of yard/parking lot; turn clockwise in circle to show entire view
- Recommended to keep same item in the bottom of frame for reference

Interior Scene Panning—Don't Forget to Pan up to Capture the Ceiling and down to the Floor

Option: Photograph from each corner
Option: Photographs from each wall in linear panning fashion
Option: Circle shape scene panning

- Stand in center of room; turn clockwise in circle to show entire room
- Try to keep same item in the bottom of frame for reference

Enhanced Overall Photographs

Option: Colored Marker/Flag

- Affix color to type of item grouping
  - Color markers: Post-it notes, flags, highlighter on stickers
  - Item groupings: Cartridge cases, footwear prints, weapons
- Take overall photographs showing color pattern
- Helps visually depict location of items
- Not for use on first set of overall photographs

Overhead Photographs (*Ideal Whenever Possible)*

Options: Ladder/nearby porch/apartment stairs/landing/drone

Mid-range Photographs

Range of Pictures

- Generally, capture 10 feet/3 m distance
- Normal lens
- Eliminate as much background as possible
- Show relationship to evidence or scene
- Can be partial body, partial room, partial yard
- Should include evidence and a fixed item
- Can include multiple evidence items
- Should include multiple angles for items
- Initially taken at natural perspective (standing height)

Close-up Photographs

It is okay to take close-up after item has been moved, after photographing original location. Examples:

- Hold item in hand in front of drawer versus inside drawer
- Hold item in front of purse versus inside purse
- Hold item with scale after being moved for examination
- Hold hat upside down to view label

Range of Pictures

- Generally, capture within 2 feet/0.6 m distance
- Fill frame; remove unnecessary content
- Can turn camera to elongate foreground and eliminate background

Natural View

- Taking a picture at standing height as it would be viewed by the subject
- Always start with natural view, then can move/squat down/step up/turn as appropriate
- Height is not factor, even if 6 feet tall
- Perspective is important—ensure you collet a 90° angle photograph, as well as move up/down/angle appropriately
- Accident vehicle and structural damages—angles show depth realistically

Panning (*Series of Overlapping Pictures to Cover Large Area)*

- 30% overlap for each picture is best practice
- Move left to right/top to bottom
- Don't forget to overlap photographs for viewers to keep reference of placement

Notes

1 Organization of Scientific Area Committees for Forensic Science (OSAC) (2020) *Standard Guide for Crime Scene Photography.*

2 Organization of Scientific Area Committees for Forensic Science (OSAC) (2020) *Standard Guide for Crime Scene Photography.*

3 American Society for Testing & Materials (2023) *ASTM E1188-11 (2017)—Standard Practice for Collection and Preservation of Information and Physical Items by a Technical Investigator.*

Specialty Scene Photography

5

After completing the initial scene photographs, attention can be directed toward taking more thorough specialty photos. These may include photogrammetry, macrophotography, or alternate light source (ALS) photography. This chapter provides detailed guidance on achieving high-quality photographs, including suggestions for ALS and steps for effective macrophotography. The section on macrophotography will cover necessary procedures for optimal imaging and provide a checklist for comprehensive scene documentation. Additionally, this chapter offers basic instruction on photogrammetry; although it is not used frequently, understanding its procedure can be beneficial in emergency situations.

Macrophotography *(Comparison Quality, Examination Quality)*

- For comparison of small patterns such as fingerprint, tire mark, footwear print, and tool mark
- Cellular phones will take significantly lower quality than camera for this purpose
- Color photographs first choice; black and white are good accompaniment, not replacement

Angle Needed for Comparison

- Strive for 90° but can vary 10°–15° and still be useable
- Bubble-level attachment helpful
- Consider small slinky or alligator clip to hold scale during photography
- Silver fingerprints can be tilted 5° to be more visible and useable

Camera Stabilization Required

- You can use tripod, mono pod, quadra pod, bean bag, ladder step, table, and so on
- Ensure tripod/monopod legs are not in photographs or leg shadows from the flash—use "fill flash" to remove leg shadows

DOI: 10.4324/9781003503897-6

Focus

- Focus on the detail in the item, NOT lines on your scale or tape measure
- Scale should be on same plane as print (dig down in dirt or use raised scale holder such as small slinky, alligator clip on platform, or wooden block)
- Place scale on long edge of frame if possible
- Use glass pane to flatten soft substrates for sharp focusing (small square piece of glass on top of plastic bag)
- Use a panning series for curved items rather than try to get one photo with all of it in focus

Lighting

- Lower angle of light gives you less depth of impression
- Hold 4–5 feet/1–1.5 m
- Take multiple photographs with multiple angles to ensure depth of field is captured—suggest across the length, across the width, and diagonal

Tire Marks

- Strive for 8-foot/2-meter section if present (length of full tire rotation)

Processing Options

Option: Bracketing

- Can do it manually or use setting
- Gives three options for lighting
- Original, underexposed, overexposed
- Helps ensure results are adequate

Option: Extension Tube

- Supplemental lens is placed between normal lens and camera
- Will allow for added zoom functions

Mirror/Window Photographs during Macrophotography

Option: Collect entire mirror/window for photography in laboratory setting

Option: Scrape silver backing off mirror over area of interest to eliminate reflection

- Area of interest should be on front and unaffected

Option: Eliminate Reflection with Painted DVD

- Paint the silver side of old DVD black
- Place over lens black side out
- Focus through holes in center
- Keep lights low
- Reduces reflection back from camera/reflection

Option: Eliminate Reflection with Paper Plate/Piece of Paper

- Poke hole in center of paper/plate
- Make it large enough to see through with camera
- Focus through hole
- F11 or smaller to reduce surrounding image clarity

Option: Eliminate Background with Solid Colored Item

- Curtains, blinds, butcher paper, large paper bag
- Place solid colored item on backside of glass to block background or add light with butcher paper
- Photograph as normal

Curved Surfaces during Macrophotography

Option: Panning Series of Curved Surface

- Start with end of print/mark
- Take photographs with scale on plane
- Turn print/mark/photograph with overlap
- Repeat until entire print is captured
- Resulting photographs can be combined

Checklist—Macrophotography

3D/2D—Tool Marks/Bite Marks/Footwear Prints/Footprints

☐ Overall/mid-range/close-up series taken PRIOR to this point

Change Camera Settings

☐ ISO 50–100
☐ RAW+JPEG or TIFF+JPEG
☐ F-stop of choice (F8–F22)
☐ Timed exposure of choice
☐ Consider flash/flash cord or remote control (set up at this time)
☐ Do you need a new digital file/cover page? (Set up at this time)
☐ Do you need labels? (Create at this time)

Lens/Filter

- ☐ Macro lens for small items
- ☐ 35 mm for footwear prints
- ☐ Polarizer filters can add depth

Affix Camera to Tripod/Camera Stand

- ☐ Overhead/perpendicular/under to item
- ☐ 90°—use bubble level

Scale

- ☐ Same plane as impression, along the long edge of frame if possible
- ☐ ABFO #2 for small areas
- ☐ 300 mm L scale for footwear prints
- ☐ Ruler stickers (not for use on humans)

Label with Case Information Visible in One Photograph

- ☐ Case number, item number, initials/ID
- ☐ Orientation arrow (up/north)

Lighting

- ☐ Block sun to have better lighting control
- ☐ Keep detached flash off hot shoe

Flash/Flashlight for 3D Prints (Soft Surface with Depth)

- ☐ 10°–45° angle best
- ☐ Hold flash 5 feet from print
- ☐ Photograph 2–4 angles/views
- ☐ Can use as burst of light or paint with light across the frame

Flash/Flashlight for 2D Prints (Hard Surface like Cement and Tile)

- ☐ Direct and bounced lighting helpful depending upon substrate
- ☐ 30°–60° angles found to be most helpful
- ☐ Hold flash 5 feet from print
- ☐ Consider bracketing
- ☐ Can use as burst of light or paint with light across the frame

Plane

- ☐ Flatten soft textured surfaces with clean glass panes (plastic bag, sheet, etc.) for better photography

- ☐ Dig down around print to place scale same level if it has depth for photography
- ☐ Panning set of photographs for curved surfaces to cover all areas of impression recommended

3D/2D Tire Marks

- ☐ Overall/mid-range/close-up series taken *prior* to this point

Change Camera Settings

- ☐ ISO 50–100
- ☐ RAW+JPEG/TIFF+JPEG
- ☐ F-stop of choice (F8–F22)
- ☐ Timed exposure of choice
- ☐ Consider flash/flash cord or remote control (set up at this time)
- ☐ Do you need a new digital file/cover page? (Set up at this time)
- ☐ Do you need labels? (Create at this time)

Label with Case Information Visible in 1 Photograph

- ☐ Case number, item number, initials/ID
- ☐ Orientation arrow (up/north)

Lens/Filter

- ☐ Macro lens for small sections
- ☐ 50 mm for tire marks
- ☐ Polarizer filters can add depth
- ☐ Affix camera to tripod/camera stand
- ☐ 90°—use bubble level

Lighting

- ☐ Two angles of light in photographs to show depth for 3D prints
- ☐ One angle of light for 2D prints

Scale

- ☐ 300 mm L scale
- ☐ Ensure scale is same plane as impression
- ☐ Flatten soft surfaces with clean glass panes (plastic bag, sheet, etc.)
- ☐ Dig down around print to place scale same level if it has depth

Short Tire Marks/Segments

- ☐ Photograph 2–4 angles/views
- ☐ Photograph 2–4 lighting variances, consider bracketing

Long Tire Marks

- ☐ Place flat, retractable tape measure, yard stick, scale stick, or marked spatter stick along entire length of tire mark being photographed and on the same plane as the lowest section of the mark. Fix in place; do not move during photographs.
- ☐ Place with needed case information and identifier
- ☐ Place 300 mm L scale or 6 inch scale across the width of mark, moving each segment
- ☐ Photograph length of mark in overlapping segments 18–20 inches/45–51 cm, minimum overlap 1 inch/2.54 cm
- ☐ 0–18 inches/0–45 cm, with 3 angles of light
- ☐ 15–33 inches/38–84 cm, with 3 angles of light
- ☐ 29–47 inches/73–119 cm, with 3 angles of light
- ☐ Repeat until the end of tire mark or 8 feet/2-m distance, whichever is first

Photogammetry

- This system is best used by experts previously trained in it, or a CSI with no equipment or other means of collecting measurements
- Done after DNA/trace evidence collection
- Overhead photographs ideal—stand on stairs, ladder, porch, and so on. Standing height acceptable but no lower. Calculations account for angle but need to be as close to 90° as possible for accurate measurements.
- Camera settings—F11–F16, good depth of field needed for accuracy
- Ensure adequate brightness for recreation accuracy

Barriers to Accuracy

- Rolling surfaces, uneven surfaces—NOT for use on stairways, bumpy/slanted roads, hilly fields
- Low angle for photographs, hard to gather accurate distance
- The higher the camera angle, the higher the accuracy of measurements—90° versus 30°

Item Used for Measurement

- Can be prior-made template or symmetrical item found in scene
- Document measurements of items used for photographs or collect to take with you
- Item options: Floor tile, sidewalk square, clipboard/posse box, homemade square piece 1 × 1 feet—make in advance if possible. Large area 2 × 2 feet good size—small area 1 × 1 feet good size.

Method

1. Place item of known size in all photographs—place item at bottom/center of frame if possible
2. Document measurements of items used in notes; consider trace evidence for scene use
3. Photograph the room with all views showing the chosen item in place from as high as possible or as close to 90° as possible
4. Repeat in each room/area/yard with 30% overlap in all photographs

ALS Photography (Alternate Light Source)

Goggles/Plastic Filter/Lens Cover

- All results will need to be viewed/photographed with filter—use same color camera lens as for viewing
- Interference filter—allows specified wavelengths through
- Common color filters—yellow, red, orange, clear (UV)
- Polarizing filter—reduces glare from light, water, windows

Finding Wavelengths for Photographs

If pictures do not match your visual, using same wavelength and filter, do the following:

- Ensure filter cover is on camera
- Move light closer, farther, angled, and so on
- Try another wavelength/filter
- Use manual focus on camera
- Eliminate all overhead/ambient light possible
- Employ timer for shutter release
- Try painting with light with ALS wand for photographs
- Substrate the sample is on will affect results

Refer to scene search for specific ALS wavelengths for use on scene.

Near Infrared Photography (NIR)

- Helps see injures **BELOW** skin level
- Bruising, scarring, bite mark impression
- Consider RAW+JPEG/TIFF+JPEG

Reflective UV

- Helps see injury **AT** skin level
- Scarring, bite mark impression, old bruises

- Will NOT show tattoos, birth marks, Mongolian spots
- Consider RAW+JPEG/TIFF+JPEG
- Consider quartz lens—transmits greater UV
- Use filter designed to transmit UV radiation, **OPTION**: Baader U-Venus Filter (350 mm)
- Minimize exposure to skin/eyes
- Can block other areas with jacket/board

UV Photography

- Likely will need to raise ISO as UV pictures are naturally dark
- White balance—consider gray chart instead of white
- Filter—consider UV transmitting bandpass filter
- Use tripod, monopod, or other stabilizing device for low light photography

Focusing the Camera While Using ALS

- Above 700 nm (IR) can use automatic focus
- Below 700 nm may need manual focus
- Digital cameras made to focus in natural light, you can add light to help autofocus but may impact camera metering
- Use tripod, monopod, or other stabilizing device for low light photography

Photographing Results

- Use the same filter/wavelength used for viewing; however, be mindful of your results. One wavelength may be sharper but another brighter.
- The more diluted the sample is, the stronger the light source needed. Try to darken your surroundings if using handheld flashlights.
- Do not move light source too close to item for brighter results—can melt plastic bags/sheeting if too close. Instead lower the F-stop or lengthen the shutter speed.

Option: ALS

- ISO 500, 10 second shutter speed, F/8, flash off, color filter/barrier

Option: Fluorescence in Visible Light

- ISO 100, F/11, aperture priority setting, −1 exposure

Procedure for Photographs—NIR, UV, ALS Photography

1. Photographs with normal lighting first with and without scale
2. Affix camera to tripod—will need to be parallel to area of interest
3. Affix detachable flash to hot shoe (or flash options of choice)
4. Adjust settings—shutter speed 1/60; use F/5.6 and F/8 and F/11
5. Affix appropriate filter/lens
6. Use light source chosen output
7. Dim overhead lighting
8. Capture photograph of area—evaluate, adjust, re-take as needed
9. Add label/scale; focus camera on area of interest, not the scale
10. Capture additional photographs of area using series of F-stops and lighting

Marking Stains While Using Alternative Lighting/Filters

Common Markers When Using ALS

- Scale stickers, scale tape, or Post-it Notes—white/fluorescent
- Circle-shaped stickers
- Arrow—sticker/plastic
- White chalk/reflective chalk
- Sharpie marker

6 Subject Photographs

Photographing subjects, both on and off scene, is essential for documenting injuries and trace evidence. This section offers guidance to help capture photographs for various scenarios, including GSR and trace evidence collection. A checklist is provided to ensure all necessary photographs are taken for both live and deceased subjects. Accurate photographing of subjects is crucial as missed photos can result in lost evidence. Identifying and photographing trace evidence on a subject is equally important. Capturing injuries accurately is necessary for any district attorney to complete a case review or a judge at sentencing. It is also important for documenting the injuries sustained by the victim with both photographs and written documentation. Adjusting photograph settings can help capture realistic images. Using a scale and a color chart for injuries is important. The color chart provides control for exposure comparison and comparison purposes for the injuries.

Reasons for Immediate Subject Photographs

- Freeing up subjects to leave the scene with no injuries
- Freeing up subjects and witnesses with injuries to obtain medical help
- Subjects needing GSR test
- Subject wearing gloves or sustained injuries
- Subjects suspected of committing a violent crime should be examined and photographed on the face, neck, shoulders, arms, chest, back, and legs as soon as possible after the crime for injuries and trace evidence

SLR Camera Settings

- Manual focus or single focus mode in autofocus
- 50 mm lens
- F/11, 1/60, ISO 250–400
- Flash exposure −0.3 to −1.0 good for bruising/scarring, +/− as needed
- Ring light has reliable results and even lighting
- Flash diffusers can be beneficial to eliminate hot spots
- Detachable flash for side lighting only; don't place on camera as it will be too bright

 DOI: 10.4324/9781003503897-7

- Use various angles to get the best contour/texture of injury
- 6 inch gray scale or ABFO #2 scale (on same plane)

Scars/Marks/Injury/Tattoo Photographs

- Multiple angles/lights for best contour/clarity—adjust exposure setting +/− as needed
- Orientation photographs (mid-range) needed—orient to joint or body "landmark",[1] can use elbow to injury, shoulder to injury, knee to injury, and so on
- Polarizing lens/filters eliminate glare/show depth—use individually or together
- Near infrared, reflective UV, and ALS help see injuries/scars/marks/tattoos. Live view will assist with focus; consider RAW+JPEG.
- Reflective UV/UV—good for scars and bite marks. Capture after taking regular photographs, using appropriate filter; live view will assist with focus.
- Scale—keep on long edge of frame if possible
- Tattoos—flash diffuser and polarizer filter beneficial
- Can use gray scale to help with color metering
- Color chart—highly recommended for injury photographs

Curved Surface Injury

- Turn the scale as you move along injury or use sticker scale that adheres to all segments
- Photograph each segment; continue until entire area is captured
- Consider side lighting for curved, raised surfaces such as scars

Child Injury Photographs

- ID photographs need to be captured fully clothed
- No undergarments are allowed in injury photographs in most court settings
  - Take a photograph showing *only* the skin/injury and scale.
  - If captured accidentally, take a better picture/*don't delete*
  - If undergarments cover obvious injury, stop and obtain medical exam

Checklist—Live Subject Photographs—*Not All Listed Photographs Are Needed for All Individuals; Verify on Case-by-Case Basis What Is Needed*

☐ CAMERA SETTINGS—File/date/time—remove detachable flash; consider ring flash

- ☐ COVER PAGE—with name/DOB—picture identification if provided
- ☐ Have clean scale and color chart ready

Front Side

- ☐ Head to shoes
- ☐ Face photograph (neck to top of head)
- ☐ With and without obscuring clothing such as hats, sunglasses, and oversize coats
- ☐ Head to shoulders (top 1/3)
- ☐ Shoulders to hips (middle 1/3)
- ☐ Hips to shoes (bottom 1/3)

Face

- ☐ EYES—closed, open, eye whites and lids, looking up, down, left, and right
- ☐ MOUTH—exterior lips/jaw, interior lips, mouth open showing throat

Right Side

- ☐ Face photograph (neck to top of head)
- ☐ Head to shoes
- ☐ Head to shoulders
- ☐ Shoulders to hips
- ☐ Hips to shoes

Back Side

- ☐ Head to shoes
- ☐ Head to shoulders
- ☐ Shoulders to hips
- ☐ Hips to shoes

Left Side

- ☐ Head to shoes
- ☐ Head to shoulders
- ☐ Shoulders to hips
- ☐ Hips to shoes

Hands

- ☐ Back of hands (hold palms to belly)
- ☐ Palms of hands (bend at elbows, palms toward camera)
- ☐ Fingernails if damaged

Close-ups

- ☐ Tattoos, piercings, jewelry, scars/marks/birthmarks
- ☐ Clothing—damages/blood/debris

Shoes

- ☐ Top of shoes if photographs are for identification
- ☐ Soles of shoes if photographs are for pattern comparison
- ☐ Any present blood, scuffing, plant matter, soil, and so on

Injuries, with and without Scale/Color Chart

- ☐ Day 1, day 3, day 7 picture series
- ☐ Scale on long edge of photograph, same plane
- ☐ Impression evidence macrophotography as needed

Subject Photos from Accident

- ☐ Face/ID
- ☐ Airbag deposit—linear/arc of small dots
- ☐ Shoulder area for bruising/impressions
- ☐ On clothing for impressions/residue transfer
- ☐ Injuries to shins/calves/legs of victim
- ☐ Bottoms of feet for pedal impressions if driving
- ☐ Glass in hair/top of head

Subject Photographs for GSR Collection

- ☐ Face/ID
- ☐ Clothing to include defects/blood/debris
- ☐ Hands with handbags and writing
- ☐ Hands without handbags to include defects/blood/debris/GSR

Subjects with Injuries—Strangulation

- ☐ Face/ID
- ☐ Clothing to include defects/blood/debris
- ☐ All visible injuries with and without scale
- ☐ Petechiae locations—eyelids, whites of eyes (have subject look left, right, up, down), backs of both ears, uvula (back of throat), inside of top and bottom lip
- ☐ Bruising locations—all sides of neck, shoulder blades/shoulders, behind ears, lower jaw/jawline, hands/wrists, feet, tongue (adjust flash exposure accordingly)
- ☐ Hands of both parties to include nails, palms, and tops of hands

- ☐ Suspect injuries to include hands, lower and upper arms, shoulder blades, back, neck and face

Checklist—Deceased Subject Photographs on Scene—Not All Photographs Will Be Possible for All Persons Though All Are Encouraged

Location in Scene with Overall/Mid-range

- ☐ All items in direct vicinity and special relationship to body
- ☐ Capture all visible injuries prior to transport if possible
- ☐ Consider bracketing for decomposition and injuries

Front

- ☐ Have clean scale and color chart handy
- ☐ Face to include spittle, dribble, drool, blood, and defects to face
- ☐ Head to shoes
- ☐ Head to shoulders (top 1/3)
- ☐ Shoulders to hips (middle 1/3)
- ☐ Hips to shoes (bottom 1/3)
- ☐ Top of shoes/feet
- ☐ Overhead if applicable

Right Side

- ☐ Face photograph (neck to top of head)
- ☐ Head to shoes
- ☐ Head to shoulders
- ☐ Shoulders to hips
- ☐ Hips to shoes

Back Side

- ☐ Head to shoes
- ☐ Head to shoulders
- ☐ Shoulders to hips
- ☐ Hips to shoes
- ☐ Bottom of shoes/feet

Left Side

- ☐ Head to shoes
- ☐ Head to shoulders
- ☐ Shoulders to hips
- ☐ Hips to shoes

Hands

- ☐ Before bagging hands—front/back, nails/defects/jewelry/hair
- ☐ After bagging hands to include case writing on exterior

Feet/Shoes

- ☐ Shoes—damages/tread/blood
- ☐ Feet (bare/socks)
- ☐ Tops/bottom—blood/dirt/debris
- ☐ Before/after bagging feet

Clothing

- ☐ Damages/blood/debris/spittle/leaves/soil
- ☐ Manufacturing tag if visible

Level of Moisture

- ☐ Wet/dry—hair/skin/clothes
- ☐ Discoloration lines from previously being wet

Mid-range and Close-up of Individual Characteristics to Include

- ☐ Injuries—with/without scale
- ☐ Weapon defects
- ☐ Medical intervention injuries/equipment
- ☐ Blood flow patterns (on/around body)
- ☐ Footwear/tire marks
- ☐ Bite marks
- ☐ Tattoos/scars/piercings/jewelry

Subject Photos from Accident

- ☐ Face/ID
- ☐ Airbag deposit—linear/arc of small dots
- ☐ Shoulder area for bruising/impressions
- ☐ On clothing for impressions/residue transfer
- ☐ Injuries to shins/calves/legs of victim
- ☐ Bottoms of feet for pedal impressions if driving
- ☐ Glass in hair/top of head

Subjects with Injuries—Strangulation

- ☐ Face/ID
- ☐ Clothing to include defects/blood/debris

- ☐ All visible injuries with and without scale
- ☐ Petechiae locations—eyelids, whites of eyes, backs of both ears, uvula (back of throat), inside of top and bottom lip
- ☐ Bruising locations—all sides of neck, shoulder blades/shoulders, behind ears, lower jaw/jawline, hands/wrists, feet, tongue (adjust flash exposure accordingly)
- ☐ Hands of both parties to include nails, palms, and tops of hands
- ☐ Suspect injuries to include hands, lower and upper arms, shoulder blades, back, neck, and face

Body Bag

- ☐ Interior body bag with contents before zipped
- ☐ Exterior bag writing/lock tag
- ☐ Area under body after removal

Cases for Consideration of Subject Photographs

The scene photographs taken of the following subjects contained valuable information for case completion:

- Kalee Bruce's body contained bloody footwear prints from stomping
- Meredith Kercher's body contained a bloody footwear print

The following suspects were photographed after the crime with attention to their injuries:

- Dan Kootz was processed after murdering Beth Kootz. He had injuries to his forearms and Beth's blood on the underside of his watch.
- While being interviewed about the stabbing deaths of Nicole Simpson and Ronald Goldman, OJ Simpson was found to have cuts to his hands.
- Craig Peyer had scratches on his face while being interviewed for the strangulation of Cara Knott.
- Johnny Lewis was suspected to have murdered Catherine Davis before falling to his death. Lewis had fingernail scratches on his face and neck when he fell.
- After the murder of Jarmecca Yvonne "Nikki" Whitehead, two juveniles were found to have unreported bite marks changing the scope of investigation, and her daughters later admitted to her murder.
- Raymond Clark had scratches to his face and arm when interviewed about the death of Annie Le.
- Darryl Littlejohn had scratches to his neck when he was questioned about the death of Imette St. Guillen.

Note

1 Organization of Scientific Area Committees for Forensic Science (OSAC) (2023) *S-0006—Standard Guide for Photographing Scars, Marks, and Tattoos.*

Body Trauma and Injuries

7

This information is intended solely for scene processing reference and evidence collection assistance; all medical determinations are made during an autopsy by a medical professional. This chapter provides guidance to help you identify and document injuries at the scene, draw preliminary conclusions, and enhance evidence collection and scene processing. It will guide you on what to photograph, help recognize normal but unusual findings, and determine which items to collect on-site. Ideally, you should secure the scene until the completion of the autopsy; however, this may not always be feasible, and preliminary decisions will need to be made.

A significant challenge encountered at scenes is accurately interpreting what you observe. For instance, how do you discern whether an individual fell or was struck and pushed down? How do you correctly interpret all the information presented by the scene? This information is designed to assist you in determining what you are observing and how to document it properly. One method that may be of use is using a color chart for injury photographs. As always injuries should be photographed with and without scale; however, using a scale with color chart attached is a beneficial way to document the color and exposure of the injury photographs.

Trauma Types

Antemortem Trauma

- Injuries occurring BEFORE death, in process of healing
- Will have visible differences in appearance from postmortem trauma which can be determined at autopsy
- Will have active blood flow to injury, active skin healing, and active bone healing which can be visible on scene

Perimortem Trauma

- Injuries occurring AT OR AROUND time of death, minimal healing process

DOI: 10.4324/9781003503897-8

Postmortem Trauma

- Injuries occurring AFTER death, no healing/bruising
- Lack of active bleeding/bruising to site/tissue at site of injury which can be visible on scene

Blunt Force Trauma

- Bruising caused by the impact of blunt object
- Can take 1–2 days to develop visible markings
- Caused by motion of acceleration or deceleration
- Blows to head can cause bleeding at ears and nose

Chemical Trauma

- Death from trauma from use of drugs/poison such as alcohol, carbon monoxide, cyanide, antifreeze, and drugs

Sharp Force Trauma

- Cuts from sharp object—knives/glass/machete

Injury Types

Abrasion

- Superficial scrape to skin that does not break skin
- Grazes, scratches, rope burns, tight handcuffs, bindings, brush burns (road rash)

Amputated

- Removal of appendage (arm, leg, foot)

Artifact

- Removed piece of body

Avulsion

- Removal of skin (cut off tattoos), generally smooth cuts in specific shaped areas

Bruising/Contusion

- Breakage of blood vessels
- Result of a blow or squeeze that crushes tissue

- Does not generally break skin unless on the head
- Can be covered by makeup, even on decedent
- Darker skin tones make bruising harder to see
- Elderly skin is thinner than younger skin
- Common color evolution: Red, violet, black, blue, brown, green, yellow
  - Color affected by depth of bruise/location of bruise
  - Yellow often found when older than 18 hours
  - Red, blue, and purple often found after 1 hour
  - Red present at any age
  - New/recent bruises will often be invisible at time of photographs
- Making a firm estimation of bruise age based upon color is not accurate nor recommended
  - Bruises on same body may not age at same rate
  - Deeper bruises can take longer to move to surface
  - Visible when closer to surface
  - Individuals' bruising development varies at different rates
  - Injuries should be evaluated multiple times after assault
- Mongolian spots
  - Birthmarks that often fade within a few years
  - Often mistaken for bruising due to dark coloring and location
  - Consistent dark blue or gray color, no green/red/purple hue
  - Found on infants/toddlers, generally the buttocks and lower back
  - Ruled out in autopsy or by medical professional

Bruising Locations

- Abdominal bruising is caused by great force due to soft areas or pinching of skin
- Always look for patterns and repetition of bruising
- Back of the hand—often defensive wounds for blunt force, often in elderly due to thin skin
- Eyelids/around the eyes (racoon eyes) can be from injury at base of skull/back of head/nose fracture and the blood pooling in the face
- Hip fracture—blood can pool in thighs causing upper leg bruising
- Pinch bruising—often symmetrical
- Tops of feet—blunt force, restriction of movement
- Tram track
  - Separation of bruise showing 2 lines on the edges of impact rather than 1 in the center often seen with baton, baseball bat, tire iron, whip
  - Gravity/blood flow moves bruise location away from injury site, leaving edges often shaped like the instrument used
- Wrist/ankles—ligature marks

- Not to be confused with hair tie marks; wrist is common storage location for hair ties/keychains

Burns

- Burns >65% of body can be fatal, even first degree
- Blisters can occur before OR after death
- Common skin conditions are often mistaken for burns
  - Scalded skin syndrome (staph)
  - Impetigo
  - Diaper rash
- Lighter skin tones
  - Appearance—red/pink
  - Scars are often darker than rest of skin tone
- Darker skin tones
  - Can appear white/peach, pink/red
  - Scars are often lighter than rest of skin tone
- Splash burns—occur when hot liquids "splash" a person
  - Photograph temperature reading from water source as well as injuries
- Accidental splash burns
  - Often found on front side head/upper chest/upper arms
  - Normally not front and back side at same time
  - Water movement often goes top to bottom
  - Often asymmetrical in shape
  - Kids reach up to pot handle, bump hot coffee cup in hand
- Intentional splash burns
  - Liquid movement from front to back, left to right
  - No movement of accidental spill
  - Often found on face/chest/neck
  - Stocking/glove burns
  - Burns in shape of socks/gloves
  - Caused by immersing hands/feet in hot water
  - Often symmetrical in shape
- Cigarette burns
  - Symmetrical if direct pressure
  - Direct pressure indicative of abuse
  - Elongated burns can indicate unintentional contact
  - Similar in appearance to impetigo (but impetigo is irregular in shape)
- Dunking burns (being dunked in scalding water)
  - Burns with linear depth absent hands/feet
  - Body is held over liquid, feet spared

    - Often upper thigh/lower abdomen line from dunking while holding hands/feet
- Fatal burns
    - Heat can shrink or expand body parts, ears often shrink, lips/tongue often expand
    - Finger/toes often curl, legs spread, knees bend, feet arch, elbows bend, wrists tighten
    - Skin splitting is often seen on scalp, hands/feet, wrists/ankles, knees/elbows
    - Skin splitting is superficial and does not include the flesh. Consider puncture wounds if there is flesh damage.
    - Fat pool can form around base of body due to becoming liquid
    - Include photographs of exterior nose/mouth and interior nose/mouth while on scene if possible
    - Results of fire heat can give appearance of injury; ensure you consult with medical professionals before making a determination

Compression Marks

- Impression made from object force to body
- Bite impressions, tool impressions, cord impressions
- Bite marks, tool marks, ligature marks

Crushing Impact

- Causes abrasions, contusions, lacerations, fractures, breaks

Chopping

- Cuts to skin/bone/tissue from large blades such as axe, machete, machinery, and lawn equipment

Cut

- Sharp object cuts skin
- Wound longer than deep, often minimal bruising
- Common cuts: Defense wounds on forearms or lower legs
- Not easy to identify tool used

Decapitated

- Removal of head

Dismemberment

- Body separated into pieces
- Tool marks may be present on bone and cartilage

Incision

- Non-jagged laceration to skin

Laceration

- Abraded edges, torn skin—puncture/ripped skin from blunt force trauma such as hit with hammer, bottle, sealed can, pistol whipping, or slamming face/head into door
- Blunt force to the abdominal wall rarely visible from looking
- Lacerations to ear/nose/throat—don't occur naturally

Scraping Marks

- Tool moving across skin with force leaving mark, can leave mark in the shape of the object

Stab Wound

- Pointed object cuts into tissue; wound is deeper than long
- Can leave shape of weapon depending upon angle
- Minimal bruising common
- There can be minimal blood on scene due to internal bleeding, heavy clothing layers, or wound location
- Self-inflicted stab wounds are less common, often have multiple locations and levels of severity but generally occur from the dominant hand
- Perpetrators often cut themselves during a blade attack due to slipping, as blood is very slippery

Weapon-Specific Injuries

Clubs/Stones

- High risk to suspect/close contact
- Cause lacerations, blunt force trauma, compression injuries
- Damage to skin, bones, brain

Knives/Swords

- High risk to suspect/close contact
- Incisions, punctures, amputations
- Damage to internal organs/damage arteries

Long Guns

- Low risk to suspect/distant contact
- Puncture wounds, perforating wounds, large chunks of damage to body

Bean Bag Guns

- Circular solid bruising in area of impact
- Redness upon impact, bruise over time
- Intent to disable not kill

Blood on Scene Can Be Deceptive to Severity—*Variables That Impact Blood Loss*

- Location of injury to body
- Amount of clothing being worn by victim
- High body fat in area of injury
- Body mobility is low or high
- Assault carried out over a long period of time or short period of time relates to amount of blood letting
- Injury pre or postmortem
- Injury to abdomen/chest little blood (goes inside)
- Injury to head/face/neck heavy blood on scene
- Victims' response to injury (fight/lay down)

Gunshot Wounds

Abrasion Collar

- Caused when bullet passes through, bullet residue wipes off on skin as passing through
- Circular dark mark

Bullet Wipe

- Impacted skin when bullet did not perforate skin, left mark as traveled
- Black soot or minor abrasion

Close Contact

- Gunshot wound from weapon being close to item when fired
- Ring around edges with sharp, defined circular shape

Contact Wound

- Gunshot wound from weapon touching item when fired
- Defect is larger than projectile size, but can retain shape of muzzle
- Contact entrance wound is often larger than exit wound
- Skin edges are torn, not smooth, searing/charring of skin
- Skull can have star-shaped wound due to gases building up between skin and skull

Close, Near Contact Wound

- Gasses/soot projected only few inches distance. Close but not touching surface.
- Blackening of skin, skin tears, dirty appearance
- Smoke can adhere to surface area, often can be wiped off wound area
- Stippling creates tiny wounds/deposits of powder that appear like tiny wounds
- Stippling cannot be wiped off wound

Distant Wound

- Distance of a few feet
- Lack of smoke, soot, stippling
- Circular skin defect, rim of abraded skin around edges

Entrance Wound

- Where the projectile enters an item
- Often smaller in size than exit wound
- Smaller amount of blood than exit wound

Exit Wound

- Where a projectile leaves an item
- Often larger than entrance wound
- Larger amount of blood than entrance wound
- Often edges are jagged, torn
- Always confirm path of projectile at autopsy; don't assume based upon size

Intermediate Wound

- Unburned powder (stippling) around defect, few inches to a few feet

Penetrating Wound

- Has entrance wound, no exit

Perforating Wound

- Has entrance and exit wound, through and through

Powder Stippling in Wound

- Postmortem—yellow brown coloring possible
- Antemortem—red brown coloring possible

Shotgun Wound

- Close range leaves one large wound with severe damage
- If less than 10 feet/3 m range—wadding may be inside wound/damage
- Distant range leaves many individual small wounds with minor damage
- CANNOT determine distance based upon distance of wounds to each other

Abuse Injuries—*Child/Elder/Domestic*

Medical Examination

- Medical examination for children/elderly should be conducted by geriatric or pediatric specialist as bodies bruise/heal differently when young/elderly
- If sexual assault is suspected, a sexual abuse examination should be conducted; ensure you have contacted the correct facility
- The level of external trauma does not always reflect the level of internal trauma, and a professional should determine the extent[1]
- Injury photographs should occur with and without a scale and with a color chart if able

Common Injury Locations on Suspect

- Hands—red knuckles, scratching, abrasions from assault, linear bruising along fingers from manual strangulation/choking, cuts to fingers/fingertips from stabbing
- Face/neck/forearms/upper back/shoulder area—linear scratching, gouging with fingernails, biting. Pay attention to directionality/location (close-ups with scale are vital).

Common Injury Locations on Victim

- Upper arms
- Abdomen/trunk/back
- Buttocks
- Upper legs
- Tops of feet
- Bruising on throat and jaw line
- Behind the ears
- Areas covered by clothing items

Common Injury Types for Victim

Bald Spots

- Self-harm of pulling hair can cause bald spots, often seen with anxiety (Trichotillomania)
- Scaly scalp could indicate medical conditions
- Bald spots that continue to change location could indicate abuse or self-harm

Bed Sores

- Causes: Circulation/pressure/thrombosis, being stationary and thinning skin
- Not always neglect, can be medical issues
- Take weeks to develop; check for signs of regular care/movement

Kennedy Ulcers

- Happen at end of life—not from neglect *(often confused for neglectful bed sores)*
- Occur suddenly, grow rapidly, mostly occur on tailbone
- Look like bed sores and when they start, they are often pear shaped/butterfly shaped
- Beginning appearance like bruise
- End appearance black/swollen

Bite Marks

- Torn flesh generally from a dog/animal
- Compressed flesh generally from a human
- Take comparison quality photographs of all bite marks

Bloating

- Physical trauma can cause fluid retention and bloating

Bruising in Soft Areas

- Abdomen, thighs, genitals, breast
- Pinch bruising—often symmetrical—2 small circles in proximity
- Circular bruising from grabbing/holding ears
- Twist/pull on ears—appears like stretch marks behind ears—bruising around ears with no other facial trauma indicative of pulling
- Trauma to forehead can cause black eyes 24–72 hours after trauma

Burns to Hands/Feet

- Common defined shapes of heater, stove, radiator, lighter, iron
- Water burns to perineum and feet but not hands can be from being held over/in water
- Water burns to hands/feet/lower legs and NOT trunk/bottom/back are common when falling in, as you stop yourself before submerging
- Consider order of actions—if it were hot would the subject willingly submerge as they did?

Cord Marks

- Electrical cords, phone cords, extension cords
- Caused by a whipping motion can leave loop-shaped injuries

Fractures

- Causes: Multiple medical conditions, physical therapy sessions, malnutrition conditions, abusive conditions
- Unrelated fractures at dissimilar stages of healing can indicate abuse or medical conditions
- Twisting fractures can be caused by pulling in and out of car seats and chairs

Internal Injuries

- Not always visible on the exterior body; medical examination is required

Myiasis

- Infestation of living body with egg/larvae/fly
- Found in bed sores, gangrene, poor hygiene, decomposition

Pin Hole Marks

- Poking with pointed instruments

Slap Marks

- Hand-shaped welting/bruising often on face/back/buttocks

Strangulation

- Injuries to the front, sides, and back of neck possible
- Bruising to the nose/lips area from facial smothering
- Petechiae on whites of the eyes, the uvula (back of throat), backs of the ears

- Injuries to the neck, even small, should be considered "significant" until you can prove they are not, as strangulation can leave minimal marks[2]

Torn Frenulum *(Upper Lip Area)*

- Forced feedings
- Sexual assault

Whip Marks

- Often buttocks/legs/abdomen/back

Sexual Assault Injuries *(Lack of Injuries Is Commonplace; This Does Not Disprove Assault)*

- Bony areas—elbows, hips, knees, spine
- Lower back/upper bottom scraping
- Circular bruising on arms/thighs
- Bruising to tops of feet
- Bruising/cuts to interior lips
- Bite marks to shoulders/back/hands/face
- Restraints marks on ankles, wrists, neck

Medical Examination Should Be Completed

- Ensure the sexual-assault-specific examination will cover NON intimate injuries and get all pictures done at one time reducing trauma
- Injuries to genitals should be captured by medical personnel only

Alternative Medical Treatment Methods[3]

These practices can leave marks often mistaken for abuse injuries:

Cupping

- Appearance:
  - Circular shaped marks with red/early bruise appearance commonly in multiple, not just 1 or 2
  - 6–8 cm size
  - Mild skin irritation
- Equipment:
  - Alcohol, matches/lighter, circular cups
  - Alcohol is ignited causing vacuum, pulling tissue into cup

Coining

- Appearance:
  - Parallel linear bruising (LIGHT) with petechiae
  - Between ribs on front/back, neck, inner arms, spine
- Equipment:
  - Coin, oil
  - Skin is massaged with oil and rubbed with coin
  - Believed to relieve fever, headache, chills, cold

Spooning

- Appearance:
  - Similar to coining but smaller, mark made from back of spoon on skin
  - Behind knees, inside elbows, between ribs on front/back, chest/clavicle
  - Believed to relieve pain
- Equipment:
  - Spoon, oil

Pinching

- Appearance:
  - Small, isolated bruising
  - Caused from pinching skin
- Equipment:
  - Mentholated rub
  - Rub is applied to skin, then pinched
  - Used for pain, minor ailments

Notes

1 Dolinak, David, et al. *Forensic Pathology, Principles and Practice*. Elsevier Academic Press, 2005.
2 Dolinak, David, et al. *Forensic Pathology, Principles and Practice*. Elsevier Academic Press, 2005.
3 Kail, Tony M. *Magico-Religious Groups and Ritualistic Activities: A Guide for First Responders*. CRC Press, 2008.

Decomposition 8

Numerous scenes involve decedents at various stages of decomposition, ranging from barely noticeable to skeletal remains. Determining details on-site can be challenging; however, having a foundational understanding can guide the processing of the rest of the scene effectively. If discrepancies arise between the narrative and the observations, discuss these differences to ensure confidence in the scene processing. Such indications may necessitate the collection of trace evidence from the body, further questioning, or significant adjustments to the scene processing methodology. Maintain open communication with your medical examiner or coroner and discuss the findings on scene before it becomes too late to collect crucial evidence.

This information is intended to aid in the scene search and documentation process and to assist in generating ideas for further evidence gathering. It should not be considered as medical advice or take precedence over any medical personnel. This document serves as a comprehensive source of information to refer to on-scene when uncertainties arise regarding timelines or nomenclature.

General Suggestions

- Consider placing body wrapped in/placed under clean sheet while in body bag to help retain trace evidence and reduce uncontrolled movement of body
- If the fire department leaves a white sheet on the body prior to your arrival: Photograph in place, mark which side is on body, remove for processing, retain sheet with the body and examine for any trace evidence. Book into property for later examination.
- Document the temperature of the decedent *by feel*—frozen/cold/hot/warm
- Body positions
    - Prone—face down
    - Supine—face up

Be mindful that all of the following information is dependent upon many variables such as humidity, temperature, season, direct sunlight, and vegetation coverage.

DOI: 10.4324/9781003503897-9

Decomposition

Timeframe

- Begins inside the body at time of death
- 1 week in air = 2 weeks in water = 8 weeks in dirt
  - *California*—a decedent in a vehicle in the summer is enough to begin skin slippage after just a couple of hours
  - *Arizona*—bloating in 2 days, gases at 3 days, partial mummification at 4 days, skeletonization 6–9 months
  - *Mississippi*—child can be skeletonized within 10 days in late summer
- Variable decomposition is impacted by
  - Bug activity/access
  - Covering/wrapping
  - Humidity/moisture exposure
  - Open air/controlled air—delayed by airtight environments
  - Sun exposure
  - Temperature—tissue frozen then thawed decomposes quicker and tissue that is hot/exposed to sun decomposes quicker
  - Tissue with trauma decomposes quicker

Eye Changes

- They should be photographed as close to arrival as possible as they can continue to change color on scene
  - If eyes are open, can photograph as soon as possible
- Cornea
  - Clear, raised portion of eyeball over iris
  - Turns cloudy with air contact
  - Cloudiness normal within 8–14 hours
  - Completely cloudy after 3 days of air contact
  - Possible to start within 3 hours after death
  - Will be absent if face is submerged underwater
  - Discoloration begins after being exposed to air
- Sclera
  - White portion of eyeball
  - Discolors with exposed air contact
  - Submerged eyes should still be white
- Tache Noir (French term meaning "black line")
  - Dark line across eyeballs after death caused from exposure to air, normally symmetrical in both eyes and matches the open position of the eyelids
  - Begins within 3 hours of death

Hair Changes

Postmortem Root Band—Discoloration of Root That Occurs during Decomposition Process

- Appearance—dark "band" section near root, occurs in humans and animals
- Collect hairs and allow laboratory to determine presence
- Delayed by water/freezing conditions, hastened by hot conditions

Body Position Changes

Cadaveric Spasm—Agonal Grasp, Dying Grasp

- Usually occurs in deaths with great panic or tension
- Body goes into instant rigor and the item in the hand at time of death stays clenched in the hand
- Examples: Clenched fist holding last items such as grass, hair, sheets, and handgun
- Not re-creatable, not stageable
- Lasts until putrefaction, does not dissipate with rigor

Pugilistic Stance (Boxer Stance)

- Caused by heat in fire, reaction to muscles' exposure to heat after death
- Arms draw toward face, knees draw toward torso

Putrefaction

Time Progression on Land—Normal Variables

- 24–30 hours—green discoloration in abdomen
- 30–40 hours—gaseous bloating, swollen tongue, green/purple face
- 36–48 hours—marbling, purge, bloating, face/trunk swelling
- 48 hours–6 days—skin slippage, bloating, more marbling, purging possible
- 18 months average—skeletonization (depending on weather/temperature)
- Factors impacting above information—ambient temperature/humidity/scavengers

Time Progression under Water 68–73°F/20–22.77°C

- 5+ hours–3 days—skin wrinkling on finger/toe pads
- 4–10 days—decomposition begins: Often head, neck, upper legs and butt begin bloating

- 2–4 weeks—bloating, marbling, peeling of epidermis/scalp
- 1–2 months—partial liquefaction and muscle separation
- 2.5–3 months—adipocere will begin
- Decomposition changes are based upon environment, bacteria, temperature, and microorganisms since bacteria growth requires moisture/humidity
- Body initially sinks and rises as gas accumulates
- While decomposition underwater is slower, once the body is exposed to air there is a quick acceleration

Changes to Body during Putrefaction

- Can cause pink discoloration of teeth due to red blood cells
- Green coloring to skin
- Dark vein coloring visible through skin
- Gas producing; great swelling can occur in face, tongue, abdomen, genitals
- Skin slippage occurs
- Can cause fetus to be expelled
- Submerged bodies float at this stage
- Purge—release of body fluids from all orifices due to internal pressure during putrefaction, can be confused with vomit or bowel release
- Butyric Fermentation—tissues and organs become liquid; odor decreases

Adipocere

- Expulsion of fat in gray/white greasy substance
- Initially it looks like white oily wax or soft cheese on skin
- Found on cheeks, chin, abdomen, buttocks primarily
- Turns hard/brittle after several months
- Requires high humidity/high temperature, typically found in wet environments or water
- Floats in water
- Normally 3 months to form; can be found as early as 3 weeks
- If present should be documented—indicates exposure to air

Algor Mortis

- Cooling of body after death; continues until body reaches ambient temperature

Time Progression

- 1.5–2°F loss per hour for first 12 hours and 1°F loss per hour after that is common rate of loss[1]

- Limbs cool quicker than body core
- Temperature collection from core rather than armpit is more accurate
- Using temperature to determine time of death is low accuracy; it should be a variable considered but not a deciding factor

Variables Affecting Algor Mortis

- Not all bodies start at 98.6°F and that can skew rate of decomposition
- Struggle prior to death can cause increased body temperature
- Heavy maggot presence can raise temperature of corpse after death
- Clothing/covering—minimal clothing in a cold environment will lower temperature of body or excessive clothing in a hot environment

Livor Mortis—Livor—Lividity—Hypostasis

- Change in skin coloring after death, pooling of blood due to gravity only
- Blue/purple coloring to skin normal
- Blanching
  - Pressure by finger squeezing causes void in purple coloring which promptly dissipates upon release
- Voids
  - Section with lack of purple coloring
  - Can be normal areas touching the ground, or could show an item was beneath body while settling
  - Voids found at point of direct contact with floor and skin
  - Rest of blood pools around pressure point
  - Body found lying on back?—chest/face should not be purple
  - Purple on top and bottom?—body was turned over after lividity started and before lividity fixed
- Co-sleeping
  - Lividity often shows pressure voids on chest/back
  - Depicts pressure above/below
  - Suffocation with body

Variables Affecting Color

- Body with extreme blood loss can show little/no lividity
- Easier to see on lighter skin
- Subjects with anemia often have light coloring
- Carbon monoxide causes cherry red lividity
- Cyanide poison causes bright scarlet red/light pink lividity
- Snow or extreme cold can cause light pink lividity
- Phosphorus poisoning can cause brown/yellow lividity

Time Progression on Land

- Begins to pool as soon as circulation stops
- Detectable 30 minutes–4 hours after death
- Blanching occurs within 4–5 hours after death
- Fixed at 8–12 hours
- Each time body is moved before livor is fixed, it will begin to pool again, forming a new pattern

Lividity of Body in Water

- Drowning often has no visible lividity
- Color change does not follow gravity like on land—instead, compression pushes blood away from area
- Contact lividity—voids from resting on rocks, branches, bottom of water present on hands, feet, knees
- Current lividity—lividity follows flow of current and water level
- If body goes in water dead with livor already setting in, the original lividity markings will remain
- If body goes in water alive, they may have no lividity markings

Rigor Mortis—Rigor

- Stiffening after death
- Small muscles affected quicker
- Can cause semen to expel from penis
- Can affect pupil dilation
- Rigor is almost never found in expelled fetus
- Can be confused with stiffening from extreme heat/cold exposure during death
- If your M.E. is not coming for several hours, gather rigor status/information from medics who pronounced. You may lose valuable information if no one touches the body for several hours.
- Rigor can be broken with force on joints
  - If fully in rigor when broken, stiffness will not return
  - If not fully in rigor when broken, some stiffness can return to the joints
  - Rigor gets broken by hand during autopsy
- If fixed position does not match body as found, it was likely moved after onset
  - Body on back with arms raised in rigor—was moved after rigor set in
  - If death is reported to be in last hour but there are signs of rigor upon arrival, do more checking

Time Progression on Land

- 1 hour—starts to be noticeable
- 3 hours—eyelids
- 5 hours—neck muscles
- 6 hours—upper limbs
- 9 hours—legs
- 12 hours—full rigor
- 12–24 hours—remains in rigor for 12 hours
- 24–36 hours—begins to dissipate over another 12–24 hours at ROOM TEMPERATURE
- 40 hours—normally gone

Rigor on Body in Water

- Starts in jaw
- Partially submerged will impact rigor
- Often absent in young/old victims
- Cold causes muscle rigidity before death, appearing like rigor

Variables Affecting Rigor

- Heat speeds up rigor, cold slows down rigor
- Desert extreme heat—can appear/disappear within first 12 hours
- Appears/dissipates quicker in children/elderly/severely malnourished due to smaller muscle mass
- Carbon monoxide poisoning can delay onset/Strychnine poisoning accelerates onset

Mummification

- Requires low humidity/high temperature
- Fingers are not good for printing unless re-hydrated; soak in water/dish soap
- Shrinkage around cuticles gives appearance that nails grew after death
- Shrinkage can cause large splits that appear as trauma
- Average conditions require 3 months for mummification

Skeletonization

- Skin and tissue decompose, leaving bones exposed
- On ground—takes 1–2 years with normal conditions
- Underground—15–20 years with normal conditions

Bug Bites

- Ant bite marks—small, shallow superficial holes/lines, can look like abrasions on exposed skin
- Cockroach marks—cockroaches feed inside diapers of living children/adults and on exposed skin of deceased persons, can be confused with abrasions or diaper rash

Animal Bites

- Can be pets or wild animals
- Gives appearance of deep injury
- Blood activity in the wound will assist with the determination, can be done at autopsy

Cases to Consider Regarding Decomposition

- 2014: Elderly male decedent in California was reported to have occurred within the last 3 hours and was cold to the touch upon arrival. He kept the temperature setting in his room to 50 degrees and he was minimally dressed, accounting for the low body temperature so close to death.
- 2011: Chris Coleman was found guilty of murdering his wife and two sons. He was immediately suspected because the officer identified signs of decomposition that were already present, which contradicted the timeline Coleman provided.
- 2008: Tommy Booth disappeared while out with friends and was found 2 weeks later in a state of rigor, in a body of water previously searched, with drag marks nearby in the soil. Authorities stated he was in water the whole time and was just missed.
- 1993: During scene processing at the death of juveniles James M. Moore, Steven Branch, and Christopher Byers the temperature of the children was not collected, further complicating their time of death findings.

Note

1 Spitz, W. U. et al. *Spitz and Fisher's Medicolegal Investigation of Death, Guidelines for the Application of Pathology to Crime Investigation*, 3rd ed. Charles C. Thomas Publisher, 1993.

Cause, Manner, Mechanism of Death

9

Accurately interpreting the signs of death and decomposition is a challenging aspect of death investigation. This chapter provides refresher information that you may have learned previously but may not immediately recall. It is important to note that this information is for reference purposes only and should not be used as a medical diagnosis or to supersede medical advice, similar to the previous chapter. This content does not apply universally to all scenes. The scene information, clues, and context should be considered alongside all aspects of the subject's life, with caution exercised in making final decisions.

> Most of the problems occur with improper response to a crime scene.
>
> —**Geberth**[1]

Cause of Death

- Disease or injury that initiated the lethal chain of events that led to death
- What did they die of? For example, heart disease, gunshot wound, car accident

Manner of Death

- Legal classification of death based on circumstances surrounding death
- Natural, accident, suicide, homicide, undetermined
- Determined by pathologist, coroner, medical examiner

Mechanism of Death

- Reason death occurred—for example, asphyxia, blood loss, sepsis

Death by Asphyxia—*Restriction of AIR*

- Most commonly strangulation/suffocation, hanging, drowning
- Does not always cause visible injuries

DOI: 10.4324/9781003503897-10

- Agonal breath—dying breath—bodies' last attempt to breathe before dying/as dying is strong and can inhale hair/silt/plants/water, can trigger vomit/convulsions. The airway is inspected at autopsy to check for this.

Asphyxia—Hanging or Hanged (Not Hung)

- If victim has been hoisted up to appear as a hanging, the rope/stabilizing item can show signs of wear from hoisting the weight
- Look for "step off" point—chair, ladder
- Ensure lividity matches hanging upright
- Urine or blood flow in the right direction?
- Photograph the back of the neck prior to transport
- Hanging can occur at any height though the ligature will likely still be at an angle
- Photograph angle of ligature, placement, and knots of ligature
- Doorknobs and closet bars are common sources
- Take note of shoes/flooring/walls when the height is low and look for scuff marks from the shoes
- If bruises are visible inside the groove line of a ligature, then it can indicate the injury occurred while the subject was alive
- Lividity above the ligature may pool in the neck, as well as legs/feet/hands

Asphyxia—Positional

- Air flow cut off due to position of throat, often low to ground
- Often accidental due to impairment/age/mechanical and subjects have the inability to correct their body position

Asphyxia—Strangulation—*Asphyxia from External Pressure*

- Manual or ligature (belt, rope, zip tie, paracord, shoelaces, phone cord)
- Can lose consciousness in 10 seconds–1 minute
- Can cause death in less than 10 minutes, but the injuries can cause death up to 36 hours later due to injuries
- Release of pressure will regain consciousness of victims—victims often tortured with repetitive strangulation

Body Indicators

- Hyoid bone fracture common, determined at autopsy
- Injuries can continue to be visible for up to a week after the assault; consider ALS/UVIR for injuries and multiple days of photographs

- May have trauma to the tongue from biting
- Injuries to back/top of head/face/neck
- Linear scratching to shoulder blades/back from scooting away on floor
- Throat—often both sides, bruising in circular marks (fingers) or linear marks (ligature), scratching from victim or suspect fingernails (top to bottom or back to front)
- Manual strangulation with crook of arm rarely leaves markings from pressure
- Petechial hemorrhages from external pressure found on the
    - exterior and interior upper eyelid, eyeballs
    - neck
    - interior ear lobes
    - internal mouth
- Subconjunctival hemorrhage
    - Red to whites of eyes from pressure
    - Bruising, cuts, scrapes, friction burns
- Impression markings
    - Cordage shape/thread
    - Jewelry—ring/watch/pin
    - Be mindful of the angle of ligature grooves. Does it match the scene?
    - Groove" from item is clearer and easier to match with smaller ligatures
- Can cause
    - urination/defecation
    - memory loss/amnesia
    - stroke/seizures
    - brain damage
    - visual changes

Scene Processing to Consider

- Swab body before placing on body bag
    - Neck/chin
    - Palms/fingers
- Hands/feet can be swabbed—ask coroner or medical examiner permission. Bag hands/feet on scene and swab at autopsy OR swab on scene ensuring you do not impact nail cuttings at autopsy.
- Examine fingers closely for hair, fiber, injuries, and impressions

Asphyxia—Suffocation

- Facial smothering/head covering
    - Inner lip/teeth/nostrils

    - Facial bruising
    - Displacement of nose
    - Often no injuries
    - Elderly people are often suffocated with a covering over their face
    - Can cause urination/defecation
- Throat blockage
    - Items present inside throat
    - Scratching/nail marks inside throat

Death by Drowning

Consider on Scene

- Drowning with weights attached can be suicide OR homicide
- Piling clothing neatly can be suicide OR homicide
- Always consider taking samples of water
- Always consider collecting water temperature

During the Act of Drowning

- Body creates foamy mucus while drowning from water trauma on air passageways
- Can indicate body alive at time of entering water

After the Act of Drowning

- Blood will escape from nose/mouth due to trauma of mucus membranes, may look like blunt force trauma
- Will continue to purge foam for several hours

Eyes—Should Be Photographed ASAP

- CORNEA—*Clear raised portion of eyeball over iris*
    - Begins after contact with air when no longer submerged, delayed by submersion
    - If no cloudiness, likely had face submerged under water
    - Cloudy after 12–14 hours deceased
    - Completely cloudy after 3 days deceased
- SCLERA—*White portion of eyeball*
    - Becomes discolored when dried out
    - Submerged eyes should still be white; darkening indicates extended air exposure

Death by Drug Overdose/Drug Toxicity

- Autopsy will provide most information

- Drug overdose is one of the leading causes of death among adults in the United States
- Scene processing affected by CSI personal bias at alarmingly high rate
- Most overdoses happen in front of others—check for witnesses
- Could be from accident, homicide, drug mule activities, and so on
- Be wary of staging
- Take fentanyl precautions when in doubt
- Meth can stay in system 5 days, giving a positive test unrelated to death
- Photograph indicators as soon as possible, as they are fragile evidence

Body Indicators

- Petechia in skin common
- Needle marks/track marks/pinpoint bruising in skin/scarring
- Hyperpigmentation common
- Bright red lividity common
- Abnormal pattern of lividity common
- Often foaming at mouth, or expel foamy vomit
- Look for evidence of malnourishment/have multiple recent injuries/ visible abscesses

Scene Indicators to Watch for

- Emergency medications are indicative of heavy use: Naloxone (inhale/inject), Narcan (inhale), Rivive (inhale), and Opvee (inhale)
- Homemade tourniquet (hair bands, exercise bands, rubber bands, belts)
- Syringes, syringe tips
- Drug residues of powders, pills, papers, liquids
- Pills, loose and in vials
- Plastic baggies (zip top, torn corners, miscellaneous plastic bags) and small airtight containers
- Cut cans, spoons, aluminum foil, scouring pads (Brillo pad, steel wool pad), cotton balls, cigarette butts
- Vape pens—can have empty cartridges to place powders and other narcotics
- Any drugs on scene should be booked and inventoried (herbal supplements included) if any doubt

Death during Electrocution

Body Indicators

- Entrance/exit sites are charred/scorched
- Can leave gray/black/blue dust on skin

- Can be affected by type of clothing/shoes
- Water (wet clothing)
- Metal objects in pockets can be fused

Scene Indicators

- Entrance/exit
- Scorch marks
- Pools/spas with lights can short out
- Electricity source/water source

Death by Excessive Temperature Change

Hypothermia

- Excessive cold, body falls below 95°F/35°C
- Not uncommon to remove clothing right before death
- High risk: Intoxicated people, homeless people, elderly, children
- Symptoms: Mental confusion, weak pulse, slow breathing, shivering, drowsiness, poor coordination, hallucinations, blue skin, large pupils, death
- Light pink to bright red lividity
- Body may retain blue coloring if moved from deep cold to warm environment

Hyperthermia

- Excessive heat, body reaches above 106°F/41°C, at risk if body temperature is over 100°F/37.7°C
- High risk: Dehydrated individuals, elderly, children younger than 4, physically impaired, over exertion in heat
- Symptoms: Cramping, heatstroke, heat rash
- Fever due to illness, hyperthermia, and heatstroke all speed up rigor due to body heat

Death by Fall

Short Distance

- Check flooring and any barriers
- Floor wet with drawers open?
- Heavy items in walking path
- Medications? Alcohol abuse? Ethanol alcohol, mouthwash, rubbing alcohol
- Document any and all material that could be consumed by smoking, drinking, eating, wearing, and so on
- Measure distance to access opening and distance of fall

Great Distance

- Landing feet first will cause greater trauma to the legs and feet
- Capture pictures along pathway to access the origin
- Capture overhead pictures to include location of fall and landing with 2 angles
- Ease of access to location of fall—realistic? Easy access?
- Measurements are important to capture—distance from building face to body, distance of height of fall as well as distance to access opening before the fall

Death with Fire

Body Indicators

- Death timing prior to fire or during fire will be determined at autopsy
- Pugilistic stance
  - From heat burning tissue/tendons
  - Draws hands toward face and knees toward abdomen
- Can cause bone shrinkage up to 25% giving height discrepancies and causing fractured/broken bones/skulls
- Can cause tissue to exude from head from gas buildup/heat
- Heat can cause blood to seep from nose, ears, vagina—will be minimal, not pooled blood. Pooled blood would still be indicative of trauma.
- Skin changes in varying degrees—burn, crack, turn red, blisters
- Hair
  - White hair turns to yellow hair at 290°F/140°C
  - Hair begins to char at 500°F/260°C

Scene Indicators

- Can cause body to fall off beds/chairs due to tissue movement—pathologist can tell the difference
- Note any items on top of the body prior to moving, such as mattress coils or wood pieces as they may indicate an item was placed on top of the body
- Photograph all different burn patterns and locations even if it just looks black to you

Death by Poison

Body Indicators

- Poison-induced seizure will speed up rigor
- Vomit appearance can indicate poisoning if brown, yellow, black, green

- Vomit can burn skin depending upon contents
- Body may have no signs of poison
- Autopsy can identify many substances such as pills or liquids

Scene Indicators

- Look for funnels, extra bottles, droppers, measuring cup, bottles with residue
- Vomit AND mucus if found on scene/around body should be collected
  - Can contain traces of the poison
  - Liquid vomit on non-porous surface—collect with cotton absorption or pour in glass jar
  - Vomit on porous surface—take cutting of upholstery/textiles

Poison Type: Anti-Freeze *(Propylene Glycol)*

- Fluorescent green in color, sweet in flavor, generally ingested as beverage
- Symptoms begin 30 minutes–12 hours after ingestion
- Early symptoms: Fatigue, slurred speech, confusion, headache, vomiting
- Late symptoms: Shallow breathing, irregular heartbeat, death
- Testing: Blood, urine, chest X-ray

Poison Type: Arsenic

- Is ingested or inhaled?
- Leaves odor of garlic to body and oral cavity
- Found in agriculture, mining, and farming
- Early symptoms: Red skin, swollen skin, new lesions, new warts, stomach pain, diarrhea, stomach cramps
- Long-term exposure: Sore throat, worsening symptoms, change in heart rhythm
- Best sources for testing: Blood, hair, nails, urine

Poison Type: Carbon Dioxide

- Asphyxiant used in food industry, beverage carbonation, used in fire extinguishers
- Dry ice is frozen carbon dioxide and when warmed rapidly it is dangerous
- Little effect at low levels—carbon dioxide baths used for medical treatment
- High concentration—respiratory rate changes, cardiac arrhythmias, impairment
- Suicide by carbon dioxide common—closed quarters with dry ice

Poison Type: Carbon Monoxide

- Inhaled
- Bright red coloring of decedent skin; lividity is not purple
- Blood levels as low as 20% can be fatal
- Symptoms of continued exposure can be headaches, fatigue, dizziness, flu-type symptoms without fever
- Hookah charcoal and indoor grills can cause carbon monoxide poisoning

Poison Type: Cyanide

- Can be found in solid, liquid, or gas form
- Can be inhaled, absorbed through skin, or ingested
- Found in manufacturing/photo development
- Breath smells like almonds
- Can be detected in concentrations as little as 1 part per million
- Symptoms: Weakness, confusion, seizures, headache, cardiac arrest
- Bright red face during early stages, blue lips after ongoing exposure
- Blood appears bright cherry red color, skin lividity red rather than purple

Poison Type: Freon

- Found in air conditioning units/refrigerators
- Colorless, smells like grass
- Highly flammable, found in liquid or gas form
- Symptoms may be mild and increase with use; single or multiple symptoms may be displayed
- Symptoms include swelling of throat, sinuses, burning of eyes, vision loss, vomiting, irregular heartbeat, and sudden death

Poison Type: Rat Poison

- Multiple colors, physical forms, and chemical formulas
- Human symptoms may take 1 week for onset if low dose: Bleeding from gums and eyes, stomach pain, chills, confusion, heart failure, extreme abdominal pain
- Dog symptoms: Pale gums, lethargy, stomach pain, bloody stool, slowed breathing, paralysis

Poison Type: Strychnine

- White odorless bitter tasting powder that can be ingested (primary), inhaled, or injected

- Symptoms appear within 15–30 minutes; death can be within several hours
- Symptoms of low dose—agitation/fear, back/neck arching, rigidity, breathing difficulty, awareness of symptoms, convulsions
- Muscles contract in mouth to resemble a grin, jaws clenched, back bent backward, arms/legs drawn together
- Symptoms of high dose—respiratory failure, brain death
- Is used in some medical procedures and is found in outdoor pesticides

Poison Type: Tetrahydrozoline

- Found in eye drops such as Visine, Eye-sine, Geneye, Murine, Opti-Clear, and Tyzine
- Colorless, odorless, generally ingested
- Symptoms include slow breathing, dizziness, blue lips, altered mental state, hypothermia, respiratory distress, and changes in blood pressure

Poison Type: Thallium

- More toxic than mercury, cadmium
- Often found in food crops
- Colorless, odorless, tasteless
- Can be inhaled, absorbed through skin, or ingested
- Symptoms begin 3 hours after exposure: Abdominal pain, vomiting, diarrhea
- After 2–3 weeks of exposure: Hair loss, vomiting, diarrhea

Death during Seizure

Body Indicators

- Often have linear scrapes/abrasions on shins
- Fingernails dig into palms leaving nail marks
- Teeth dig into lips/tongue, leaving bite marks
- Can choke on tongue or food debris
- Trauma to face/extremities from repeated contact with floor or furniture
- Photographs should include shins, hands, inside of mouth, and tongue
- Epileptic seizure/poison-induced seizure speed up rigor

Scene Indicators

- Family may move pillows or blankets under their heads to reduce blunt trauma

- Photographs should include any bedding/cordage/furniture nearby that may have injured or suffocated subject

Self-inflicted Death, Accidental

Self-caused behavior but accidental results:

- Drug/alcohol overdose
- Game with weapons
- Literature/bondage situation
- Dangerous stunts
- Erratic driving in a vehicle
- Positional asphyxia

Self-inflicted Death, Suicide

Facts to Consider

- National Suicide Prevention Lifeline, 1-800-273-TALK (8255)
- Police officers and firefighters are more likely to commit suicide than be injured in the line of duty
- EMS personnel are more likely to commit suicide than members of the public
- 80% of veterinarians suffer from clinical depression during their career, and are 5 times more likely to die by suicide than the general public
- 20% of physicians in the United States suffer from depression
- 24% of dispatchers report suffering from PTSD
- Healthcare support workers are at higher risk of suicide than the general public

Many Reasons/Triggers

- Suicide can be premeditated or an act of passion
- Financial reasons to include loss of financial security
- Occupational stress to include loss of job or bullying at work
- Family/marriage stress to include loss of loved ones or friction
- Blackmail demand/outside pressure
- Depression/distress/PTSD/mental health
- Punish self or others

Self-harm/Self-sabotage Behaviors

- Professionally/personally/mentally
- Lack of routine self-care

- Self-isolation
- Refusal of medical treatment or mental health treatment

Body Indicators on Scene

- Is it possible that all injuries are committed by the decedent?
  - Are all injuries in reach of decedent? Wound grouping—together or sporadic? Are injuries on the dominant side of decedent?
  - Injury to the back and face is often NOT self-inflicted
  - Stab wounds to the heart/chest—reachable, realistic
- Presence of hesitation marks
  - Non-lethal, shallower, smaller injuries next to lethal injuries
  - Caused by hesitation of force
  - Could be hesitation of self-harm OR hesitation of non-experienced suspects in homicide
  - Are stageable
- Is the cause of death physically realistic for the subject?
  - Example: Ill patient at home on oxygen/medication. Could they have physically carried the oxygen tanks from their original location to the location they were recovered if the patient is ill?
  - Could they have physically administered the medication dosage for an overdose if they could not reach the medication and were ambulatory?
  - Absence of back spatter does NOT exclude suicide or mandate homicide—only 35% suicides by firearm have reported back spatter
  - Gunshot wounds from a distance would have to be rigged and present on scene
- Asphyxia with a ligature
  - marks on neck made while alive will have indentions/redness/swelling and placement consistent with ligature
  - ligature placed on a deceased person often will not leave a lasting impression in the tissue
  - marks on back of neck resemble shape of V if point of tension above
  - marks on back of neck straight across if point of tension directly behind
- Self-harm locations (small thin cuts)
  - Often covered by clothing to keep private
  - Small thin razor cuts to forearm, upper arm, ankles, back of hands
- Torture locations (small thin cuts)
  - Underside of feet/arms/palms of hands
  - Back of torso/back of knees

Scene Indicators

- Pay attention to cause, mechanism, and manner of death if known. Do they all seem logical and possible. Does your scene support it?
- Are any cameras present?
- Are all weapons present and near decedent?
  - Gunshot wounds with no guns in the room? Gun only remains in hand for a brief time if at all.
  - Cut/stab wounds with no blade within short walking distance or blood trail to resting place?
- Any evidence of intent?
  - Effort to learn procedures, how to tie knots, chemical formulas, and so on from books, online articles, or journals
  - Evidence of trial runs, practice
  - Tips for staff at hotels or businesses
  - Preparations made for animals and/or children
  - Medication schedules
  - Blanket placed over broken glass
  - Apology notes
  - To do list for self or others
  - Giving away belongings
  - Leaving phone unlocked
  - Documents gathered for legal and financial issues
  - Attempts to reduce mess around body made in advance such as hoodie closed around head when shot in head, relocation to hotel rather than home, and pre-wrapping body in containment materials
- Any evidence of note writing/receiving? Check for indented writing
- Are important documents still on scene or are they missing?
- Inventory all medications—photographs of labels and contents
- Evidence ligatures were tied by decedent.
  - Padding inside ligatures
  - Simple knots
  - Knots within decedent's reach
- Hanging
  - Should have no wear/marks from hoisting—should have no marks on suspension point
  - Hoist marks could indicate hoisting a rope with weight attached
- Sexual indicators related to hanging
  - Is there evidence of a second person or autoerotic asphyxiation?
  - Is self-rescue realistic/in reach?
- Be wary if female body found from suicide in home who is healthy, has prior DV, is found deceased by a partner/ex-partner

- Suicide by helium common, suicide by stabbing, or electrocution uncommon
- Suicide by drowning
  - Make neat pile of clothing, personal items at entry point
  - Can bind self, place weights on self
  - Can tie rope from body to shore so body is found
  - Don't untie knots, cut rope instead—identify ends of rope cut if needed
- Suicide inside vehicle
  - Photograph/document gas level, key location, window/locks, tail-pipe, radio, valuables

Cases to Consider for Cause/Manner of Death

- 2021: In Minnesota, a family died of carbon monoxide poisoning, and all were reported to display red colored skin. The blood tests confirmed, and the incident was ruled accidental.
- 2020: Dry ice was added to a warm swimming pool at a birthday party with innocent intentions. Unfortunately, it created a large amount of carbon dioxide in gas form and 3 people were killed.
- 2011: Chris Coleman was suspected of murdering his family at initial arrival as he reported a timeline that contradicted the scene facts. The family was already showing signs of lividity and rigor when police arrived.
- 2007: Tony Thompson was using Freon to get high and overdosed. He was found between 2 air conditioners on the exterior of a residence.
- 1982: A series of deaths known as the Tylenol Murders; multiple bottles of Tylenol were tampered with in Chicago, causing death in at least 7 individuals.
  - The medication was laced with potassium cyanide and to this date no one has been held responsible.
  - The bottles of Tylenol are maintained in the property room and continue to be the subject of discussion.
- 1916: Hannah Peck's initial cause of death was kidney failure, and her husband John Peck's cause of death was heart disease, later to be changed to poisoning with germs for Hannah and suffocation for John. Their son-in-law was found guilty, and a search of his home turned up samples of bacteria and influenza germs which killed Hannah.

Cases that lack trauma to the body can confuse even a seasoned investigator without an autopsy.

- 2022: Steve Clayton initially assumed cardiac event, later determined to be Tetrahydrozoline poisoning.
- 2019: Tammy Daybell initially assumed to be cardiac event in her sleep, later determined to be homicide.
- 2017: A teenager suffocated her newborn with a rock down the throat in Denver Colorado, initially unknown cause.
- 2015: Mary Yoder initially assumed cardiac event, later determined she was poisoned with colchicine. Her initial symptoms included vomiting and diarrhea.
- 2002: Respiratory therapist Efren Saldivar—responsible for 200+ patients' deaths, confessed to 60+ patients' deaths who did not have visible physical trauma.
- 1998: Dr. Harold Shipman—responsible for estimated 200 patients' deaths that did not have visible physical trauma.
- 1995: Regina Krieger initially assumed self-harm and runaway, later determined kidnapped/murdered.
- 1994: Orit Cooper initially assumed overdose, later determined homicide at the hands of her husband.
- 1979: 13-year-old John Pius was suffocated when rocks were shoved into his throat by other teenagers in Long Island New York, initially unknown cause.

It is often hard to determine suicide, accident, or homicide when you are not present at the time the individual went missing. The struggle is real. One series of deaths started being tracked in 1997 by many separate individuals for multiple "drowning" victims and continues today.

- 1997–2006: 24 males drowned in rivers and lakes in Minnesota, Wisconsin, Michigan, Illinois, Indiana (not counting Texas cases). SIMILARITIES: Males, 18–27, no visible injuries, good health, out with friends, drinking, 10 pm–4 am. Males go missing when out with friends, found days to weeks later in area that they went missing.
- 2005: Michigan, Todd Geib was found deceased, floating upright in a previously searched lake, with minimal insect activity 3 weeks after his disappearance. The cause of death was determined to be drowning. His mother has been unable to have his case reopened even though a second review of the autopsy disagreed with the original findings.

Note

1 Fenster, Jordan. "Homicide Scene Missteps: How Not to Investigate a Murder." *Westchester Journal News*, 20 Jun. 2017.

Search Practices 10

Searching is fundamental part of almost every scene. Whether it's a large-scale outdoor search with multiple participants or a focused hunt for a single piece of evidence like a projectile in a confined space, every search has its own scope, style, and challenges. No matter the style chosen the goal remains the same: To uncover missing items or establish meaningful connections between items. Success in searching isn't just about what you see; it's about how you perceive the scene. Your eyes, ears, nose, and even canine or machine assistance can all play a role depending on the environment and circumstances. However, this chapter isn't about teaching you how to search; rather it's a guide to help you refocus when you find yourself outside your usual element or struggling to make progress.

Sometimes the suspect was exceptionally skilled at covering their tracks, leaving little behind. In these cases, a keen eye and sharp critical thinking are essential. It's not just about what you find; it's about understanding the relationship between the evidence, the scene, and the crime itself. Stay methodical, trust your instincts, and let the details tell the story.

Search Suggestions

- Ensure photographs of area to be searched are captured prior to moving, touching, or searching anything[1]
- Capture photographs of search participants for missing parties—suspects often assist with searches to gather information
- Scene search requires a minimal hypothesis to be formed—why are you there? Why are you searching? Be open to all possibilities; let the evidence tell you, not the other way around.
- Verbally articulate to a lead coordinator (and document) who is searching which area; do not assume.
- Never blindly reach into an area or crevice—pat clothing/coat/backpack pockets before reaching in. Look in tight areas before reaching in (mirrors, endoscope camera).
- Wear specialty gloves (thicker) so you do not get poked or cut with broken glass/sharps.
- Change disposable gloves after 1–2 hours while searching so that you do not leave your own fingerprint in the scene.

DOI: 10.4324/9781003503897-11

- Always search
  - down (floor/ground/underneath)
  - eye level (in bushes, on shelves)
  - up (ceiling/roof/trees)
- When you search outside facing the sun, conduct a second search of the area with the sun to your back. You will potentially see items you would have otherwise missed in the shadows.
- Possible false positives for metal detectors: Ketchup packets, foil gum wrappers, foil candy wrappers, cigar pouches, lug nuts, sprinklers, bottle caps, and so on—remove the item and run it over again to see if that was the culprit or if there is still another hit.

Checklist—Exterior Scene Search

Exterior

☐ Outbuildings, sheds, storage, new construction
☐ Drainpipes, sewer systems, gutters, drainage ditches
☐ Shrubbery along edges of scene/through scene/along path of travel
☐ Vents—roof vents, basement, under house crawl spaces
☐ Fence—broken fence tops? Bent chain link fence?
☐ Mailbox—when was mail last collected?
☐ Cameras—tampered with? Line of site for incident?
☐ Underneath/around porches and entryways

Identify Entry/Exits

☐ Tire marks—vehicle, bicycle, dolly, carts, wheelbarrow, wheelchairs, luggage
☐ If a single tire mark is located, search for opposite side tire 2–15 feet away
☐ Rocks/bricks used to break windows—compare to landscaping of neighbors, preserve for DNA
☐ Broken fence tops?/Bent chain link fence? Ladders present?
☐ Pry marks on windows and doors? Footwear prints under windows?
☐ Removed screens? Light bulbs removed?
☐ Security system—armed/unalarmed/damaged; follow wiring line if applicable

Search along Path of Travel for Discards—Search beyond the Perimeter

☐ Pile of cigarette butts/wrappers/seed shells?
☐ Urine/feces/spit puddles
☐ Used band aids or first aid items
☐ Trail of blood

- ☐ Trail of stolen items/currency/jewelry
- ☐ Trail of footwear prints
- ☐ Dropped items/tools/supplies
- ☐ Dropped IDs and cell phones
- ☐ Electronics/tracking devices/binoculars
- ☐ Rope, twine, zip ties
- ☐ Screwdrivers, hammers, pliers, pry bars
- ☐ Wire cutters, bolt cutters, blowtorch, tanks
- ☐ Glass cutters, spark plugs, glass breakers
- ☐ Lockpick tools, dental tool

Checklist—Interior Scene Search

- ☐ Identify path for foot travel—stick to single path
- ☐ Try not to touch doorknobs prior to them being swabbed, but if you do retain your gloves to book in evidence if policy
- ☐ Search down/eye level/up

Each Bedroom—*Search in*

- ☐ Clothing hampers, clean and dirty
- ☐ Clothing pockets
- ☐ Mattresses—under/between/on, check sides for cut pockets
- ☐ Drawers—check for false backs/bottoms
- ☐ Closets—top shelf, racks of clothing, on floor; look for false walls

Kitchen

- ☐ Trash can/bag—inside and under the bag
- ☐ Fast food bags resembling trash, food boxes
- ☐ Inside and behind refrigerator—produce drawer, cheese drawer, egg cartons
- ☐ Inside freezer—inside food boxes, ice bucket
- ☐ Inside and behind oven—drawers/burners
- ☐ Inside microwave
- ☐ Inside cupboards/pantry, on top of suspended cupboards
- ☐ Inside dry goods/food containers/Tupperware/cereal/oatmeal, coffee cans, and so on
- ☐ Inside animal food bags/totes

General

- ☐ Electronics—videos, tapes, cameras, hidden cameras, CD/DVD, memory sticks, USB, hard drives, and so on

- ☐ Plants/planters—recently disturbed? Dirt on floor?
- ☐ Bookshelves—what books/periodicals/journals present? Anything in books? Behind books?
- ☐ Washing machine/dryer
- ☐ Light fixtures
- ☐ Behind blinds/curtains
- ☐ Above suspended ceiling tiles
- ☐ Behind mirrors/pictures
- ☐ Inside vents/ducts
- ☐ Inside toilet tank, behind toilet
- ☐ Medications/medical records
- ☐ Hidden areas—false drawer fronts/drawer bottoms, false compartments/cabinets, hollow shelving/items/books, glasses with removeable arms

Search under

- ☐ Couch cushions/chair cushions
- ☐ Couches/chairs
- ☐ Mattresses/beds
- ☐ Carpets/rugs
- ☐ Behind curtains/blinds
- ☐ Piles of laundry
- ☐ Intermingled items—be gentle, one layer at a time, slowly and methodical
- ☐ If many items are on the floor, remove one at a time and place it in another location/bin so you can clearly see the floor/wall
- ☐ Often scenes are in disarray/small items become entangled

Blind Search Types

Line Search Method—Multiple Searchers

- Walk the scene in lines together approximately at arm's length OR shoulder to shoulder.
- Everyone walks together, side A to side B.
- Keep the pace of the slowest searcher; too much gap between can allow for small items to be missed.
- Flag items as found, all parties stop to place flag, maintain line, and keep moving to retain structure of searchers. Items will be picked up by others after photographed with flags.
- Get used to searching visually in a structured pattern to ensure you do not leave blank spots.

Good for

- Uneven terrain
- Exterior scenes with large physical search area with many searchers
- Visual search of any area

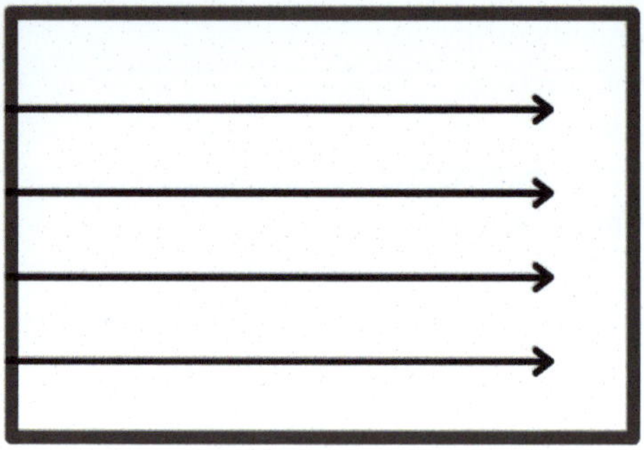

Figure 10.1 Line Search method: Depicting search pattern of a line search with multiple searchers.

Line Search Method—Just You

- Same as above, but only one searcher—searching area at arm's width in linear fashion.
- Walk side A to side B, take two steps to the right, walk side B to side A moving in a serpentine fashion.
- Continue to turn and search entire area, leaving no gaps between search lines.
- Keep eyes to the ground and stay within search area.
- Flag or mark items as found and continue searching to avoid leaving gaps/missing areas.

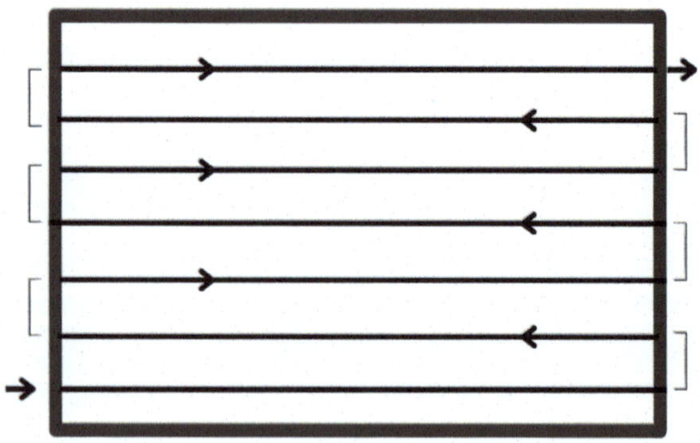

Figure 10.2 Line Search method: Depicting search pattern of a line search with one searcher.

Good for

- Yards/parking lots/any scene/any situation

Grid Method—Just You Searching

- Walk the scene boundary north to south THEN east to west covering same ground.
- Walk/search arm's width area.
- Continue to turn and search entire area in linear fashion, leaving no gaps between search lines.
- Keep eyes to the ground and stay within search area.
- Flag or mark items as found and continue searching to avoid leaving gaps/missing areas.

Grid Method—2+ Person Search

- 1+ person walk north to south, 1+ person walk east to west, covering the same ground.
- Walk/search arm's width area.
- Continue to turn and search entire area in linear fashion, leaving no gaps between search lines.

Good for

- searching large areas—can be done alone or in groups.
- all scenes—ensures the sections methodically checked twice.

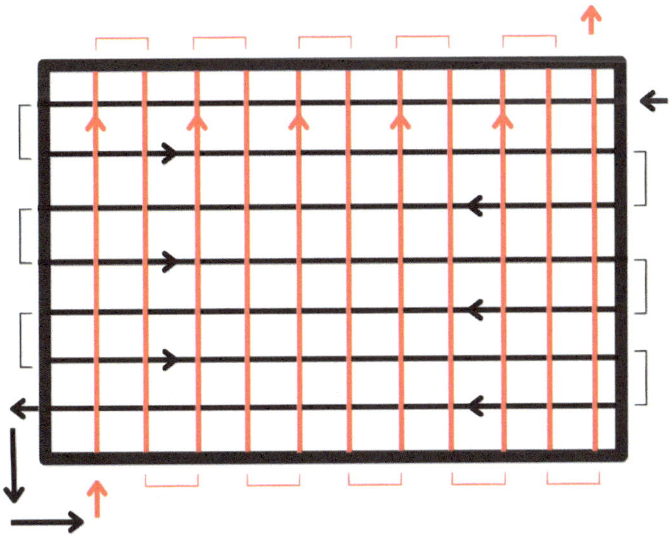

Figure 10.3 Grid Search method: Depicting search pattern of a grid search.

Spiral Method—Single Searcher Only

- Search in a spiral fashion—from center out OR from exterior to center.
- Not commonly recommended for land searching since it is not as efficient as a grid search.

Good for

- Underwater search

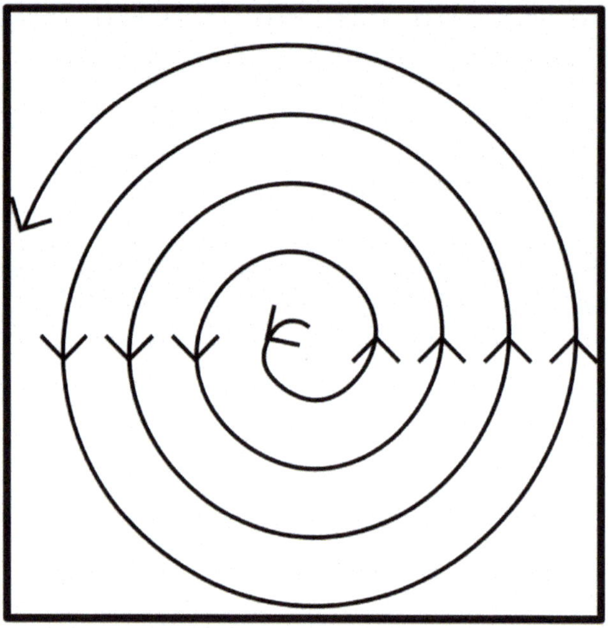

Figure 10.4 Spiral Search method: Depicting search pattern of a spiral search.

Wheel Method—Multiple Searchers

- All parties start in circle, backs together at location body found/murder occurred. Each person walks forward, like spokes on a wheel.
- Be mindful; once individuals get too far from each other they can miss small items.

Good for

- Large outdoor field/junkyard setting.
- Not often used—easy to damage and miss items of evidence.

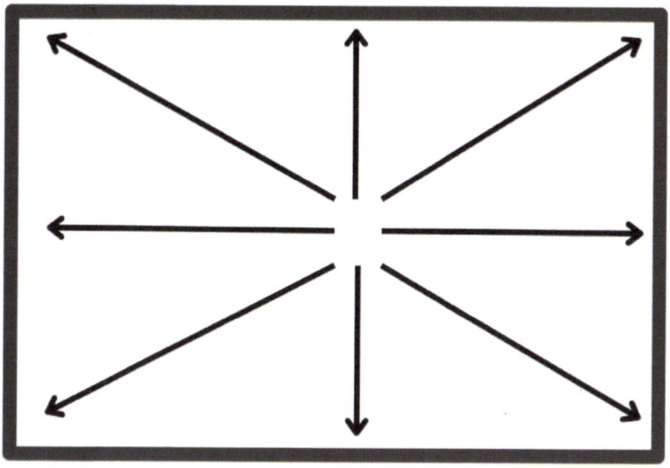

Figure 10.5 Wheel Search method: Depicting search pattern of a wheel type search.

Quadrant/Zone Search Method

- It is easier to break up indoor areas.
- Large yards can be broken into smaller zones.
- 6–10 feet area decent size for quadrants if overwhelmed.
- Draw diagram with zone area to keep notes straight.
- Estimated or measured depending on scene needs.

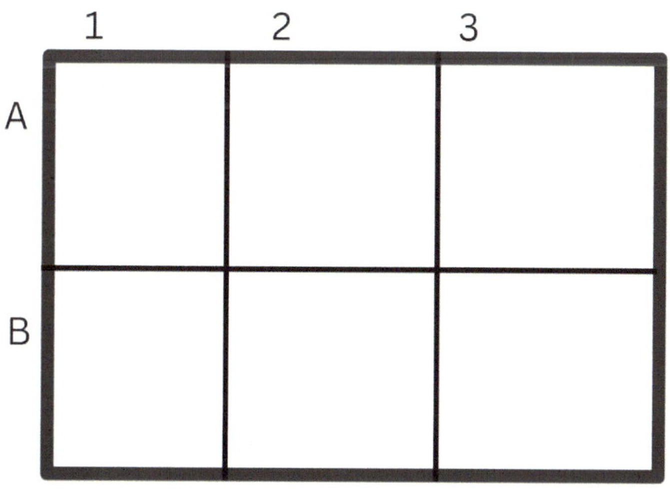

Figure 10.6 Quadrant Search method: Depicting search sections of a quadrant type search with larger sections.

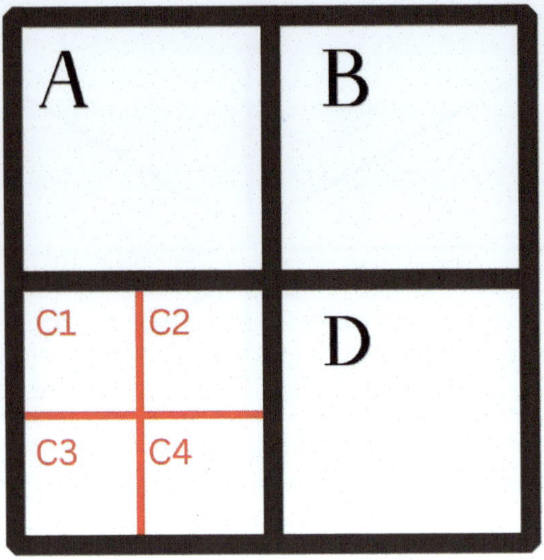

Figure 10.7 Quadrant Search method: Depicting search sections of a quadrant type search with smaller sections.

Zone Labeling Options

Vehicles

- Zone A: Interior driver area
- Zone B: Interior passenger area
- Zone C: Interior rear passenger area
- Zone D: Interior rear driver area
- Zone E: Engine/undercarriage
- Zone F: Cargo area/trunk/truck bed

Residence/Rooms

- Zone 1: Exterior front porch
- Zone 2: Front living room/entryway
- Zone 3: Kitchen
- Zone 4: North bathroom

Yard/Field

- Assign letters to the X axis zones
- Assign numbers to the Y axis zone

Focused Search

- Most used by experienced detectives/small scenes

- Combined with quadrant/zone method—search room by room
  - Move methodically, slowly, layer by layer
  - Looking for correlations, items of significance—in a shooting look for guns. If the door was pried open look for pry bar and tools; keep all things in context
  - Broken down to a quadrant of vehicles, rooms of residence, or individual outbuildings which are then searched one at a time
- It is okay to lay down butcher paper on the floor of a room to search thoroughly without contamination
- If you find unexpected evidence, you must reassess the scene
- Consider switching for second check—switch sections with co-worker if an option; complete second search
- Use endoscope camera—for small hard-to-see areas
  - inside door panels
  - under vehicle seats
  - behind light switch plates
  - inside vent systems
  - behind vent door
  - above suspended ceiling
- Can use canine to search for deceased bodies, live bodies, accelerant, drugs, explosives, firearms, and electronics. Consult expert in your area for your individual needs.

Searching with ALS (Alternate Light Source)

- ALS is considered presumptive testing and still needs a confirmatory test from the laboratory
- Documentation should be completed with photographs using the same wavelength/filter as found as well as detailed written descriptions

Steps for Searching for Biological Fluids (Suggested)

1. Areas/bedding/vehicle as found
2. Move items and examine individually layer by layer
3. Examine area of interest with all small items removed (mattress/cushion, chair, etc.)
4. Document wavelengths and filters used for the search, orientation of bedding, and all positive and negative results
5. Label areas of interest found with labels, direct marking on item, painters tape label, scale tape, or other medium of choice for your agency
6. Ensure directionality of all bedding is included in notes

Method

- Turn down lights as dim as possible
- Hold light source 2–12 inches from area of search; be mindful of heat coming off light
- Plastic bags and thin plastic will melt/shrink if too close; hold approximately 6 inch/15.24 cm from light source
- Keep light beam thin for stronger results on non-skin surfaces; vary angle for best results
- If too bright on skin will eliminate results—can turn down light or use different light

Wavelengths for Searching

- Sunlight contains all wavelengths/colors
- Do not stick to one wavelength/filter—run through series of light/filter choices because the material the sample is on will affect the results
- Same color lens/filter and light = lighter results
- Opposite color lens/filter and light = darker results

Common Wavelengths

CSS Settings—Crime Scene Search Settings on Equipment

- Between 200nm and 700 nm
- Use orange filter

180–415 nm—*UV Light—"Very Short" Wavelength*

180–280 nm—Disinfectant Level Wavelength

- Limit exposure to evidence and eyes
- Good for
  - Luminol enhancement
  - Latent prints prior to processing

280–315 nm—Sunburn Level Wavelength (Includes Sunlight)

- Sunlight contains all wavelengths/colors

315–400 nm—Tanning Level Wavelength

- UV light exposure for greater than 30 seconds can degrade DNA
- Good for
  - Latent prints prior to processing
  - Bruising/below skin bruising—can be seen 1–9 months after injury

  - Darker skin tones
  - Mummification/decomposition

415 nm

- Good for untreated blood

455 nm

- Good for blood treated with fluorescein and body fluids—use orange filter

485–530 nm—*Blue Light—"Short Wavelength"*

- Orange filter common
- Good for
  - Rhodamine results viewing
  - Fluorescent powder viewing
  - Biological stain searching

495–570 nm—*Green Light—"Medium" Wavelength*

- Good with yellow filter
- Good for fingerprints on scene; filter can change depending upon substrate

570–700 nm—*Orange/Red—"Long" Wavelength*

- Good for inks/documents
- Good with red filter

700–1100 nm—*(IR) Infrared—"Very Long" Wavelength*

- Makes black cloth appear white
- Must be used in darkness, hard to use on scene
- Good for
  - Blood
  - Seeing beneath paint for blood/writing
  - Inks/papers
  - Regular/burned/charred documents
  - GSR

Wavelengths for Scene/Subjects—*Move through a Range of Settings to See What Works Best for Your Lighting and Substrate*

- Capture photographs with the wavelength/filter that is best for viewing/searching

- Use tripod, monopod, or other stabilizing device for low light photography

Bruising/Bite Marks/Strangulation Marks

- 260–400 nm with clear filter (with caution, very short intervals)
- 380–495 nm with yellow filter
- 450–490 nm with orange filter
- 490–560 nm with red filter
- Try range of light/filters to get best results
- Reflective UVIR camera shows bruises/bites greater than 6 weeks aged
- Strangulation bruising often shows up with ALS that is not visible to the naked eye

Blood

- Untreated dry blood will normally not fluoresce; it absorbs light
- Appears as a dark spot with lighter background
- 395–435 nm range for search, most absorption for background distinction
- 415 nm with yellow filter recommended
- 447 nm for aged blood—sometimes will fluoresce
- 700–1100 nm (IR)

Documents (Charred and Ink Comparison)

- 700–900 (IR)

Fingerprints

- 180–280 nm with yellow filter
- 315–400 nm with yellow or orange filter
- 495–570 nm with orange or red filter

Fluorescein Enhancement

- 455 nm with orange filter

Fluorescence in Visible Light

- ISO 100, F/11, 1/60, −1 flash exposure setting

Fly Feces

- Feces will fluoresce
- 465 nm with orange filter

Fly Spots (Regurgitated Blood)

- Will NOT fluoresce
- Will appear dark in color—like blood
- Will have different shape than blood spatter

General Search

- 350–500nm with yellow and orange filter

GSR—Gunshot Residue

- 415 nm with yellow filter
- 450–490 nm with orange filter
- 700–1100 nm (IR)
- CSS light with orange filter

Hair/Fibers

- 260–490 nm with yellow or orange filter (try the whole range)
- 490–560 nm with red filter

Human Bones and Teeth

- Will fluoresce, rocks/stones will not
- UV light with no filter
- CSS light with orange filter
- 400–490 nm with orange filter

Luminol Enhancement

- 180–280 nm

Residue from Removed Decals on Vehicle Exterior

- 365–490 with yellow or orange filter (try the range)

Saliva

- Looks like semen but fluoresces at lower intensity
- 450 nm with orange goggles
- 470 nm with interference filter
- 415 nm with yellow filter
- UV light with yellow filter

Semen

- 260–400 nm with clear filter

- 420–450 nm with orange goggles, fluoresces white
- 532 nm with orange goggles, fluoresces yellow green
- Fresh semen generally does NOT fluoresce
- The older it is, the brighter it glows

Shoe Prints

- White light with oblique angle or white light with yellow filter
- Treated with DFO 535 nm with red filter

Skin

- UV, violet, blue lights best
- Reflective UVIR camera shows bruises/bites greater than 6 weeks aged
- Skin tone affected by light wavelength
- Avoid going below 400 nm on skin

Urine

- Will fluoresce with correct light wavelength
- 415 nm with yellow goggles/filter
- 450 nm with orange goggles
- 505 nm with red goggles

Cases to Consider for Scene Searching

During the SECONDARY scene search for several investigations evidence was recovered that had been overlooked during the INITIAL scene search that was integral to their case. No pictures were captured showing the items present during the first set of photographs throwing their integrity into question during trial.

- Teresa Halbach—her car keys were located in suspect's home during a second search.
- Annie Le—sweatpants with biological stains of the suspect and victim found in a laundry basket.

In a sexual assault case, a blanket was used for an assault that contained plant material on the back. The exact location of the scene was unknown, so an analysis of the type of plant material was conducted.

- They were identified and triangulated to find the location that contained all five plants on the blanket.
- The scene was successfully located and processed.

Searches beyond the perimeter turned up integral evidence during the following scene searches:

- 1998: Serial killer Luis Garavito—handwritten note contained the address of his girlfriend found outside the direct scene.
- 1990: After the murder of Nickie Lowe the suspect dumped items in a dumpster a mile from the scene, containing the suspect's fingerprint.
- 1984: Killer of Melanie Road Hampton cut himself during the attack and touched the wall down the street while fleeing from the scene.
- 1980: When a dingo stole Lindy Chamberlain's child the initial search didn't locate any items of interest. However, the child's clothing was found just outside the search area in 1986.
- Killer of Krystal Steadman cut himself during the attack and left his DNA on a fence down the street from the crime scene.
- Randal Comeaux—a serial rapist known for not leaving evidence left cigarette butts behind outside the scene at several locations.

Note

1 Organization of Scientific Area Committees for Forensic Science (OSAC) *2021-N-0019 Standard Practice for the Documentation and Processing of Shooting Scenes.*

General Scene Processing 11

Crime scene processing requires a meticulous and systematic approach to preserve and analyze all potential evidence. This process begins with documenting the scene through photographs and notes, ensuring no contamination occurs and that all items are accounted for. It continues until all evidence is preserved for its potential value. This section begins with a list for on-scene processing, as well as providing suggestions and options for basic scene processing including marking defects on scene, labeling areas being processed, and glass examination. All crime scenes should be handled with integrity and should be processed as if you were the victim. What would you expect if you were the person wronged today, or if it was your grandmother, your father, or your friend. Would you do anything differently?

Crime scene processing involves a wide range of specialties due to the diverse nature of evidence involved. Over time, this field has expanded to include many specialists across different areas. Recent professional crossovers have highlighted new challenges, including external pressures on individuals conducting the reviews. In 2009, the National Academy of Sciences published a report titled called "Strengthening Forensic Science in the United States: A Path Forward".[1] This report emphasized the importance of maintaining the autonomy of investigators from government influence. It also recognized the value of obtaining findings from an independent professional outside the investigating agency, ensuring that their conclusions remain free from external pressures and biases.

> Confusion, incompetence, and imprudence may result in a failed investigation.[2]
>
> **—Barry Fisher**

Suggestions for Basic Scene Processing

Do

- Wait to form conclusions until you have spent time in the scene and observed all items of evidence. Be open to changing your mind and be open to what the evidence is showing you.
- Reassess and re-evaluate continuously.

DOI: 10.4324/9781003503897-12

- Always be mindful of your surroundings; it's a crime scene to you but someone's home or neighborhood.
- When evidence is located, consider the timeline for its arrival. Was it prior to crime, during the crime, or after the crime?
- Consider multiple hypothesis. Look for evidence for ALL POSSIBILITIES while on scene. Consider evidence that will SUPPORT AND REFUTE your hypothesis.
- Take notes continuously as you process the scene; do not try to fill them all out from memory when you return back from the scene. Contemporaneous notes are going to be more reliable. REMEMBER notes are discoverable in court!!
- Consider giving your notes to the relieving team or having them take a photograph of your notes and measurements for their continued reference while they finish up.
- Maintain your "clean" and "dirty" areas, no crossover. Clean gloves touch your clipboard, flashlight, ink pen, exterior evidence packaging, adjust glasses, zip coat, and so on. Dirty gloves touch evidence items, dirty equipment, dirty ink pens, place items inside clean packaging.
    - *Clean area*—supply of clean PPE, clean packaging, ink pens/markers, clean equipment.
    - *Dirty area*—collected evidence, used equipment, dirty markers, trash bag, biohazard bag.
- Drop something in the scene or in the body bag? Say aloud and show when you grab. Don't quickly put in your pocket; it can eliminate the appearance of impropriety.
- Consider using a red light inside vehicles for use during night shift and darkness. Using a red light to see equipment and take notes will reduce the shock to your vision and is vital for night shift safety.
- Break down larger scenes; make it convenient for bystanders as well as yourself.

1. Process street evidence first
2. Open the street and process the porch
3. Open the sidewalks and process the building entryway
4. Open the yard and process the first-floor interior residence
5. Open the first floor and process the second floor

Don't

- Skip scene processing due to CCTV or witness statements; video can get thrown out or contested.

- Replace bodycam with a scene video or photography. It does not capture the same content as well as can be thrown out leaving you in need of documentation.
- Discount information that seems useless now; later the story may change.

Purpose of Scene Processing Is to Determine

- What happened
- When did it happen
- Where did it happen
- Who was involved
- How was it done
- Why was it done

Order of Crime Steps—*You May Find Items of Evidence from Each Step*

1. Suspect prepares for crime
2. Approach to victim/scene
3. Control of or detention of victim occurs
4. Crime against victim occurs
5. Response of victim—voluntary/involuntary, fight/flight, panic, urinate, vomit, and so on
6. Disposal/display—stage scene, dump victim
7. Flee scene

Order of Crime Scene Processing—*Adjust Depending upon Scene*

1. Photographs/video prior to touching items or adding to the scene
2. Search
3. Marker placement for evidence items, bullet holes, blood spatter, and so on
4. Photographs/video after search and with all markers
5. Sketch and measure
6. Evidence collection
7. Chemical enhancement processing

Notes

- Notes and documentation are one of the main reasons for scene attendance. The notes are best when made contemporaneous with processing for more accurate observations. The notes are to include observations, ideas, conclusions, and measurements. The notes can be in the following forms: Writing, drawing, photographs, digital scan, audio recording, video recording.

Labeling/Marking Options on Scene

Labeling with Many Rooms/Cars/Aisles/Bodies

- Labeling can be done using letters or numbers, determined by your agency policy. Place markers facing same direction/angle for better photographs and easier visibility.
- Room A, markers 1, 2, 3
- Room 1, markers 1, 2, 3
- Body A, items A1, A2
- Bullet defects
  - Defect 1A, 1B
  - Defects A, A1, A2
- Vehicle A, markers 1, 2, 3
- Section A/aisle 1, aisle 2, aisle 3

Labeling Blood/Blood Trails

- Place at intervals to show path traveled with notation of where samples are collected along path
- Keep a wide berth when marking trail to prevent contamination from the bottom of shoes
- Option: Green or red cones placed along trail
- Option: Reflective markers to enhance nighttime blood trail photographs
- Option: Lawn markers in a field
- Option: Reflective chalk on hard surfaces

Labeling Animal Hoarding Scene

- Labels placed on crates/cages/boxes AND IN NOTES (duct tape ideal)
- If animal is deceased, add a "D" to the numbering
- Room A, Crate 1, cat 1—A.1.1
- Room 1, Crate A, deceased cat—1.A.D1

When to Use Markers versus Just Pick up Item

- Markers are used when you need to identify individual locations for evidence. Each agency has their own set of criteria to rely upon.

Each agency is different, and various geographic locations will be different.

- Some locations consistently have concrete buildings and do not have to follow bullet paths through a house.
- Other locations have wooden housing affected so often they are marked with a permanent marker instead of a sticker to assist with record keeping between shootings.

Evidence Marker Options

- Plastic pre-formed markers—tents, cones, arrows, squares, circle stickers, reflective tape, and so on
- Cone shaped, arrows, squares, triangles, and so on
- Green, red, yellow, reflective cones
- Fold coin envelope in half to make tent, write on it with Sharpie
- Pre-printed paper disposable foldable markers, write on it with Sharpie
- Markers with lights or reflectors
- Chalk (reflective or white) on vehicles/walls/asphalt
- Flags in yards, fields, landfills, and so on
- Consider reflective driveway markers in large areas/fields for ease of visibility
- Consider placing reflective tape on bullet hole scales or markers so they can be seen in overall photographs

Staged Scenes

- Can be staged by suspects to ensure they are not caught
- Can be staged by decedent to change cause of death
- Can be staged by family due to shame surrounding death
- Can be staged by family to retain resources of decedent such as checks and residence

Types of Death Investigations

Death Investigation

- The purpose is to determine the cause, manner, mechanism, and time of death.

Institution-Based Death Investigation

- Performed by/for institutions
- Hospitals, nursing homes, medical facilities

- Usually required permission from next of kin
- Generally conducted on site in hospital/morgue
- Organs not normally retained but destroyed after examination unless requested, rendering no further testing available

Medicolegal Death Investigation

- Conducted because required by law and performed by government officials
- Homicide, suicide, accidents, unexplained/unattended deaths
- Usually conducted by medical examiner or coroner
- Organs returned to body unless samples retained for examination
- Some jurisdictions use hospital morgues for homicides
- Rules/procedures will vary per location

Private Death Investigation

- Family can hire private attorney and other professionals for death investigation and obtain private autopsy

Commonly Encountered Roles in Forensic Science

Accountant

- Analyze financial records to identify fraud and embezzlement

Animal Control Officer

- Specialist in animal abuse/neglect investigations and related crime scenes

Anthropologist

- Can assist with time of death and cause of death

Archaeologist

- Perform excavations, respond to burial sites/body dumps, or answer questions about the age of remains
- Use archaeological techniques to locate evidence and burial grounds to include mass graves and historical crimes/burial grounds

Arson Investigator

- Specialist in fire investigation, development, and protection
- Will lead investigation with fire death

- Relies upon CSI to
  - collect the right samples and preserve the samples appropriately on scene
  - ensure photographs are decent quality for later reconstruction
  - ensure all burn patterns are accurately photographed
  - ensure measurements are accurate from sketch

Ballistics Expert

- Examine firearms and ammunition to link weapons to crimes

Behavior Analyst

- Can provide psychological autopsy, profile of suspect/victims, assist with line of questioning

Botanist

- Provides analysis of plants, pollens, flowers, wood from crime scene
- Relies upon CSI to collect and preserve the right samples

Climatologist

- Scientist who studies/predicts weather patterns and long-term weather impacts
- Can be helpful in missing persons' cases or body dump inquiries

Coroner

- Elected official, determined by state laws
- No required medical background
- Determines manner/cause of death
- Relies upon CSI to
  - provide accurate case information
  - provide photographs which are accurate to assist with determination
  - provide needed weapons to the morgue for examination
  - retain appropriate chain of custody

Crime Scene Investigator

- Can be sworn or civilian
- Can involve body manipulation/examination
- Main tasks[3]
  - Document, search for, identify, collect, interpret, and preserve items of evidentiary value

- Professional duties[4]
    - Act thoroughly and produce results and conclusions within the scope of the expertise of the individual practitioner
    - Mitigate your own biases
    - Use contextual information to formulate hypotheses

Digital Examiner

- Recovers and analyzes data from electronic devices to include computers and phones

Document Examiner

- Specialist with questioned documents
- Relies upon CSI to collect all needed evidence without damage

Engineer

- Investigates failures in structures, materials, and products to determine cause of accident or malfunction

Entomologist

- Specialist with insect activity
- Relies upon CSI to collect and preserve the right samples

Forensic Geologist

- Analyzes soils, minerals, and other materials to link or locate crime scenes

Meteorology

- Meteorologists can provide testimony on weather conditions at the time of a crime

Medical Examiner

- Physician appointed to conduct autopsies, determined by state laws
- Can determine autopsy not needed
- Determines manner/cause of death
- Is often a forensic pathologist
- Relies upon CSI to
    - provide accurate case information
    - provide photographs which are accurate to assist with determination
    - provide requested weapons to the morgue for examination
    - retain appropriate chain of custody

Naturalist/Field Biologist

- Can be helpful with plants/soils and determining timelines

Odontologist

- Dentists that can use bite mark analysis and dental records to identify victims or suspects

Linguist

- Analyzes language used in written or spoken form to help identify authorship or deception

Palynology

- Study of microorganisms (pollen and spores) to help solve crimes, locate crime scenes, and identify regions of travel

Pathologist

- Physician with specialty training on autopsy procedures/death investigations/violent death
- Determines manner/cause/mechanism of death while conducting autopsies, determined by state law
- Relies upon CSI to
  - provide accurate case information to include photographs
  - provide needed weapons to the morgue for examination and retain chain of custody

Psychologist

- Assesses the mental state of suspects and victims, provides court testimony

Serologist

- Analyzes blood and other bodily fluids for ID and DNA analysis

Taphonomy

- Can provide data on death events, including tampering with remains and postmortem timelines

Toxicologist

- Collaborates with a forensic pathologist to determine the cause/manner of death

- Reviews toxicology of decedent
- Analyzes bodily fluids and tissues to identify drugs, poisons, and other chemicals

Veterinarian Pathologist

- Collaborates with scene investigators to find cause of death, extent of injuries, medical health
- Their work includes necropsy, histopathology, microbiology, serology, parasitology, virology, toxicology, entomology, and DNA testing

Cases to Consider for Scene Processing

- 2019: CSI McArthur was convicted of murder for the murder of her friend, a law enforcement officer. McArthur was convicted for taking her money, killing her, and dumping her out on the family property.
- 2014: When Cassy Farrington was murdered in her bathtub, scuff marks were left behind during the struggle. No DNA swabs were collected during processing though the water faucet was still running upon arrival, casting doubt on the thoroughness of processing later.
- 2010: When a warrant was served on the home of Lonnie Franklin (serial killer) over 650 pieces of evidence were collected, including seat cuttings and over 1,000 photographs and videos. The crime scene processing was long and meticulous, resulting in his conviction.
- 1998: Vladimir Pokhilko (co-creator of the game Tetris) was found dead alongside his wife and son in the family home. While it was concluded murder/suicide, the evidence points to the possibility that it was 3 murders.
- 1994: Orit Cooper was found deceased in her home, and the cause of death was listed as unknown with the manner of death listed suicide. Multiple sleeping pills were thrown around her body giving the appearance of a suicide though the autopsy showed no presence of sleeping pills in her system.
- 1989: Cheryl Ann Commesso went missing at the age of 18; in 1995 her skeletal remains were found alongside the road in brush with tree roots having grown through and around the bones. A suspect was identified based upon her previous relationships, but the detectives could not prove the timeline.
  - They used an anthropologist to determine the age of the tree that grew through her bones to determine the year her body was placed in the field.
  - This timeframe placed her body being dumped while the suspect still lived in the area, and in 2002 Franklin Delano Floyd, a previously unknown serial killer, received the death penalty that ended his list of victims.

Notes

1 Committee on Identifying the Needs of the Forensic Sciences Community, National Research Council. *Strengthening Forensic Science in the United States: A Path Forward.* National Academies Press, 2008.
2 Fisher, Barry. *Techniques of Crime Scene Investigation*, 7th ed. CRC Press, 2004.
3 Organization of Scientific Area Committees for Forensic Science (OSAC) (2020) *Guiding Principles for Crime Scene Investigation and Reconstruction.*
4 Organization of Scientific Area Committees for Forensic Science (OSAC) *2021-N-0015—Guiding Principles for Crime Scene Investigation and Reconstruction: Transparency and Ethics Proposed Standard.*

Scene-Specific Considerations

12

This chapter addresses key considerations for various types of crime scenes, including accident sites, scenes involving deceased individuals, aquatic environments, incidents of animal abuse, child abuse, and sexual assault. Each section will present critical reminders and fundamental information necessary for processing these specific crime scenes. When handling crime scenes, it is essential to remain vigilant, follow established training protocols, learn from past case successes and failures, and be mindful of potential biases.

Between 1977 and 2000 in Illinois, 12 individuals were executed for their crimes while 13 were exonerated from death row, highlighting concerns regarding the reliability of the justice system and forensic processes. This led to the exoneration of death penalty cases and ultimately the abolition of the death penalty in Illinois. Effective crime scene processing is critical to the outcome of criminal trials, and once public confidence is undermined, it becomes challenging to restore trust in the system. Crime scene forensics, collection, and analysis are conducted according to strict protocols by CSI professionals to ensure the thorough collection of all relevant evidence.

Checklist—Scene Processing

- ☐ Photographs to include overall, mid-range, close-ups, vehicles, damages, and subjects
- ☐ Mark area designators if applicable (room number/letter, vehicle number, etc.)
- ☐ Collect touch DNA from doorknobs, cupboard handles, or any known needed areas prior to search
- ☐ Collect temperatures needed: Water, body, soil, and so on
- ☐ Conduct search of scene/areas of interest
- ☐ Take detailed notes of what was searched, results, damages incurred while searching
- ☐ Mark items of evidence located, bullet defects, blood spatter, tool marks, anything of interest to be noted
- ☐ Take crime scene video
- ☐ Complete **SCENE PHOTOGRAPHY CHECKLIST—AFTER SEARCH**, to include macrophotography
- ☐ Complete rough sketch/measurements/scan

DOI: 10.4324/9781003503897-13

- ☐ Collect DNA samples identified to include touch DNA from doorknobs, light switches, and alarm pads
- ☐ Gather and pre-mark needed packaging or box to bring through scene
- ☐ Collect tangible items of evidence identified, taking photographs to document evidence identified during this process
- ☐ Create evidence list of items collected/sampled
- ☐ Body on scene should be collected (if not already) prior to any further procedures completed
- ☐ Complete enhancement procedures if necessary
- ☐ Complete fingerprinting of identified areas of interest
- ☐ Complete trajectory/re-enactment procedures
- ☐ Photograph any newly found evidence/relationships
- ☐ Collect needed wall cuttings/samples from trajectory
- ☐ Collect all equipment/trash
- ☐ Conduct walkthrough before leaving scene with scene detective for anything left behind or not noticed already; look closely as there is still time for collection/processing
- ☐ Mark/collect/document any additional samples/evidence identified
- ☐ Take equipment and all trash/debris/labels with you when you leave

I. Accident Scene Processing

Skid Marks

- Follow skid marks backward to find location of impact if present. Newer vehicles with anti-lock brakes may have lighter, interrupted, or missing skid marks at an accident scene.
- Fresh skid marks may show up on thermal cameras for a short period of time
- Caused from tire sliding, NOT rotating, locked wheel
- Appearance: Usually the full width of the tire with linear marks run parallel to tire

Searching

- Glass is often found in pants cuffs/shoes/hoods/hair of subjects after crime
- Hats and headwear often fall near the point of impact
- Shoes often scuff the pavement with vehicle/pedestrian accidents. Search the pavement/roadway for scuff marks, scrape marks, tire marks, footwear marks, flesh scraping and so on.
- The speedometer needle can stick upon impact and freeze in place, or the needle can make a “stamp” mark on the dial upon impact.[1] This information is good to note and document, though it may not be exact.

Lighting

- Sunlight searches help to find damage to buildings, bullets in holes, evidence on the ground, skid marks in roadway from victim footwear/bicycle tires
- LED lights show liquid blood in an alley puddle better than a flashlight
- Pelican lights or flood lighting can help find projectiles, cartridge cases

Checklist—Vehicle Accident Scene Photographs

- ☐ Camera settings accurate—date/time, new file, settings, normal lens (50 mm), detachable flash, additional lighting
- ☐ Cover page

Scene Photos

- ☐ Show approach for all parties and viewpoint from all witness locations
- ☐ Fixed location—intersection signs/utility pole with number/hydrant with number
- ☐ Series moving along path of travel from approach to impact for all vehicles/pedestrians
- ☐ Resting location of vehicle in scene—show from more than 1 angle
- ☐ All points of impact to roadway and/or vehicles
- ☐ Roadway before AND after moving vehicles to include gauge marks, tire marks, skid marks, rim marks, footwear marks, and flesh/blood
- ☐ Trail of damages along route of travel
- ☐ Tire marks of all vehicles if present
- ☐ Debris in roadway to include hats, shoes, plastic, glass, and so on

Vehicle Photos

Exterior Vehicle Condition

- ☐ Vehicles in place, 4 sides and 4 corners if possible
- ☐ Include ID photographs—plates/VIN, make/model, stickers/decals/ornaments
- ☐ All tires showing placement, tread (use coin/oblique lighting), wear/separation, and printed information on side
- ☐ Defects to vehicle exterior
- ☐ Light filaments

Interior Vehicle Condition

- ☐ Remove detachable flash for interior photographs
- ☐ Speedometer and dashboard
- ☐ Driver pedals—damaged/blocked? Shoe prints/footprints? Shoe stuck in pedals?
- ☐ Air bags deployed? Do they have makeup/facial marks? Blood?
- ☐ Blood on interior/dome/steering wheel/windows
- ☐ Makeup marks/face marks on A pillars/interior windshield/backside of headrests
- ☐ Photograph from height of driver showing view from sitting (is it obstructed?)

Vehicle versus Pedestrian

- ☐ Scuff marks in roadway from shoes/feet
- ☐ Debris in roadway to include hats, backpacks, purses, canes, and synthetic hair
- ☐ Windshield/windshield wipers/edges of hood (scrape skin/hair)
- ☐ License plate/holder
- ☐ Front bumper/hood/grill
- ☐ Top/bottom of windshield
- ☐ Sideview mirrors
- ☐ Undercarriage if applicable
- ☐ Consider black powder on exterior vehicle as it will stick to body fluids and show possible path

Vehicle versus Vehicle

- ☐ Paint transfer/glass transfer
- ☐ Defects/oil smears
- ☐ Vehicle parts transfer
- ☐ Damages

Evidence Collection on Scene

- Airbags, if deployed or manipulated
- Touch DNA from each interior door panel, at minimum driver door panel to include handle
- Touch DNA from the steering wheel and tilt control, gear shift, driver seat controls, emergency brake, rear view mirror, radio/AC buttons, A pillar handle, visor, keys, ignition button
- Blood DNA from each compartment if present
- Condition of seatbelts from each compartment (locked in place, moveable, buckled, etc.)

Measurements Needed

- Location of final resting place of vehicle
- Location of pedestrian and all pieces of evidence located
- Start/stop location of skid marks
- Distance from vehicle to all points of impact
- Overall scene dimensions

II. Animal Abuse: Neglect/Hoarding Scene/Sexual Assault

Good on Scene Resource

- Maxwell, Virginia, and Martha Smith-Blackmore. *Investigating Animal Abuse Crime Scenes; A Field Guide. CRC Press*, 2023.

Checklist—Photograph Series for Small Animals

- ☐ Consider also video with FULL SOUND (can have second person document the photography session with a video camera)
- ☐ Camera settings—date/time, new file, settings, normal lens (50 mm), on camera flash (or no flash if nervous animal)
- ☐ Cover sheet with identifying information (dry erase board/laminated paper acceptable with many animals)
  - ☐ Case number, date, location, name ID of photographer
  - ☐ Animal ID or name, ID assigned to cage, kennel, tag, and so on or identifying information
- ☐ Animal as found/location found with overall/mid-range
- ☐ Animal's face with coversheet in frame if possible
- ☐ Capture teeth if showing
- ☐ Overhead view with dog standing (if possible)—nose to tail
- ☐ Side view with dog standing—nose to tail
- ☐ Back side view with dog sitting—head to hips—if docile
- ☐ Pads of feet/nails
- ☐ Injuries—mid-range and close-ups with scale if possible (ABFO #2 with circles showing)
- ☐ Soot patterns if present

Enclosure after Animal Removed (Can Use Detachable Flash)

- ☐ Overall/mid-range photographs of living environment
- ☐ Food/water containers and storage/supply
- ☐ Bathroom needs including location and hygiene
- ☐ Feces found to include close-ups showing content, nonfood items, parasites, diarrhea, blood
- ☐ Vomit locations, spit up locations

- ☐ Nonfood items present in their living area to include bedding, weapons, and drugs
- ☐ Repeat for ALL animals on scene not just the reported animal

Behavioral Suggestions with Injured Animals/Scared Animals on Scene

- Remain calm, breathe slowly, move slowly
- Baby talk can be calming; use soft slow speech
- Consider using a muzzle as the animal is likely afraid and potentially in pain

Evidence Suggestions

- Consider using an ammonia reader at locations with large amounts of animals indoors, photograph results
- Don't open any doors or windows for ventilation until you are sure no animals are free roaming the interior
- Write animal ID (found or given) on duct tape on enclosure
- Capture video of animal to show behavior, noises, response to photographs/handlers
- Scan with microchip scanner and photograph the results. If you don't have one consider purchasing one, or any veterinary office or shelter can scan the animals if they are willing to do so.
- Consider using an ALS to search for trace evidence or DNA
- Search for restraints; abuse often requires a restraint to overpower the animal.
- Check for injury to the feet and nails from possible struggle
- If animals are burned and it is not a fire scene, look for nearby cords with damage or outlets that are in reach of the animal
- Branding and controlled burns of the animal—collect all tools and process for DNA of the victim and suspect
- Consider using pre-drawn forms or templates of body outlines for injury drawing
- Canine CODIS is a system run by ASPCA and used for law enforcement entry and can be helpful with dog fighting and abuse scenes[2]

Facts to Consider

- 71% of domestic violence victims report animal abuse in the home[3,4]
- 88% of families with substantiated child abuse report animal abuse in the home
- Injured does not always equate to abused or neglected; investigation is vital.

- Canine CODIS system run by ASPCA, for law enforcement entry. Contact your local law enforcement if you are not affiliated with one.
- Animals can display pain by decreased sleep, decreased appetite, posture/gait, excessive licking/chewing on self, vocal noise, reluctance to move or cuddle, aggression
- Funereal abandonment—disposing of an animal after death (natural causes, euthanasia, accident, etc.) often includes animal comforts with the body such as blankets and bedding
- The animal can be receiving excellent care from their main caregiver, but being abused/neglected by another party. Be mindful of signs beyond nutrition.

Documentation

- Document date, time, temperature of scene, temperature of sleeping area, and location of residence
- Document all animals on scene, even if they are in reasonable condition
- Scan microchip with scanner for ID/owner information
- Document access to water to include if toilet seats are raised, height/location of food/water—is it in reach? Bowls/troughs/bottles, working condition? Appropriate amount? Fresh?
- Document number of feces piles or lack of feces piles
- Document bedding/shelter or lack of
- Document the presence of bones, bone piles, carcasses, skin/hair, and so on

Labeling Scene with Large Amount of Animals

- Labels placed on crates/cages/boxes AND IN NOTES (duct tape ideal)
- If animal is deceased, add a "D" to the numbering
- Room A, Crate 1, cat 1—A.1.1
- Room 1, Crate 1, cat 1–1.1.1
- Room 1, Crate A, deceased cat—1.A.D1

Evidence Collection[5]

- Take photographs of scene prior to manipulation of any items
- Collect water/food bowls and storage containers
- Collect all medicine, drugs, narcotics, over the counter, prescription, unknown powders, or liquids, and so on
- Dog fighting paraphernalia—wash tubs (wash dogs prior to fighting), weight scales, steroids, medical supplies, treadmills, large

sticks, forced breeding items such as hobbles or stands, fighting pits or arenas

- Chicken/rooster fighting paraphernalia—blades/leather to affix blades to the legs, weight scales, carriers, piles of dead birds, training materials
- Sexual assault—take recent stool sample, bedding, lubricants, electronic recording equipment, drugs, treats/food, pain killers, restraints, towel/rags
- Severely matted hair can be shaved and retained (can be weighed if body is severely malnourished)
- Consider tape lift or vacuum on the animal body for hair/fiber collection
- Don't unbuckle collars; cut the collar to retain DNA in the buckle
- Don't untie knots if cordage is included; cut the rope to retain DNA in the knot
- If tape is wrapped or layered around an animal, cut in one strip and initial (don't unwrap if possible)

No Visible Injuries

- Consider asphyxiation, drowning, or poison
- Consider necropsy based upon scene needs

Visible Injuries

- Photograph with and without scale if possible, can be completed with a veterinarian if needed
- Sharp and blunt force trauma will appear the same as on human bodies
- Consider using muzzle as injured/scared animals may bite
- Photograph prior to and with muzzle (if used) to ensure all facial injuries are documented

Deceased Animals

- General practice veterinarian can conduct necropsy, but forensic veterinarian pathologist is suggested. They will not determine if a crime is committed but will determine severity of injuries and likely potential causes.
- Animals that will have necropsy within 72 hours should be refrigerated, otherwise frozen until exam
- Place bags over all paws, and secure with tape or rubber bands
- Collect visible trace evidence prior to transport
- Document any foam in nose and mouth prior to transport

- Postmortem hair banding applies to animals as well as humans—collect hair if animal is suspected deceased
- Decomposition of animals does not follow the same timeline as that of humans
- Rigor in animals can last less than a day up to 7 days after death
- Livor can be visible after animal has hair removed
- Bloating, green discoloration, and marbling can occur within 1 day of death for dogs

Starvation

- Emaciated does not always mean starved; sometimes medical issues play a role.
- Abandoned, starving animals are often loud with repeated barking; starving to death is slow and painful.
- Animals with access to water and no food: Will take 3–5 weeks to slowly die
- Animals with access to no food and no water: Will take several days to die and may not appear malnourished
- Animals with access to minimal food and water: Can remain emaciated and starving for months/years

Neglect Signs

- Missing hair/matted hair/unkempt hair/dirty hair
- Overgrown nails, claws, hooves
- Dental disease, broken teeth, missing teeth
- Lack of nourishment, underweight
- Document access to outside area, sunlight, grass, and so on
- Document area for bathroom needs

Fighting Injuries

Dog

- Small thin nail scars/wounds on face/front chest/shoulders/neck
- Bite mark/small punctures to face/neck
- Infected/untreated wounds
- Limping/limb injuries
- Molds for bite mark comparison are not made on scene

Bird

- Small thin nail scars/wounds to the face/neck/chest/wings
- Broken nails and beak

Sexual Assault Examinations for Animals—Evidence Collection

- Conducted the same as for humans
- Samples collected/packaged/stored/submitted just like human samples
- Can use specialty trained veterinarian, or any willing local veterinarian (expensive to fly in for exam)
- Woods lamps are found in many vet offices and are suitable for ALS use during examination (300–400 nm, orange goggles if you have them)
- Consider using muzzle as animal can be scared and/or in pain
- Remain calm yourself and speak calmly to animals to reduce aggression/trauma for all parties
- Urine can be collected for up to 96 hours for drug use samples (no catheter, free fall collection to avoid contamination of sample)

Examination Includes

- Overall photographs
- Scan of microchip
- Exterior examination with ALS for semen and biological secretions
- Photographs of injuries, with and without scale
  - Injuries often include dog fighting scars, neglect, overall abuse, restraint markings, underweight, lack of muscle development, pressure sores, infected wounds, limping/not using limbs
- Buccal swab for DNA exclusion
- Sample swab of oral cavity to include gums, under the tongue, crevice between gums and cheek, and teeth crevices
- Swab of nails for suspect DNA
- Vaginal/anal examination and swabs
- Check the hair around genitals AND scruff of neck for semen/blood DNA
- Note behaviors and demeanor during examinations
- Note tail use or non-use, any wagging present. Could have suffered pulling/trauma during assault
- Collection of any foreign bodies, weapons, projectiles, restraints, and so on

III. Body on Scene *(Human or Animal)*

How to Handle

- Ensure family/friends not alone in scene/with body
- If a sheet is placed on body prior to your arrival

  - Collect sheet if it is removed for examination (fold in half on itself, retain for trace)
  - Place sheet in body bag with body if no examination of body is taking place on scene
- Body found inside container
  - Will go to autopsy inside container
  - Can collect touch DNA/blood DNA/trace evidence from outer container while on scene
  - Retain flat surfaces for fingerprint processing if compatible surface
- Decomposition rates—take note/document
  - Does decomposition match the position of body?
  - Does decomposition match reported timeline?
  - Do visible injuries match reported story?
  - Are stages of decomposition consistent across body? (e.g., no rigor in ring finger only)

Bagging Hands/Feet

- Ensure snug (not tight) around wrist/ankle so bags don't fall off—morgue will cut off at autopsy
- Don't remove jewelry/synthetic fingernails before the bags
- Can collect GSR/swab hands on scene if not planning to place bags on hands
- Write case information on bag exterior
  - Case number
  - Investigator
  - Which hand/foot (right/left)
  - Date/time applied

Option: Place Lunch Size Paper Bags over Hands/Feet

- Use fingerprint tape to secure at wrist area
- Tape touches bags only, not skin/hair
- Pull edges of bag to open, and don't place your hands inside the bag

Option: Prefabricated Drawstring Handbags

- Place over hand/foot
- Use drawstrings to tie with knot ensuring bag stays closed

Body Removal (Regular Conditions)

- Ensure body is fully photographed, measured, and documented prior to moving

- Ensure all clothing/jewelry are fully documented/photographed (consider leaving all jewelry and placing handbags over decedent's hands until autopsy)
- Don't remove body from/pry body off anything it is attached to: Cut mattress if fused, cut chair cushion if fused, leave in box, and so on
- If jewelry is being removed ensure touch DNA has been collected from decedent's hands
- Ensure all contact DNA has been collected from pockets prior to removing pocket contents
- Ensure all approved forensic processing of body has been completed prior to placing in body bag
- Watch body removal leave the scene, and document or video any blood drip trail/gurney tire marks along path
- Don't spray body with deodorant/air freshener or alter the chemical state of body
- Don't return personal items while on scene until fully determined to be not relevant to crime. A necklace or ring can be very important to a story line. Ensure fully photographed prior to return to family members.
- Photograph body bag with writing/lock tag/tag #

Immediate Body Removal (Emergency, Direct Sunlight, Hostile Surroundings, etc.)

1. Take initial set of photographs without markers/scales at entrance and along path to body
2. Take body-specific photographs, clothing/position/injuries
3. Take mid-range and close-ups of area surrounding body to include drag marks or footwear prints
4. Take mid-range and close-ups along the path between the body and the entrance
5. Identify, mark, photograph, sketch, and collect evidence that would be in the way of body removal
6. Take macrophotography of any marks of interest
7. Photograph body bag documentation and seal/lock tag #
8. Closely watch body removal pass through scene path, and document any blood drip trail/gurney tire marks/glove dropping along path
9. After body removal, continue processing scene as if just arrived, following normal procedures

IV. Body in Water—Scene Processing

Body Decomposition

- Rate of decomposition impacted by month of the year with variables such as water temperature, sun exposure, and environmental activity

- Common changes
  - Body will sink initially but rise after gas accumulates (except in extremely cold water, in which case body may never rise)
  - Color change of body (may appear different race—darker or lighter)
  - Hair loss
  - Nail loss
  - Skin wrinkling/slippage/loss
  - Swelling
- Adipocere
  - Possible in water over 65°
  - If present should be documented
- Agonal breath
  - Bodies' last attempt to breathe before/as dying
  - Can inhale hair/silt/plants/water
  - Can trigger vomit/convulsions
- Algor Mortis
  - Faster in water than air
  - Not all bodies start at 98.6°F
  - Struggle prior to death can cause increased body temperature
- Babies generally float due to high fat content
- Cadaveric spasm
  - Death grip, hand clutch
  - Instant at time of death, voluntary muscles only
  - Caused by extreme mental stress
  - Does not dissipate with rigor
- Use body bag with mesh bottom for water recovery. Helps prevent items/insects/trace evidence/vomit directly at/below body from getting lost.

Body in Natural Water—Lake/Canal/Bayou/Lagoon

- Adults can drown in less than 3 feet/1 m of water and children can drown in less than 6 inch/15 cm of water—double check mobility barriers
- Any bodies in water should be investigated as a homicide
- Bodies found on back should go to autopsy on back—don't turn face down to drain body on scene as you may lose valuable trace evidence, vomit or items placed in throat
- Body will be heavier than normal if water in lungs—lungs will be measured in autopsy
- External body should be allowed to dry and be re-examined for wounds at autopsy as they may appear different than they did immediately out of water[6]

- Consider using waterproof camera/video camera
- Lungs will contain plankton from water, should be collected during autopsy
- Skeletal remains—collect everything in the immediate vicinity
- Wet scenes are great candidates for Small Particle Reagent—apply while area still wet
- Look for vomit on water before moving body/head
- Look for dirt/silt inside mouth/along gumline/teeth—photograph in depth

Body in Controlled Water—Bathtub/Pool/Hot Tub/Sauna

Collect the Following

- Blood (can retain shape under water for some time, examine carefully)
- Depth of water
- Look for hairs/skin floating at top of/in water
- Photographs of water heater settings if applicable
- Temperature of water at time of arrival/departure
- Water sample

Draining Bathtub/Pool/Hot Tub

- Skim top of water for trace evidence if applicable
- Collect water sample prior to draining
- Place filter over drain (single use), drain water, and check/collect debris
- Search/photo bottom of tub
- Look for evidence/scuff marks/gouges, and so on
- Transport collected debris to laboratory in water from source using buckets, Tupperware with lids, vials/plastic tubs with lids, Ziplock bags
- Bodies removed from water on back should go to autopsy on back—don't turn over to drain water
- Consider/check all electrical sources

V. Child/Elder Death Scene/Abuse/Neglect Processing—*See Also "Abuse/Neglect Injuries"*

Capture Photographs of

- Access to others, access to dangerous items, access to toiletries
- Damages to wall/ceiling near child sleeping area with scale
- Food and hygiene items present and available. Are the necessary essentials present for their care?

- Medications prescribed/over the counter
  - New and recently taken
  - Tissues? Other vomiting incidents?
  - Recent soiled diapers?
  - Sibling illness?
- Medical equipment
  - Machines, oxygen
  - Supplies (mouthpiece, knobs, etc.)
  - Physical therapy equipment
  - Medical devices to be worn/location of devices
- Recent doctor notes/discharge paperwork. Calendar/schedule regarding feeding, medication, and so on
- Diet plan/calorie plan, nutrition information. Breast fed/bottle fed—recent can of food, bottles, cups, and so on
- Rodent and bug activity: Housing, food, feces, damages with scale if significant

Option: Turn Off Lights for Rodent/Cockroach Activity[7]

- Document activity with notes and photographs
- Turn off lights in residence/structure for 10 minutes and keep noise down
- Turn on lights and document activity present in room on walls, ceiling, light fixtures, corners, closets, and so on
- Photography or video camera use recommended for documentation

Collect Samples of

- Swab bottles/cups/food containers for contact, saliva, and contents inside
- Liquid sample of contents if suspicious
- Swab or collect discolored sleeping items—pillowcase, blanket with red stains, liquid stains
- Temperature of water if burning or water involved in injuries
- Temperature of body of water, temperature coming from faucet, temperature setting on hot water heater

Search/Examine

- Bedding—look under blanket/top sheets
- Bedroom of parent and child
- Car seat—check under padding for stains
- Clothing/undergarments—bloody/soiled/damaged? Are they appropriate for size/weather?

- Coughing/choking/vomiting cause debris to be "flung"—look for formula/vomit/food spray on walls/ceilings/clothing of caregiver, hair of victim/caregiver
- Document child/elder's identity as member of the home
- Environment is or is not age appropriate—food, hygiene supplies, sleeping area, freedom of movement in home, access to emergency services, safety concerns addressed?
- Favorite toys/clothing/books/dishes, and so on
- Food found in the scene to be compared to stomach contents—dinner on the table, last food eaten, and so on
- Glasses/dentures/braces
- Individual care and identity in home—included on school registration forms? Presence of personal items, personal hygiene items, defined personal space
- Laundry basket/back of closet for soiled items
- Locations of discipline, items used for regular discipline: Belts, cords, hangers, weapons, brushes, sticks, and so on
- Medical history/medical equipment/medications/dispensers—over the counter/prescription/herbal
- Personal information displayed publicly in home—bank statements on dinner table, will and legal forms on counter
- Restraints—leave knotted if tied and cut other location. Mark where you cut and document in notes.
- Pillow markings—linear stains along pillow common in suffocation
- Trash/complex dumpster/neighbor trash can for soiled items, weapons, restrains, first aid debris, and so on
- Water temperature/water heater settings

If Decedent Found in Bed

- Document sleeping area
- Check for damage to wall/ceiling near body location
- Check for damages to dishes/pictures/mirrors/lights/items near body
- Obtain photos and measurements of space between mattress/crib OR space between mattress/wall

If Decedent at Hospital

- You must also return to the scene for processing
- Be sure to collect all removed items to include diapers and medical equipment that hospital staff removed on their arrival. Be sure to check the trash can in the room for accidental disposal.

Modified Scene

- Be mindful of altered areas—dirty body but clean clothing, dirty mattress but clean sheets, and so on

Re-enactments

- Should be *conducted* by detective doing interviews—can be *filmed* by CSI with video camera
- Can use dolls to be drawn on with marker for child's statement and depict injury locations. Photograph all sides and book into evidence. Refer to your local children's advocacy center for more information or trained staff.
- Can use dolls to be laid in bed/bedding for parental statement. Use cover sheet indicating staged photographs and case details. Depicts how baby was put to bed/in stroller, in swing, and so on.

VI. Clandestine Grave Scene Processing

Additional Resources

- Clandestine Laboratory Investigators Association (CLIA)—clialabs.com

Finding the Gravesite

- Likely near a vehicle accessible location—remote but accessible
- Cracks/shrinkage in soil with age creating depressed soil in area. Decomposition can create a secondary depression from settling after the soil is compressed. Graves older than 5 years tend to have more compact soil.
- Carefully evaluate ground cover/shrubbery/leaf cover for anything recently disturbed—shrubbery can make soil disturbance invisible. Newer dig sites lack vegetation due to ground disturbance and lack of seeding activity.
- Water-retentive soil or nutrient-deprived soil will grow vegetation back lusher than its surroundings. Soil that is dry will regrow vegetation browner than its surroundings due to lack of nutrients.
- Check for inconsistencies. Can collect plants from topsoil to help determine age of hole.
- Digging with heavy equipment is not recommended, may disturb smaller items
- Consider using sonar technology to scan the ground prior to digging if available.

Test Hole

- Test hole dig options *(before you dig the big hole)*
- Option 1: Scrape down 2 feet and check for odor of decomposition
- Option 2: Put small PVC pipe down in dirt to check for odor—odor will come out end of PVC
- Option 3: Take dowels and push them down into soil in multiple locations, checking for voids or soft soil

Search of Gravesite

1. Narrow down search area and set perimeter with tape/rope
2. Processing is not time sensitive so do not rush, create strong plans, and set up stations for processing
3. Take detailed photographs prior to dig to capture trees, surroundings, and plant life
4. Take photographs of any test sites or pipes
5. Create grid/line system with string, wire, line, or tape
6. Scape away small layers (don't dig down)—2–4 inches layers of soil for each scrape across
7. Place all removed soil and rock directly onto a screen for sifting—1/4 inch mesh recommended
8. Collect measurements for each item located if known, to include depth/height
9. Watch for evidence as you dig to include casings and weapons
10. Watch for tool marks in roots already present prior to your processing
11. All dirt under, around, and above the body should be removed and screened prior to discarding

Body Removal

- Slide board or body bag underneath body to aid in removal
- After all items removed—including body:
    1. End digging if earth below body is compact and undisturbed
    2. Continue digging if earth below body is not compact
    3. Continue to dig and look for artifacts until soil compact/undisturbed
    4. Photograph final bottom layer of dig

VII. Dismemberment Scene Processing

Intentional Dismemberment

- Not accidents such as train accidents, vehicle accidents, and wildlife encounters

- Concealment of body/crime and ease of disposal
- Religious ritual or remnants of parts procurement for spells/ceremonies
- Warning to others from gangs, cartels, other groups
- Retribution/punishment

Processing Options

- Consider fingerprinting the floor if any locations are clear of blood
- Consider contact DNA collection from the floor (touched during crime)
- Consider contact DNA from body in areas the suspect would hold to steady the mass before cutting (where did they grab?)
- Look for footwear prints around body parts
- Check trash for evidence
- Consider blood collection from each type of pattern as suspect may have cut themselves/each other

VIII. Exhumation Scene Processing

Area/Exterior—*Photographs Needed*

- Overalls of area prior to digging
- Overhead of casket prior to opening

Interior (If Opening on Scene)—*Photographs Needed*

- Overhead of casket after opening, before touching anything
- Mid-range of items present
- Facial ID photograph
- Head to shoulders, shoulders to hips, hips to feet
- Any visible injuries
- Close-ups inside casket, end to end
- Each item removed from casket, each sample collected

IX. Hazardous Scene Processing/Evidence Collection

On Scene Resources Available

- WMD Response Guidebook—suggest obtaining book in advance
- CDC 800-232-4636
- Nationwide poison control—800-222-1222

Facts to Consider

- Always remain uphill, upwind, upstream
- Take all precautions for all identified dangers, don't skimp at this time
- Ensure all items are clean to the touch on the exterior
- All collected evidence must follow hazardous collection procedures
- All equipment must be decontaminated OR discarded
- Household bleach mixture—can decontaminate semi and non-porous items—1 part bleach, 10 parts water
- Follow your agency protocol for collaboration with the health department, ATF, or fire department depending upon scene factors

Biological Hazard Response

- Identify response route issues/dangers
- Identify site characteristics/variables to relay to responders
- Identify ability to seek direct cover
- Consider staging area issues/locations
- Identify weather factors—wind direction/rain/and so on.

Clandestine Laboratory Scene Processing

- Once aware of setting as drug laboratory immediately obtain chemist or clandestine lab-trained personnel if possible
- Keep full PPE on at all times due to possible exposure or booby traps. Instead of removing when it impedes you, take additional breaks, make personnel switches, and lengthen the time spent on scene.
- Be mindful of common booby traps
  - Traps to doors/light switches—can be explosives
  - Trip lines
  - Poisonous spiders/snakes in area
  - Dogs loose in area
  - Pipe bombs attached to equipment

Put on PPE (In Order)

1. Put on face mask (and beard mask if applicable)
2. Put on hairnet (and hard hat if applicable)
3. Put on safety glasses/eye cover
4. Put on disposable gloves (your inner layer)
5. Put on Tyvek or long-sleeved laboratory coat (depending on scene needs)
6. Place gloves on exterior of sleeves, tape together holding arms outstretched (for mobility)
7. Put on footwear covering/boots/overshoes, and so on
8. Tape bottom of suit to top of boots (if applicable)
9. Put on second pair of disposable/collection gloves

Remove PPE (In Order)

1. Get large trash bag/biohazard bag/box ready and open
2. Move slowly and deliberately, avoid excess air movement
3. Remove second layer of gloves (outer layer only)—start at wrist, turn inside out, slowly
4. Remove Tyvek/laboratory coat/apron—Fold (don't crumple) soiled side in on itself keeping exterior cleanest, place in plastic bag. Move slowly to reduce air movement of contaminants. Place gown in disposal.
5. Remove hair covering and dispose
6. Remove shoe coverings slowly, don't fling—fold in on itself and dispose
7. Remove last set of gloves—inside out, slowly—dispose
8. Remove facial mask/covering and dispose
9. Put on CLEAN GLOVES/MASK to close/secure bag opening—DON'T squeeze air out of bag—will release all the contaminants into your face
   - All removed PPE should be thrown in the same trash, not carried to your car in your pocket
   - Don't forget, it is possible to transfer blood from scene to scene, scene to home

Maintain Clean/Dirty Areas

While all scenes can be considered "dirty," you will greatly reduce contamination and exposure to yourself and others if you are mindful of maintaining clean and dirty boundaries. The evidence you pass on to others needs to be clean enough to touch with bare hands (because people will). The majority of your equipment is not single use, so it will need to remain "clean," maintained and cared for. Common practice—your dominant hand remains "clean."

CLEAN—Has Not Touched ANYTHING Dirty—Often Dominant Hand

- Clean items—clean hand, clean swab, posse box/note pages, camera, ink pens, flashlight, exterior FINAL packaging
- Clean actions—hand/receive equipment from others, take notes, remain "clean," touch swab *not packaging,* hold exterior packaging while dirty hand places items inside

DIRTY—Touches Non Clean Items, Collects Evidence, Opens Packaging

- Dirty items—gloves that have touched anything, equipment that has collected samples, inner packaging, latent processing equipment

- Dirty actions—collecting items, open swab packaging for clean hand to grab clean swab, place items inside packaging without touching exterior packaging

Hazardous Evidence Packaging

- Keep exterior of all packaging “clean”
- Writing goes on each layer of packaging
- Maintain “dirty” and “clean” packaging, equipment, and hand placement
- Ensure all evidence is double bagged to ensure exterior packaging is “clean”
- Item must be placed inside heat seal packaging and heat sealed on scene (don’t forget to bring your heat sealing equipment and extension cords)
- Decontaminate the exterior of all sealed evidence packages
- Place appropriate hazard stickers on exterior packaging

X. Hostile Crowd

- Body can be processed/removed as priority—as it can reduce the emotions on scene and loved ones often wait to see removal
- Be prepared to accommodate the emotional processing of friends/family of victims. Denial and anger are the first 2 stages of grief, which can occur immediately (i.e., while you are processing the scene)
- Common symptoms/indicators of beginning grief/shock (be mindful of these actions with their intention)
    - Screaming/rage/crying/yelling/fainting
    - Refusal to accept current reality/scene scenario
    - Refusal to accept boundaries of scene tape
    - Inability to negotiate movement of vehicles for scene personnel

XI. In Custody Death Scene Processing

Facts to Consider

- If decedent dies at a hospital you must return to original scene for processing (collect all items from hospital). Be sure to check the trash can in the room for accidental disposal.
- Most common means of suicide in custody is hanging by means of kneeling, sitting, standing, leaning, hanging.

Possible Injuries

- Stomping/standing on back—look for footwear marks on back

- Blunt force injuries to the head/forehead can be caused during "terminal fall" at time of death OR separate blunt force injury
- Pattern injuries should ALWAYS include examination quality or scaled photography (at scene and autopsy if possible)—baton, handcuffs, footwear, bite marks

XII. OIS—Officer-Involved Incident Scene Processing

- Consider collecting uniforms for further examination in the laboratory with ALS or other specialty equipment
- If using GSR, collect from all parties to include officers even if you don't think you will run them
- Search/process all evidence the same—show no preferential treatment, search officer's bags as any other subject's bags
- Bullet holes can be tested if it is unknown to be bullet hole or other damage
- Processed like a homicide scene
  - Overall photographs/video if applicable
  - Search/mark items of evidence
  - Overall photographs/video if applicable
  - Sketch/laser measure items of evidence
  - Collect items of evidence
  - Weapons charting for officers on scene

Checklist—OIS Scene Processing

Not All Options Apply to All Scenes

☐ Complete initial arrival actions checklist
☐ Establish equipment staging area (NOT near media staging area)
☐ Establish trash—transport ALL trash back with you, don't use local trash cans
☐ Establish officer photograph/charting area
☐ Complete initial documentation checklist
☐ Conduct walk-through with detectives—consider video tape of initial walk-through
☐ View CCTV if available
☐ Establish inner and outer perimeter—if already established, re-evaluate with initial information
☐ Photograph any emergency vehicles needing to leave the scene—placement, light status, vehicle numbers/license plates
☐ Complete photographs of weapons charting for all officers
☐ Complete initial photographs of scene prior to any searching/labeling/marking

- ☐ Search areas of interest
- ☐ Identify all items of evidence
- ☐ Collect measurements of overall scene and identified items of evidence
- ☐ Bullet defects—mark with scale/label, width/length of holes if needed
- ☐ GSR or preliminary testing of holes needed? GSR from any parties on scene needed?
- ☐ Blood stains—mark with scale/label, width/length of stains if needed
- ☐ Collect all clothing/shoes with defects, stains, writing, and so on
- ☐ Comparison samples—tire marks/impressions, shoes marks/impressions, hair/fiber, DNA
- ☐ Complete scene photographs checklist—ensure 4 angles for full capture
- ☐ Capture photographs with real lighting and added lighting
- ☐ Overalls from viewpoint of all parties
  - ☐ Shooter to victim
  - ☐ Witness to crime
  - ☐ With and without visual obstructions
- ☐ Consider holding the scene until autopsy is completed and all variables have been considered

Hospital—Respond as Soon as Possible

- ☐ Projectiles may already be in plastic sealed cup—leave sealed, book as received
- ☐ Taser barbs—may be present in clothing, don't separate, photograph barbs in place with/without scale
- ☐ Check all room trash cans and floors for accidental disposal of important items
- ☐ Ask staff if any belongings have been returned to family prior to your arrival

Clothing

In Bag Already

- ☐ Photograph exterior bag both sides and visible contents through bag opening
- ☐ Gather contents list from hospital staff that bagged it, name for chain of custody
- ☐ Transport to office for itemization drying as soon as possible.

In Pile Already

- ☐ Photograph as is upon arrival even if on floor or tray, check pockets prior to leaving by feeling exterior for sharps/weapons

- ☐ Wrap clothing in butcher paper to prevent stains from transferring if still wet and applicable
- ☐ Place in paper bags individually if able, or collect as received if needed
- ☐ After transport back to office/controlled environment lay out for better examination

Photographs of Officers

- ☐ COVER SHEET with name/badge number for EACH officer photographed
- ☐ Full length view on all 4 sides

Front

- ☐ Face shot for identification
- ☐ Close-up of badge/name ID
- ☐ Front and back in third segments—raise arms for full view of belt to include items present/missing
- ☐ Close-ups of any blood with/without scale—adjust flash exposure as needed
- ☐ Duty belt/holster

Shoes

- ☐ Close-up photographs of front/back/top/blood/dirt/debris/trace evidence—with/without scale
- ☐ Collect shoes if needed
- ☐ Tread if applicable—with/without 300 mm L scale

Gloves (Polyester or Disposable)

- ☐ Close-up photographs of damages/defects/blood/debris/trace evidence
- ☐ Collect entire glove if above items are pertinent

Injuries

- ☐ Close-ups of all injuries (new or old) with/without scale
- ☐ Photograph any visible trace evidence

Evidence Being Collected from Officer

- ☐ Trace evidence—uniform/shoes/equipment/blood/spit/hair/fiber
- ☐ Touch DNA from body if physical contact
- ☐ Weapons to include all firearms/magazines/tasers

OIS Weapons Charting—*Handle Weapons Minimally, If Not Weapons Trained Have Sworn Officer Unload Weapons with Clean Gloves*

Non-Lethal Weapons (Consider Touch DNA on Multiple Locations)

- ☐ Placement on belt if not seen in overall photos
- ☐ Exterior of both sides
- ☐ SN/model #
- ☐ Damages/defects
- ☐ If weapon is deployed include wiring and barbs

Mace

- ☐ Placement on belt if not seen in overalls
- ☐ Photographs of lids/defects/blood present

Extra Magazine

- ☐ Placement on belt if not seen in overalls
- ☐ On table, not unloaded
- ☐ On table next to unloaded ammunition
- ☐ Return to officer for reload

Firearms on Duty Belt (Consider Touch DNA on Multiple Locations)

- ☐ Placement on belt if not seen in overall photographs
- ☐ On table/box, not manipulated
- ☐ On table/box next to magazine
- ☐ Exterior of both sides
- ☐ SN: Model #
- ☐ Any blood/defects/defects/dirt/debris/hair/fiber

DNA

- ☐ Swab exterior firearm where touched by suspect, where blood is present, prior to rendering safe OR
- ☐ Render firearm safe with clean/unused disposable gloves and book the gloves together, turned inside out, in a 6 × 9 envelope or small bag. Collect remaining trace evidence once firearm is safe to do so.

Firearms in Vehicle (Consider Touch DNA on Multiple Locations)

- ☐ Placement in vehicle and lock/release
- ☐ On table/rifle bag, not manipulated

- ☐ On table/rifle bag next to ammunition
- ☐ SN #, model #
- ☐ Any blood/defects, swab/collect if blood present
- ☐ Touch DNA if concern the weapon was touched

XIII. Property Crime Scene Processing

Ensure All of the Following Documented/Investigated

- Entry, tool marks, items left behind
- Transfer of trace evidence entering
- Transfer of trace evidence during commission
- Is the exit realistic? Where did the projectile travel?
- Check toilet/refrigerator/food/drinks/cigarettes
- If blood is left behind during entry or crime, collect and store until your agency has the funds for processing rather than leave on scene due to classification of minor crime

XIV. Religious Artifacts Found on Scene

This section is merely a reference to help identify what you are looking at in a stranger's home and does not in any way imply a correlation between religion and violence nor an inference of guilt when searching. These are common religious artifacts that are kept in homes. Prior to processing you should ensure collection or processing is necessary, maybe photograph documentation is sufficient. If collection is necessary, be mindful that artifacts may contain traces of mercury and blood.

Processing Options

- Ensure collection is necessary—is photograph documentation sufficient?
- Shrines often contain items with saliva, blood, touch DNA, and mercury
- Look for artifacts as well as books, manuals, and bibles that are present or open to specific sections
- Collect photographs from several angles, overall/mid-range/close-ups
- Artifacts may contain traces of mercury; only touch if necessary and don't separate on scene. If mercury is present, collect with chemical spill kit.

Gangs/Cartels

- Gangs/cartels often use religious ceremonies for good luck. Saint Santa Muerte protects from law enforcement.

Hoodoo—*Does Not Have a Religious Structure*

- Evolved with African traditions/American traditions
- Evolved to include folk magic in SE United States
- Can include animal sacrifice, rituals, and drums
- Does not pray to specific spirits

Kongo Religions

Common Artifacts—Kept in Private Area, Not in Main Room

- Items placed in cauldron or container, may involve catholic saints
- Blood/animal sacrifices
- Cane filled with mercury and sealed
- Human and animal bones—primarily skull, tibia, femur, skullcap may be the cauldron

WICCA—*Neopaganism Religion*

COMMON ARTIFACTS
- Burnt sage (resembles burnt marijuana)
- Candles/incense
- Candy/fruit/vegetables/salt
- Dolls, photographs with names/images, stone figurines
- Items that represent 4 elements (earth, air, fire, water)
- Pentagram

Santeria *(from West Africa)—A Mixture of African Yoruba/Roman Catholic Traditions*

COMMON ARTIFACTS
- Beaded stick/straw hat
- Candy/toys
- Doll figures
- Herbs/mercury
- Oils
- Tools

Voodoo—*Can Include Catholic Saints, Prays to Specific Spirits, Used in Human Trafficking Rituals*

COMMON ARTIFACTS
- Animal offerings
- Bottles, beads, food, jewelry of many colors
- Drums
- Zombies

XV. Sexual Assault/Kidnapping Scene Processing. *See Also "Sexual Assault Injuries"*

Scene Processing Considerations

- Date indicators of last time victim was seen
  - Date on milk cartons or perishable goods
  - Mail in house and in mailbox
  - Newspapers in house and on porch/in yard
  - Clocks—stopped/running
  - Food—state of freshness
- After overall photographs taken, use ALS before and after moving anything
  - Positive results—collect items with stains at this time
  - Negative results—can move items to view all sides, continue processing
- Sometimes it helps the victim to walk you through the events/scene with fewer viewers (pick 1–2 people to be present) while rest of personnel wait outside
- Don't store victims and suspect items together, ensure no appearance of contamination
- Touch DNA can be vital to the case, on items in the scene as well as on the victim and their clothing
- Drug use
  - When drugs are used during a sexual assault they are most often given through a beverage
  - Look for bottles, containers, glasses, medicine vials, and so on
  - Swab residue or collect item

Commonly Involved Sexual Assault Drugs and Their Interaction

Rohypnol

- Odorless/tasteless
- Sometimes colored blue, often comes in pill form
- Effects in 15 minutes, effects last 12 hours
- Slow psychomotor performance, confusion, muscle relaxation, sleepiness, mentally/physically paralyzed, amnesia, blackouts common
- Not routinely tested for in autopsy
- Detectable in blood 1–24 hours for live subject
- Detectable in urine 72–96 hours for live subject
- Detectable in hair, can show history of ingestion, if applicable

GHB

- Clear/odorless liquid is most common form, can be powder or pill form as well
- Slightly soapy/salts taste
- Effects in 15–30 minutes, effects last 3–6 hours
- Slowed motor coordination, inhibited balance, impaired speech, unconsciousness, amnesia
- Not routinely tested for in autopsy
- Detectable in blood 1–4 hours after ingestion
- Detectable in urine 4–12 hours after ingestion
- Detectable in saliva 1–6 hours after ingestion

Search Considerations

- Doors and locks—which side are locks on? height of locks? evidence of force applied/tool marks?
- Common for strangulation victims to urinate—look for pool OR trail of urine
- Hygiene items used, removed, or discarded since assault
- Personal items: Jock strap, underwear, diapers, lingerie, feminine hygiene items
- Towels, shirts, socks, thrown or dropped that could have been used to wipe down assailants' genitals/hands prior to dressing
- Drains/filters/sink screens
- Trash cans—restraints, condoms, weapons, tissue for clean up
- Washer/dryer and hampers (to the bottom of the hamper)

Sexual Assault Evidence Collection

- Whole item collection is ideal if realistic

Bedding

Option: Mattress, Whole

- Wrap mattress in butcher paper or craft paper in its entirety
- Mark exterior packaging for top and front

Option: Mattress, Top Only

- Place butcher paper over top of mattress to preserve and mark accordingly
- Cut the sides of the mattress to remove the top in one piece like a sheet
- Roll or fold to preserve DNA
- Leave mattress frame and springs

Option: Butcher Paper Covering Bedding

- NEED: Butcher paper/Sharpie/large bag
  1. Lay butcher paper over top of bed with sheets and blankets—you can collect blankets and sheets separate or together based upon size/condition
  2. Mark top of paper with Sharpie: Directional arrow and description (head/feet with arrow OR side by wall with arrow or north with arrow), case number, evidence item or description, date, collector
  3. Untuck corners of sheet and flip corners up over paper
  4. Roll sheet from feet to head like carpet or fold in small segments (paper will prevent bedding from touching)
  5. Final roll can be bent in half since ends exposed will be the part on corners
  6. Place in large lawn and leaf size paper bag for transport (or paper grocery bag if child bed)

Option: Larger Bedding/Comforters

- Collect as found—if found flat, fold soiled side in, can wrap in butcher paper
- Packaging: Large paper lawn and leaf bag

Option: Pillows

- Place in large bag, individually, can wrap in butcher paper

Option: Clothing

- Package in paper bags, individually. If intermingled on scene, collect as 1 item and leave intermingled.
- Wrap in butcher paper if available

Option: Wet Items/Towels

- Collect as found, wrap in butcher paper
- Option: Place wet items in paper bag, write needed case information on bag. Place paper bag in plastic biohazard bag until you reach your drying cabinet location.

Persons Not Having Examinations—Evidence Collection

- Swabs of hands/arms/legs
- Scrapings/swabs underneath/on nailbed/nails/fingers of suspect/victim

- Swabs of head/hair
- Any noninvasive swabs
- Collection of non-vital clothing such as scarves, gloves, shoes, hat, and face mask/COVID mask

Persons Having Exam—Evidence Collection

- Should always be conducted by medical personnel—SANE specifically
- Oral swabs for buccal sample—stick to inside of cheeks for collection
- Oral swabs for assault sample
    - Get gum lines
    - Along front/back of teeth
    - Under tongue
    - Inside cheeks

Medical Exam—Evidence Collection

- Will receive sealed/signed in paper bag/box from medical personnel with chain of custody written on packaging or separate (either is fine)
- Don't break seal—book as received
- Can place in additional packaging, without opening original

XVI. Weather

Rain/Hail

- Tent/cover/umbrellas—over body or fragile evidence
- Use camera covers—prefabricated or home made with plastic bags/rain poncho/tape
- Change order of processing if needed
- Place cones over casings to stop wind movement/rain
- Place boxes over footwear/tire marks
- Ammunition can rust during scene processing due to humidity/fog/rain within 2 hours

Direct Sunlight

- Deceased body in direct sunlight will impact decomposition
- Take first set of photographs as found, no manipulation, then cover with tent to reduce direct sunlight
- Can process body on scene as priority for early removal

Cases to Consider Regarding Scene Processing

Animal Abuse

- 2023: Jennafer Glaesemann was cited with 37 counts of neglect after 17 horses died of poor nutrition in her care and many were placed in the back of her veterinary clinic in Nebraska, unburied. Necropsies were utilized for evidence as well as the documented quick recovery of the remaining animals with only food and water.

Sexual Assault

- 2011: Touch DNA off the clothing of a sexual assault "groping" victim was analyzed and used for the suspect's identification and conviction.
- 2006: When Imette St. Guillen was murdered and sexually assaulted her killer left his blood on her restraints, and his carpet fibers were stuck to her tape bindings.
- 1987: Grace Hayden was suffocated during a sexual assault when her own dentures dislodged causing her death. DNA was left behind, but no matches were found. Kevin Ford was a suspect, but his DNA was not on file. A single fingerprint was collected off the kitchen stove because the entire home was processed where he was present and moved about, not just the area of the assault. That fingerprint matched Kevin Ford, which allowed for a DNA warrant, and they found out the semen left behind matched Kevin. While fingerprinting the items in the surrounding area may seem "extra" to some, this case clearly shows the value in finding surrounding clues outside immediate assault area.

Eyewitness Statements

- 1984: Dennis Maher of Massachusetts was convicted of three rapes based solely on eyewitness identification then validated by circumstantial evidence. In 2003 Maher was exonerated as the testing showed that he was not the source of the DNA.
- 1983: Calvin Johnson of Georgia was convicted of rape based solely on eyewitness identification and again no samples were tested until The Innocence Project facilitated the testing. Calvin Johnson was exonerated in 1999 after he was excluded as the source.
- 1976: 16-year-old Randall Adams was reported by an eyewitness (David Harris) to be responsible for the homicide of a police officer. Just prior to his execution he was granted a new trial with further investigation resulting in all charges being dropped in 1989. Turned out David Harris was responsible for the murder all along.

Notes

1 Zeldes, I., and D. Stoner. "Speedometer Examination—an Aid in Accident Investigation." *FBI Law Enforcement Bulletin*, vol. 49, no. 3, 1980, pp. 11–15.

2 ASPCA. "Dog-Fighting DNA Database Breaks New Ground In Crackdown on Animal Cruelty." *ASPCA*, 15 Jun. 2010, www.aspca.org.
3 Humane Society.ORG, 2024.
4 American Humane.ORG, 2024.
5 Maxwell, Virginia, and Martha Smith-Blackmore. *Investigating Animal Abuse Crime Scenes: A Field Guide*. CRC Press, 2023.
6 Dolinak, David, et al. *Forensic Pathology, Principles and Practice*. Elsevier Academic Press, 2005.
7 Maloney, Michael S., and Donald G. Housman. *Crime Scene Investigation Procedural Guide*. CRC Press, 2014.

Fire Scene Processing and Evidence Collection 13

Fire can be encountered in a variety of scenarios, ranging from large-scale structural fires to small, localized fires within a scene. The causes of these fires can vary widely, from intentional acts such as concealing a crime to accidental spills. While crime scene investigators typically do not determine the origins of fires or analyze burn patterns, they often collaborate closely with fire investigation experts. Their responsibilities include collecting and packaging evidence from fire scenes and handling scenes with minor fires that may not require any fire department involvement. This guide provides essential information to navigate a fire scene effectively, from capturing photographs to collecting evidence.

Scene Resources

- Evidence and fire scene processing guide from International Association for Arson Investigators (IAAI)—https://iaaievidence-guide.com
- NFPA 921—Guide for Fire and Explosion Investigations

Checklist—Photographs of Structural Fire

Personal Preparation

- ☐ *Grab a partner—mandatory for safety in structures*
- ☐ Ensure equipment is clean or single use
- ☐ Ensure uniform was not worn on previous scene—long pants and long sleeves recommended
- ☐ Hard hat if needed while on scene
- ☐ Boots with traction/steel sole lining recommended (rubber recommended, uniform acceptable)
- ☐ N95 mask recommended at minimum, R95 mask or a respirator with P100 filter will block vapors and odor, reducing headaches and strain
- ☐ Create an evidence collection list while on scene—gather all needed note forms prior
- ☐ Bring monopod or tripod into scene as you will likely need it at some point during photographs

DOI: 10.4324/9781003503897-14

- ☐ Bring extra batteries for flashes and extra light sources as they are drained faster in dark scenes when used often or continuously
- ☐ Ensure utilities are disconnected by the supplier if possible, at minimum turned off at source for safety
- ☐ Ensure a site safety assessment has been completed, or do it now prior to entering

Photography

- ☐ Cover page
- ☐ Settings—consider indoor/outdoor scene, extent of damages, additional lighting
- ☐ Auto or flash white balance recommended
- ☐ Close-ups—ring flash or two oblique angled flashes recommended
- ☐ Bracketing recommended (manual or as a setting, adjust +/− 1 F-stop)
- ☐ Overlap photographs in a panning fashion

Exterior Structure

- ☐ Fire in progress if you are present
- ☐ Address/entrance to structure
- ☐ 4 sides and 4 corners of structure/yard/vehicle showing ground to roof
- ☐ Pathway entrance and exit from location
- ☐ Any entry/exits (threshold barrier and tool marks if present) to include access and barriers to access
- ☐ Yard and structures if applicable
- ☐ Tire marks in yard/driveway
- ☐ Footwear prints below windows/outside doors
- ☐ Windows/windowpanes to include broken glass on ground below, charring/soot above
- ☐ Any ignitable liquids/rags/paper/lighters/matches/bombs/cordage and so on
- ☐ Containers/piles of debris directly surrounding fire area
- ☐ Clothing/partially burnt clothing to include label
- ☐ Electrical panels, fuse boxes/breakers and equipment—controls and overall condition
- ☐ Electrical cords and extension cords
- ☐ Power poles/transformers/drops
- ☐ Gas connections/meters—controls and overall condition
- ☐ Propane connections/storage—controls and overall condition
- ☐ Heat-producing appliances located on exterior—controls and overall condition

- ☐ Phone lines (cut anywhere along length?)
- ☐ Roof (burn patterns and access to/barriers)
- ☐ Burn/soot patterns over doors/windows, venting, porches, garages
- ☐ If on a night shift scene, take additional set of pictures once the sun comes up
- ☐ Witness perspective photographs—their location in relation to the scene and from their location viewing scene
- ☐ Overhead photographs of scene if possible—see if you can access a tall ladder

Interior Structure

- ☐ Entry and exit path if known
- ☐ Overall and mid-range photographs floor to ceiling
- ☐ All char/soot/burn patterns visible
- ☐ Can push water off floor to view patterns (manual focus, be quick)
- ☐ Soot voids and non-voids
- ☐ Damaged/minimally damaged items/undamaged items

Overall and Mid-range of Each Room

- ☐ Uninvolved/undamaged rooms need at least overall photo and their threshold/entrance to the room including over the door/window
- ☐ Sprinkler system
- ☐ Alarm panels
- ☐ 360° photographs—all corners and walls—floor to ceiling view
- ☐ Behind each door/threshold of each room—tool marks? Doors open/closed? Soot/burn patterns?
- ☐ Ceiling—smoke detectors, smoke patterns, light bulbs
- ☐ Doors—locks, magnetic locks, automatic closers, and open/closed position
- ☐ Floor (as found and debris removed)
- ☐ Furniture/behind all furniture as found and any voids surrounding
- ☐ Inside cabinets, cupboards, closets, medicine cabinets, and so on
- ☐ Walls—clocks, pictures, light sockets, electrical sockets
- ☐ Windows/locks and open/closed position
- ☐ Fire extinguishers
- ☐ Furnace/stove and other heat-producing appliances
- ☐ Electrical cords and extension cords
- ☐ Close-up of suspected items involved, evidence, damage, and so on
- ☐ Partially burnt clothing—include labels/tags of materials
- ☐ Valuables—safe, jewelry box, firearms, and so on
- ☐ All fire patterns inside/outside room

- ☐ Any reconstruction efforts taken and visible voids during reconstruction/collection
- ☐ Any suspected points of origin/ignition sources

Evidence Collection Photographs

- ☐ Set up tool cleaning station before collecting evidence
- ☐ Item before collection in place
- ☐ Item with scale
- ☐ Place container next to item being photographed and take picture with the interior empty container and item both visible
- ☐ Place item inside can/bag
- ☐ Take picture showing the interior container and empty void next to can both visible
- ☐ Seal can or bag
- ☐ Take picture of container and written case information—case #, date, collector, item/description, marker #, *time of collection*

Exit Checklist—Second Walkthrough

- ☐ Ensure evidence packages match the evidence list, are all accounted for, and are all sealed
- ☐ Ensure all evidence items are included on sketch and have 2 measurements + height/depth
- ☐ Ensure sketch legend and all notes are completed
- ☐ Ensure all trash, soap, and equipment are picked up

Subjects on Scene

- ☐ Cover page with name, DOB
- ☐ Overall head to toe
- ☐ Face for ID (shoulders to top of head)
- ☐ Head to shoulders, shoulders to hips, hips to feet
- ☐ Hair—possible singe/burn (look closely)
- ☐ Hands/wrists on both sides—look for burns/cuts/missing nails
- ☐ Pants—accelerant spillage, burns, singe
- ☐ Shoes—melting/burning, accelerant spillage, residue (check the bottom)
- ☐ Deceased subjects can include broken bones, torn skin, ripped skin, and the pugilistic stance
- ☐ Subject location found in scene to include all surrounding items and area underneath body
- ☐ Crowd photographs—consider video of crowd as well

Photograph Suggestions

- Be systematic with photographs to make them easier to follow among all the dark colored background (overlapping panning by 30%)—helps the viewer keep track of location in scene
- Use timed settings, raise ISO, lower F-stop
- Polarizer filter helps reduce flash glare off charred wood and wet items
- Moisture in air is common with fire suppression which hinders pictures because the flash/added lighting reflects off moisture—avoid the flash and adjust your settings instead
- Detachable flash/oblique or added lighting can assist with photography
- Use detachable flash, ISO 400, F/8—adjust flash output and settings for scene
- Digital scan should be done in black and white rather than color
- LEICA, FARO can capture burn/char patterns well
- Be mindful of soot voids indicating an item has been moved intentionally or by falling during fire activities (hose spray, firemen with big boots, items falling due to shelves burning)

Burn Pit Scene Processing

Photographs

- Photograph burn pit as is before manipulation to include surrounding area
- Photograph with section designators applied prior to search
- Photograph during processing to include sifting area, grid area
- Photograph the resulting items found and marked

Sifting through Burn Pit

- Process all contents of burn pit through screen if human remains suspected, 1/4 inch screen good for sifting ashes
- Human body has approximately 206 bones in the body, 32 teeth
- Bones change color when exposed to extreme heat
- Search for false teeth, dental work/implants, hardware from joints/bones, medical devices
- Document who helped and was on scene

ALS for Pit Search

- Human bones and teeth will fluoresce, rocks/stones will not
    - CSS light with orange filter
    - 400–490 nm with orange filter
    - Blacklight with no filter

Facts about Fire Scenes

Fire Origin—Will Be Determined by the Fire Department Personnel

- Where the fire started often has heaviest amount of damage
- Fire moves away from origin by path of least resistance, horizontally and vertically

Possible Sources of Fire Combustion

- Chemical mixtures, electricity, matches/lighter, liquid accelerant, natural gas, bottled gas
- Accelerant can still be present in soil, carpet, seat cushions, and so on after fire

Burn Patterns

- Structural fire burn patterns differ from vehicle fires due to the compact size and different fuel sources found in vehicles
- Vehicle fires tend to ignite quicker due to the close proximity and large amount of flammable items
- Structural fires contain several basic burn patterns the fire investigator will evaluate
  - V shape—wider at the top than the base
  - Inverted cone—resembles an upside down V
  - Protected surface—void, lack of soot due to an item covering that space
  - Ignitable liquid patterns—locations where a burning liquid was placed, often clean lines with unburnt portion of substrate
- While you do not need to interpret the burn patterns, it is important to capture them in your photographs for later analysis and review

Canine

- Search for accelerants in scene
- Screen tools and packaging to ensure they are clean after evidence collection
- Screen debris or soil for accelerants

PPE

- Has tremendous value for your own protection inside and around a fire scene
- Hard hat should be worn until the structure is deemed stable

- Boots should be rubber with steel shank and steel toe and good traction
- Mask should be minimum N95, R95 helpful, half-mask air purifying respirator highly recommended
- Protective goggles and work gloves needed for sample collection if using hand tools
- Disposable gloves will be needed for some sample collection

Glass

- Will melt and/or soften bending toward source of heat (light bulbs/windows/bottle necks)
- Melts at 1400°F/750°C
- Breaking glass can fly up to 10 feet/3 m
- Once glass is heated and cooled it is much more fragile than original; it will shatter easily
- If it is still able to be processed for fingerprints after that amount of heat exposure, prints will be baked onto glass and able to be photographed not lifted
- Determining direction of force on broken windows/glass
    - Look for Wallner lines on glass break surface—doesn't happen with thermal breaks
    - Collect and submit for examination—expert can tell if window broken before/during fire
- Heat-distorted light bulbs ("pulled" bulb)
    - Incandescent light bulb of greater than 25 watts—portion of the bulb that bulges out will point in the direction of the heating
    - Incandescent bulbs of less than 25 watts—push inward on the side closest to the heat source

Grass Fires

- Wind will affect the burn patterns and can cause confusion with expected results
- Fire will move away from the source after fire ignition. It is possible and quite likely that paper/wooden matches or a lighter are still present and unburned due to the fire moving quickly away.
- Stem fall: During a grass fire, the grass stems fall in the direction of the fire origin due to quick movement and can literally point the way back to the fire source

Paper

- Not all paper burns the same—thick or coated paper burns slower
- Can turn yellow as low as 100°F/37°C or char at 300°F/148°C

Plastic

- Plastic clocks melting on scene can give temperature estimation, time, direction
- Melted trash bags in fire can still have prints on bottom (superglue processing recommended)

Soot

- Color/density of soot deposits are more related to ventilation than accelerant
- Move doors to see soot void on flooring for door placement
- Document soot voids/no voids when items are collected
- Bloodstains can get covered with soot and not be seen—LCV can be used on soot covered blood washing off soot covering leaving blood enhanced
- Soot can be cleared off items successfully with such items as ninhydrin, SPR, physical developer, LVC, Amido Black, Magic Eraser pads, and Silly Putty

Search with ALS

- Human bones and teeth will fluoresce, rocks/stones will not
    - CSS light with orange filter
    - 400–490 nm with orange filter
    - Blacklight with no filter

Temperatures

- Aluminum melts at 1220°F/660°C
- Boats/mobile homes/travel trailers engulf in flames quickly due to fiberglass and other materials
- Body turns to ash at approximately 1800°F/982°C
- Bonfire temperature 2,012°F/1,100°C
- Blood exposed to heat over 425°F/200°C will degrade
- Brass melts at 1625–1780°F/875–980°C
- Campfire temperature 1650°F/900°C
- Cast iron melts at 2200°F/1204°C
- Charcoal burns at temperatures 2,012°F/1,100°C
- Copper melts at 1981°F/1080°C
- Glass melts at 1400°F/750°C
- Housefire temperature 1,200–1,800°F/649–982°C
- Housefire can reach 1100°F in less than 5 minutes
- Lead melts at 621°F/327°C

- Steel melts at 2,200–2,500°F/1,205–1,370°C
- Melted firearm can be X-rayed to see location of ammunition (not a scene activity)

Vehicle Fires

- Passenger compartment fires often results in a failure at the top of the windshield
- Engine compartment fires often result in failure at the bottom passenger side of the windshield

Video

- Can move through scenes showing burn patterns in a systematic fashion
- Does NOT replace photographs or sketches
- Effective way to document a fire scene, often easier for viewer to follow than the photographs when using good lighting

Your Safety

- Eat, wash, make calls, and take breaks in the cold zone or outside the red tape
- Breaks mandatory—but take them in the cold zone
- Be prepared—the scene will always be changing as people move and put out fires
- Hold the scene if it needs it—take your breaks and confirm your actions, don't feel rushed to release the scene
- Common errors—not cleaning tools sufficiently, rushing due to being exhausted
- If you want to bring in heavy lights and equipment, ensure the flooring can adequately hold it
- Assess oxygen levels prior to entering if not already done
- Wear nitrile gloves under leather gloves to protect yourself
- Post fire does not mean no PPE, still required for your health
- Assess hazards such as
    - Holes in the floor and ceiling (if doors are laying on the floor, likely covering holes). Ask the firemen if they are present.
    - Chimneys that could collapse
    - Standing water that can cover holes or carry electricity
    - Inhalation hazards due to burning items and low oxygen levels
    - Weather issues like heat stress, frostbite, dehydration, heavy rain, and heavy wind blowing debris

- Chemical/radiological hazards from room contents that have burned
- Hanging wires you may trip on or touch

Evidence Collection on Fire Scenes

- Be mindful that heat can etch fingerprints onto surfaces, and soot can protect them from heat preventing evaporation and allowing latent comparison and DNA. Even after a fire the items can still provide valuable evidence.
- When collecting for accelerant samples, search closer to the center of the fire
- When collecting for fingerprint/DNA samples, search the outer perimeter for evidence to process
- If trying to determine whether broken glass be processed for accelerant or fingerprints, go with accelerant. That is more likely to obtain a useful result.
- Glass becomes extremely fragile after exposure to extreme heat even though it remains intact. Transport with care.

Prior to Collection, Complete the Following

1. Photographs with and without scale
2. Sketch to include two measurements AND height/depth
3. Video of scene and evidence items
4. Creation of evidence list entry
5. Fill out packaging prior to collection

Collection Tools/Equipment—*Steel Recommended*

- Shovel, trowel, chisel, hoe, sand scoop, screen with wood frame for sifting
- No gas-powered tools, should be electric or battery powered
- Never coat with tools with a rust preventative/sealant
- Never store with regular crime scene hand tools
- Provide appropriate storage and maintenance for optimum performance/collection—don't let your tools get rusty and dirty, don't let your handles dry out or you can get punctured on scene
- Can place a clean glove or new plastic bag over tool for soft item collection

Tool Maintenance

Tools MUST be decontaminated between EACH sample collection

- Ultra Dawn concentrated dishwashing liquid commonly used
- Good rinse with continuous flow of water required
- Fully dry tool between each collection sample
- Retain sample of dishwashing soap for substrate control samples suggested—swab sample acceptable
- NO waterless cleaners

METHOD—Set up wash chain with 3 tubs: Soapy water and 2 rinse tubs (in cold zone or outside tape)

Common Sampling Errors—*According to Interfire.org (2024)*

The most common ignitable liquid residue sampling errors:

- Sample size too small
- Samples from wrong place/materials
- Poor sample preservation techniques
- No comparison or control samples
- Not maintaining chain of custody

Comparison Samples

- Sample of like item from scene to compare scene sample
- Nearby undamaged area, if possible
- Flooring, roofing, soil, doorway, carpet

Control Samples

- Sample of an item used during processing—swab blank, can blank, water blank
- Sample of contaminants you introduce—cleanser sample

Packaging Options for Fire Evidence *(Must Be Vapor Free)*

- All containers/packaging MUST be labeled/sealed on scene
- Max fill for ALL CONTAINERS—2/3 FULL
- ARSON BAG
  - Nylon, Kapak, aluminized bags
  - Reduce the smell and release of vapors
  - Can be in roll or pre-cut bags
  - All heat sealed—don't forget sealer
- CAN
  - Unlined or Teflon lining only
  - Other lining can cause chemical contamination

- Paint can or gas can size
- Denting can during closure can cause leakage
- Don't reuse cans for evidence collection
- GLASS
  - Glass jar or mason jar
  - Teflon-lined lid ideal—metal lid or Bakelite lid good, screw top only
  - No rubber seals
- PLASTIC—Only DOT approved accelerant/gas cans

Storage for Fire Evidence

- Upright position, not jostled or easily disturb able
- Temperature-controlled environment only
- Do not store at temperature above 100°F/40°C due to vapor buildup or further heat damage to documents and fragile evidence
- Avoid direct sunlight storage
- Accelerant samples in soil should be frozen as soon as possible

Collection Options

Whole Items Samples (Clothing, Shoes, Cans, Weapons, Burnt Cloth, etc.)

Option: Whole Tangible Item/Textiles—Paint Can Size

- Photograph empty can next to item being collected from overhead (don't move can)
- Place item being collected in paint can—max fill 2/3 full
- Take additional overhead photographs with the item now in the can to include the original collection area (don't move can)
- Wipe rim of can of any debris preventing closure of lid
- Immediately place lid on can and seal with rubber mallet
- Mark with appropriate information on can/lid and photograph writing
  - Case #/date
  - Collector/ID
  - Item/description
  - Time of collection

Option: Whole Tangible Items—Nylon Self Cut or Pre-cut Bags—Bigger than a Paint Can

- Place photographed item in plastic bag of appropriate size, fill bag approximately 2/3 full

- Heat seal closed on scene if possible
- Mark with appropriate information on bag and photograph writing (recommend placing tape over writing)
  - Case #/date
  - Collector/ID
  - Item/description
  - Time of collection

Accelerant Samples

Accelerant Goes 3 Places When Used at a Scene

- Part of it stays in intended material
- Part of it wicks into surrounding material
- Part of it evaporates while burning

Search Tools for Accelerants

- Electronic detector/air reader
- Canine—canines can search a scene for accelerants, screen your equipment after cleaning, screen packaging for new equipment or your own uniform to prevent cross contamination
- Nose—your own sense of smell is a powerful tool for finding sample locations
- ALS—450–490 nm with orange filter

Common Collection Areas for Accelerants

- Accelerant can be found as a liquid, gas, or solid
- Areas protected by fire that liquid accelerant could have pooled such as underneath furniture legs, under threshold barrier/trim, joints in baseboards/floorboards, and carpet/cushion backing
- Cloth/porous materials in contact with pour pattern are good for sampling, area to sample: Inside the edge of burn pattern
- Concrete and plaster holds sample well
- Drains from clean-up or water run-off
- Lightly charred material
- Residue on bottom of shoes/pant legs/cuffs/ankles splashed with liquid accelerant onto subjects when starting a fire
- Seams/cracks/joints/hinge in substrate
- Sand and soil are good for sampling though search lower than normal as it will flow down into material
- Soil outside threshold can hold accelerant even after the fire has been put out—must be stored frozen

- Wood—sampling good with raw, untreated/unsealed wood, area around nail holes and cracks, ends of wood

Burned/Charred Document Collection

- Photograph documents *as discovered, prior to packaging, after removal from packaging*

Option: Collection for Document Content

- Don't separate on scene if found together, transport as 1 item—slide rigid item underneath pile/documents, lift carefully (file folder, cardboard, box lid)
- Transport in box—can use fabric padding to reduce damage—don't fold documents to fit
- Hand carry box/don't stack

Option: Collection for Accelerant Testing

- Place immediately in arson can, metal fireproof box—can fold to fit
- Seal can (with rubber mallet) fully at time of collection
- Take picture of can lid sealed with case information written—case #, date, collector, item/description, marker #, TIME OF COLLECTION

Chemicals from Clandestine Laboratories/Chemical Incendiary Mixtures

- Place sample in glass jars then place jar in arson can
- May corrode cans

Carpet-Absorbed Accelerant Samples

- Photograph item before collection before manipulation
- Place can/bag next to item being photographed, take picture with the interior empty can/bag and item both visible
- Using clean/new blade cut sample to include padding/lining as needed
- Chimney roll sample if larger, allow excess liquid to drain off
- Place in arson can or bag, max 2/3 full
- Take picture showing the interior can/bag and empty void next to can after collection
- Seal can (with rubber mallet) fully at time of collection or heat seal arson bags on scene
- Take picture of can lid adhered/bag sealed with case information written—case #, date, collector, item/description, marker #, TIME OF COLLECTION

- Ensure photographs of empty area after collection is taken
- Comparison sample collection—sample from other section of same substrate with NO burn/accelerant using CLEAN/NEW blade—package separately

Textile/Wood-Absorbed Accelerant Samples (Door Frames, Window Frames, Floorboards)

- Photograph item before collection before manipulation
- Place can next to item being photographed, take picture with the interior empty can and item both visible
- Arson bags not recommended for wooden samples
- Using clean/new chisel collect sample from wooden area, as much as possible/suspected to be stained
  - Edge of charring adequate but deep charring recommended for sampling
  - Within 1/2 inch of seam if possible, liquid pools in seams
  - Consider crevices, areas underneath furniture legs, threshold trim, and so on
  - Place sample in arson can—max 2/3 full
- Take picture showing the interior can and sample area in same frame
- Seal can (with rubber mallet) fully at time of collection
- Take picture of can lid sealed with case information written—case #, date, collector, item/description, marker #, TIME OF COLLECTION
- Ensure photographs of sample area with scale is collected
- Collect comparison sample from other section of same substrate with NO burn/accelerant using CLEAN/NEW chisel following the same procedures above—package separately

Liquid Accelerant Samples

Option: Accelerant in Container

- Photograph original container with liquid
- Pour liquid directly into glass jar or metal gas collection can depending upon size, max 2/3 full, clean funnel acceptable
- Place glass jar into arson can, can place padding inside can to prevent jarring movement
- Mark with appropriate information on can/lid and photograph writing—case #, date, collector, item/description, marker #, TIME OF COLLECTION
- No control samples needed
- Package and collect original container

Option: Liquid/Gel Accelerant—Puddle Sample

- Photograph sample in place
- Soak up liquid sample off non-porous surface with swabs, cotton pad, gauze, filter paper
- Gel can be scooped onto gauze/cotton pad
- Place cotton in small paint can and seal paint can immediately
- Mark with appropriate information on can/lid and photograph writing—case #, date, collector, item/description, marker #, TIME OF COLLECTION
- Comparison sample of swab from same substrate should be collected

Autopsy Attendance 14

Many CSIs, both sworn and unsworn, are tasked with attending autopsies. It is important to remember to take essential photographs while present as you will not have a second opportunity. This chapter provides reminders of areas to photograph such as the face and all injuries, as well as items to collect as a precaution they are not forgotten. You can ask the morgue if you can lay items removed from the body on clean plastic or butcher paper which reduces the risk of contamination.

While attending an autopsy is one of many duties for some crime scene investigators (CSIs), it is the primary responsibility for others in the forensic field. Medical examiners and coroners face pressure regarding their findings, as shown by a study conducted by the National Association of Medical Examiners (NAME), where over 70% of their members reported feeling such pressure.[1] Cooperation is essential to ensure that the truth is discovered, and it is important to share evidence with all parties involved. Verifying that they have seen scene pictures and know the medical history might be crucial. The 2009 National Academy of Sciences Report, Strengthening Forensic Science in the United States: A Path Forward, recommended direct autonomy of investigators from the government to reduce pressure and accessibility.[2] Pathologists play a necessary role and face similar ethical, work, and personal obligations.

Suggestions

- Do not attend the autopsy of a co-worker, friend, or family member in an official capacity
- If bringing evidence to the morgue for the pathologist to examine make sure it is fully processed FIRST
- If bringing photographs for pathologist to examine—ensure COPIED to CD prior to arrival, never bring original as accidents happen
- Ask pathologist questions, use their expertise—is wound behavior consistent with scene conditions? Any ideas on trajectory? Any suggestions on weapons search on scene?
- Bring butcher paper to wrap items collected if needed and to lay on table if allowed

DOI: 10.4324/9781003503897-15

- If a body is brought to morgue in a container, be prepared to take the container at this time. All extended sampling and processing should be done at the lab/office.
- Non-injury photographs should be taken at a distance of 4–8 feet/1–2.4 m (no farther back)
- Injury photographs should be taken with and without scale. Consider using color chart for injuries, or a scale with included color chart.

PPE

- Wearing PPE is non-negotiable, put on the mask
- *Minimum* PPE—surgeon's mask and gloves (pieces and fluids DO fly, bone powder is hazardous)
- *Recommended* PPE—N95 mask, double gloves, maintain clean/dirty hazardous protocol

Wound Documentation Recommended

- Location on body—check all wrists, ankles, shoulders, neck, hip, and other joints
- Overall shape and color
- Pattern
- Direction of injury
- Width/length/depth, use a scale for reference
- Number of wounds

Evidence to Collect

- Blood card, nail clippings, inked fingerprint cards/strips
- Any trace evidence
- All clothing/shoes/jewelry the body arrived with
- Oral swabs if suspected sexual activity or biting—gums, gum line, teeth cracks, cheek interior—consider flossing teeth if biting suspected
- GSR or pepper spray samples from wounds/hair using filter/gauze/swabs
- Container body arrived in if applicable (trash can, tote box, cardboard box, etc.)
- Water from lungs if present

Checklist—Autopsy Photographs

☐ Ensure all unnecessary background is removed from your frame when taking pictures—staff, tools, blood, and so on
  ☐ Camera settings—date/time/file/flash (do you want bracketing?)

- ☐ Suggest—ISO 400, 1/60, F/11, remove detachable flash
- ☐ Cover sheet with name/DOB if known
- ☐ Apply PPE if you have not already
- ☐ Grab scale and color chart

Exterior Body Bag While Sealed

- ☐ Exterior body bag or container with all seals
- ☐ Lock tag/case writing
- ☐ Document any insect/larvae/egg activity present, collect needed samples

Interior Body Bag (Open with Body Inside)

- ☐ Body—head to feet
- ☐ Insect/larvae/egg activity if applicable
- ☐ Trace evidence in place if applicable
- ☐ Blood/purge/vomit/dirt/vegetation/debris on body

Body after Removal from Bag/Prior to Being Cleaned (Consider Placing Items on Butcher Paper)

- ☐ Empty body bag from which the body just came out of
- ☐ Consider X-ray if body is burnt or involved in gunfire
- ☐ Overhead of body if able
- ☐ Face—front and side—spittle, blood, defects to face
- ☐ Head to shoes, head to shoulders (top 1/3), shoulders to hips (middle 1/3), hips to shoes (bottom 1/3)
- ☐ Body—close-ups of face/hair/hands/head/feet
- ☐ Body—medical intervention equipment and injuries with scale
- ☐ Body—underneath breasts, scrotum, between buttocks if additional injuries
- ☐ Hand bags and foot bags in place on body to include any writing
- ☐ Hands and feet after bag removal to include debris/blood/soot/etc.
- ☐ Clothing/shoes—defects/stains/blood/spittle—manufacturing tag if not already photographed
- ☐ Pocket contents
- ☐ Any remaining trace evidence on body/inside wounds (COLLECT AT THIS TIME)
- ☐ Item close-ups as removed from body, consider lying flat on table for additional photographs

Body after Being Cleaned, Before Cut

- ☐ Overhead of body if able

- ☐ Face—front and side—spittle, blood, defects to face
- ☐ Capture face as is, then capture face with eyes open, mouth closed (if possible, for ID purposes)
- ☐ Eyes—eyeballs, interior/exterior eyelids
- ☐ Ears—front and back, check for bruising/injury
- ☐ Mouth—interior/exterior mouth, lips, teeth/gums
- ☐ Neck—front and side
- ☐ Head to shoes, head to shoulders (top 1/3), shoulders to hips (middle 1/3), hips to shoes (bottom 1/3)
- ☐ Body—close-ups of face/hair/hands/head/feet all sides and all defects
- ☐ Palms/soles of feet—check for injury/bruising/small cuts/glass debris
- ☐ Hands—nail beds (check for evidence of injury, poison, or torture), broken nails, fingertip cuts
- ☐ Body—medical intervention equipment and injuries
- ☐ Body—underneath breasts, scrotum, between buttocks if additional injuries
- ☐ Tattoos/scars/visible injuries—with/without scale
- ☐ Coloring/decomposition changes—consider bracketing
- ☐ Footwear/tire marks on subject—use a 300 mm L scale
- ☐ Injuries found with and without scale

Body after Being Cut

- ☐ Chest cavity before/after being cut
- ☐ Visible injuries with/without scale, and after dissection if done
- ☐ All organs/items of interest
- ☐ Gastric contents—look for undissolved pills/medication—consider contents sample
- ☐ Trajectory rods in place if applicable
- ☐ All removed samples and cuttings

Ending Photographs

- ☐ Body closed/sewn
- ☐ Body bag re-secured
- ☐ Photographs of all collected items—to include blood card, jewelry

Known Print/Inked Print Collection

Additional Resources

- *https://fbibiospecs.fbi.gov/video-respository*—Video series of post-mortem fingerprinting techniques

Options

- Black ink (in a tube)
- Black ink pads
- Black powder
- Inkless fingerprint pads
- Casting material—AccuTrans, Mikrosil, or molding clay

Autopsy Print Suggestions

- Wait for hands to turn room temperature
- Break rigor in fingers/hands/wrists prior to beginning
- Print fingers before the palm
- Use card strips rather than full 10 print card
- Note all missing or unprintable fingers in your written notes
- Use large tube or your forearm to roll full palm prints

Regular Conditions

1. Apply black ink to hands/feet of subject with even coverage using rubber roller
2. Use separate metal spoon form for each set needed, put a strip in each spoon prior to beginning
3. Complete all sets of first finger
4. Move card to next opening once all cards are printed in order (so the ink dries)
5. Complete all sets of second finger
6. Move card to next opening once all cards are printed in order (so the ink dries)
7. Continue until completed

Charred Hands

Option: Inside Out

- Remove dermal layer and turn skin inside out
- Photograph fingerprints/footprints using macrophotography if possible

Option: Submerge in Water

- Remove dermal layer
- Submerge in water 15 seconds
- Apply black fingerprint powder and lift with method of choice or photograph with macro photography

Embalmed Hands

- Formaldehyde causes tissue shrinkage
- Fingertips/ridges smaller but still printable

Putrified Bodies/Mummified Bodies

- Likely no useable known print lift obtainment
- Consider footprints if possible
- Consider lifting fingerprints or footprints from the scene or items within the scene to assist with ID/investigation

Option: Photograph Finger Pads

- Use camera or cell phone to photograph finger and footpads

Waterlogged Hands

GOOD *Skin Condition*

OPTION—BLACK INK
- Apply with roller and lift as normal on card strips

OPTION 2—BLACK POWDER
- Apply powder to hand with camel hair/foam brush/fiberglass brush (keep brush separate from scene use brushes)
- Lift with adhesive paper/gel lift/fingerprint tape

WRINKLED *Skin Condition*

OPTION 1—INJECT AIR BELOW SURFACE OF SKIN WITH 28-GAUGE NEEDLE
- Once skin is flatter process with method of choice

OPTION 2—SWELL FINGERTIP
- Wrap string/fishing line/disposable glove around finger moving toward the tip. Pressure will swell fingertip. Process with method of choice. Remove string upon completion.

SUBMERGED *Skin Condition—(Epidermis Coming Off, Recommended in the Lab)*

OPTION: BOILING WATER
- Remove dermal layer slowly in one piece if possible (can do one finger at a time if needed)
- Submerge epidermis in boiling water for 15 seconds, remove
- Process with method of choice

Necropsy Photographs (for Animals)

- Ensure all unnecessary background is removed from your frame when taking pictures—staff, tools, blood, and so on
  - Camera settings—date/time/file/flash (do you want bracketing?) Suggest—ISO 400, 1/60, F11, remove detachable flash
  - Cover sheet with name/DOB if known
  - Apply PPE if you have not already
  - Grab scale and color chart for injuries

Exterior Body Bag or Packaging/Container

- Overall body bag or packaging/container
- Close-up of label/tag/writing on packaging
- Photograph each layer as unwrapped (bodies often arrive in several layers)
- Trace evidence as encountered
- Overall body once unwrapped at multiple angles, ensure all sides/limbs pictured
- Microchip scanner results if chip present

Overall Exterior Body—*before and after Shaved*

- Top of head
- Close-up of face, ears, neck
- Teeth, gums
- Chest/belly/genitals
- Bottom/tail/back of legs
- Left side
- Right side
- Feet (top/bottom), nails

Close-ups

- Ear tags, collars, ropes, harness, and so on in place and after CUT AWAY
- Tattoos, brands, scars
- Injuries with/without scale (ABFO #2 scale, ensure circle visible) and label, ensure all have orientation (mid-range) photographs—broken bones, bruises, gunshot wounds, and so on
- Injuries with color chart if applicable

Body after Being Cut

- Chest cavity before/after being cut

- Visible injuries with/without scale, and after dissection if done
- All organs/items of interest
- Gastric contents—look for undissolved pills/medication—consider contents sample
- Trajectory rods in place if applicable

Evidence Collection

- If accelerant is suspected, a sample of hair should be collected for analysis (unsinged hair, plucked) and secured in a paint can, marked, and sealed on scene
- Tape lift results if used
- Photographs of all layers of wrapping or items searched for projectiles, weapon defects, trace evidence, accelerants

Ending Photographs

- Body closed/sewn
- Body re-secured in container/bag
- Removed tissue being sent for further analysis
- All collected items

Cases to Consider Regarding Autopsies

- 2016: Vanessa Marcotte was murdered while on a jog along her normal route. DNA was collected from underneath her fingernails which identified her killer.
- 1990s: Serial killer Donna Perry was tied to one of her juvenile victims when Perry's DNA was found under the fingernails of the decedent.
- In 1980 Lindy Chamberlain claimed a dingo kidnapped her child, and officers did not believe her story.
  - 1981 coroner ruled the baby taken by animal, not homicide. Authorities disagreed and continued to work on the case.
  - 1982 second coroner ruled homicide and Lindy went to prison.
  - 1986 Lindy was exonerated, and it was proven a dingo had taken the baby.
  - 2012 the coroner report was again changed to reflect the child was taken by an animal.

Notes

1 Melinek, J., et al. "National Association of Medical Examiners Position Paper: Medical Examiner, Coroner, and Forensic Pathologist Independence."

Academic Forensic Pathology, vol. 3, no. 1, 2013, pp. 93–98, https://doi.org/10.23907/2013.013.

2 National Research Council. 2009. *Strengthening Forensic Science in the United States: A Path Forward.* Washington, DC: The National Academies Press, https://doi.org/10.17226/12589.

15 Sketch and Measure

There is a wide range for when sketches are used based upon agency requirements and known details of the crime. Some agencies sketch all scenes to include burglaries and scenes with no evidence while other agencies rarely rely upon sketches. Sketches have proven their value repeatedly, and many seasoned CSIs recommend having them completed in all scenes regardless of how much evidence is present, and even if no evidence is initially found.[1] Juries still tend to give credibility to a hand-drawn sketch/measurements rather than a computer-generated rendering because they cannot measure the validity of the computer whereas with a human artist they can judge their competence.

The sketch must be reproducible by any other party based upon your information. Your reference points, measurement style, and legend must be clear, even when it seems obvious to you. A sketch can be completed for an entire scene or the contents of a kitchen table. Anytime distance is relevant be sure to measure it. This chapter will include a checklist for quick reference on scene to be sure nothing is forgotten as well as instructions for collecting measurements if you have forgotten, or suggestions for reference points if you are on scene and cannot find any.

Sketch Checklist—Scene Rough Sketch

Header (Include the Following Information on Drawing Before Leaving Scene)

- ☐ Directional arrow with notation: North, up, top, cashier side, and so on
- ☐ Address/location information
- ☐ Date of drawing/measurement collection
- ☐ Author of drawing/ID #
- ☐ Case #
- ☐ Not to Scale if applicable

Overall Drawing

- ☐ Reference points used—location/name/ID (minimum of 2)
- ☐ Overall scene measurements (yard dimensions, room dimensions, etc.)
- ☐ Exterior boundaries/exterior surroundings of interest

DOI: 10.4324/9781003503897-16

- ☐ Witness viewpoint distance to point of impact
- ☐ Height measurement of ceiling if indoors
- ☐ Height of above ground access—parking garage/balcony/roof
- ☐ Doors/windows of interest
- ☐ Furniture—height/width/length, relationship to room and other furniture
- ☐ Staircase—length of stair steps and height of top step
- ☐ Barriers if interest to include location and/or size

Evidence—2 Measurements and Height/Depth for

- ☐ All items of evidence
- ☐ All recovered projectile locations
- ☐ All bullet holes/defects
- ☐ All tool marks/impressions
- ☐ All bloody impressions
- ☐ Height/depth measurement for any defect/item not ground level
- ☐ Identify on sketch which ones were sampled/processed if any

Body

- ☐ Head
- ☐ Torso
- ☐ Right hand
- ☐ Left hand
- ☐ Right foot
- ☐ Left foot

Vehicle Placement 2 Minimum, 4 Optimal

- ☐ Front driver tire or bumper
- ☐ Rear driver tire or bumper
- ☐ Passenger tire or bumper
- ☐ Rear passenger tire or bumper
- ☐ Vehicle wheelbase measurement, tire track width (front tire to front tire OR rear tire to rear tire)
- ☐ Directional arrows for facing direction

Legend (Include the Following Information on Drawing Before Leaving Scene)

- ☐ Furniture/trash can/CCTV/vehicle shapes/meanings
- ☐ Vehicle identifiers (plate/make/color, etc.)
- ☐ Roadways/sidewalks/grass/shrubbery, etc.

Scene Specific

Fall from Building/Room/Hotel Room

☐ Measure height of window to ground on exterior
☐ Measure height of window to floor on interior
☐ Measure width of window if a ledge
☐ Measure roof to ground

Fall from Bed/Dresser/Counter

☐ Measure height of fall surface
☐ Measure width of standing area
☐ Measure distance of item to wall

Child Death—Death in Bed

☐ Measure space between wall/mattress or crib frame/mattress
☐ Measure width/height of mattress
☐ Measure the height/width of any damage surrounding bed to wall/ceiling

Kidnapping/Neglect

☐ Height of door locks/window locks
☐ Sides of doors with locks notated

Blood Trails

☐ Measure beginning and end of known trails
☐ Measure spots of DNA collection along trails

Tools for Measurement Collection

- Paper—graph paper/blank/lined/waterproof paper
- Pencil/waterproof pencil—ink pen not recommended unless erasable

Use Correct Measuring Tools

- Path of blood/bullet travel through air—use laser measurer along path
- Path of foot/vehicle travel—use walking wheel (Rolly wheel) on ground along path
- Distance around scene and overall measurements—use either method

Handheld Scales

- Keep on same plane as item and keep angle correct
- L scales—ABFO NO. 2 and 300 mm

- 6 inch ruler and yardstick
- Measuring tape 50 feet AND 100 feet
- Keep tape taut when gathering measurements—clean with bleach wipes prior to retracting if bloody/contaminated

Laser Measuring Tool/GPS Tool

- Be mindful of laser placement
- Keep line straight when gathering measurements
- Keep accurate starting point

Rolling Wheel—Measuring Tool

- Be mindful of start/stop point on wheel—do not start at the back of the wheel and measure to the front of the wheel
- Can roll outside PASSENGER window of vehicle, on bike, on foot to measure path of travel that is a short distance (around a corner, from house to house, from bank to house, etc.)

Known Items of Consistent Size to Use in a Pinch

- Quarter, US currency, ink pen, clipboard
- Can be used in emergencies, maintain 90°

Reference Points—*Document All Identifying Information/ Numbers with Notes and Photographs*

Do Use

- Streetlights/telephone poles—photograph pole number
- Street sign—photograph signs with functional lighting
- Corners—photograph signs with functional lighting
- Driveway line—ensure shows in overall photographs
- Curb lines—for example, West curbline of Clay Street—ensure visible in overall photographs
- Fencing—for example, South fence of backyard—ensure visible in overall photographs
- Walls of rooms—for example, South wall of primary bedroom
- Property stake—ensure stake information readable in a photograph
- Fire hydrant—photograph hydrant number
- Walls of structure—NOT outbuildings/temporary sheds

Don't Use

- Furniture
- Rocks

- Trash cans
- Trees
- Vehicles
- If above items are related to crime scene, gather measurements in relation to items of evidence as additional measurements, but do not use as reference points

Exceptions—Because There Always Are . . .

- When sketching the placement of items at moveable locations such as furniture and doors, you can use the edges as reference points, for example, West table edge or top edge of door

Sketch Notes

Legend Required on Scene

- Case number, date, artist name/ID, location, directional arrow
- Trash cans, furniture, vehicles, evidence markers, and other symbols must be identified in a legend
- Use designated short cuts with drawings/shapes: N for north, circle for trash can, triangle for evidence marker, vehicle drawing with directional arrow
- Use any diagram shortcut you decide, as long as you also write a legend entry of what that picture is depicting. You may forget, DO IT ON SCENE.

Directional Arrow with Written Explanation

- North
- Up
- Cashier side
- Front door

Measurement List

- Can be a structured list or drawn into picture
- Two measurements for each item, height/depth if applicable
- List of reference points/location/identifications
- Reference point identification—pole #, hydrant #, and so on

Sketch Views

Overhead View

- Shows scene as the crow flies, most common
- Nice visual for path of travel or blood trail

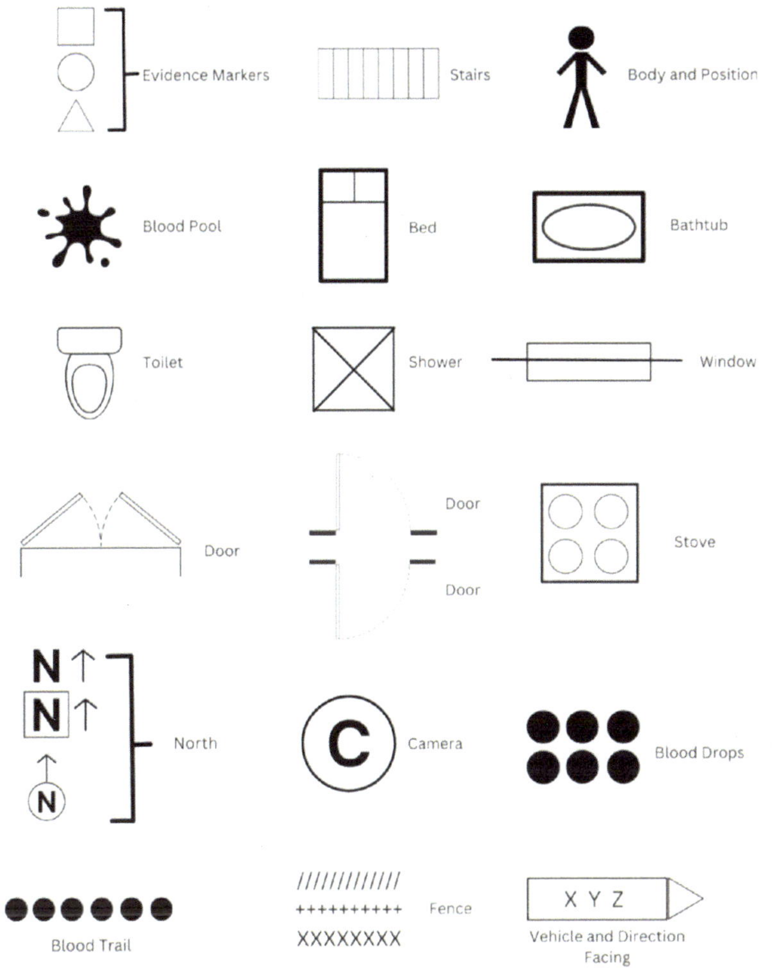

Figure 15.1 Sketch legend: Depicting several options of drawings for a scene sketch key.

Elevated View Sketching—Projected Viewpoint

- 1 viewpoint, 1 plane
- Shows view as if standing in front of it—bullet holes in a wall, grave depth, door/wall/house/window
- Reference points will be height/width
- Results reporting: 2 feet east of west side, 3 feet high

Detailed View

- Enlarged section of area with chosen details (driveway, countertop, etc.)

Vehicle Sketches

- Elevated view of vehicle door defects
- Overhead view of vehicle interior
- Good for showing evidence placement and subject reach distance

Types of Measurements

Baseline Measurement

- Works well in fields, farms, desert, long distance scenes, school/malls, and places with long hallways
- Needs 2 measuring tapes to be the 2 reference points (RP)
- 1 tape fixed in scene along length and 1 tape moving to measure width to items of evidence
- Measure with right angles
- Keep tape taut, no angles—straight distance only—will skew distance measurements

Method

- Use ruler/measuring tape 1 to:
  - establish single line by securing measuring tape, rope, string, across the length of the room/area—location along this plane is a reference point
  - keep ruler/measuring tape in place until finished with sketching/measuring
- Use ruler 2 to:
  - locate items of evidence
  - measure across the width, distance from item over to baseline tape
  - Results reporting: 1 feet north along baseline, 2 feet west of baseline, 6 inch high

Triangulation Measurement

- Works well in parking lots, residences, stores, intersections
- Item of evidence measured to 2 fixed reference points (RP), must be single stationary point, measure to center mass
- RP examples: Streetlight, fire hydrant, corner of wall, mailbox pole
- The points must have clear visual from point to point, and create triangle with all 3 points
- The points cannot be along same plane, or right next to each other (triangle should not be small)

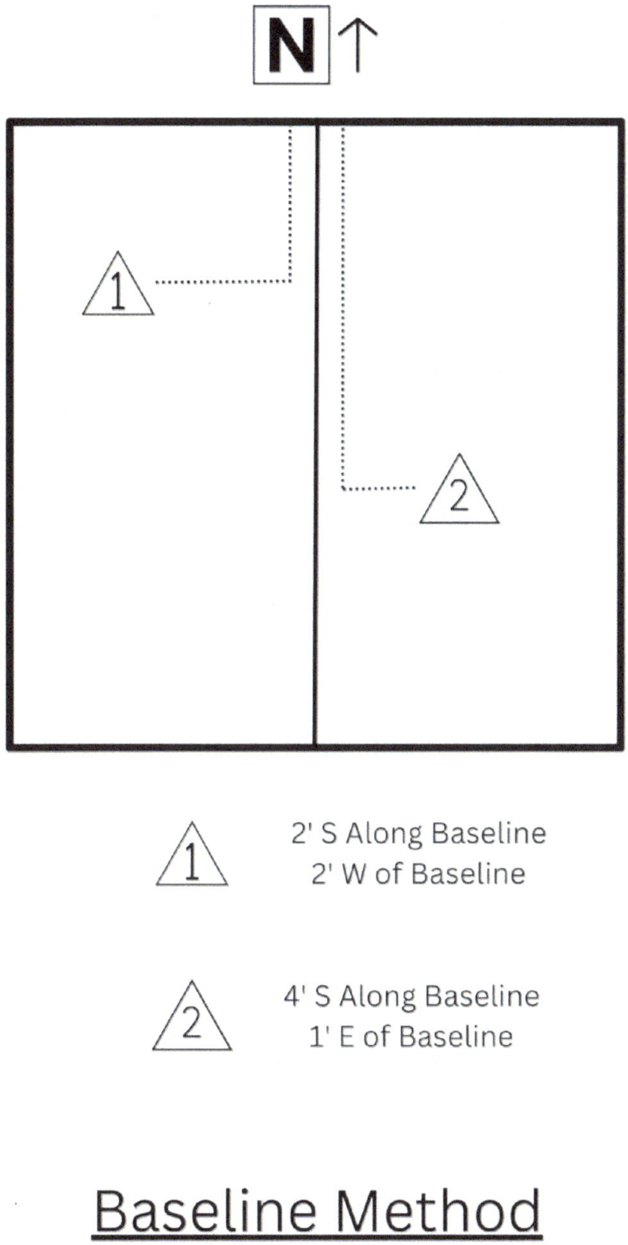

Figure 15.2 Baseline Method of measuring: Depicting the process for capturing measurements using the baseline method.

Method

- Measure from RP1 to each item of evidence
- Measure from RP2 to each item of evidence
- Measure distance from RP1 to RP2
- Measure height/depth if above/below ground level
- Results reporting: 10 feet from RP1, 2 feet from RP2, RP1 is 50 feet to RP2

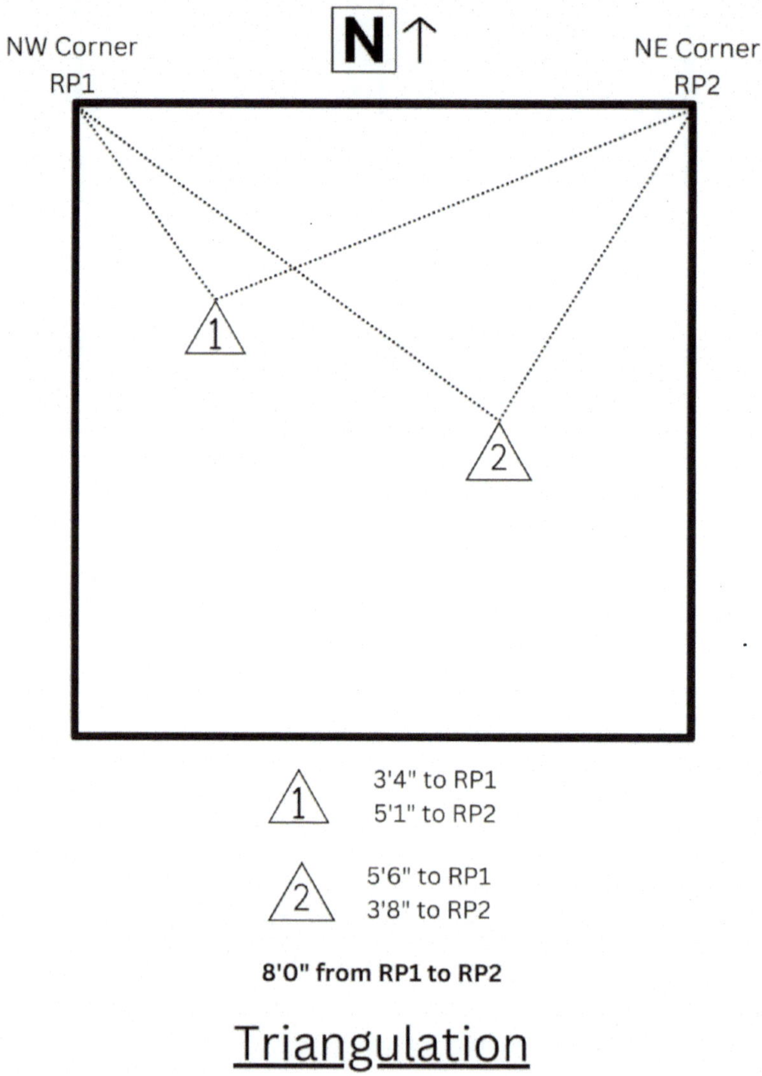

Figure 15.3 Triangulation Method of measuring: Depicting the process for capturing measurements using the triangulation method.

Rectangular Coordinates

- Works well in rooms, homes, yards, parking lots, gas stations, banks, schools
- Item of evidence measured to 2 perpendicular reference points (RP) creating right angle between RPs and evidence
- Keep tape taut/lines straight
- RP EXAMPLES: Curbline, parking lot line, west wall of bedroom, north wall of garage, exterior north wall of residence

Method

- Measure from RP1 to each item of evidence
- Measure from RP2 to each item of evidence

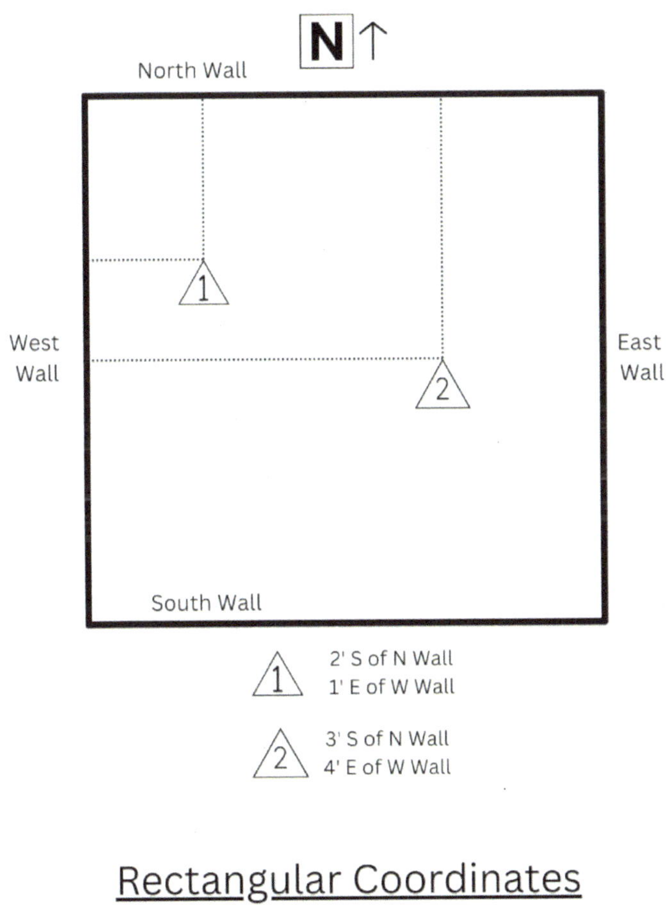

Figure 15.4 Rectangular Coordinates Method of measuring: Depicting the process for capturing measurements using rectangular coordinates.

- Measure height/depth if above/below ground level
- Results reporting: 2 feet east of west wall, 1 feet south of north wall

Coordinate Based

Polar Coordinates

- Best for large outdoor areas with scattered items
- Use a reference point of choice, gather coordinates for that point, and measure item distance to that point

Method

- Select 1 fixed point (permanent if possible) and obtain coordinates from compass point/GPS as well as identifying information
- Measure all items to point with distance and angle, height if above/below ground level
- Results reporting: 10 feet from north wall of house, 100° west of N

Forensic Mapping/GPS Mapping

- Good for bike paths, campgrounds, farm fields, forests, and so on. Inexpensive and accurate.
- Digital sketch/scan—use of GPS (Global Positioning System)
- Gather individual coordinates for all items of evidence

Method

- Collect coordinates for each piece of evidence and can take screenshots of GPS coordinates on phone/device or document in notes

Vehicle Sketch—Interior of Vehicle with Measurements

- Consider keeping a template for an overhead view of vehicle seating compartments
- Baseline or triangulation recommended, consider digital scanning of interior

Baseline inside Vehicle

1. Measure front driver doorjamb to front passenger doorjamb and find center
2. String paper measuring tape (or string, marked ribbon, etc.) along center of vehicle and attach at base of both windshields. This is your baseline and all measurements will be down/along baseline and off/out from baseline. Double check you are affixed at center at two separate locations prior to measuring all evidence.

3. Baseline at front windshield will be 0 and move down to rear windshield, record total distance.
4. Measure all items of evidence along baseline (down towards rear windshield) and from baseline (out towards doors).
5. Measure all items that are relevant to your situation. Location of seats, width/height of seat, distance to glove box handle, distance between front passenger/rear driver seat, and so on.
6. Add center console, glove box, trays, and other fixed points as needed according to your situation and policy

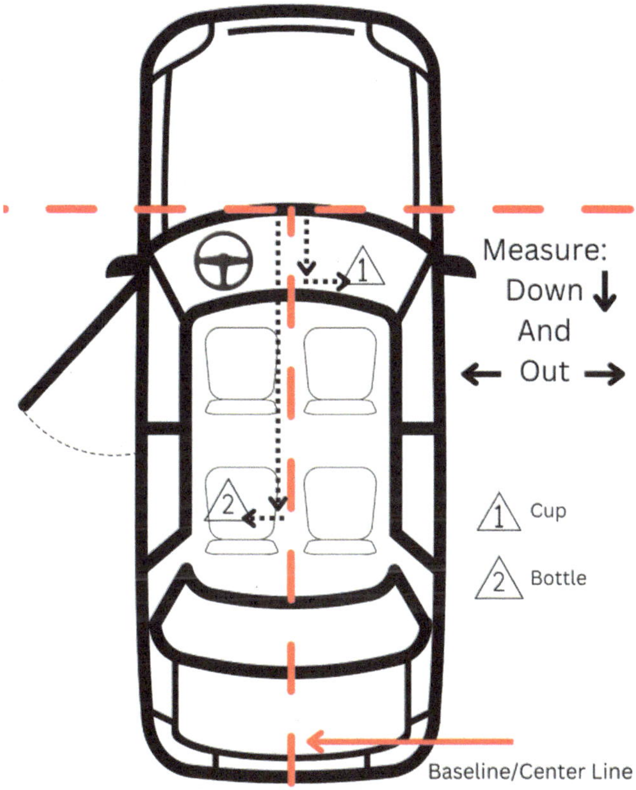

Figure 15.5 Vehicle Sketch: Depicting the process for collecting measurements on the interior vehicle.

Scanning Devices—Total Station/Leica/Faro

- Most often used for accident scenes and scenes with substantial amounts of blood spatter and bullet holes
- Records distance/slope/angles as well as records distance between station and moveable "targets"

- It can be used inside vehicles, under beds, and in other small areas as well as large scenes
- When used in vehicles: Can set on center console if larger vehicle, don't forget to close the doors during the scan when possible
- Consider making yourself a pre-made list of settings you like and how to set up your file.
- Don't forget reference measurements, can lay a ruler on the floor in scan if needed

Note

1 Rynearson, Joseph M. *Evidence and Crime Scene Reconstruction*, 7th ed. 2015.

Scene Video 16

A scene video is an essential component of on-site documentation, offering critical material for subsequent investigations. It is not advisable to replace a purposefully created scene video with body camera footage or CCTV recordings. The controlled lighting, deliberate pacing, and multiple angles provided by a dedicated scene video ensure comprehensive documentation. Although body camera footage is highly valuable, it cannot substitute the detailed perspective required for thorough scene documentation. Some agencies utilize videos to record the evidence collection process, which is crucial for documenting the personal protective equipment (PPE) worn and the procedures used. Additionally, some agencies use videos to document the body removal and manipulation process, which has proven vital for recording what was present beneath or absent from the body. There are various applications for videos as long as they remain viewable.

Possible Purposes for Video

- Video tour of the crime scene
- Initial walk-through or walk-through by subjects/witnesses
- Before placards/after placards
- During evidence collection
- During interviews
- Highlight areas of special interest or high detail
- Path of travel through scene/between scenes
- Show viewpoint from witness/subjects
- Animal scene conditions and animal physical conditions to include ability to walk, response level, strength of voice, or response to handler
- Audio recording
- Can show 360° view from victim location smoothly
- Video of area to show for briefing/tactical planning

Video Camera versus Digital Camera

- Both can be used to collect scene videos
- Memory card formatted to a camera should not be used for video during scene processing, can override pictures when moved from digital camera to video camera and back

DOI: 10.4324/9781003503897-17

- Video camera recommended for regular crime scene video with sound off

Cell Phone Camera

- Cell phone camera (ON YOUR WORK PHONE) is alternative option if there is no other video camera available
- Better option than no video at all
- Use stabilizer functions if available
- Cover page A MUST when using this option

Cover Page

Option: Cover Page Sheet

- Can be the original cover page from scene photographs
- Case #, date, location, videographer

Option: Investigator Verbal Statement

- Investigator makes verbal statement on video
- Case #, date, location given verbally

Movement through Scene

- Film with normal view at standing height (regardless of height)
  - No special lens, 50 mm recommended
  - Can use tripod/added lighting
- Begin in same location as initial photographs—follow same path if realistic
- Move smoothly and with intention
- Pan each room slowly—horizontal and vertical
- Mid-range of all locations—close-up of items of interest
- Don't forget close-ups for sketch reference items
- Include thresholds/doorways of rooms/areas
- Keep camera shake to a minimum—makes it hard to view

STABILITY OPTION: Bend knees and roll feet when stepping down to reduce bounce

STABILITY OPTION: Tuck elbows tight against stomach/chest to hold arms steady to reduce shake

Zoom

Mid-range Video

- Zoom in, pan area, zoom out
- Dressers, floor, shelf, and so on

Close-ups on Video

- Zoom in and out from same location (close-ups) for continuity of viewer; don't forget to pause on each item for viewing

Option: Zoom Function/Button

- Can be shaky and too fast for viewer
- Easier for videographer

Option: Physically Move Camera Closer to Object

- Smoother for viewer
- Harder for videographer

Audio

Crime Scene Video—*No Audio Unless Intentional Narration*

- Verbalize to all parties that audio is being recorded when it is not turned off
- Can place headset cord in plug to stop sound on video
- If you are narrating the scene, take scene video with NO narration first, then second video WITH narration
- For animal abuse scenes—take video with full sound

Interview/Statement Video

- Ensure microphone IS working
- Consider tripod unless moving narration/re-creation

Lighting

Lighting Options

- Handheld light/LED light
- Light stand
- Flashlight
- EMS/fire/PD vehicle lighting (headlights and spotlights) helps for outdoor scenes
- Be mindful of hotspots created with flashlights
- Adequate lighting is needed for video to focus and take sharp footage
- If crime happened in low light or dark light a second video is recommended
  1. Take video with lighting at time of crime or arrival
  2. Take second video with additional lights for investigation

Style Options

Option: Overall Scenario Only

- Slow walk-through to show path traveled
- Not recommended if items of evidence are present

Option: Mid-range and Close-up Like Photographs

- Ensure reference items are seen in video
- Same as mid-range photographs
- Ensure you have several angles of important items/rooms

Option: Path of Travel

- Follow suspected path of travel in real time
- On foot or from passenger seat of vehicle

Single Video versus Multiple Short Videos

Try for single continuous video rather than multiple short videos, if possible

- Both are acceptable forms of crime scene video
- Turn in all videos; never delete/alter/edit ANY VIDEO
- If video stops or dies, start again with camera overlap

Vehicle Processing 17

Vehicles are often involved in crimes for several reasons, whether they serve as the primary crime scene or as a means of transporting people or objects. The extent of processing required depends on the nature of the crime and the information sought. Just like a crime scene, a vehicle must be processed methodically. However, due to the confined space and prolonged contact within a vehicle, there are typically more areas and items to collect evidence from. This chapter will guide you on where to search and where to swab or fingerprint when processing a vehicle and with checklists for needed photographs to help ensure you don't miss a thing while processing a vehicle.

Cars hold more value to crime scene process than they are often given credit for and are often intricately involved in the process of and movement between crime scenes. An abandoned vehicle is often involved in some phase of criminal activity, and an abandoned vehicle is rarely just abandoned. The decision will need to be made if it is processed on scene where it is found or if it will be towed to a new location.[1] In the United States, the "automobile exception" to the Fourth Amendment and the "plain view" rule do not apply to vehicles once they are moved from the scene. This exception does not extend to storage locations and tow yards. Because of the location change you now need consent or warrant. Refer to your local DA if you have legal questions and be mindful of this when determining what to do on scene.

Vehicle Processing Order

1. Ensure vehicle is adequately secured and stable
2. Photographs/documentation of EXTERIOR
3. Hands-free search of EXTERIOR with ALS if applicable
4. Collect biological swabs/trace samples from EXTERIOR vehicle
5. Fingerprints from exterior if all windows raised/doors closed, otherwise wait until after interior processing due to risk of contamination
6. Unlock doors if needed; use clean tools if applicable
7. Photographs/documentation of INTERIOR without touching anything
8. Collect contact DNA/trace samples from immediate areas
9. Search of interior areas of interest to include ALS if applicable
10. Mark/label areas of interest/defects/blood/hair, and so on
11. Photographs of identified evidence/labeled defects, and so on

DOI: 10.4324/9781003503897-18

12. Collect identified biological samples/tangible items
13. Process for blood enhancements
14. Photograph/swab/collect results
15. Process for latent prints
16. Photograph of any damage caused during processing with scale
17. Collect vehicle's black box (or EDR), infotainment equipment

Checklist—Basic Vehicle Photography

- ☐ Camera settings accurate—date/time, file, settings: ISO (400–800 for exterior, 200–500 for interior, 100–200 for documents), shutter speed, lens cover if needed
- ☐ Cover page

Exterior Vehicle (Overall/Mid-range/Close-up)

- ☐ 4 sides AND 4 corners[2]
- ☐ Exterior roof, if able—may have writing or relevant damages
- ☐ Doors open/closed, windows raised/lowered, windshields intact/damaged front end
- ☐ Moonroof/sunroof open/closed/damaged
- ☐ Standing height looking down and 90°
- ☐ Damages/lack of damages
- ☐ Graffiti, dust writing, wax crayon writing, and so on
- ☐ Point of entry if applicable

Front END—*Standing Height Looking down and 90°*

- ☐ Hood ornament
- ☐ Close-up of license plate (slight angle for reflection) AND VIN (polarizer lens for reflection)
- ☐ Close-up of any stickers on windshield

Driver Side

- ☐ Bumper to bumper in one shot
- ☐ Front bumper and front quarter panel
- ☐ Driver door and rear driver door
- ☐ Rear quarter panel and rear bumper

REAR END—*Standing Height Looking down and 90°*

- ☐ Close-up of license plate
- ☐ Close-up of any stickers on windshield
- ☐ Make, model, stickers, decals, decorations

Passenger Side

- ☐ Bumper to bumper in one shot
- ☐ Front bumper to front quarter panel
- ☐ Driver door to rear driver door
- ☐ Rear quarter panel and rear bumper

Tires

- ☐ Damages, sidewall markings
- ☐ Tread/wear if applicable/can place coin in tread for photographs
- ☐ Hubcaps/lug nuts

Interior Vehicle

- ☐ Interior of each compartment (driver, rear driver, trunk, etc.)
- ☐ Seating and flooring of each compartment
- ☐ Interior of each door panel to include pockets/door button/window/lock positions
- ☐ Stand at 90° and 45° to see inside door pockets
- ☐ Keys/keychain/key fob if present
- ☐ Steering wheel column/ignition to include damages/wires
- ☐ Dashboard/radio area to include speedometer and odometer if visible
- ☐ Rear view mirror/windshield area
- ☐ Dome/headliner of interior vehicle—dome lights/trays/handles/visors/damages/spatter/scuff marks
- ☐ On/interior of center console and glove box—beverages/items in cupholders
- ☐ Ledge behind rear seats—over trunk
- ☐ Engine compartment
- ☐ Undercarriage area
- ☐ Interior of trunk/rear cargo area
- ☐ Truck bed interior/sides/lining/contents—2 sides or 2 corners should cover all interior area
- ☐ Presence of any items that are subject of search—cell phones, weapons, drugs, and so on

Checklist—Accident Vehicle Photography

Exterior Damages—*at Least 2 Angles—Adjust Lighting/Shadows to Show Depth*

- ☐ Paint transfers/denting
- ☐ Glass fractures/breaking
- ☐ Mirrors

- ☐ Headlights/bumper/grill
- ☐ Any voids from missing pieces

Trace Evidence Present in Damages If Accident Vehicle

- ☐ Hair, fiber, blood
- ☐ License plate/holder
- ☐ Front bumper
- ☐ Edges of hood
- ☐ Windshield wipers
- ☐ Top/bottom of windshield
- ☐ Sideview mirrors

Checklist—Submerged Vehicle Photography

- ☐ Cover page with identified location (consider photograph of GPS coordinates)
- ☐ Settings—polarizer filter if needed, consider settings and wet surfaces
- ☐ Overall photographs of area to include all roadways, entrances, barriers, easements, tire marks, and so on
- ☐ Photographs of vehicles while being removed from water, if possible
- ☐ Photographs of vehicles after being removed from water to include VIN, license plate, 4 corners, 4 sides
- ☐ Collect DNA from the exterior at this time if applicable
- ☐ Apply SPR to the exterior and rinse at this time if applicable (will dry while processing interior)
- ☐ Photographs of interior vehicle (search as soon as possible due to preservation of evidence and oxidation of wet metal)
- ☐ Firearms, cell phones, tools present while in place and after being removed to place in water for collection
- ☐ Document moving vehicle to secure location for further processing

Checklist—Vehicle Fire Photography

Prior to Towing Vehicle Off Scene

- ☐ Vehicle in place, immediate surroundings, roads, vegetation/trees, area around tires
- ☐ Exterior vehicle: 4 sides/4 corners if possible, to include tires, lug nuts, interior wheel wells, and front windshield
- ☐ Area directly surrounding vehicle—vegetation, nearby roads/walkways, footwear/tire marks, towing material, dead grass patch, and so on

- ☐ All equipment—trailer, boat, top mechanism for convertible, and so on
- ☐ All parts that have fallen off to the ground before being picked back up and thrown inside vehicle—lights, metals, glass pieces, door handles, and so on
- ☐ Ground below vehicle—consider soil samples below tires and note any glass on ground

After Towing Vehicle Off Scene

- ☐ Ground that contained the vehicle—consider soil samples, container collection
- ☐ Store vehicles indoors as rust will obscure the burn patterns

Exterior Vehicle ***(Even If It Is Crispy)***

- ☐ Ensure vehicle is adequately secure and stable
- ☐ 6 sides and 4 corners (including top and undercarriage)
- ☐ Hood to include burn patterns and soot. If hood is missing, photograph hinges
- ☐ Hood ornament, emblems, specialty pieces
- ☐ Engine compartment—battery/hoses/plugs—overall mid-range of area
- ☐ Engine compartment—liquid spray residue, spray patterns, melted materials, melted wiring
- ☐ Bulkhead—wall between engine compartment and seating compartment
- ☐ Doors—handles, locks, and switches
- ☐ Panel below doors (damaged/missing?)
- ☐ License plates
- ☐ Radio antenna
- ☐ Wheels—tires/rims/hubcaps—present or missing?
- ☐ Tire tread—close-up of tread if able, portion touching ground may still be present
- ☐ Wheel wells—look for wear, damage from impact, or evidence of leaks
- ☐ Top mechanism if convertible
- ☐ VIN
- ☐ Visible burn patterns and path of fire spread if known
- ☐ Window placement/condition
- ☐ Windshield damage or final resting place
- ☐ Undercarriage—fuel/exhaust system, oil pan, transmission, leakage residue/spray, consider fluid samples
- ☐ All damaged and undamaged areas

Interior Vehicle *(Even If Crispy)*

- ☐ All damaged and undamaged areas
- ☐ Airbags deployed/missing
- ☐ Emergency brake/gear shift
- ☐ Close-ups of visible damages/trace evidence
- ☐ Door panels—locks/buttons/levers/arm even if melted/charred
- ☐ Driver floor and debris—as found and as sifted (need to if below debris or on debris)
- ☐ Remaining floor area—guns/metal can be melted to floor frame
- ☐ Ignition/key placement/damage
- ☐ Dashboard area/steering column area
- ☐ Lock cylinder or ignition lock
- ☐ Odometer and speedometer if visible
- ☐ Ceiling/dome area
- ☐ Seating compartments individually, all interior trays and compartments
- ☐ Condition of seats
- ☐ Burn pattern/soot pattern on interior windows
- ☐ Cracks/creases/joints/hinges—can retain blood and trace evidence, look closely
- ☐ Radio/speakers/and so on
- ☐ Event data recorder

Trunk Area

- ☐ Are expensive items still present? Radio/screen/speaker
- ☐ Presence of accelerants/debris—cans/containers/rags
- ☐ Metal fragments of melted items

Lights

- ☐ Mechanical components in question

Possible Sources—Process for Prints

Exterior Areas to Fingerprint

- Doors
- Front and rear quarter panels
- Gas tank door
- Hood/trunk/tailgate
- License plates, front and back
- Roof above doors to include the luggage racks
- Sideview mirrors
- Windows/window trim

Interior Areas to Fingerprint

- Ashtray/trim
- Dashboard/trim
- Dome lights
- Door handle (can DNA backside of handle and fingerprint front side of handle)
- Door panel (metal edges, door handle, smooth trim even fake wood)
- Gear shift button/trim
- Infotainment touch screen
- Radio screen
- Rear view mirror
- Seat belt buckles (metal)
- Steering wheel—smooth trim
- Sunroof/moonroof and controls
- Vinyl (magnetic powder and/or superglue fuming)
- Visor mirrors
- Windows and windshields

Possible Sources—Swab for Contact DNA

Exterior Vehicle

- Area around license plates and bumper if plates switched, exterior license plates, and screws
- Area around wheel well if tires removed
- Cargo racks and accessories
- Exterior door edge—area touched to swing door shut
- Exterior door handles
  - rough plastic—DNA front and backside
  - shiny plastic—DNA backside, fingerprint front side
- Exterior hood or trunk if sat on or leaned on
- Trunk/rear cargo door handle and trunk/door edges, where you grab to swing the door shut

Interior Vehicle

- A, B, C pillar handles
- Air vents
- Center console top/sides/buttons
- Dashboard area drawers/trays
- Door panel/window
  - arm rest
  - buttons/handles/levers

- mirror adjustment controls
- rough plastic—DNA front and backside
- shiny plastic—DNA backside, fingerprint front shiny side
- Ignition button
- Steering column if altered/damaged
- Gas cap door release if had longer than 1 day
- Gear shift/emergency brake
- Glove box/handle
- Navigation system buttons
- Radio buttons/AC/heat buttons
- Rear view mirror (edges/back)
- Rear view mirror wiring system if pulled out
- Seat belt/buckle/clasp—consider pulling belt out short distance
- Seats/headrests/seat adjustments
- Steering wheel/adjustment lever—consider collecting entire wheel cover if present
- Trunk release/hood release
- Vehicle lights switch/controls and dome lights
- Visor edge/visor mirror

Possible Sources—Search for Blood DNA

After a Clean-up Blood Is Commonly Found

- Door panel by window/lock buttons
- Steering wheel—on and around
- Gear shift—on and around
- Rear view mirror
- Seatbelt buckle/seat belt, pull out seat belt as far as you can and check both sides
- Leg area
- Under floor mats/carpeting, consider looking under carpet if suspected
- Fly spots and bug/rodent footprints and trails
- Check spots along edges and seams
- Check spots where items meet—seat meets carpet/floor/center console, pillar trim meet dome fabric, door trim meets fabric, seat belt buckle meets seat

Possible Sources—Search for Semen DNA

- Carpet
- Dashboard
- Dome/visors/dome lights

- Door pockets and buttons
- Seat front/sides by leg space/seams
- Seatbacks/headrests

Checklist—Searching a Vehicle for Contraband—*Use What Applies to Your Scene*

Exterior Vehicle Search

☐ Gas tank/gas line interior
☐ Roof racks—inside tubing and/or attached roof topper
☐ Inside retractable side rails/stairs—be mindful of fresh welding/paint/carpet
☐ Front bumper to dashboard firewall
☐ Behind radiator

Front End/Engine Compartment

☐ Washer fluid reservoir interior
☐ Under firewall/foam
☐ Inside bumper—can use mirror
☐ Space between grill/radiator
☐ Empty space inside/behind lights
☐ Inside air assembly

Tracker/GPS Tracker Equipment Search (Several Inches in Size, Often Magnetic/Black)

☐ Inside wheel well
☐ Beneath undercarriage
☐ Behind bumper
☐ Under seats/dashboard

Interior Vehicle Search Checklist

Disturbed Areas—Be Mindful of the Following While Searching

☐ Worn carpet, worn plastic
☐ Carpet/items tucked under console/door trim
☐ Items partially under seat cushion
☐ Seat cushion ajar
☐ Loose screws/bolts/trim
☐ SD cards—often in consoles/trays/fuse boxes

Seating Areas—Repeat List for Each Seating Compartment

☐ Door pockets

- ☐ Under/behind steering wheel
- ☐ Floor mats—under, behind, between layers
- ☐ Inside floor storage—door pocket, ashtrays—inside, under, behind
- ☐ On/under seat and seat cover
- ☐ Along sides of seat by console area—no blind reaching
- ☐ Underside of seat cushion—lift bench seat/fold individual seats
- ☐ Inside front seatback pockets
- ☐ Along seatbelt track/plastic covering—pull seatbelt out to see if anything attached or stains present
- ☐ Dashboard trays
- ☐ Under/behind steering wheel
- ☐ Vents/vent recess
- ☐ Speaker/speaker recess
- ☐ Under headliner (dome)—flat-palm feel along entire dome of vehicle
- ☐ Under visors/inside overhead compartments
- ☐ Sunglasses holder by dome lights
- ☐ Fuse box area—can hold SD cards, small items behind cover
- ☐ Center console—interior/under/around, under trays/behind trim, look for SD cards plugged in
- ☐ Inside cupholders, under cupholder/trim
- ☐ Glove box—interior AND behind glove box tray
- ☐ Cameras/recording equipment
- ☐ SD cards/memory sticks plugged in to vehicle
- ☐ Under A, B, C pillar trim
- ☐ Ledge behind seats/over trunk

Trunk/Rear Cargo Area

- ☐ Behind carpet lining on walls, door
- ☐ Under floor mats/carpet
- ☐ Spare tire area/tool area—under spare tire/tool
- ☐ Inside first aid kits/tool kits/hazard kits
- ☐ Inside taillights/headlights
- ☐ Look for false floors/walls
- ☐ Inside homemade speaker boxes
- ☐ Truck bed—inside/behind/under toolboxes

Collection Variables

- Vehicles treated with WD40, Armor All, and other oily cleaning products have lower chances of getting fingerprints and DNA
- When a suspect breaks a window with the intent of driving it, it's rarely the driver's window (keeps seat glass free)

- Tools often used to break into a vehicle—spark plugs, rocks, wedges, wire hanger, slim jims, electronic equipment such as "Flipper Zero" and homemade devices, gloves, and socks (used as gloves)
- Some agencies choose to seal the doors and hood/trunk with tape when transported off scene for processing. Ensure you document with photographs and writing the condition of the tape upon your arrival for processing or if leaving the vehicle with the tow driver.

Common reason for vehicle processing regarding crimes—*knowing why helps you prioritize evidence*

- Crimes committed inside vehicles and then abandoned
- Used to flee from scene of crime
- Used to practice criminal skillset
- Breaking/entering
- Getaway driver practice
- Shooting practice with drive by shootings
- Working up nerve to commit robberies
- Adrenaline management for younger kids

Processing Suggestions

- Vehicles broken down into 3 sections for notes and processing:
    - Engine compartment (under the hood, front grill, undercarriage)
    - Passenger compartment (seating, floors)
    - Cargo compartment (trunk, cargo, truck bed)
- LEICA/FARO use are encouraged for vehicles with blood spatter or bullet holes that need further analysis as it can also provide seat/item measurements
- Black box, AKA Event Data Recorder (EDR) collection—typically under dashboard on driver side, inside center console, in steering column, near engine control module, or under front seats
- SD cards in fuse box area store video footage from 360 cameras installed in vehicle
- Check the user manual for other SD card locations; some are found in rear cargo area such as Cadillac.
- Many vehicles have a recording system that records the exterior area surrounding the vehicle 24/7, even if the vehicle is off and unattended. Check the vehicles in the parking lot at your shootings, and you may be able to capture some video. Tesla, Toyota, Mercedes, and Cadillac are some of the vehicles to check into.
- Consider ALS and/or specialty powders for latent print processing of dashboard and other textured surfaces

- Crime-Lite from Foster+Freeman is reported to work on a vehicle interior to find fingerprints to include the dashboard and other textured areas[3]
- Consider a drive-in size superglue chamber for vehicle processing—can be DIY style
- Consider using magnetic powder to highlight damages to exterior vehicle if light colored or in accident with pedestrian
- Submerged vehicle—if latent print processing is needed it should be done as soon as vehicle is lifted from water, prior to drying. Once the vehicle has dried powder is recommended; however, immediate processing with SPR may produce better results.
- Markers: Evidence markers can be made small by using small plastic arrows or triangles and placing a piece of scale tape or scale sticker on arrow. You can also use scale stickers without plastic arrows assigning number/letter.
- Consider orienting your markers toward the front of the vehicle for orientation and clarity

VIN

- VIN information can be found in U.S. Code of Federal Regulations which began in 1981—ISO standards available for review
- 17 digits—consists of all capital letters and numbers—NEVER INCLUDES LETTER O, Q, I
- Digits 1–3—manufacturing information
- Digit 4–8—specifics about vehicle—size, brakes, make, and so on
- Digit 9—security digit
- Digit 10—year of manufacturing
- Digit 11—plant of final assembly
- Digits 12–17—production information
- Digits 18–19—location and chassis manufacturer

VIN Locations (Suggest F/11–16 for Sharpness)

- Dashboard on metal plate below or near steering wheel (visible through windshield)
- Steering column (often a plate attached)
- Driver door frame
- Driver door jamb by B pillar
- Frame under driver seat and under front passenger seat
- Under the bonnet
- Rear wheel well on vehicle frame
- Under front chassis
- Spare tire compartment in trunk, under spare tire

- Interior trunk lid
- Hood by windshield, passenger side
- Passenger front and rear door jambs
- Passenger quarter panel by rear windshield
- Glovebox (inside, often a sticker)
- Firewall separating passenger compartment and engine block
- Engine block
- Passenger fender well, under the hood
- Radiator support bracket
- Sometimes etched in windows/windshields

Tires

Tire sidewall markings: P 195/65 R 15

- P—vehicle type (passenger vehicle, light truck, etc.)
- 195—width in millimeters
- 65—aspect ratio
- R—radial tire
- 15—rim diameter in inches

Searching a Vehicle

Consider Using the Following Equipment

- Endoscope approved for liquid submersion for tanks/reservoirs/tight spots
- Flashlight to enhance your vision
- Handheld extendable mirrors to see between snug spots
- Floor jack to get a good look underneath
- Butcher paper to lay your body on
- Butcher paper to lay evidence on

Search Suggestions

- Open all containers—cigarette boxes, cigar pouches, fast-food trash bags/containers, plastic trash bags, shoe boxes
- Search for footwear prints—hood, exterior roof/interior dome/headliner, dashboard, interior windows/windshields
- Look for hidden compartments: Hollow headrests, hidden drawers, removable vents, false bottoms, or false backs of shelves, under seats, behind trim, under gear shift cover, and so on
- If sexual assault is possible, view entire inside of vehicle with ALS as found prior to moving ANY ITEMS. If all negative, then you may begin moving items one by one.

Vehicle Section Designation Options

- Driver, passenger, rear driver, rear passenger, engine, rear cargo/trunk
- Zone 1—driver, Zone 2—passenger, Zone 3—rear driver, and so on
- Section 1—engine, Section 2—seating, Section 3—trunk/cargo

Cases for Consideration Involving Vehicle Processing

- 2017: After the murder of Eric Garcia, receipts located inside a vehicle helped solve the crime.
- 2012: When Betty Wheeler was hit and killed the vehicle left behind part of the front grill which was matched to the suspect's vehicle.
- 2011: Jayna Murray's murder was unraveled after DNA was found inside her vehicle.
- 2000: After the murder and disappearance of Beth Kootz, her vehicle was processed for evidence, and it was determined her vehicle was wiped down on the interior. A print was found on the exterior door handle and small traces of blood were found inside the vehicle which matched the suspect.
- 1994: When the vehicle of OJ Simpson was collected as authorized and placed into secure storage there were multiple unauthorized and unreported personnel inside the vehicle because they wanted to "look." During formal authorized processing, blood belonging to Ron Goldman and Nicole Simpson was located inside the Bronco in multiple locations. The transferred blood located inside the Bronco was no longer useable in court due to the chain of custody being broken from unauthorized personnel entering the vehicle.
- 1989: Fibers from victim Melissa Brannen's sweater were found in her abductor's vehicle.
- 1983: Caria Lowe was killed in hit and run with no leads. In 2021 the case was reopened and re-examined with new technology, resulting in the original suspect now being tied to the scene.

Notes

1 Fisher, Barry. *Techniques of Crime Scene Investigation*, 7th ed. CRC Press, 2004.

2 Organization of Scientific Area Committees for Forensic Science (OSAC) (2020) *Standard Guide for Crime Scene Photography.*

3 https://fosterfreeman.com/crime-lite-auto/.

Evidence Values 18

Evidence can hold different values for the same items based upon the variables of the crime. Even with the best crime scene processing you will rarely find the "smoking gun" on your scene, and often the most important items to your case are easy to overlook. The value of the items present is gauged in context, and that context can be different to each professional. They can assign different weights to the same information as well as come to different conclusions.

You do not have to pick just one value for items; you can obtain multiple values for items with the correct choice of procedures. If you are careful, you can obtain DNA AND fingerprints from an item increasing your chances of identification. The following list will help you identify what options you have with items from your scene. For best results and value of the information, it is recommended that you review this chapter in advance a couple of times so that when you are looking around a scene or vehicle you recognize the value of what you have.

Evidence Can

- Prove or disprove a crime was committed
- Prove or disprove a fact's legitimacy
- Incriminate or exonerate a suspect
- Demonstrate the sequence of events
- Aid the continuing investigation
- Provide timeline for crime or subsequent acts

Evidence Items and Their Possible Value—*Does Not Mean That Each Piece Will Always Have All Values*

Airbags from Vehicle

- Contact DNA/blood DNA on airbag
- Makeup transfer from occupant to airbag
- Transfer of gas/residue/singe to subject—round pattern often driver side, linear pattern often passenger side
- Chemical composition of driver/passenger airbag residue can be different—deposits on hands/clothing
- Helps show positions of occupants at time of collision

DOI: 10.4324/9781003503897-19

Air Samples

- Chemical analysis of air

Airsoft Gun, Pellet Gun, BB Gun

- Contact DNA from exterior
- Fingerprints on exterior
- Visual match to eyewitness/photographs/CCTV
- Visual match to ammunition type

***Airsoft Gun Ammunition* (Pellets, BBS, Cartridges, Air Canisters)**

- Can indicate a sport gun was used during crime, collect
- Contact DNA can be collected from the ammunition
- Inspect for presence of blood/trace evidence
- Airsoft and other sport guns are often found from robberies in get-away vehicles, backpacks, and so on

Ashtray

- Fingerprints from bottom/sides
- Saliva DNA from butts inside ashtray
- Cigarette butt/cigar butt contents for toxicology
- Heat of contents can contribute to timeline (feel exterior bottom or hover hand over top)

***Bag* (Plastic, Trash, Zip Lock)**

- Contact DNA from openings
- Fingerprints exterior bag/interior edges

Ballistic Evidence

- Range from which it was fired
- Position and orientation when fired
- Position and orientation of victims at impact
- Number and sequence of shots
- Presence and nature of intervening material
- Flight path of projectile

Bandana

- DNA
- Hair/fiber and residue from hair/fiber

- Odor
- Visual match

Baseball

- Contact DNA
- Fingerprints

Baseball Bat

- Contact DNA on both ends, blood DNA if present
- Fingerprints
- Impressions in wood/metal
- Trace evidence embedded in wood and impressions

Bedding

- Hair/fiber
- DNA from sweat, saliva, blood, semen, urine
- Presence of lubricants, lotions, oils, foods, and so on

***Beverage Containers* (Cans, Bottles, Cups, Straws, Pouches)**

- Liquid sample of contents for medication/poison
- Contact DNA from exterior lid/cap/tab from opening
- Saliva DNA from mouth of bottle/can/cup/straw
- Fingerprints from exterior can/bottle/cup/pouch from holding

Bite Marks

- Saliva DNA from impression and surrounding area
- Cast impression or macro photography for comparison

Bloodstain Pattern Analysis

- Direction/angle/distance of blood travel
- Type/direction of impact
- Whether arterial or not for level of injury to victim (if victim not present)
- Approximate minimum number of impacts
- Sequence of events
- Positions of participants and distance between locations
- Left/right-handed suspect

Body Fluids

- Location of crime
- Validate claims of severity

- Corroborate/refute story
- Type of blood
- DNA of contributor

Bones

- DNA for identification
- Sex/race/age of deceased
- Tool marks used for destruction

Books

- Fingerprints from cover and pages
- Content can show you preferences and interests
- Pages with handwriting/markings can have locations, numbers, dates, and so on

***Botanical Specimens* (Leaves, Flowers, etc.)**

- Match between scene and locations

Bracelet

- Contact DNA/blood DNA
- Hair/fiber in joints/small cracks
- Match to photo/description/manufacturer/store that sold item

Bullet Defects

- Angle of impact/path of projectile travel
- Lead test could confirm if bullet traveled through defect
- Trace evidence carried through bullet path left behind in defect

Burned Matches

- Physical match to matchbook
- Origin of matches from packaging
- Contact DNA

Calendar

- Handwriting analysis
- Fingerprints/contact DNA on pages
- Timeline information, stalking activity, cultivation activity

Cartridge **(Unfired Bullet, Bullet, Round, Ammo)**

- Type/brand of ammunition match
- Contact DNA
- Fingerprints

Cartridge **(Chambered, Misfired)**

- Matched to gun with marks from ejection port, extractors, ramp, primer, chambering
- Match to gun with malfunction marks—sustain damage to the side and marks to headstamp from malfunction
- Match to semi-automatic gun magazine with individual use markings

Cartridge Case **(Fired Semi-Automatic, Some Revolvers, Some Long Guns)**

- Casing can be matched to firearm
- Casing can be matched to other casings/cases
- Contact DNA
- Etched fingerprints

Cartridge Case **(From Revolver)**

- Match to caliber, brand, manufacturer
- Contact DNA
- Etched fingerprints

Cell Phones

- Contact DNA from edges/buttons/back
- Saliva DNA/lipstick/lip balm from microphone area
- Ear wax from speaker area
- Fingerprints on screen/battery/interior case
- Digital content from phone

Cell Phone Case

- Contact DNA from interior and exterior
- Fingerprints from interior and exterior
- Saliva DNA from area by microphone
- Physical match to pictures/video

Cell Phone Box, Packaging

- Fingerprints—waxy surface good for prints

- Contact DNA from interior packaging and exterior box
- Serial numbers and other identifying information

Charging Cords for Phones/Electronics

- Contact DNA from exterior ends
- Visual match to victim/suspect items

Cigarette Box/Cigar Pouch

- Contact DNA from opening/exterior
- Fingerprints on exterior packaging
- Sample of contents for drugs
- Tax stamp

Cigar/Cigarette/Pipe/Hookah

- Saliva DNA from mouth
- Sample of contents for drugs
- Fingerprints from exterior non-porous areas

Clothing, Worn

- DNA from wearer/transfer during assault
- DNA from exterior pockets/biological deposit/blood
- GSR/other contaminants on clothing that left a deposit
- Visual match to scene/friend group/social media
- UV stamp from drycleaners
- Purchase information from tag/barcode
- Damages and marks from weapons can show position of wearer

Computer

- Digital information from source
- Contact DNA
- Fingerprints from screen/flat surfaces

Comparison of Items

- Class characteristics—can tell if same type but not same item, can only be used for exclusion
- Individual characteristics—exact match to 2 broken pieces, fingerprints, DNA profiles, impressions, footwear prints, fracture matches—can be used for identification or exclusion

Condom, Used

- Chemical match to suspect/victim lubricant
- DNA on interior of wearer
- DNA on exterior of contributor

Condom, in Wrapper

- Contact DNA from edges/perforation
- Fingerprints from flat sides
- Brand match

Condom Wrapper

- Physical match to wrapper/torn corner
- Contact DNA from exterior
- Fingerprints if large enough piece

Cup

- Saliva DNA from mouth of cup/lid/straw
- Contact DNA from sides of cup
- Liquid analysis from contents of cup
- Fingerprints from exterior/interior

Crime Scene Video

- Record the crime scene, witness/suspect statement, interview given, walk-through of an incident by victim or parent
- Provide second view of crime scene and contents
- Document evidence collection process and actions taken while on scene
- Arson scene video can show video of fire fighting in progress and better viewing of burn patterns/sizes

Diapers, Adult and Child

- Entomology samples
- Toxicology samples—drugs/poisons
- Presence of blood in urine from trauma
- Food history samples
- DNA samples from previous assault
- Duration of neglectful incident
- Location of diapers in residence—disposed of or piled around one subject's bed?

Digital Evidence

- Contents of communications, social media, contacts
- Match to server information

DNA

- Confirmed matches can be the product of direct contact between the subject/item, secondary transfer, pre-crime/post crime contamination

Documents

- Fingerprints from paper
- Contact DNA from edges of papers
- Content information/alteration of content
- Origin of document
- Hidden writing/indented writing/obliterated writing
- Fracture match from edges if torn/cut (physical fit)
- Handwriting analysis
- Cannot determine age of ink on document

***Documents*—Charred**

- Content on paper, can be enhanced
- Accelerant testing

***Documents*—Shredded**

- Content on paper, can be reassembled in lab—not scene work
- Collect as a whole item, do not separate

Drains/Sink Traps

- Blood/hair/tissue

Ear Buds

- Ear wax is DNA worthy
- Contact DNA on exterior ear buds

Entomology Samples

- Duration of neglect incident
- Time elapsed since death/deposit
- ID of species being eaten (human or not human)
- ID of victim if comparison sample is available

- Toxicology results of the eaten area—did they ingest drugs or poison?
- Tell if the body has been moved based on the geographical location of bugs found on body

Envelope

- Fingerprints
- Saliva DNA
- Handwriting analysis
- Contact information

Eyeglasses

- Contact DNA
- Fingerprints from lens
- Prescription information from packaging/label/sticker
- Physical match to picture

Fabric Marks

- Match to a victim/suspect's clothing
- Footwear/tire marks on clothing, blankets, tarps, and so on

Feathers

- Class characteristics match to species
- Match to materials from crime scene
- Match to known suspect's pet

Fetus, Terminated or Miscarried

- DNA from both parents
- Injuries/lack of injuries
- Lung/heart activity
- Secured by medical personnel, analyzed in autopsy

Fibers

- Color, type of cloth
- Dye of fabric
- Comparison of fabric shape, size, twist

Filament

- Can tell if light bulb was exposed to force

Fingerprints

- Match/elimination to fingerprint source
- Contact DNA from print residue/ridges
- Does not provide class characteristics of depositor

Firearms

- Class characteristics—caliber, size, size/shape of firing pin, breech face marks, shape of extractor and ejector
- Individual/specific characteristics—firing pin impression, side contact point, extractor mark, drag marks, aperture marks
- Fingerprints
- Contact DNA, Blood DNA
- Hair/fibers
- Physical match to photographs/video if individually marked or accessorized

***Food Packaging* (Containers, Chip Bags, Candy Wrappers, Sucker Sticks)**

- Contact DNA from opening of container/crease/zipper
- Fingerprints from labels on foil packaging (gas station food, chip/jerky bags)
- Saliva DNA from sticks, spit out gum, half-chewed hard candy
- Sample of contents

Food, Partially Eaten

- Saliva DNA from bite mark
- Teeth marks in soft food
- Fingerprints in soft food

Footwear Prints/Impressions

- Route of entrance/exit
- Direction of travel before, during, after crime
- Number of parties present
- Speed, injury (limp), gait of subject
- Other crimes to be linked
- Identification/elimination of a specific shoe
- Class characteristics—type of shoe, size of shoe, brand of shoe, shape, design, logos, mold shape from manufacturing process, elimination can be completed
- Individual characteristics—wear and tear, arch pressure, defects, damages, gum/poop/rocks stuck to bottom, elimination, and identification possible

Fibers

- Class characteristics comparison
- Match brand, type, color, and so on
- Manufacturer information

Fire Soot Voids

- Soot-covered item with no soot underneath (void present) indicates the item was present before the soot covered the room
- Soot-covered item with soot underneath indicates the item was placed there after soot covered the room

Fly Feces (Fly Spots)

- DNA value intact, good for sample collection
- Location of body/activity

Furniture

- Hair/fiber
- Contact DNA
- Fingerprints if non-porous
- Sequencing of events based upon location

Glass

- Physical match to pieces of broken glass
- Physical match to deposits of broken glass, linking driver to scene or vehicle to scene
- Fingerprints
- Contact DNA
- Type of glass
- Chemical composition of glass pieces
- Estimate of fire temperature

Glass Fracture Analysis

- Order of damages
- Direction of force
- Approximate angle of impact

Glove Marks/Impressions

- Individual match to pair of gloves
- Type/pattern of type of gloves

***Gloves*—Disposable**

- Contact DNA on interior/exterior glove
- Fingerprints on interior/exterior glove

***Gloves*—Fabric**

- Touch/biological DNA from interior/exterior
- Visual match to CCTV
- Imprint match to impressions left on scene (material, stitching, individual wear marks)

***GSR—Presence of* Possibly Tells You**

- Subject was near firearm upon discharge
- Subject touched object/person with GSR on it
- Distance of fired shot
- Ammunition used deposits detectable GSR

***GSR—Lack of* Possibly Tells You**

- Subject did not discharge firearm
- Weapon used does not deposit GSR
- GSR was already removed from hands
- Shot was fired from distance

Gun Magazine

- Contact DNA
- Blood DNA
- Fingerprints
- Match to cartridges from markings

Hair, Human with a Root

- Nuclear DNA likely present and can be matched to individual
- DNA profile
- Can find match or exclusion to owner
- Method removed from body, possibly indicating a struggle if all pulled out

Hair, Human with No Root

- Mitochondrial DNA likely present and can be grouped to family not an individual
- Exclusion to owner
- Class characteristics: Ethnicity, color, artificial/real
- Determine animal or human

Hair, Animal

- Can provide DNA match, familial information
- Can link victim/suspect to a location where animal resides

Handcuffs

- Contact/blood DNA from suspect and/or victim
- Fingerprints from flat side
- Hair/fibers

Hand Tools

- Contact DNA from handle/controls
- Possible blood from edges/cracks/gears
- Store stickers with purchase information/bar codes
- Tool mark impression comparison

Hat

- Hair strands
- DNA from skin/sweat (bills and bands are best)
- Physical match to known owner
- Visual match

Ink Pen

- Contact DNA on exterior pen/lid
- Saliva DNA on end of pen
- Ink sample for comparison

Ink—Liquid

- Ink sample for comparison

Insulation

- From interior safe/structure—physical match to scene
- In pants cuffs/socks/shoes—can corroborate/refute story, match to person to scene
- At scene—provide path of travel leaving scene

Jewelry

- Contact DNA
- Fiber/hair stuck in joints
- Physical match to picture

- Manufacturing information
- Purchase information from engraving

Keys/Keychain/Key Fob/Lanyard

- Contact DNA from exterior
- Fingerprints on sides of keys/fob
- Physical match from keys to residences/rooms/safes/vehicles

Lamps

- Contact DNA on switches/cords/lightbulb
- Turned on/off details events
- Fingerprints on light bulb

Lamp Filaments

- Can tell if lights were on or off at impact of vehicle

Leash/Collar

- DNA
- Hair/fiber

License Plate

- Contact DNA from edges/screws
- Fingerprints from flat surfaces, front/back

***Lid* (Beverage Lid)**

- Saliva DNA from mouth of lid/straw
- Fingerprints from exterior
- Contents from interior lid

Ligatures

- Touch/blood/saliva DNA
- Match to injury marks
- Match to pictures/descriptions

Light Bulbs

- Possible heat damage from fire
- Fingerprints/contact DNA from both ends

Light Switches

- Turned on/off details events
- Contact DNA from switches
- Fingerprints from switch and plate cover

Lip Balm/Lipstick/Chapstick/Lip Gloss

- Saliva DNA from applicator area, contact DNA from exterior
- Color match with known/unknown sample or named product

Lip Print

- Match substance worn to known product
- Saliva DNA from sample

Locks

- Physical match of key to lock
- Physical match of combination to lock
- Physical match of broken pieces
- Tool marks from damage to lock
- Touch/blood DNA from exterior lock

Lubricant

- Chemical match between scene sample/known sample
- Evidence of possible sexual activity

Mail

- Fingerprints from paper envelope
- Fingerprints from cellophane window
- Saliva DNA from envelope/stamp
- Names for theft trail
- Location of post offices impacted during service

Mask (Ski Mask, Party Mask, Disposable Mask)

- Hair strands
- Saliva DNA from breathing
- Contact DNA from face/hands touching

Metal Fragments

- Lead can give original caliber based upon size
- Copper jacket is examinable for comparison to casing

Mineral Grains

- Can be used to link soil/environment
- Known sample/unknown sample comparison

Necklace

- Contact DNA
- Match to photographs/description
- Hair/fibers

Paint Samples

- Physical match when broken off, source ID
- Make/model/year of vehicle
- Match to tool/object when transferred

Pepper Spray

- Chemical match of known sample to scene sample
- Contact DNA and fingerprints from exterior container

Scene Photographs

- Accurate and factual documentation of scene
- Can show relationships/distances of items
- Document conditions of scene
- Document damages of scene
- Document injuries to victims without medical treatment
- Provide time stamp for changes in scene, items moved, taken, damaged
- Re-create the scene for viewing
- Prove/disprove memory or written notes

Pictures

- Confirm or refute story of contact
- Relationships of subjects in photographs
- Fingerprints from exterior of photographs or frame
- Contact DNA from backside of photographs or frame

Pillows

- DNA from saliva, sweat, dandruff, blood, ear wax, body fluids
- Hair sample
- Makeup sample

Pipe (Smoking Pipe)

- Contents/residue from bowl
- Saliva DNA from mouth
- Contact or blood DNA from exterior
- Fingerprints from exterior
- Trace evidence

Pipe (Metal, PVC, Plastic, Glass)

- Contact DNA from exterior
- Fingerprints from exterior

Plants

- Age of plants under body/through body can tell you when body dumped
- Physical match to known source of plant material
- Path of travel by dropped plant material

Pollen

- Match to specific location
- Can corroborate/refute story

Poster

- Fingerprints on front side
- Fingerprints on backside/in sticky tape
- DNA from front side

Printer/Copy Machines

- Class characteristics—grabber marks, paper edge depressions, specialized paper, paper type, toner type
- Individual characteristics—marks on drum, cover, glass plate, camera lens

Projectiles

- Comparison to firearm
- Trace evidence from path of travel (fibers, hairs, bone, DNA, drywall, wood)
- Headstamp from manufacturer
- Examination of projectile can tell you caliber, rifling features, physical match to firearm, match to related cases

Receipt

- Fingerprints (thermal or non-thermal paper depending upon chemicals available)
- Date/location for follow up or to confirm timeline

Ricochet Marks

- Direction of projectile path
- Sometimes it contains rifling marks for comparison to projectile

Rocks/Stones/Bricks

- Physical match to broken pieces
- Contact DNA if compatible exterior
- Fingerprints if compatible exterior

Rope/Zip Ties/Wiring

- Contact/blood DNA from suspect and/or victim
- Type of knot tied—related cases? Sufficient to restrain victim? Tied for easy release?
- Physical match from ends of rope/wiring/ties
- Comparison of scene/known samples
- Manufacturer of rope from strands

Semen Sample

- DNA of contributor
- Location of crime occurrence
- Evidence of sexual activity

Pre-ejaculate Fluid

- Can contain traces of semen, blood, and skin cells
- Can contain traces of Acid Phosphatase
- Don't discount collection of fluids if no ejaculation reported

Sterile Semen

- Can still lead to DNA match
- 85% of males secrete blood group factors in seminal fluid

Vasectomy Semen

- Some sperm can still be present in minimal amounts
- Skin cells with carrier DNA are present in semen with no sperm
- Can still use presumptive testing for semen after a vasectomy

Sketch

- Removes clutter, blood, and bodies, showing relevant items only
- Accurately documents relationships/distances of items
- Quick reference for window/door count, evidence placement, item relationships, entrance/exit/pathway layout
- Court exhibit for a visual reference

Shoes

- Footwear print/tread pattern
- Size/color for elimination
- Urine, blood, sweat, vomit, spatter on exterior
- DNA from sole of shoe (transfer) AND DNA from wearer of shoe
- Soil/shrubbery deposits from being outside

Shot Pellet, Buckshot, Slugs

- Manufacturer, size of the shot, gauge of slug

Shotgun Wadding

- Gauge
- Type of shot

Sim Card

- Information from card
- Contact DNA from exterior card

Socks

- Sweat/skin DNA—often used as gloves

Soil

- Match soil composition of known/unknown samples and scene location/elimination
- Can link/eliminate—vehicle to scene, scene to scene, subject to scene, subject to vehicle

Steering Wheel Cover

- Physical match to photos/descriptors
- Touch/saliva/blood DNA
- Hair/fiber transfer

Steering Wheel

- Contact DNA from wheel/buttons
- Contact DNA from adjustment lever
- Fingerprints if smooth trim

Straw

- Saliva DNA from mouth of straw
- Contact DNA from side of straw

***Styrofoam Containers* (Food, Drink, Egg Carton)**

- Latent prints from exterior
- Contact DNA from exterior
- Saliva DNA from mouth of cup
- Collection of what was carried in cooler (preserves for good amount of time)

Syringe with Needle

- Toxicology of contents
- Blood DNA from needle
- Contact DNA from syringe
- Fingerprints from syringe

***Tape* (Torn-Off Piece or on Roll)**

- Contact DNA and saliva DNA if torn with teeth/mouth
- Fingerprints
- Physical match to tape roll

Taser

- Confirmation of working/non-working and identifying information (SN, model)
- Contact DNA/prints if involved in struggle or if barbs made contact

Taser Barbs/Wires

- Confirmation of contact

Taser AFID

- Serial number of taser that fired

Teeth

- Dental record comparison for ID
- DNA sample for comparison/match
- Bitemark comparison if intact mouth
- Fingerprints on exterior teeth if removed from mouth
- Contact DNA on exterior teeth if removed from mouth

Television

- Fingerprints off screen and exterior surface
- Contact DNA from surface and cords
- Viewing history

Tire Tracks

- Make/model of tires
- Number of vehicles
- Identification/elimination of specific tire
- Size of vehicle driving

Tool

- Match to wounds on body/marks left on scene
- DNA from exterior handle from user of tool
- DNA from end of tool for receiver of injuries from tool
- Fingerprints on flat parts from either party touching tool
- Trace evidence in cracks/joints of tool

Tool Marks

- Physical match to the tool
- Corroborate or refute story
- May still have trace in the tool mark (paint, fibers, wood, oil, safe insulation)
- Can help identify weapons used

Toothpick

- Saliva DNA, contact DNA

***Trace Evidence* (Fibers)**

- Source of fibers (synthetic, clothing, carpet)
- Comparison of known/unknown sample
- Determination of same source items

***Trace Evidence* (Fragile Evidence)**

- Physical match to scene/victim
- Class characteristics to type of item/vehicle

***Trace Evidence,* Examples of**

- DNA (hair, saliva, touch, blood, biological fluids)
- Fibers—clothing/bedding/furniture/curtains/carpet/flooring/insulation
- Hair/synthetic hair
- Soil/plant
- Gas/vapor
- Glass
- Paint
- Adhesives
- Ink/paper
- GSR
- Lamp filament
- Tool marks
- Metal/wood shavings and fragments
- Building materials—concrete, plastic, insulation, Styrofoam, sheet rock, leather, wood
- Chemicals—cleaning, poison, hazardous, hygiene products, makeup

Tracker

- Contact DNA
- Physical location of stolen items
- Physical match to person/crime items

Transient Evidence

- Can assist with timeline of events, evidence that will dissipate quickly and is not retainable
- Temperature, odors, steam, condensation, and so on
- Shoeprints still wet, ice cream not melted, food still steaming, ice cubes not melted, and so on

Trash Bags

- Contact DNA
- Fingerprints
- Physical match to tear strip on roll of bags

Trash Receptacle Contents

- Can show recent activities/timeline of events
- Receipts—sources of CCTV, direction of travel, ATM trips, tool/disguise procurement, number of eaters for food orders
- Tool packaging, cigarettes, alcohol used
- Handwritten addresses, times, dates, and so on
- First aid debris if recently injured
- Crime items can be hidden among trash debris

Typewriter

- Can make physical match from typed document to typewriter
- Ribbon retains carbon copy of typed letters
- Keys can make specific marks on paper
- DNA/fingerprints from user of typewriter

Urine

- Presence of drugs—GHB present for 12 hours
- Blood DNA in urine content
- Urine running down the body can pick up skin cells along path
- Shows placement of crime location

Video

- Helps visualize the scene
- Good memory refresh before court
- Captures crowd and reactions of crowd
- Provides natural view of scene as well as entrance/egress from scene
- Can capture witness statement with visual aid
- Can capture dying declarations
- Provides demeanor when giving statement
- Can capture animal response to stimuli and sounds of communication
- Can include clock/compass at beginning of video
- Assists with bloodstain analysis
- Captures unaltered lighting/weather conditions
- Can capture evidence collection process
- Can capture body manipulation process

Walls

- Fingerprints (paint, wallpaper, paneling, mirror/glass)
- Damages and their location can detail events
- Small spots can remain on walls for years undetected
- Contact DNA from common traveled areas

Watch

- Watchmaker information from engraving on back
- SN often on inside of back
- Contact DNA
- Physical match to photograph
- Hair/fiber in joints
- Fingerprints on smooth parts of exterior

Windows

- DNA on locks/handles
- Fingerprints on panes and dividers/frame
- Footwear prints on panes/frame
- Footwear/fingerprints on screen/frame
- Directionality of broken glass from window

Window Frame/Putty/Caulking

- Contact DNA from smooth surfaces
- Fingerprints from soft/smooth surfaces

Window Screen

- Fingerprints on frame
- Hair/fiber on screen
- Pry marks from tools for comparison

Wood (Bats, Signs, Sticks, Furniture, Fencing)

- Raw wood—fingerprints with ninhydrin/iodine/silver
- Varnished wood—DNA, fingerprints
- Match to wood source
- Wood particles on suspect from tape lift, cuff of pants, interior shoes

Wrapping Paper

- Fingerprints on paper from opening/wrapping
- Handwriting analysis
- Contact DNA from ribbons/bows/adornments

Wrappers, Food/Candy

- Contact DNA from exterior
- Fingerprints from flat surfaces

Cases to Consider Regarding Evidence Values

- Tiago da Rocha was a serial killer in Brazil over a 4-year span, claiming 39 victims. Da Rocha was not a suspect in any murders until he was seen stealing a license plate near a scene.
- During the scene processing of juveniles James M. Moore, Steven Branch, and Christopher Byers, their clothing, which had been thrown in a drainage ditch, were held down in the water by sticks. Those sticks were not examined or collected. Blood was located in the water; however, it was not collected.
- 2009: After the body of Annie Le was removed from the crime scene, an ink pen was beneath her that contained the killer's DNA.
- 2001: After the murder of Krystal Steadman the case went cold as the normal DNA items did not produce a match. The investigators decided to think outside the box in 2013 and processed the granite rock used in her murder which provided a full profile and match.

General Evidence Collection, Packaging, Transport 19

The value you can obtain from evidence is only as good as the collection and preservation efforts used during collection and transportation. The vast variety of evidence makes it impossible to have one all-encompassing guidebook for collection and preservation, but this handbook will get the CSI through basic situations. There are a growing variety of resources that are beneficial to use and keep at your disposal. While collecting items, keep in mind that you want to collect items that not only prove your theory, but also challenge your theory. Collect and document the evidence at the scene to be able to fully evaluate their value later. This chapter will cover some of the basic evidence, while other chapters will cover evidence that is more complex and requires more explanation such as fire evidence.

> Physical evidence cannot be over-documented.
>
> **—Federal Bureau of Investigation**[1]

> Improper collection, labeling, or preservation of evidence, or the less than complete processing of a crime scene, can be the first steps on the road to conviction for an innocent person.
>
> **—NCCAI—North Carolina Center on Actual Innocence**[2]

Do

- Have 1 main collector per scene—others can assist
- Keep evidence log on scene
- Package all items individually
- Use porous packaging for most items
- Seal containers on scene or prior to transfer for chain of custody
- Use biohazard bags when needed
- Keep packaging loose without squishing or rubbing off latent prints, but not so loose they are rolling around
- Cover any writing on plastic with tape so it does not rub off

Don't

- Store item in hot vehicle without air conditioning
- Store items in vehicle with canine inside vehicle

 DOI: 10.4324/9781003503897-20

- Touch hair/face/shirt/phone during collection and packaging procedures
- Use staples for evidence bags
- Wrap packaging tight, but should be loose enough to not rub off prints or trace evidence

Packaging Documentation

Information Needed on Exterior Packaging

- Individual marker# on scene if used
- Case number/date
- Collector
- Quantity/description
- If information is written on plastic bag or tube, place piece of fingerprint tape over top so it does not rub off with handling

Collecting Items of Evidence *(Not Including Trace)*

Storage Temperature Ranges

- Frozen: 14°F/−10°C to −4°F/−20°C
- Refrigerated: 36°F/2°C to 46°F/8°C, less than 25% humid
- Temperature controlled: 59°F/15°C to 75°F/24°C, less than 60% humid
- Room temperature: Ambient temperature around you

Airbags, **Deployed**

- Keep front of air bag folded in on itself, wrap in butcher paper, place in paper bag or arson can
- Store temperature controlled

COLLECTION OPTION: Remove steering wheel cover and remove air bag

COLLECTION OPTION: Cut deployed air bag at base, use clean scalpel/razor blade for each bag

Airbags, **Undeployed**

- Do not dismantle undeployed airbag unless fully trained

Airbag Residue

- Use GSR stubs on hands/clothing to collect possible airbag residue. Collect within 5 hours of accident, otherwise residue may dissipate with normal activities.[3]

***Blood Sample,* Liquid**

- Refrigerate only
- Do not keep room temperature longer than 1 hour—have a runner take back to refrigeration

***Blood Sample,* Absorbed on Cotton**

- STORAGE OPTION: Temperature controlled—dry the sample first
- STORAGE OPTION: Freezer—wet items can be frozen until hung/laid to dry

***Bloody Items,* Heavy Contamination (Textiles/Larger Items)**

- TRANSPORTATION OPTION: Place items in biohazard bag, place the biohazard bag in a paper bag, write information on paper bag, and transport to laboratory for immediate drying
- DRYING OPTION: Freezer—wet items can be frozen until hung/laid to dry
- Store temperature controlled in paper bag/box/envelope dry
- Consider retaining original collection packaging even if blood soaked and dried as it may retain trace evidence

***Bloody Items,* Mild Contamination**

- Double bag or double envelope—document contents on both envelopes
- Transport to laboratory to assess drying needs
- Consider Tyvek tubes, bags, or other breathable packaging

***Body Tissue,* (Scalp, Ear, Appendage, Finger, etc.)**

- Turn over to medical examiner if applicable
- Collect in plastic if wet, do not seal
- Store frozen

Bone

- Place in paper bag/envelope/unlined cardboard box. May need to be wrapped several times as bone marrow can leave a greasy residue on the packaging that will bleed through and upset the property department.
- Do not store it in plastic, will mold
- Store frozen or temperature controlled

Buccal Swabs

- Store temperature controlled or frozen after drying

Cartridge Cases

- Should always be packaged individually

Collection Option: Swab Stick

- Place end of stick inside opening of cartridge case
- Lift up at an angle
- Visually examine for blood DNA
- Package individually
- Stick can be discarded or retained; no DNA found on interior cartridge case

Collection Option: By Hand

- Pick up cartridge case by hand, with clean glove for each cartridge case
- Pick up on each short open end, not headstamp
- Avoid touching long sides
- Examine for blood DNA

Collection Option: Frisc Caps[4]

- Purchase seal caps for cartridge cases from Signature Science
- Stops GSR contamination of DNA prior to laboratory processing

Collection Option: Special Collection Container IBIS Clear Case[5] *or Case Grabber*[6]

- Use metal to collect cartridge cases from the open end
- Place in secure container, mark packaging accordingly

Cell Phones

- Secure in faraday bag as soon as possible or book in 6 × 9 envelope
- Touch minimally, hold on sides if processing
- Turn off after DNA collection, fingerprint search

Clothing

- Loose paper bag or envelope ideal
- Can wrap in butcher paper prior to placing in bag—can wrap as found or wrap flat and fold
- Examine for trace evidence upon return to controlled environment

Clothing Removal for Clothing Collection

- Must be done in non-public view regardless of case type, location, or subject

Collection Option: Butcher Paper on Floor Beneath Subject

- If possible turn off AC vents around subject to restrict air flow (only during this process)
- Have subject stand on butcher paper during photographs/undress
- Collect items from subject
- Have subject step off paper
- Provide cover such as Tyvek or secondary clothing for re-dress
- Collect butcher paper/trace evidence/footwear prints—slowly fold paper in on itself, wind will lose all trace evidence

***Condom* (Used, Still Wet)**

- Interior/exterior have different DNA profiles
- Liquid semen of volume should be immediately frozen

Option: Swab exterior and interior separately prior to storage—recommend completing in controlled environment

Option: Place whole item in plastic tube/jar/bag—immediately freeze

Option: Absorb contents from interior condom with swab/gauze/cotton pad

Option: Pour liquid semen in test tube/gauze pad—freeze immediately, retain frozen

Option: Place in jar with lid off/glassine envelope, allow to air dry—store temperature controlled

***Condom* (Used, Floating in Water/Toilet)**

Option: Absorb Water and Contents From Interior Condom

- Grab 2 edges of condom (with tweezers) lifting to retain all water inside of condom when found
- Insert gauze pad to collect all liquid until absorbed
- Collect DNA swab sample from exterior condom (extra focus on rolled edge)
- Freeze or air-dry all samples

SECONDARY OPTION: Run cotton pad or filter paper through water bowl/along edge of water to "grab" any semen present in water in addition to collection condom from water

***Condom* (Used, Dry)**

Option: Collect Entirely, Send to Laboratory for Swabbing

- Keep flat/upright in glassine and paper envelopes

- Store at room temperature
- Don't store in hot vehicle on scene longer than 1 hour, send to laboratory for DNA collection asap

Option: Swab Exterior and Interior Separately Prior to Storage

- Place swabs in separate packaging
- Place condom in glassine envelope/paper envelope for storage

Option: Place Condom in Plastic Specimen Jar with Lid

- Keep upright to avoid any leakage
- Freeze immediately/store frozen
- Don't let sit in hot van during processing

Diaper **(Soiled, Adult/Child/Animal)**

- Collect in paper bag, individually
- Will never fully dry (by design), go right to freezing the item

Documents, **Charred**

- Attempt to collect pile as 1 item

1. Slide clean cardboard underneath bottom of pile and lift it as one item to avoid breakage
2. Place whole item in box, don't bend/fold/roll
3. Mark exterior packaging; up and fragile, keep upright.

Documents, **with Indented Writing**

- Fill out packaging prior to placing items inside packaging
- Double packaging suggested
- Envelope in envelope
- Envelope in bag
- Bag in box
- Preserves integrity if indented surface
- Keep at top of evidence piles

Doors and Other Large Items

- Wrap in butcher paper (partially wrap side of interest)
- Preserves prints/DNA/blood evidence/tool marks
- Photos of prior to leaving scene and arrival to laboratory showing damage/lack of damages

Drugs/Drug Evidence

- Narcotics should be booked in original container found in and seal on scene
- Determine the value the item has to the scene—is it narcotic charges or DNA/fingerprint evidence? If fingerprints or contact DNA are needed collect prior to submitting drugs for storage.

Possible Evidence from Drug Manufacturing/Processing

- Diluting agents—baking soda, sugar, other drugs, water, decongestants
- Tablet press
- Disinfectants
- Sterilization liquids/equipment
- Glassware
- Electronics
- Calendars
- Spreadsheets
- Water bottles with a white and yellow substance, or bottles that appear to be melting
- PET bottles
- Lithium batteries
- Chemicals such as ammonium nitrate, sodium hydroxide, and sodium chloride
- Camping fuel, kerosene, cyclohexane, or diethyl ether

Paraphernalia from Drug Use/Minor Drug Dealers

- Aluminum foil
- Beverage lids with debris/soot
- Bottles, bags, empty capsules
- Cardboard tubes from the foil, wrap, and toilet paper
- Cling wrap
- Containers with false bottoms, odor free—soda cans, beer cans, disinfectant wipe tubs, aerosol spray canisters such as WD40 and Lysol
- Copper wire, copper shavings
- Currency—in rolls for use and flat for purchase
- Dryer sheets and dryer sheet boxes, together or separately
- Filter paper
- Glassine envelopes
- Ink pen tubes—emptied out
- Needles
- Odor/smell-free backpacks

- Pipe
- Rubber hose, belts, ropes, exercise bands
- Plastic bags, big/small, zip top/fold top
- Plastic bag corners torn off
- Scales, balances
- Scoops
- Shelf paper
- Spoon with char/soot
- Steel wool/Brillo pads
- Straws
- Tape

Fabric/Clothing

- Can separate layers or wrap in butcher paper if blood evidence is present
- Don't cut out stains of collectable items, collect whole item instead
- Don't shake/tear/stretch
- Photograph label during collection photographs for later reference
- Store in bag/envelope/box in room temperature or temperature controlled

Fabric with Accelerant **(See Also Fire Evidence)**

- Place in arson can/arson bag to prevent evaporation, seal immediately
- Store temperature controlled

Feathers **(Bloody or Non-Bloody)**

- Package in glassine envelopes preferred, paper bag/envelope acceptable

Feces

- Animal feces—if dry store temperature controlled, if wet store frozen
- Human feces—store frozen with substrate found on

Fetus **(Umbilical Cord/Birthing Material)**

- Option: Turn over to medical examiner/coroner office if possible
- Option: Collect/transport in plastic—immediately freeze

Finger Skin Collection from Submerged Body

- Can place each finger sleeve in test tube with water—send for comparison/evaluation

- Can place entire hand skin in plastic Tupperware with water—send for comparison/evaluation

Firearms

- Keep chamber round kept separate from magazine rounds (misfire markings?)
- Unload and collect DNA prior to transportation (unless jammed)—can use orange zip ties or red rubber rope ties when secured

Revolver

- **DOCUMENTATION OPTION**: Mark cylinder position with China marker or wax pencil with a single line across the cylinder and frame
- **DOCUMENTATION OPTION**: Diagram for direction of cylinder
    - Draw diagram of cylinder filling in headstamps in order of cylinder with arrow showing direction of rotation
    - Mark packaging of cartridges being removed as to their placement in cylinder chart
- **REVOLVER SECURE OPTION**: Secure cylinder in place in firearm[7]
    - Cut small strip out of side of clean Styrofoam cup
    - Slide cup over cylinder of revolver prohibiting movement
    - Can transport safely once placed inside gun box

Firearms Packaging

- Always mark barrel direction on exterior packaging
- Can mark barrel of revolver position with China marker or wax marker
- Packaging/transportation options
    - Rifle bag for long guns (recommended)
    - Lawn bag for long guns
    - Gun box for handguns (recommended)
    - Envelope for handguns
    - Paper bag for handguns
    - Plastic Ziplock bag for handguns

***Firearms*, under Water**

Option 1—Keep Submerged in Original Liquid Source

- Collect in sample of water submerged in to keep wet (keep in bucket or Tupperware)
- Remove from water only long enough to unload weapon

- Return firearm and ammunition to water
- Transport to lab

Option 2—Remove from Liquid Source (Raw Sewage or "No Liquids" Policy)

- Remove from water/mud
- Render gun safe
- Place in plastic bag/seal to keep moisture inside bag and prevent oxidation
- Transport to laboratory for further examination
- Will keep moist until test fired

Option 3—Alcohol/Acetone DIP with Kerosene Storage (Raw Sewage)

- Place immediately in clean water, fully submerge then quickly remove
- Unload weapon
- Place weapon in container of alcohol or acetone, fully submerge then quickly remove
- Surface will dry quickly as liquid will displace water from surface
- Gather all written information, SN, model, and so on for notes
- Submerge weapon fully in kerosene and store in airtight container
- Transport to lab

Option 4—Collect without Water Sample (Raw Sewage or "No Liquids" Policy)

- Immediately spray barrel with WD40 to coat interior barrel prior to rust/oxidation. Spray coat of exterior gun suggested to prevent rust of remaining firearm.

Gel Lifters

- PACKAGING: Tall medium paper bag or legal-size envelope will hold footwear size without bending
- COLLECTION: Keep clear cover intact (can retain in place with tape)
- DOCUMENTATION—writing goes on back of gel lift, not clear cover
    - Needed documentation for hair/fiber lift: Case number, name/ID, date, time, location
    - Needed documentation for footwear/fingerprint lift: Case number, name/ID, date, time, location, directional arrow, drawing of area with lift placement

Knife

Packaging Options

- Knife box (made for securing knives)
  - If bloody, loosely wrap knife in butcher paper, loosely secure in box with zip tie (enough to keep paper closed, not enough to rub knife)
- Knife tube (made for securing knives)
- Envelope with cardboard folded over knife point

Light Bulb

- Option: Cut x in top of box or bottom of cup, place foot of light bulb in hole, leave in place
- Option: Place in Styrofoam cup, tray, or box for transportation
- Option: Place cotton pad in bottom of arson can, lay on cotton
- Option: Place vehicle lights in box

Liquid Sample

- Soak with gauze/swabs
- Collect with pipette and place in jar or liquids vial

Machete

- Place in rifle bag, handle up
- Place in bag, cardboard secured over sharp end

Medication

- Collect inside the container found in inventory at scene and at office

***Pepper Spray Sample* (Sprayed Person/Item)**

Option: If textile, submit whole item

Option: Wet gauze/swab with rubbing alcohol, rub swab/gauze over spray covered area

- Dry swab/gauze, submit unused swab/gauze as control

Plant Matter

- Should be dried completely prior to storage
- Don't package in plastic or other airtight container—will decompose

Pillow

- Collect whole, paper grocery bag is good packaging
- Can wrap in butcher paper if hair is of value

Powder, Unknown Material

- Collect physical sample of powder rather than a swab sample of powder. Scoop into disc container, test tube, jar with lid, arson can.

Rope

- If CSI cuts rope on scene mark, identify which end was cut
- Can wrap length of rope in butcher paper or place in bag as whole item, depending on scene needs

Rubber Stamps

- Submit to laboratory as is, don't clean/wipe off

Saliva

- Soak with gauze/swabs
- Collect with pipette and place in jar or liquids vial

Shotgun Wadding/Cups

- Place in individual paper envelope or small bags

Syringe

- Place in sharps tube
- Consider collecting contents only if that is focus
- Consider processing on scene and leaving

Tape

- Place in plastic bag
- Place sticky side down on sheet protector, then in paper bag
- Place in arson can
- If tape is cut for removal from person/place mark tape accordingly with pen/Sharpie

Temperature/Humidity Collection

- Collect as soon as possible upon arrival, prior to opening doors/windows/draining water

- You can use liquid thermometer, laser thermometer, or mercury thermometer
- Don't take in direct sunlight
- See Entomology section for locations of sampling

Tools, Hand Tools

- Wrap bag around ends or secure in box to prevent additional marks being made—place item in box/bag/envelope

Typewriter

- Collect as whole item, leave ribbon in place
- Box is ideal

Urine—Human or Unknown Source

- Option: Soak with gauze/swabs, keep frozen
- Option: Urine-soaked item samples, dry and retain dry or frozen
- Option: Collect with pipette and place in jar or liquids vial

Urine—Animal

- Store liquid animal urine frozen[8]
- Store swabs of animal urine dry at room temperature

Wet Bloody Clothing Items

- PACKAGING/TRANSPORTATION: Place in plastic biohazard bag, then in paper bag, place item/case information on paper bag, transport to laboratory to be dried

Wet Items That Cannot Be Dried Immediately

- Place items in plastic bags, unsealed or non-porous container
- Transport to refrigerated storage until dried or laboratory submission

Window/Windshield

- Option: Large piece—secure between cardboard/plywood, mark interior/exterior, directional arrow
- Option: Small piece, debris on ground of accident—scoop handful amount into small envelope, sample from each location
- Option: Small piece, known window sample (collect from frame seam if possible)—place tape on one side of glass being collected, mark interior/exterior, directional arrow prior to collection, place collected piece in small envelope, mark sharp and fragile

Notes

1 *FBI Handbook of Crime Scene Forensics*. Skyhorse Publishing, 2008.

2 "Evidentiary Errors." *North Carolina Center on Actual Innocence*, nccai.org/causes/evidence-error/.

3 *Trace Materials Crime Scene Investigation Guide*. OSAC, NIST.

4 https://www.signaturescience.com/press/signature-sciences-frisc-service-enables-dna-recovery-from-spent-shell-casings/.

5 https://leadsonline.com/clearcase.

6 https://casegrabber.com/.

7 Rynearson, Joe. "Tips and Tricks." *National Crime Investigation and Training*, ncit.com.

8 "Sample Collection." *US Davis Veterinary Genetics Laboratory*, vgl.ucdavis.edu/sample-collection.

Trace Evidence Types and Collection

20

In countless investigations, trace evidence has been pivotal in solving crimes, securing convictions, and preventing wrongful verdicts. By collecting minute materials such as fibers, hair, glass fragments, and other small substances, investigators significantly increase the likelihood that the apprehended suspect is indeed the one responsible. This meticulous approach ensures no piece of evidence is overlooked, and every fragment is thoroughly analyzed to provide crucial insights into the crime. It underscores the importance of trained forensic teams who adhere to stringent protocols to maintain the integrity of evidence from discovery to courtroom presentation. Like other types of evidence, there are numerous methods to collect and preserve trace evidence. This section will outline various collection techniques applicable to the different forms found. Additionally, it will provide a list of forms and locations for discovering this evidence at a scene, serving as a helpful reminder.

It is important to note that the list of obtainable trace evidence goes way beyond the information found here, and I hope that you use this information to help you find stronger connections between your suspect and your crime scene. While there are several options and method choices for collection, you will need to determine which methods are acceptable for your own agency.

> Finding trace evidence on a crime scene will depend on the experience/skill of the investigator and scene supervisor.
>
> **—Geberth**[1]

Reference Samples for Trace Evidence

Comparison Samples

- Collected for comparison/elimination of the item sample collected from areas such as carpet, upholstery, and soil
  - Sample of nearby area, "like item" as scene sample
  - Same method of collection as scene sample—cutting, scraping, scooping, swabbing

DOI: 10.4324/9781003503897-21

Control Samples

- Sample of clean item used for scene sample collection/tool maintenance
  - Swab blank—unused swab, piece of cloth, and so on
  - Arson can blank—unused piece of can or empty can
  - Water blank—sample from your water source
  - Cleanser sample—sample of soap or disinfectant used for evidence collection

Types of Trace Evidence (*What to Collect*)

Examples of Trace Evidence

- Air samples
- Building materials/insulation
- Feathers
- Fiber
- Glass fragments
- GSR—gunshot residue
- Hair
- Oil/grease and residue
- Paint
- Plant material/pollen/leaves/type
- Residue from explosive, accelerant, makeup, lotion, hair care products, pepper spray, ink/dye pack
- Soils
- Wax and wax residue
- Wood

Air Samples

Scene Sample Methods of Air Collection

Option: Empty Water Bottle for Collection Medium

- Begin with sealed, unused water bottle
- Open bottle, pour out water in area that air sample is wanted while ambient air replaces water in bottle
- Seal on bottle on scene (tape around lid)
- Book control sample of unopened water bottle from same source

Option: Air Pump through Filter

- Attach filter of choice to end of air pump hose (filter/cotton/gauze/charcoal piece)
- Turn on, let air pass through filter for predetermined amount of time
- Filter/charcoal are packaged/booked

Option: Syringe from Air Compartment (Trunk, Room, Bottle)

- Using clean, new syringe collect sample of air in contained area by emptying syringe then drawing full of air in area of choice
- Cap syringe immediately
- Place in arson can and seal on scene
- Submit syringe of air for analysis

Option: Evacuated air canister (new/unused)

Comparison/Control Samples of Air Collection (Known Sample)

- Consider taking a comparison sample from ambient air in a nearby area, collect in the same manner as scene samples
- Consider taking a control sample of any used filter, bottle, can, and so on

Example of Needed Samples for Trunk Sample Collection

- Scene sample of air from inside trunk of vehicle in garage
- Comparison sample of air in garage, area not near trunk
- Control sample of machine blank/filter blank

Documentation Needed for All Samples

- Sketch collection location of all samples/GPS coordinates of all samples optional
- Time/date of collection
- Collector information
- Description of sample, area sampled, sample method

Fiber

Scene Sample Methods of Fiber Collection (See below for Instructions)

- Lift (tape, gel lift, GSR stub), vacuum

Comparison Samples of Fiber Collection (Known Sample)

- OPTION: Cut section of item in question
- OPTION: Collect adhesive lift of item in question using same method as scene sample

Comparison Sample Examples ***(2”×2” Sample or Larger If Possible)***

- Carpet sample—cut sample of carpet, backing not needed for fiber analysis

- Fabric sample—cut sample of fabric
- Vehicle fibers—cut sample from each quadrant of vehicle, cut sample from each type of upholstery/carpet
- Residence carpet—cut sample from each possible room/type of carpet

Documentation Needed for All Samples

- Sketch collection location of all samples/GPS coordinates of all samples optional
- Time/date of collection
- Collector information
- Marker number or letter
- Description of sample, area sampled, sample size/amounts

Glass

Scene Sample Method of Glass Collection (Unknown Source)

- Sample from each type/location of "found glass" in scene
- Sample size—minimum 1×1 inches, maximum size 8.5×11 inch
- Collection—scoop with envelope or pick up with hand
- Document location carefully: Exterior of broken window, interior residence floor, driver seating area, and so on
- Fill out packaging prior to placing sample inside, if using envelope consider double packaging

Documentation Needed for All Samples

- Sketch collection location of all samples/GPS coordinates of all samples optional
- Time/date of collection
- Collector information
- Marker number or letter
- Description of sample, area sampled, sample size/amounts

Comparison Samples of Glass Collection (Known Source)

- Need 1–2 inches minimum, try for 4 inch sample from each source—collect from area still attached to frame, generally by trim/frame: Window frame, mirror frame, kitchen door frame, and so on

Vehicle

- Collect as close to source of impact as possible AND separate sample from each impact location

- Windshield glass will need collection from each side of windshield pane (2 panes)—interior/exterior of vehicle, store separately, and designate which side is interior pane/exterior pane

Method

- Place tape on 1 side of glass on the section for collection, mark directionality (inside/outside, up)
- Remove glass from frame directly if possible, tape should cover most of sample (in case of further breakage)
- Place in glassine envelope/envelope, double package
- Mark envelope with collection information prior to placing sample inside

Types of Glass

Plate Glass

- Structure windows, mirrors, display cases
- Single pane of glass, breaks in large pieces that are sharp
- Fractures show sequence of defects

Tempered Glass, Safety Glass

Vehicle Windows

- Single pane of glass that breaks into small squares
- Initial defect will have radial fracture lines and the next defects break up broken glass
- Often window remains intact with fracture lines until more than 1 impact
- Direction of force (inside/outside) from markings on glass not possible with tempered glass

Vehicle Windshields

- 2 layers of safety glass with laminate in the middle
- Large radial fracture lines
- Additional impact can lengthen the lines rather than make new ones
- Each side can have separate fracture lines (interior/exterior)

GSR—Gunshot Residue

- Collection does not give immediate results

What It Is

- 2 TYPES of GUNSHOT residue—primer residue from combustion AND gunpowder residue from the gunpowder combustion

Where Is It Found

- Point of discharge AND point of impact and several feet surrounding

Persons within 3 Feet of Gunfire

- Hair
- Hands—thumb/forefinger
- Face—nostrils, facial hair
- Face mask worn after/during shooting
- Gloves
- Long sleeved sweatshirt—arms/front/pockets
- Pants—pockets/front of legs

Vehicle Compartments If Shooting Occurred inside Vehicle

- Dome/headliner
- Dashboard
- Trim/window
- Seatbelt
- Seats/headrest
- A, B, C pillars

When Is It Found

- Will exist indefinitely but does not remain in one place indefinitely
- Collect GSR PRIOR to: Handcuffing—transporting—shaking hands

Hands

- Remains until washed/wiped off
- Reliable up to 4 hours after shooting
- Hands have more direct contact for secondary transfer

Nostrils

- Reliable up to 48 hours after shooting[2]

Clothing

- Remains until washed/wiped
- Lasts longer on clothing than hands

Who Should Collect

- CSI who has NOT handled a firearm recently nor has ridden in any law enforcement vehicle due to contamination issues

Known Barriers with GSR

Variables to Sample Deposit

- Long guns leave less GSR behind on hands/clothing
- Certain types of ammo leave bigger GSR deposit than others
- Most contain lead, barium, and antimony—not all ammunition contains all 3

Transfer

- Very easily transferred (like DNA) from contact
- Primary transfer—GSR transferred from gun to subject when fired
- Secondary transfer—GSR transferred from hands of shooter to other object/person

Contamination/False Positives Caused by

- Wearing handcuffs with GSR already present
- Touching the hands of someone with GSR already present
- Sitting in the back of a police car with GSR already present
- Being near someone who fired a weapon
- Airbag deployment
- Brake/brake pad work
- Firework handling
- Any other environment where barium, antimony, and/or lead may be deposited on the person

Prevention of Contamination

- Bag hands prior to any handcuffing/movement
- Collect handbags before GSR collection—can be paper bag/tape—can be premade bag with drawstrings

Documentation Needed for All Samples

- Time/date of collection
- Time of crime, estimated
- Collector information
- If from a person: Their name and DOB
- If from items: Description of area sampled

Scene Sample Method of GSR Collection

Option: GSR Stubs on Live/Deceased Subjects

- Gather information for enclosed form if pre-packaged kit
  - Name, DOB, right/left hand dominant, last time washed hands, and so on. Ensure your agency has deemed your questioning acceptable if subject has refused to speak.
  - Time of crime AND Time of collection
- Cover sheet photograph, with ID if available
- Subject photographs—face ID (shoulder to top of hair/hat)
  - Overall photographs of front/back—include blood/dirt/debris on clothing
  - Close-up of hands with any bags if present
- Collect bags—ensure packaging dictates right/left hand—okay to write on bags exterior
- Close-up photographs of bare hands—include any injuries/blood/dirt/soot
- Collect any blood on hands/hair stuck in fingers
- Change gloves before touching collection stubs
- Mark stub individually with case number, date, collector, location, time (mark time in notes as well)
- Collect stubs from hands on thumb/forefinger area—keep right/left accurate
- Put lid on stub FIRMLY and place in same envelope
- Seal on scene

Option: Stubs on Items, Not Persons

- Avoid areas heavy with blood/soot/debris

Apply to
- Clothing items, vehicle areas, furniture

Method
- New gloves before touching stubs
- Press/raise until no longer sticky in area of interest
- 1 stub per area/1 stub each hand/1 stub each shirt sleeve/1 stub each vehicle seating area
- Mark stub individually with case number, date, collector, location, time (mark time in notes as well)
- Place in envelope with lid intact
- Seal on scene

Option: Tape

Apply to

- Thumb/forefinger area
- Vehicle seats
- Carpet
- Furniture
- Clothing items
- Bedding

Method

- Take several passes over area of interest with tape (can loop over hand or keep straight strip)
- Press/raise until no longer sticky
- 1 tape per area/1 tape for each hand/1 tape for each shirt sleeve/1 tape for each vehicle area
- Secure in sheet protector/plastic bag

Option: Vacuum

Apply to

- Vehicle seats
- Carpet
- Furniture
- Clothing items
- Flooring

Method

- Use new forensic filter in vacuum
- Use forensic vacuum over area of interest
- Place entire sample in bag/paper wrapping for examination, do not separate/inspect on scene
- Use new filter per area of interest

Option: Elmers Clear Glue/Clear/White AccuTrans

Apply to

- Non-porous surface
- Skin
- NOT for use clothing/fabrics/textiles

Method

- Cover area in question slowly and deliberately with liquid glue or AccuTrans and allow to dry

- Once dried, lift slowly in 1 piece
- Package entire lift in glassine envelope or plastic zip lock bag

Option: Swabbing

- Use swab/gauze/cotton of choice
- Run wet substrate over area in question
- Fold sample on itself or place in packaging immediately

Option: Human Mucus

- Have subject blow nose into tissue/gauze—5 × 5 inches approximate size
- Fold tissue in on sample and place in glassine envelope
- Retain/store entire sample

Option: Collect Clothing Items Entirely

- Shirts, gloves, sweatshirts, face masks
- Ensure all layers are covered with butcher paper or fold in on itself
- Submit entire shirt/hoodie to laboratory for analysis

Option: Photographs of Enhancement

- Use enhancement option of choice from next section
- Photograph results prior to sending for laboratory analysis or as part of laboratory analysis

GSR Enhancement

Option: IR—700–1100 nm

- Photograph results with appropriate filters
- Control tests of IR lighting should be conducted

Option: Vinegar Solution[3]

- Premix vinegar solution—5 parts water, 1 part vinegar
- Apply solution to blotter paper/coffee filter until fully moist/not dripping
- Lay flat on suspected surface
- Leave 5–10 minutes to absorb
- Mark pattern orientation/directional arrow before removal from surface
- Dry flat OR package between 2 pieces of paper for later photography/analysis
- Can show patterns to help determine distance and trajectory

Option: Sodium Rhodizonate (Reacts with Lead)

- Color change from pink to blue violet indicates positive results
- Good for clothing, drywall, carpet, furniture, and so on
- Can show patterns of GSR to help determine distance and trajectory
- Can confirm if a hole is from a bullet due to presence of lead
- Control tests should be conducted
- Results should be photographed

Hair

- Secondary transfer is possible, you can pick up deposited hairs at one location and deposit at second location
- Be mindful of leaving your own hair on scene, utilize hair nets and lint rollers on your own uniform

All Types of Hair Suitable for Sample Collection

- Head hair
- Pubic hair
- Body hair
- Nose hair
- Eyelashes
- Eyebrows

Documentation Needed for All Samples

- Sketch collection location of all samples/GPS coordinates of all samples optional
- Time/date of collection
- Collector information
- Marker number or letter
- Description of sample, area sampled, sample size/amounts

Scene Sample Method of Hair Collection (See Section below for Instructions)

- Lift (tape, gel lift, GSR stub), vacuum, combing

Comparison Samples of Hair Collection (Known Sample)

Human Sample

- 1 or more regions on body
- 10–20 hairs per region common
- 25 per region recommended by FBI

Collection Options

Option: Pull hair (recommended)
Option: Comb hair—collect comb as well as hair sample
Option: Hairbrush of known person—package entire hairbrush without separation of hair

Animal Sample

LARGE ANIMAL SAMPLE—HORSE, COW

- Pull hair, retain root if possible—10–20 hairs from mane, tail, neck
- Package in paper or glassine envelope, no plastic
- Air-dry at room temperature

SMALL ANIMAL SAMPLE—CAT, DOG

- Pull hairs, retain root if possible—10–20 hairs
- Shed hairs are an acceptable alternative (likely still contain nuclear DNA due to grooming process)
- If animal is not available/cooperative—collect tape lift or hair from pet brush, bed, comb, collar

DECEASED ANIMAL

- Over 2 hours—don't collect hair, too deteriorated already
- Under 2 hours—can take hair sample from body

Paint

- Common paint types encountered for sampling
  - House paint
  - Spray paint
  - Craft paint
  - Vehicle paint
- All collection equipment must be single use or properly cleaned between samples
- When collecting tools for paint transfer analysis, submit entire tool without removing sample if possible
  - Consider covering the tip of tool for preservation (coin envelope or paper over tip)
- If transfer is suspected from 2 vehicles, be sure to collect[4]:
  - comparison sample (paint known to be from this vehicle) from each vehicle
  - unknown paint sample from each vehicle (paint appearing to be transfer)

- IR photography can be used to identify areas on vehicles that have been repainted/repaired
  - 700 nm–900 nm ideal range to start viewing

Scene Sample Method of Paint Collection Options (See below for Instructions)

- Scraping, cutting, whole item collection
- Picking off flaking paint with hands/tweezers
- Tape collection should only be done with fingerprint tape, otherwise the adhesive may be too strong

Comparison Samples of Paint Collection (Known Sample)

When Scraping Paint

- Avoid curved surfaces on vehicles (often contains touched-up paint spots)
- Be as close to area of transfer/damage as you can WITHOUT collecting sample from INSIDE area of transfer/damage

If Multiple Layers of Paint Suspected or Present[5]

- Collect from adjacent areas
- Wall and ceiling
- Door and window
- Fender and hood
- Vehicle paint sample—suggest 1 sample from each panel for each vehicle involved

Documentation Needed for All Samples

- Sketch collection location of all samples/GPS coordinates of all samples optional
- Time/date of collection
- Collector information
- Marker number or letter
- Description of sample, area sampled, sample size/amounts

Plant/Shrubbery

Scene Sample Method of Plant Collection Options, Unknown Source

Method

- Whole item collection (if shrubbery is dropped into scene), scooping if pieces are small

Option: Small Pieces in Scene

- Close-ups of area prior to lifting
- Tape lift of area with shrubbery
- Package as normal tape lift
- Allow to air dry before storage

Option: Larger Pieces in Scene

- Close-up photographs needed prior to drying
- Scoop or pick up with hands
- Allow to air dry before storage

Burial Site Plant Collection

Body Dumped on Top of Vegetation

- Collect sample of plants directly beneath body

Body Buried under Vegetation

- Collect sample of plants directly above body
- If digging scrape top layer of plants/grass/weeds/roots/soil with flat shovel
- Retain sample as collected
- Photograph to include close-ups for visual examination
- Air-dry for storage

Comparison Samples of Plant/Shrubbery Collection (Known Source)

Option: Cuttings

- Cut small branches to include wood and leaf
- Look for areas that are disturbed already to find source
- Only bring roots if soil is of interest

Option: Large Plants in Ground

- Cut from roots, take stalk only
- Consider taking a sample of leaves

Documentation Needed for All Samples

- Sketch collection location of all samples/GPS coordinates of all samples optional
- Time/date of collection
- Collector information

- Marker number or letter
- Description of sample, area sampled, sample size/amounts

Packaging of Plant/Shrubbery Sample

- Bag, envelope, box of breathable material—if appearance is important do not crush sample
- Store dried/temperature controlled not frozen

Soil

- Subsoil and topsoil are different—topsoil soil samples 1/4–1/2 inch depth
- Tire/footwear/footprint generally from topsoil, burial/body dump generally from subsoil and topsoil
- Burial—collect sample from each visible layer of soil
- Collection should be done as soon as possible—soil content changes quickly, consider doing earlier on in processing sequence
- Keep clumps as intact as possible for soil samples
- Must be air dried OR frozen within 24 hours
- Can cover with butcher paper/clean paper towel to eliminate contamination during air-drying process
- Clean tools or collection equipment with water rinse or wipe down between samples[6]
- SAMPLE AMOUNT—collect about 5 samples from each area on scene—range could be 3–20 samples
- SAMPLE SIZE—collect minimum 2–3 tablespoons[7]—1 cup per sample

Documentation Needed for All Samples

- Sketch collection location of all samples
- GPS coordinates of all samples AS WELL
- Time/date of collection
- Collector information
- Slope of site (if applicable)
- Description of sample, area sampled, sample size/amounts

Packaging for Soil—Store Air Dried or Frozen

- Rigid plastic cups or tubes with screw on lids for frozen storage or dry storage
- Glass jars with screw on lids for dry storage only
- Small arson can, lined only
- Secured in box for larger items

Sample Location Options

Collection from Scene

- Entry/escape routes, along path of travel, inside footwear/tire marks
- At base of furniture
- Areas of soil disturbance

Collection from Suspect Location

- Digging tools, trays/pans/buckets with soil debris
- Samples of soil from their property in areas similar to questioned samples

Collection from Vehicle

- Carpet, pedals, doorways, doorjambs
- Tires

Scene Sample Method of Collection Options, Unknown Source

Method

- Scooping/picking, vacuum, whole item collection (most common). Make all attempts to keep soil intact.
- Tape lifting not recommended due to adhesive, can impact soil analysis
- Swab/wipe with polyurethane swab rather than cotton, preferred with soil samples
- One sample per site on body before transport
- One sample from body bag interior after transport

Comparison Samples of Soil Collection (Known Source)

Scooping

OPTION: SAMPLE FROM TOPSOIL

- Scoop with clean fingerprint card, cleaned shovel or gloved hand
- Only go down to needed depth—same as tread or weapon placement depending upon scene sample
- Collect in shallow plastic or glass jar
- Air-dry before storage within 24 hours
- Don't separate chunks/debris, leave as collected

Vacuum

OPTION: VACUUM CARPET/SEATING/CLOTHING/FLOORING

- Remove forensic filters for soil collection as the fine powder will clog filters

- Vacuum area of interest
- Package filter in envelope, allow to air dry

Whole Item Collection

OPTION: HAIR WITH SOIL—HUMAN/ANIMAL, LIVE/DECEASED
- Cut the hair with soil deposit
- Package hair/soil as 1 item
- Handle with care

OPTION: BODY WITH SOIL—HUMAN/ANIMAL, LIVE/DECEASED
- Swab the area of interest with polyurethane rather than cotton, if possible

OPTION: SOIL FROM LIVE SUBJECT—WITH SOIL ON CLOTHING/SHOES
- Have subject stand on new butcher paper
- Remove clothing with soil deposit OR remove soil deposit from clothing
- Pant cuffs, shoe edges, collar, seams
- Slowly fold butcher paper in on itself and book paper inside an envelope
- Collect sample from scene for comparison

OPTION: FLOOR MATS WITH SOIL DEPOSIT
- Collect/wrap entire floor mat with butcher paper, keep flat if possible

OPTION: SOIL CLUMPS SAMPLE
- Collect from wheel wells, undercarriage, floor mats, truck beds
- Don't break clump, can wrap clumps in butcher paper prior to packaging

OPTION: SOIL OFF FOOTWEAR/TIRE MARK CASTING
- Place whole item in box/butcher paper for transport
- Collect sample from subject for comparison

Burial Site Soil Samples

- If soil samples with blood are collected, also collect soil sample with no visible biological matter
- Consider rough sketch with letter designators/measurements of each layer sample site
- Consider grid system top to bottom
- Samples should include layers of soil for burial, sample from body, sample from container body is in, if applicable

Option: Samples from Layers of Soil (Burial Scene)

- Photograph sequence for dig
- Collect sample from each layer/change in dirt
- Avoid samples with body fluids
- Mark depth collected on each container
- Store in rigid container
- Allow to air dry prior to sealing (upon arrival back from scene)

Methods of Trace Evidence Collection *(How to Collect It)*

- Block all air drafts if possible during collection to prevent contamination and loss
- Glassine envelopes do not carry a static charge and are great for trace evidence collection
- Trace evidence collection from bodies should be done on scene prior to transport or placement inside a body bag
- Bodies that have a white sheet placed on them prior to your arrival should have the sheet collected (slowly fold in on self) or sent to morgue with body to retain the trace evidence
  1. Picking (hands or tweezers)
  2. Cutting
  3. Adhesive lifting
  4. Scraping
  5. Scooping
  6. Vacuum

Picking

Option: Using Sterile Toothpick/Collection Pick/Swab Gently Move across Area of Sample Knocking Off Loose Material

- Consider placing glassine paper/envelope below area of sample so the sample has a controlled fall to the collection medium
- If single use collection medium, retain those tweezers or pick as well

Option: Picking up Item with Gloved Hands, Tweezers, Forceps

- Tweezers should be flat edge, not angled to a point for more secure grip on items
- Tweezers must be cleaned with bleach wipes/bleach solution/alcohol wipes between collections

Cutting

- Using clean or new blade, cut small piece of object for collection—pocketknife, razorblade, scalpel blade

Cutting Options

Option: Soft Porous Items

- Cut area around stain almost to completion allowing a 1–2 inch barrier around stain
- On front and back side of cutting add directional arrow
- Complete cutting around stain (retain whole)—can wrap in butcher paper/glassine envelope
- Cut the comparison sample near area of stain—directional arrow not needed

Option: Metal/Wood Items

- Keyhole saw 1 inch blade will give sample size of quarter which is the minimum sample size needed
- Good for paint sample off vehicle, wood sample from structure

Comparison Samples

- Collect in the same manner from other section of metal/wood item
- Example: Section of mattress near stain but not stained, section of vehicle near paint transfer but didn't get any transfer, section of wood near blood stain but not stained

Adhesive Lifting

- BAD for paint/soil collection due to adhesive (can be used if needed)
- GOOD for hair/skin cells/fibers/powder

Lifting Options

- GSR stubs
- Silicone casting
- Tape
- Adhesive paper
- Post-it notes
- Lint roller
- Gel lifters

GSR Stubs

Good for—Small Areas, Hair/Fiber

- Residue from airbag, 5 hours or less
- Residue from gunfire, 4 hours or less
- Fibers/hair/feather, sample size 5 strands or less
- Granules

Control Sample

- Retain unused GSR stub if control sample needed

Stub Method

- Apply singular stub to each area, press and repeat until full coverage of desired area
- Small sample area recommended (set of hands, singular sweatshirt, seating area of vehicle, set of gloves)

Silicone Casting/Flexible Casting

Good for

- small sample area—hairs/fibers
- clear or white recommended, not for use on fabrics/textiles

Control Sample

- Sample of unused AccuTrans or mixed Mikrosil from tubes used for sample collection

AccuTrans

- No hand mixing, use extruder gun with spreading tip
- Sets in about 4 minutes at 68°F/20°C
- AccuTrans Ice—use range −10°F/23.3°C to 10°F/−12°C, sets in 8 minutes

Accutrans Collection

1. Photograph with/without scale prior to this point
2. Use tip spreader or tongue depressor to even out coverage, gentle pressure to remove air bubbles
3. Start outside mark and move inward
4. Place directional arrow and item # on back before lifting
5. Take photograph of defects with casting material/markings
6. Gently remove from defect
7. Package all lifts separately or adhere to fingerprint card
8. Can distort each other by sticking

Mikrosil

- Hand mixing required
- Normal conditions set in 5 minutes
- Works below freezing—sets in 15 minutes

Mikrosil Collection

1. Photograph with/without scale prior to this point
2. Mix casting materials—even length lines of both materials—approximately 4 inch length each
3. Brown recommended for tool marks
4. Spread evenly with gentle pressure across tool mark, beginning on exterior, fill in gaps with wooden tongue depressor
5. Leave depressor stuck to back when done—won't distort, use as handle/marker
6. Mark with directional arrow before removing with ball point pen
7. Package all lifts separately in envelope OR adhere to fingerprint card and place in envelope

Tape Lift—*Large Sample Size Collection*

Types of Tape

- Masking, packing, scotch, fingerprint tape, painters tape (least recommended)
- Recommended to discard first strip of tape

Packaging

- Write on all final packaging before placing lifts inside
- Place in a glassine envelope, wrap in paper, plastic page protector, plastic bag with airflow cut, or place in envelope directly

Control Sample

- Piece of tape from the roll used for sample collection

Recommended Sample Area

- Vehicle—1 tape/sample per quadrant—driver, passenger, rear driver, and so on
- Bed with bedding/pillows—1 tape/sample for bed/pillows/blankets
- Couch—1 tape/sample for couch/pillows
- Collected items from bed to be processed at lab—1 tape/sample per item collected

Tape Formation Options

Option: Tape Loop

- Wrap tape around 4 fingers, sticky side out and adhere to self, creating a loop shape

- With hand inside loop, press tape against surface repeating until entire area needed has had contact with tape, turning tape if needed
- Leaving on hand, place entire piece of tape inside plastic bag/in sheet protector

Option: Single Tape Strip

- Cut/tear single strip of tape for use
- Place on surface, press down for contact, repeat until entire area needed has had contact with tape
- Place tape sticky side down in sheet protector or cut open plastic bag

Option: Multiple Tape Strips Overlapped

- Cut multiple strips of tape
- Lay across area until covered creating a tape blanket (can number strips)
- Overlap tape on edges to create 1 big blanket of tape
- Ensure entire area has contact with tape, PUSH IT DOWN
- Draw orientation arrow prior to removal, photograph recommended
- Remove tape blanket, place on sheet of plastic
- Ensure all sticky portions of tape are adhered to a non-stick surface

Option: Hinged Tape

- Write needed information on attached label and packaging
- Open hinge and remove backing to allow adhesive to be exposed
- Press and repeat on surface of choice and close when complete
- Place in envelope and seal

Adhesive Paper/2D Impression Paper

Method

- Gently adhere to surface
- Rub back gently to ensure complete coverage
- Repeat for all desired coverage area
- Place in sheet protector or in plastic bag

Control Sample

- Piece of adhesive paper from batch used for sample collection (small cut piece is okay)

Lint Roller/Sticky Roller

- Use single or multiple sheets per area depending on substrate and scene needs

Roller Option: Single Use Lint Rollers

- Store clean and in bags until use, use for all samples in scene, book remaining roller with evidence

Roller Option: Re-useable Lint Roller

- Store in sealable plastic bag between uses, discard top sheet and use next sheet

Style Option: Can Repeat with New Papers Until Desired Area Returns Clean Pass of Roller

- Book all collected sheets as 1 sample for specific area

Style Option: Can Use 1 Sheet of Paper Per Section

CONTROL SAMPLE

- Piece of adhesive paper from roller used for sample collection (small cut piece is okay)
- If entire roller is booked, no control sample is needed

Post-It Note Paper

- Write on final packaging prior to placing Post-it inside
- Use Post-it from clean pad (multiple of needed)
- Press and raise until entire area is covered

Control Sample

- Post-it (unused) from pad used for sample collection

Gel Lifter

- Apply small piece of tape over small edges covering plastic cover and backing of gel lifter to avoid complete separation
- Remove gel lifter cover without breaking tape, allow to sit 60 seconds for stretch to return to normal
- Apply gel lifter to area in question, pressing/removing as much as needed, repeat until entire area covered
- Reattach gel lifter cover
- Label information on backside of lifter—area applied to, case number, collector/ID, date, time of collection, no orientation arrow needed
- Place in large envelope or tall paper bag, optional to wrap in butcher paper

Control Sample

- Piece of gel lifter (small cut piece is okay) from same manufacturer (individually packaged)

Scraping

- Always use new OR cleaned blade for sharp scraping—pocketknife OR dull butter knife, scalpel, razor blade
- Only use if no other option, may not be needed
- Can use plastic scraping tool/spatula for dull scraping—commonly used for putty, wax, residues, or unknown substance collection
- SAMPLE SIZE: Minimum of quarter size, or 1 × 1 inches
- Okay if plastic/metal/wood/drywall is attached, can be separated in laboratory during analysis
- SAMPLE LOCATION suggestions: All places of impact/transfer
- COMPARISON SAMPLE locations: Each quadrant and/or each possible source of transfer

Method

Option: For Sharp Scraping Collection

- Use scalpel/razor blade/knife
- Place glassine envelope/butcher paper below sample to grab what falls
- Scrape/repeat surface repeatedly to collect paint off surface
- Repeat until base metal reached AND sample size is at least size of quarter/1 inch
- Place all in petri dish with lid, plastic tub with lid, glassine envelope, fold in paper/place in envelope

Option: For Dull Scraping Collection

- Using dull rubber/plastic spatula or wooden tongue depressor, slowly scrape item of interest and place in applicable container
- If single use spatula, package in glassine envelope and book with sample

Scooping

- Can use clean gloves/shovel/trowel/fingerprint card/lid/tweezers/tongue depressor
- Wipe clean before/after each collection

- GOOD FOR—soil, unknown powders, fire pit contents, gelatinous substances

Control Sample

- Depending upon your method, retain an unused sample from the same batch

Vacuum

Good for

- Collecting hairs/fibers from small surfaces (shirt/hoodie, pillow, car seat) and large surfaces (floor, vehicle trunk)
- Use single use filters
- Retain and submit entire sample after collection (don't pick out pieces and throw away rest)

Control Sample

- Consider retaining sample of unused filter as control

Method

- Change filter and clean collection receptacle
- Vacuum area in question methodically and slowly
- Empty entire collection with filter in glassine envelope or plastic bag

Cases to Consider for Trace Evidence

- During the scene processing of the murder of Nicole Simpson, CSIs were viewed on video cleaning their tweezers with soiled gloves, as well as dropping swabs of DNA samples which later impacted the value of the evidence.
- During the scene processing of juveniles James M. Moore, Steven Branch, and Christopher Byers in a wooded area, a hair belonging to a known party was collected from a nearby tree. Though this hair was not afforded adequate value in the court, it may still be integral in the case outcome and required thorough CSI searching to locate.

Animal Evidence

- 1999: When John Helble was murdered the suspect was found with a gun box containing the murder weapon and dog hair from the missing dog of the victim. Samples were collected from the scene for comparison.

- 1994: After Shirley Duguay was murdered her previous spouse was linked by a bag of clothing containing her blood and his cat's hair.

Trace Evidence Played a Key Role in the Following Cases

- 2012: Betty Wheeler was hit and killed by a vehicle, leaving behind a small piece of the front grill. The vehicle was identified by the appearance of the piece and when the search warrant was served for the truck it was still missing the piece of the grill from the accident. A comparison was conducted, and it was matched to the vehicle with fracture matches.
- 2009: Chris Coleman was staging his family's homicide scene and spray-painted writing on the interior residence wall which also deposited onto the pictures hanging. Paint was scraped off a picture from the wall and detectives determined a color and brand of spray paint from analysis.
- 2003: Paint from a Green River killer case was re-examined and matched from transfer to his victim utilizing Microtrace.
- 2000: Giuseppina Martorana was shot and killed in her driveway during a robbery. Her husband followed the suspect and hit their vehicle with his vehicle causing a paint transfer which was later matched. When the suspects were located one of them had fibers matching the stolen vehicle on his clothing.
- 1996: John Joubert was executed for the murder of 3 boys during the 1980s. After an eyewitness led detectives to him he was found in possession of a rope (having an abnormal appearance) that matched the victim's bindings. This led to a search of his vehicle which contained hair matching one of his victims.
- 1986: Betty Wolsieffer was murdered in her home. Fibers from her husband's blue jeans were found under her fingernails and were used to convict him for her murder, while he maintained his innocence.
- 1986: When Cara Knott was murdered by her assailant (a highway patrol officer) and her body dumped in bushes over the side of a cliff, fibers matching his uniform and rope were found on her body and neck.
- 1985: Tonya McKinley was sexually assaulted, murdered, and dumped in a parking lot. A cigarette butt was discarded at the scene and was collected, with a match identified in 2023.
- 1984: Serial killer Bobby Joe Long left red carpet fibers on multiple victims. His only surviving victim was able to lead authorities to him and the carpet fibers helped seal his fate. Long was executed in 2019.
- 1979–1981: Atlanta child murders: Multiple victims retained fibers from the suspect's carpet.

Notes

1 Geberth, Vernon. *Practical Homicide Investigation: Tactics, Procedures and Forensic Techniques*. CRC Press, 1996.

2 Shrivastava, Priya, V. K. Jain and Suman Nagpal. "Gunshot Residue Detection Technologies-a Review." *Egyptian Journal of Forensic Sciences*, 2021.

3 Rynearson, Joseph M. *Evidence and Crime Scene Reconstruction*, 7th ed. 2015.

4 Organization of Scientific Area Committees for Forensic Science (OSAC) (2020) *Trace Materials Crime Scene Investigation Guide* (NIST.GOV).

5 American Society for Testing & Materials (2023) *ASTM E1610-18—Standard Guide for Forensic Paint Analysis and Comparison.*

6 American Society for Testing & Materials (2019) *ASTM E3272-23—Standard Guide for Collection of Soils and Other Geological Evidence for Criminal Forensic Applications.*

7 Organization of Scientific Area Committees for Forensic Science (OSAC) (2020) *Trace Materials Crime Scene Investigation Guide* (NIST.GOV).

DNA Evidence Collection

21

DNA can appear in various forms and locations at a crime scene, and each location requires specific methods for collection. DNA is transient and can vanish in an instant or be inadvertently transferred to other objects, people, or places within the scene. This makes it crucial for CSIs to identify and handle it properly, as improper collection or oversight can result in its destruction or loss. For example, it is easy enough to keep a supply of butcher paper in the vehicle to set items on, or to change gloves before picking up each item you are processing. Many items of evidence collected for DNA on crime scenes around the world were done in the years prior to the validation of DNA's value. Many of the samples contained comparison samples and control samples which later helped validate the results. It was collected because the CSI knew it should be: Follow your intuition and do what you know the scene requires.

Types of DNA Found on Scene

- Blood
- Contact DNA—area touched by a person that contains sweats, oils, anywhere touched
- Ear/nose secretions—sneezing releases up to 3,000 cells, nasal secretions contain blood and skin cells
- Fecal matter
- Hair—every day we shed 40–100 hairs
- Saliva
- Semen
- Sweat—armpits sweat 30 times more than normal when under stress, suspects have been known to take off hoodies or gloves to lower their body heat
- Tears—contain epithelial cells
- Tissue—every minute we shed enough skin to cover a football field
- Urine
- More than 1 suspect at a scene is quite common—be generous with processing and sample collection

DOI: 10.4324/9781003503897-22

Blood DNA

Possible Sources on Scene

- Blood pools, wipes, spatter sources all could transfer on items, wet or dry, new, or old—check all patterns and locations as the suspect often bleeds in addition to the victim within the scene
- Ceilings, along joints and inside texture
- Ear and nasal secretions—snot or used tissue
- Firearms—look inside barrel, cracks, grip edges
- Flip the blinds and curtains to check the other side, check cords/rods
- Fly spots and bug/rodent footprints and trails
- Projectiles/weapons that travel through or into body
- Shrine items/religious artifacts
- Sinks/drains/drain traps/faucets/showers/tubs/laundry machines
- Snow
- Tissue paper and toilet paper used as tissue (look inside the tube)
- Tools—inside scratches, grooves, edges, under grips
- Urine and fecal matter
- Where items meet: Baseboard meets floor/wall, outlet covers/light switches/covers, where couch/furniture meets wall, behind doors

Blood Collection—See Collection Methods Section below for Instructions

- Liquid blood can remain in standing water for considerable time and remain collectable with swabs/gauze
- Blood in snow can be collected in a container with gauze/cotton at the bottom for it to melt into, then air-dry the gauze/cotton.[1] Eliminate as much white snow as possible to reduce watering the sample down.
- Fill out packaging prior to collection
- Appearance of blood
  - Colorless, red, brown, green, orange—many variables affect the appearance of blood, don't discount on color alone
  - When dry it will flake/chip—will not remain thick/sticky or liquid like sauces/condiments/juices
- Photograph all stains prior to collection
  - If it's hard to explain exact location of item/area swabbed, photo area with swab (area on gun or something that you can't mark with evidence marker)

Presumptive Tests for Blood

- Should be completed ON scene but not IN the scene. Stay at your vehicle or step outside the tape for blood control testing.

- Blood DNA can still be beneficial even after washing/cleaning
- Blue Star and Luminol use—DNA CAN be collected after use for several hours without degradation but always be mindful that blood enhancement CAN affect the DNA value

Results

- False positives are possible, ALWAYS get laboratory confirmation
- Positive result—indicates blood MAY be present but still needs laboratory confirmation
- False positive—requires additional testing/collection
- False negative—can result in missed evidence collection

Chemical Controls

- Photographs of results optional

Positive Control—Should Have Appropriate Color Change You Expect

- Collect the known blood sample from your PREPARED BLOOD CARD you brought with you
- Apply chosen chemical to sample
- Verify appropriate results

Negative Control—Should Have No Color Change

- Apply 1 drop chosen chemical to sample with no blood/contaminants
- Verify appropriate results

Comparison Sample

- When collecting a sample for comparison of the substrate, swab/cut area that is also treated with chemical but showed no reaction to account for all variables

Tests

Benzidine *(Alder Test)*

- Blue results are positive
- Results must be photographed immediately as they will fade
- Not recommended for use on scene due to carcinogenic properties, must be used in well-ventilated area

Hemastix

- Testing strips, blue/green color change of positive
- Recommended method for wildlife crime testing
- False positives—tomato, bleach, potato, rust, avian uric acid, red onion, saliva

Hematrace

- Can test for the presence of human DNA
- False positive: Some animal blood

HEMIDENT *(McPhail's Reagent)*

- Easy to use on scene, easy to interpret results, appear within seconds
- Positive reaction will fluoresce blue, will not distinguish between human and animal
- Photograph results before fading, will last over 15 minutes
- False positives—semen, red onion

Hexagon OBTI

- Test tells you if blood is human's
- Testing easy to read, easy to collect—results in 2–3 minutes

Leucomalachite Green (LMG)

- Turns blue/green with a positive result, easy to read and identify results
- Results must be photographed immediately because they fade

Orthotolidine *(Kohn and O'Kelly Test)*

- Blue or yellow color changes if positive results, no color changes if negative
- Less sensitive than TMB but safer than Benzidine
- False positives—fruit, vegetables, metal, milk, body fluids/puss

Phenolphthalein Test *(Kastle Meyer)*

- Harder to use on scene due to application method
- Reacts with heme in blood
- Pink color change for positive results
- More sensitive than Hemastix
- Sunlight can ruin chemical formula, store in brown bottles

- False positives—rust, horseradish, potato, tomato, red onion, turmeric, cobalt, manganese, iron, lead, semen, saliva, puss, bleach, Oxiclean brand cleaning products
- False negatives—blood deposited on leather

Tetramethylbenzidine *(TMB)*

- Immediate dark blue color change for positive results
- Enhancement reagent as well as presumptive testing
- Detects peroxidase activity
- Safe to use on skin/bodies
- Results should be photographed immediately since they will fade
- Use in a well-ventilated area
- False positives—horseradish, garlic, green grapes, typing paper, saliva, coriander, tomato, onion, beet, multiple fruits

Contact DNA *(Touch DNA, Trace DNA)*

- Potentially any item touched by the skin can leave contact DNA
- DNA can be collected after fingerprinting if using clean powder/equipment
- If the equipment is dirty, DNA can still be analyzed but may contain additional profiles from transfer
- Fill out packaging prior to collection

Possible Sources on Scene

Exterior

- Cameras
- Doorbells
- Doorknobs/handles
- Light bulbs/lighting equipment
- Window/frames/screens

Interior

- Anything touched/dropped/moved with skin contact
- Clothing/bedding
- Cups, bottles, exterior of bottle caps, dishes, silverware
- Curtain rods/cords
- Decedent body—collect BEFORE placing in body bag
    - swab throat/chest/hands/knuckles if physical violence possible (consider GSR collection as well)
    - swab clothing, pockets/pocket lining, gloves
    - swab ligatures/restraints

- Doorknobs/window handles, shutters/handles, locks/knobs/keys/levers
- Drawer handles/sink handles
- Eyeglasses, used contact lenses, sunglasses
- Faucets
- Fingernails/clippings/manicure tools
- Firearms
- Fuse panel door/switches
- Hat—interior ring contains substantial amounts of sweat DNA
- Keypad buttons—door alarms, door pad codes, vehicle door code, safe code pad
- Keypad/switches for AC/heating system
- Keys/key fobs/garage door openers
- Ligatures/restraints
- Perspiration found on most clothing items/hats—stress causes heavier perspiration
- Plug ends, electrical cords, phone chargers
- Purse—handle/lock/clasp
- Q-Tips, tissue, anything in bathroom trash can likely
- Refrigerator handles if food/drink obtained
- Shoes, inside and bottom of sole
    - Contact DNA can be found/transferred/carried on the sole of a shoe up to 400 steps
    - Sweat DNA can be found on the interior shoe
- Shrines/religious artifacts
- Switches/pull cords for lights or fans
- Tape/ligature
- Tears—contain epithelial cells
- Wallet—exterior side flaps/edges/stitching and interior edges
- Weapons/tools
- Your own gloves if you opened doors/windows—book your gloves as you remove them, inside out
- What was touched during crime, what was moved, where would you touch to move where they moved?

Fecal Matter DNA

Facts to Consider regarding Collection

- Has good likelihood of blood and skin cells
- Always requires frozen storage until submitted to the lab
- Can be diaper collection, clothing collection, tissue, or sample swab collection

- Can swab exterior of a solid "log" shaped fecal sample or visible blood
- Fecal matter often left behind in burglary crimes by suspects trying to make a statement, assault scenes when suspects receive injuries and sexual assault crimes
- Very few laboratories will process due to high biohazard
  - more hazardous than any other biological substance
  - can contain *E. coli*, polio, dysentery, cholera, parasites, viruses
  - can harbor pathogens for weeks, still spreadable when touched
- Weigh the pros and cons for each case involving fecal matter as it poses a health hazard
- Fill out packaging prior to collection

Saliva DNA

Possible Sources

- Bite marks on any surface
- Chapstick, lipstick, toothbrushes, dental pick, anything put in mouth
- Cigarette/cigar/joint/smoking pipe/filters—partial smoked or butts
- Drink/food container eaten off during crime (partial fruit, food from refrigerator)
- Face mask, ski mask, Halloween mask, facial coverings, COVID mask
- Licked stamps, envelopes
- Liquid candy applicator
- Locations of spit/dribble
- Mouth of bottles/cans/cups/water bottles
- Open condiment packets—people open with their mouth—(especially if driving and eating at the same time)
- Shrines/religious artifacts
- Silverware eaten with during crime
- Sunflower seed shells—likely spit out of mouth
- Tissue paper, toilet paper
- Toothpicks, lollipop/ice cream sticks, sucker sticks, popsicle sticks
- Torn fingernails—likely spit out of mouth if stuck to object
- Tape/ligature torn/held with mouth
- Vape pens mouthpiece/hookah mouthpiece

Suggestions about Saliva Collection—See Collection Methods Section below for Instructions

- If the victim was spit upon by the suspect—collect the suspect spit sample AND a buccal sample from the victim

- Saliva collection from containers (mouth of can/bottle/cup)—swab for saliva PRIOR to dumping contents or liquid sample collection
- If buccal swabs cannot be collected for comparison, collect toothbrushes or clothing known to be worn solely by the individual needing to provide buccal swab sample
- Fill out packaging prior to collection

Buccal Swab Collection

- Collect from suspects/victims for elimination/comparison
- Human, canine, feline samples collected the same

Method

- Use 2 swabs simultaneously
- Swab the interior of both cheeks with both swabs at the same time—5–10 seconds collection time
- If you can see the swab pushing the cheek from the outside, it is hard enough for collection
- Package all buccal swab samples separately/store temperature controlled

Presumptive Tests for Saliva—Recommend Photographing Results

Phadebas

- Tests for presence of amylase (enzyme present in saliva and other body fluids)
- Positive result will turn blue on paper
- False positives—semen, urine, feces

Saligae

- Tests for presence of amylase
- Positive results turn yellow, results in approximately 10 minutes
- Test is sensitive and will respond to diluted samples
- Positive reaction—liquid will turn yellow
- False positive for pigs, rodents, human urine/feces

Immunochromatographic Strip Tests

- Tests for presence of amylase
- Marking on test kit will tell you test results
- Allow 5–15 minutes for processing

Semen DNA

Facts about Semen

- Average amount of male ejaculate 3.5 ml each time
- Lifespan—sperm can really last, don't discount samples just because it has been a while
  - Intact sperm in vagina can last 5 hours
  - Sperm heads in vagina can last 7 days
  - Sperm inside rectum can last 18 hours
  - Sperm in the mouth can last 5 hours
  - Survival of sperm depends on variables such as the surface, recent activities, and the environment
- Sterile semen can still lead to a DNA match
  - 85% of males secrete blood group factors in their seminal fluid
- Pre-ejaculate fluid can still lead to a DNA match
  - Can contain traces of semen, blood, and skin cells
  - Can contain traces of Acid Phosphatase
  - Collect fluids even when victim does not report ejaculation during assault

Possible Sources on Scene

- Bedding/clothing/towels/underclothing/bedsheets—semen continues to travel after deposit and heads toward a seam
- Touched items—sperm on hands can leave semen fingerprints on towel/paper towel/napkin

Appearance

Dry

- Clear to off white to yellow in color
- Brittle in texture
- Turns yellow/brittle with age

Wet

- Can be colorless liquid in small amounts
- Cream to cottage cheese texture in large amounts
- Clear to white/off white color or could just appear as wet spot-on clothing
- Minimal amounts may not be visible to naked eye

Searching for Semen with ALS

ALS Response

- Not all semen reacts with ALS
- Factors that cause reaction failure: Fabric treatments, heat, humidity, mold
- Fresh semen often does NOT fluoresce, aged semen glows brighter as it ages
- Semen on hands can leave fingerprints with seminal/vaginal fluid and fingerprints will glow with ALS

Wavelengths

- 260–400 nm with clear filter
- 420–450 nm with orange goggles—fluoresces white
- 532 nm with orange goggles—fluoresces yellow/green

Presumptive Testing for Semen

RSID Semen Detection Kit, Sirchie

- No false positives, no cross reactivity
- Tests for human semen
- For use in field

Acid Phosphatase Test (Walker Test)

- Color can be impacted by age of stain
- Dark blue/purple color result will occur in less than 1 minute
- Positive for mammal/human
- Reaction diminished due to age and storage conditions
- False positives: Vaginal secretions, contraceptive creams, fungi, vegetables

Collection

Call your processing laboratory to find out:

- What type of DNA samples will they accept? Contact DNA? Homicides only?
- How do they want it packaged/marked? Separate or together?
- Storage temperature requirements
- Packaging options—individual boxes, glassine envelope, envelope?

Documentation—*All DNA/Trace Samples Must Have the Following Documentation*

- Time/date of collection
- Name/ID of collector
- Case #, item # (if applicable)
- Description of sample and collection location
- Document if water was added for sample collection or no water was used (because sample was wet)

Control Samples/Comparison Samples

- Comparison samples allow you to compare the results to the substrate a sample is on
- Control samples can validate/refute the sample results
- Substrate control samples confirm the chemical content of the item being sampled
- Collection control samples confirm the presence of or lack of DNA on the medium for collection
- Water control samples confirm the chemical composition of the added liquid to the sample

Method Instructions

Water for Dry Sample Collection

- 1–2 drops for sample ONLY
- Too much water—will wick into the stick and remain there, losing sample unless the stick gets analyzed
- Too little water—dry sample will not stick to swab
- Distilled water/sterile water only—NOT tap water—may have chemical contaminants that will impact DNA
- Can use individual ampules OR refillable containers
- Allow water to free fall onto surface—don't touch water dispenser to swab as the dispenser is then considered contaminated

Swab

Equipment Options: Sterile and/or DNA-Free Absorbent Material

- Polyurethane foam swabs or Nylon flocked swabs (for cartridge cases/small items)
- Cotton swabs, cotton gauze, cotton pads, #8 cotton thread
- Toothpick
- Filter paper/coffee filter

- Acrilan cloth
- Can purchase swabs treated with ethylene oxide to prevent any manufacturing contamination[2]

Swab Option: 2 Swab Collection

- Use 2 simultaneous swabs/pads/cloth for each sample
- 1–2 drops of water per swab
- Package/store as 1 sample

Swab Option: 1 Swab Collection

- Wet 1 swab/pad/cloth with 1–2 drops of water
- Swab the area of interest
- Package individually

Swab Option: Wet/Dry Swab Method (2 Swabs/Pads Needed)

- Can be used with swabs/gauze/pads/cotton/filter paper

Method

- Wet 1 swab/pad and swab the area of interest as normal, keep swab in other hand
- Take the 1 dry swab/pad and go over the visible wet line where you just swabbed and cover the same area
  - This wet trail leaves a high amount of DNA
  - Swabbing cartridge cases with this method increases chances of getting DNA profiles up to 25%
- Place them together in the same container (box, envelope) for booking
  - They do not need to be separated

Liquid Pool/Stain Sample Collection*: Pool of Liquid (Urine, Blood, Semen, Spit, Unknown Liquid)*

Option: Liquid Blood in Standing Water

- If it's visible, it's collectable (rocks in river, grate in bayou)
- Swabs/gauze/pipette will still absorb sample
- Move quickly and with intention to collect sample

Option: Pipette

- Single use or sterilized only
- Suck up as much sample as possible into pipette
- Transfer to vial/glass jar/test tube/cotton
- If small sample, can retain/dry/book pipette as well as sample

Option: Soak up Liquid

- USE: Cotton pads/gauze pad/cotton swabs/#8 cotton thread/filter paper/coffee filter/toothpick/Acrilan cloth
- Sterile or individually wrapped only
- Absorb generous amount liquid with medium of choice
- No water needed
- Collect a sample from any pools directly beneath body/direct flow from the body
- If questionable pattern, collect sample from NEAR the body

Option: Cutting

- If the liquid sample is on a moveable substrate cut around sample
- Collect whole sample, allow to dry

Drying Samples

- Some agencies prefer to dry swab/gauze samples while on scene which eliminates samples bleeding into packaging but allows for air blown contamination
- OPTION: DRY RACKS
    - Small stands with multiple small holes
    - Place swabs in holes to stand upright
    - Allow sample to air dry prior to packaging
- OPTION: AIR-DRY WITH ENVELOPE
    - Partial fold coin envelope
    - Pierce small hole
    - Prop up swab to dry
    - Mark envelope sample number

Dry Stain Sample Collection

Option: Swab

- USE: Cotton pads/gauze pad/cotton swabs/#8 cotton thread/filter paper/coffee filter/Acrilan cloth/polyurethane foam swabs
- Wet swabs with 1–2 drops water ONLY/wet other medium as needed
- Place item being processed on clean butcher paper
- Use intentional wiping motion, cover area of interest entirely
- Move slowly for maximum absorption
- Move with the grain for maximum sample collection
- Consider comparison sample of item being swabbed

Option: Cutting of Item Containing Stain

- Vehicle seat, carpet, mattress, drywall

- Leaving at least 1 inch around stain, cut out area of interest
- Cut comparison sample of the item or enlarge cutting to include unstained content

Option: Small Whole Item Collection (Clothing, Purse/Wallet, Shoes, Coat/Scarf, Pillow/Pillowcase)

- Lay item on butcher paper
- Wrap in a way it is not touching anything but paper (cover completely before folding)
- Dry before submission to property room
- Butcher paper needs to be retained with submitted item

Option: Large Whole Item Collection (Chair, Mattress, Nightstand, Bicycle)

- Wrap with butcher paper
- If it is too large, preserve stain area by taping butcher paper to portion of concern only

Option: Tape Lift

- Skin cells will adhere to tape with other trace items
- Does not require a substrate control sample from item surface
- Blank tape sample could be retained for tape control
- Place in plastic bag, glassine envelope, or plastic page cover
- Method: Using clean fingerprint tape or other designated tape, touch adhesive side to surface as if collecting hair/fibers

Option: Picking

- Nail scrapings—nail scrapings of area directly below/at nailbed collected at autopsy/sexual assault examination.
- Nail clippings—using new pair of nail clippers cut the nail to the quick collecting the nail and skin below of decedent. Place nails from each hand separately, book the nail clippers with the sample.

Packaging for DNA Samples

OPTION: Place Back in Swab Sleeve

- Can dry in sleeve
- Don't close/seal end of sleeve
- Place sleeves in envelope for storage

OPTION: Place Swabs/Gauze in Coin Envelope

- Allow to dry in coin envelope
- Place coin envelope inside 6 × 9 envelope for storage

OPTION: Boxes

- Place swabs in boxes to dry
- Place box in 6 × 9 envelope for storage

OPTION: Glassine Envelope

- Place swabs/gauze in glassine envelope
- Place glassine envelope in 6 × 9 envelope for storage

OPTION: Cuttings

- Wrap sample in butcher paper or place in glassine envelope
- Place wrapped items in envelope or bag for storage
- Place item in arson can

Cases to Consider regarding DNA

- Contact DNA was transferred by medical equipment resulting in the DNA of Lukis Anderson being found under the fingernails during the autopsy of Raveesh Kumra. Anderson was initially charged and later released and exonerated.

Control Swabs Have Been Highly Beneficial during the Investigation of Many Cases

- 2009: A factory worker in Europe was ruled out as a new serial killer due to the use of control samples taken from crime scenes, and it was determined to be contamination during the manufacturing process.
- 2007: During the scene processing of Meredith Kercher blood swabs were being collected without a glove change in between samples with no control samples taken, casting doubt during trial.
- 2005: Halbach murder investigation—a supervisor contaminated swabs by talking without a mask near where swabbing was being completed by another CSI, highlighting the need to be mindful.

Many Suspects Leave DNA behind That Is Collected and Analyzed to Include the Following

- 2021: Burglary in Harris County Texas—suspect left behind urine leading to his arrest.

- 2018: At the murder scene of Steven Pitt, DNA was collected and analyzed off a cartridge case fired on scene. Within days they had a match to the suspect; unfortunately, several more people died in the meantime.
- 2016: Murder of Vanessa Marcotte—suspect left DNA under Marcotte's fingernails leading to his arrest.
- 2015: Murder of Amy, Savvas and Philip Savopoulos, and Veralicia Figueroa—suspect left behind partial pizza and box.
- 2012: Murder of Raveesh Kumra—one of the suspects left DNA behind inside gloves laying in soapy water leading to his arrest.
- 2005: BTK Dennis Rader left behind multiple DNA samples including semen, leading to his arrest.
- 2002: Murder of Kevin Jackson—Jackson was stabbed in the head with a screwdriver and when the suspect was arrested blood was in the joints of the handle of the screwdriver.
- 2001: Murder of Raquel Carter—suspect left urine on Carter's clothing leading to his arrest.
- 2001: Murder of Kevin Butler—suspect left his blood on the claws and beak of Butler's cockatoo leading to identification.
- 1995: Murder of Krystal Beslanowitch—suspect left DNA on granite rocks and cigarette butts.
- 1990s: Donna Perry left DNA under the fingernails of her (unnamed) victims.
- 1989: Murder of K. Martin—the suspect left behind DNA samples.
- 1987: Murder of Jay Cook and Tonya Van Cuylenborg—the suspect left behind several DNA samples.
- 1985: Murder of Tonya McKinly—the suspect left behind cigarette butts with DNA.
- 1977: Murder of Christine Eadie and Helen Scott—a ligature with knots retained the DNA of both suspects.
- 1974–2005: BTK Dennis Rader left a string of DNA at multiple crime scenes to include semen and was not identified until 2005.
- 1971: Murder of Rita Curran—the suspect left behind cigarette butts with DNA providing a match.

Several Suspects Have Been Identified by Having Their DNA Collected from Food without Their Knowledge

- Eugene Gligor 2024—water bottle at airport
- Rex Heuermann 2023—pizza crust
- Robert Plympton 2021—chewing gum
- Jerry Westrom 2019—used napkin
- Joseph James DeAngelo 2018—contact DNA from his vehicle and used tissue

- William Talbott 2018—used cup
- Raymond Rowe 2018—water bottle and chewing gum
- Chanel Lewis 2016—pizza crust
- Grim Sleeper Lonnie Franklin 2010—pizza crust

Notes

1 *FBI Handbook of Crime Scene Forensics*. Skyhorse Publishing, 2008.
2 Shaw, Kirsty, et al. "Comparison of the Effects of Sterilisation Techniques on Subsequent DNA Profiling." *International Journal of Legal Medicine*, vol. 122, 2008, pp. 29–33.

Fingerprint Evidence

22

Fingerprints play a crucial role in crime scene investigations and are routinely discovered at various types of crime scenes. The primary value of fingerprints lies in their ability to generate a list of suspects for further investigation and to corroborate or refute statements. However, the challenge lies in locating these prints and successfully retrieving them. Fingerprinting necessitates the development of techniques and an understanding of different substrates and development options, including the use of powders and chemicals. Knowledge can also tell you when NOT to mess with fingerprints, as was determined when fingerprints left in dew were photographed resulting in a match.[1] Despite practice, certain items, such as firearms, present inherent difficulties due to their rough surfaces and frequent handling. Significant technological advancements, such as digital scanners and innovative powders, have been made to assist investigators.

Types of Fingerprints

Etched Prints

- Oxidation can cause permanent fingerprints on metal such as cartridge cases, weapons, statues, and tools. Will need to be photographed rather than lifted.

Inked Print

- Known fingerprint collected with black ink or inkless products or using a mobile live scan device
- Elimination prints should be collected from all parties known to be in the scene

Latent Print

- Fingerprint that requires additional processing or light to be visible, collected, and compared

Patent Print

- Fingerprint that is left behind in the residue of a substance like paint, blood, and powder

 DOI: 10.4324/9781003503897-23

- May need chemical enhancement, can be photographed or lifted on occasion

Plastic Print

- Impression left in soft surface (cheese, clay)
- Can be photographed with macrophotography or cast with silicone casting to lift

Take Away Print—Fingerprint Void

- When a surface is touched it removes the layer of dust and does not leave an oil residue behind
- Dust void—common on furniture tops, exterior vehicles, exterior residence doors, and windows

Searching for Prints

- What did the suspect touch, move, or destroy during the commission of the crime. Search there for fingerprints.
- Always begin with:
    1. Ambient light and naked eye search for patent prints in blood, ink, and so on
    2. Flashlight and naked eye
    3. LED handheld light
    4. ALS to include UV light as sometimes fingerprints can inherently fluoresce or quench under UV light if contaminated with blood
- Try different lighting sources and angles when searching for latent prints, for best results
    - Indirect sunlight is good for visualizing powder results, and direct sunlight can make it harder to see most prints
    - 70° good angle for exterior vehicles
    - 45°–90° good angle for window with powder
    - 45° good for dust prints
- Static lifts can be used for blind lifts in hard-to-reach areas
- Items contaminated with suspected fentanyl should only be fingerprinted while on scene if necessary. Otherwise, you can package and process later during controlled conditions. If done on scene CSI should wear half- or full-faced respirator.

Checklist—Scene Locations to Process for Prints

Exterior Areas

- Gates/fence and handles
- Removed light bulbs

- Light switches
- Screen frames/screens and putty/rubber
- Window/frames and pane dividers
- Broken window pieces on ground
- Broken window frame/lock
- Doors/frames
- Door handles
- Fuse boxes if disturbed

Interior Areas

- Entryways/point of entry if known
- Windows/doors
- Ledge below window/near doors
- Walls
- Light switches
- Plugs
- Lamps
- Removed light bulbs
- Sink faucets and handles
- Toilet handles, toilet seats, top of toilet tank lid
- Decorations: Turned over, knocked down, out of place (moved room to room), picture frames moved
- Look at dust marks—it shows what items were recently moved/picked up/touched
- Furniture that has been moved/used
- Food items can be printed: Smooth fruit and vegetables, wrappers, drink bottles
- Interior refrigerator can be printed if it has been open for a while and condensation is gone
- Batteries inside items
- Phones, flashlights, electric tools
- Floor (for assaults that occur on floor or if suspect fell)
- Areas of damage and tools nearby
- Items along path of travel

Fingerprint Station

- Can gather items to be fingerprinted AFTER first set of photographs taken and set up printing area. If victim is present and alive they can assist you with determining items that have been moved/altered.
- Can minimize amount of damage to scene from processing or items being overlooked/forgotten for processing

Item Collection

- Items can be collected for processing at laboratory in controlled environment. Transport with great care, as valuable prints are often lost at this stage.

Fingerprinting Options

- Consider taking mid-range photographs of developed prints prior to lifting showing placement of hands and actions
- Helpful scene reference—*Latent Fingerprint Processing Techniques Selection and Sequencing Guide.* Chesapeake Bay Division International Association for Identification. www.cbdiai.org/

Bloody Fingerprints/Footprints

- Amido black
- LCV

Bloodstained Non-porous Items

- Amido black
- COA with dye
- LCV
- Powders

Bloodstained Porous Items

- Amido Black
- DAB
- Ninhydrin
- Physical Developer

Cartridge Cases

- Latent processing should be done in laboratory environment
- Etched prints—fingerprints often have reaction imprinting on cartridge or cartridge cases leaving a visible print behind that must be photographed

Curved Surfaces

- Photograph with a panning series for each plane
- Lift with AccuTrans/Mikrosil/Diff lift
- Collect entire item for laboratory processing
- Lift with fingerprint tape in segments: 1–2 inch tape for each lift, lift in small strips right next to each other, repeat until entire print collected

Fire Evidence

- Heat from fire often "fixes" prints and preserves rather than destroys
- Amido Black, LCV, and ninhydrin have all shown to remove soot when processing
- SPR and Physical Developer have both shown to develop latent prints while removing the soot around the prints by processing

Option: SPR Method for Glass or Metal

- Spray thick coverage on item
- Rinse under faucet or with water spray bottle—may require heavy/multiple rinses
- Allow to air dry
- Use multiple successive tape lifts to remove excess soot, discard tape
- Repeat, if necessary, until prints visible
- Photograph results if they don't lift

Option: Rinse Method for Glass or Metal

- Rinse item under running cold water for several minutes
- Can use spray bottle with repeated spray to remove loose soot
- Can gently blot soot to view print on glass
- Photograph resulting prints if they don't lift

Option: Ninhydrin for Paper/Cardboard

- Spray lightly charred documents with ninhydrin
- Will immediately remove loose soot/darkening
- Can spray glass items, less effective though fewer studies have been completed
- Will help remove loose soot
- Rinse, air-dry, photograph results

Option: Silly Putty,[2] AccuTrans

- Apply substrate to glass/cans with soot
- Use blotting motion to remove excess soot exposing prints beneath
- Photograph results

Option: Melamine Foam Pads (Magic Eraser)

- Apply water and pad to area with soot
- Use gently wiping motion to wipe off soot

Firearms Evidence

- Double check with your firearms examiner to see if they have any preferred method as their preference can impact your results

Option: Black powder and lift

Option: Sciluminate Powder Processing

- DO NOT superglue fume
- Apply Sciluminate powder sparingly with feather brush
- Clean off excess powder with separate feather brush, may need additional removal of background powder
- View/photographs with UV light 254 nm

Option: Superglue Fuming with Dye Stain or Black Powder Application

- Ensure firearms are room temperature
- Process with superglue chamber
- View/photograph results if present
- Apply Rhodamine 6G/black powder/bi-chromatic powder
- Lift or photograph results accordingly

Floor (Laminate/Tile/Wood)

- Magnetic powder
- Static lifter if prints are in dust

Food

- Exterior of fruit skin—magnetic powder, black powder, silver powder
- Exterior plastic packaging—superglue and magnetic powder
- Soft food for plastic prints, teeth impressions (cheese, mushrooms, putty)—photographs, AccuTrans, Mikrosil

Frozen Surfaces

- Will smear when frozen, allow to warm to room temperature and dry entirely before processing
- Do not superglue fume until room temperature
- Process according to surface type

Furniture

- Magnetic powder on polished wood/metal
- Black powder on glass tops, smooth trim

High Humidity Items—Condensation

- Will stick to brush and smear, don't powder process when wet
- Will need to introduce to air conditioning to remove condensation
- Transport with care
- If on scene dry prior to transport if possible—close all doors/windows and turn on AC system

Hot Surface/Direct Sun

- Allow hot item to become room temperature before processing: Shield surface from direct sunlight and allow to dry entirely
- Prints can bake onto surface, especially metals and vehicles
- Transport to laboratory if possible for processing
- Huffing to add moisture is a successful technique
- Process according to surface

Leather

- ALS
- Superglue
- Luminescent powder

License Plates

- Black powder or bi-chromatic powder

Metal Surfaces/Items

- Smoke (camphor, masking tape, etc.)
- Superglue
- SPR
- Luminescent powders

Multicolored Surfaces

- Bi-chromatic powder
- SPR
- Sciluminate powder with UV light
- Fluorescent powder with ALS
- Superglue with or without dye

Non-porous Surfaces

- ALS, UV, IR, Laser
- Cyanoacrylate fuming
- Powders

Non-porous Textured

- Cyanoacrylate fuming then powder OR dye stain

Non-porous Smooth

- Powder/brush/lift with tape
- Cyanoacrylate fuming then powder OR dye stain
- SPR if appropriate surface

Oily Surfaces

- ALS
- Superglue
- SPR

Old Fingerprints—Not Holding Powder

- Both methods reintroduce condensation to help powder adhere

Option: Freezer

- Place in freezer long enough to cool surface, then remove from freezer and keep room temperature while printing

Option: Huffing

- Gently release a fair amount of your own hot breath on print causing condensation, allow to sit 5 seconds for some moisture to dissipate, then apply powder
- Has proven successful for many years
- Use only with prints not being processed for DNA

Painted Surface

- Latex paint—porous evidence procedures
- Semi-gloss/enamel paint—non-porous procedures
- Sciluminate powder with UV light all painted surfaces

Paper

- VERY fresh (within 10 hours)—Mag powder
- OLDER prints—ninhydrin
- DFO
- Silver nitrate
- Iodine fuming

Option: Loose Black Powder (No Brush)

- Drop powder on paper and move paper at an angle moving the powder across the surface
- Dump loose powder back in container after all areas coated with powder as needed
- Photograph and/or transport resulting paper
- Glossy paper—magnetic powder, luminescent powder, superglue fuming with black powder, physical developer
- Cardboard—ninhydrin ethanol formula, DFO, silver nitrate, physical developer

Photographs—Developed or Polaroid

- ALS
- Oblique lighting
- Superglue
- Powders (photograph, don't lift)

Plant Material

- Magnetic powder or luminescent powder
- Smooth flat leaves best

Plastic Bags—Trash/Grocery

- Superglue then dye stain or magnetic powder
- Fluorescent powder or luminescent powder if minimal folding/crumpling
- Not recommended during scene processing, transport to laboratory for best results

Records

- Black magnetic powder
- Sciluminate powder

Rocks

- Smooth surface—magnetic powder
- Smooth and NOT dusty—superglue wand and magnetic powder
- Superglue and dye stain/powder

Rubber/Latex/Nitrile Gloves

- Latent processing should be done in laboratory environment, collect and transport

Skin

- Best results found when
  - Body is 70°F/21°C and above
  - Lifting medium maintains 90°F/32°C and above
  - Done within several hours of contact
- Use various lighting angles/techniques to be successful
- Recommend handheld magnifying glass
- Obtain permission from medical examiner first

Options for Skin Processing

- Complete all trace evidence and injury photographs prior to this point
- Areas of skin most likely to provide good prints are smooth hairless areas such as neck, wrists/ankles, upper arms, and upper legs

Option: Patent Prints

- Macrophotography with scale, should be completed as soon as possible as they may dry, flake, or smear
- Gel lift/tape lift for bloody print lifting

Option: Transfer of Latent Print to Non-porous Surface

- Warm skin surface to 72–80°F/22–26°C
- Warm substrate to 86+°F/30+°C (can use hairdryer)
- Place non-porous substrate on skin (mirror, plastic, glass, metal plate) and apply against skin for 15–20 seconds
- Transport substrate to superglue chamber with transferred prints, process accordingly

Option: Transfer of Latent Print to Sticky Side of Tape

- Stick tape directly to the area, sticky side to skin
- Print will transfer to sticky side of tape
- Process tape with Wetwop or sticky side powder
- Photograph results
- Newer prints provide the best results

Option: Transfer of Print to Receipt Paper/Fingerprint Card/ Kromekote Paper

- Lay thermal paper or glossy side of fingerprint card over area of interest
- Hold in place with hand for 30 seconds
- Rub backside of thermal paper with warm hand (or use hand warmer)

- Mark backside with directional arrow
- Remove substrate
- Enhance with magnetic powder, ninhydrin, DFO, physical developer

Option: Powders

- Apply mag powder or Sciluminate powder directly to the skin
- Clean excess with feather brush/gauze
- Photograph results, lift may be possible

Option: Cyanoacrylate Fuming Directly to Skin

- Apply CA to the skin with life size chamber or wand
- Can use superglue with dye or enhance with powders
- View/photograph/lift results as soon as possible
- Should ONLY be used on deceased subjects

Option: ALS of Skin

- 180–200 nm provide the best results
- Photograph the results

Option: Amido Black Directly to Skin

- Apply as normal
- Should ONLY be used on deceased subjects

Option: Iodine Fuming Development Directly to Skin

- Complete iodine fuming/spraying of area in question
- Photograph results as soon as possible
- Should ONLY be used on deceased subjects

Sticky/Greasy Surfaces—Gas Station Bathroom/Door/Floor

- Black magnetic powder (sticky)
- Sudan Black (greasy/oily)
- SPR (sticky/greasy)

Styrofoam

- Magnetic powder
- SPR

Tape/Stickers

- For best results don't complete processing on scene

- If there are no other options, following are some suggestions for processing tape/stickers/labels/sticky side items
- If you are printing both sides of the tape, print the un-sticky side first

Tape Separation—Not Recommended for On-scene Processing

Option: Undu (Heptane)

- Heptane works great for items like labels and stickers. With duct tape can dissolve adhesive depending upon brand, test similar item prior to using.

Option: Aerosol Duster (Canned Air)

- Hold can upside down, direct spray to tape
- Will chill adhesive, making it removable

Option: Rubbing Alcohol to Remove Stickers/Labels/Stamps/Tape

- Slowly pour/dab over area until item is removable, taking approximately 5–20 seconds

Option: Place It in Freezer to Freeze/Separate

- Place in freezer 1 hour—check adhesive
- Continue as needed
- Separate 1 layer at a time, retaining in freezer until finished

Tape/Poster Processing—Sticky Side

- Wetwop (black or white)
- Sticky side powder
- Gentian violet—dip tray recommended
- SPR (good for scotch tape/packing tape)

Walls

- Flat paint—iodine, ninhydrin
- Glossy paint—powders
- Latex paint—use porous evidence procedures
- Semi-gloss/enamel paint
  - Magnetic powder or black powder with silicone lifter
  - Sciluminate powder with UV light collected with photographs
- Wallpaper—ALS, Iodine fume, ninhydrin spray, silver nitrate

Wet Surfaces

Option: Process Wet

- Spray with SPR or physical developer while wet on scene
- Rinse
- Repeat if needed
- Photograph or allow to dry and lift results
- Recommended for submerged vehicles and safes, wet leather, condensation covered items

Option: Process Dry

- Allow entire item to dry naturally
- Process with powders or preferred method

Windows

- Interior—black powder, tape lift
- Exterior—minor dust
  - Black powder, tape lift
  - Black powder, gel lift
- Exterior—heavy dust
  - No powder, black gel lifter for dust lift
  - No powder, black fingerprint card with tape dust lift
  - Black powder, tape lift
- Vehicle—exterior
  - Lift dust prints with gel lifter
  - Black powder, tape lift
  - Bi-chromatic powder, tape lift
- Vehicle—interior with tint
  - Photographs
  - Gel lift
  - Tape (pull SLOWLY)
- Vehicle—interior, no tint—black powder, tape lift

Wood (Untreated)

- Ninhydrin ethanol formula
- Magnetic powder—clean excess powder off and lift with gel lift/silicone casting
- Iodine fuming

Wood (Varnished)

- Black powder, black magnetic powder—clean excess powder off and lift with gel lift/silicone casting

- Superglue
- Luminescent powder

Wood (Oiled)

- SPR or photographs if visible

Facts for Consideration

- You can still leave examination quality fingerprints when wearing nitrile or latex gloves. Once your gloves have been on for an hour or so and your hands start to sweat they will adhere to the shape of your ridges.
- Stress affects fingerprint deposits which often cause subjects to leave wetter, thicker prints on scene
- Newer fingerprints hold more moisture, causing heavier powder retention and may require removal of extra powder
- Older fingerprints are drier and may require extra powder application or addition of moisture (huffing) for powder retention
- Clean powder/clean brush can be used for latent print development, after which any prints that do not contain detail can be swabbed for DNA content. DNA-free powder and brushes are treated with ethylene oxide, eliminating any potential DNA contamination during manufacturing.[3]
- Some agencies photograph all developed prints prior to lifting them in case they do not lift as expected. Consider your agency protocol prior to lifting.

Temperature

- Ideal temperature for latent preservation is 40°F/4°C and 55% humidity
- Latent prints deteriorate fastest above 70°F/21°C and less than 25% humidity
- Quick temperature change can cause condensation destroying latent prints. Allow item to become room temperature prior to printing if possible.

Factors That Degrade Fingerprints

- Direct sunlight
- Dust/dirt contact
- Excessive/improper handling
- Heat/cold
- Humidity
- Rain/dew

- Processing with powder makes latent prints easier to destroy and wipe off. Don't add powder if you are going to move to another location before lifting them.

Deciding Which Method to Use

Variables to Determine Technique

- Location—laboratory or on scene
- Type of print—latent/patent/bloody
- Type of substrate/surface
- Horizontal or vertical surface
- Condition of surface—sticky, scratched/extreme temperature
- Weather/environment—is it raining on top of you?
- Any possible subsequent processing—don't powder on scene if you are wanting DNA later
- If lift cannot be obtained on scene—collect the item and transport to the laboratory for further processing

Small Items—*Can Be Transported or Processed on Scene*

- Loose packaging
- Bags/boxes versus envelopes
- Handle carefully—don't hold item as you normally would, because so did the suspect
    - Touch the rough areas of handgun, not smooth
    - Touch the bottom/top of bottle, not neck
    - Touch the corners of box, not sides
- Latent prints wipe off easier once print powder has been applied, so don't transport after powder application if you can help it

Large/Stationary or Extremely Fragile—*Items Must Be Done on Scene*

- You will need to determine what processing the evidence needs, but don't be too quick to dismiss multiple options as you don't always have to pick between DNA and fingerprints.

Fingerprinting with Powder

Facts to Consider

- Powder not recommended for oily, sticky substances such as chip bags, food packaging, and meat stick wrappers. Consider collection for laboratory processing/chemicals for better results.

- Test multiple powders/mixtures on unimportant surface area and determine best powder to use for substrate
- After your last lift—check surface again. Repeat until you are really done.
- Prints with a thicker deposit can be lifted twice which is good for vehicles that have a layer of dirt/pollen on the surface. Powder and lift two times. The first lift will remove debris and the second or third lift is often cleaner and more detailed.

Powder Options

- Black powder (black carbon), magnetic powder, black magnetic, dragon's blood, fluorescent, Sciluminate (UV), bi-chromatic, silver, aluminum flake/copper flake powder
- Nano-engineered, nanoparticle, nano-technology—small particles that hold powder better, reports of up to 30% improvement than conventional powders[4]
- Volcanic powder 20 times finer than talcum powder
- In an emergency crushed charcoal into a fine powder or other homemade remedies may substitute for black power

Bi-chromatic Powder

- Mixture of *silver* (sticks to most surfaces) and *black powder* (visible and liftable)
- Can be photographed, lifted with tape/AccuTrans/gel lifters
- Regular or magnetic
- Good for multicolored backgrounds, vehicles with multiple surfaces/paints, older prints
- Can be made darker by adding black powder to the mixture or lighter with silver added, find combination you like most—2/3 black powder, 1/3 bi-chromatic powder—better coverage, retains dark results

Black Powder *(Most Commonly Used)*

- It can be used on dark and light non-porous surfaces
- Can be photographed or lifted with tape/flexible casting material/gel lifters
- Results are often viewed with an oblique flashlight angle. Move the light several angles before you determine no detail is present, as the lighting can make a huge visibility difference.
- Good for windows, mirrors, glass bottles, porcelain surfaces, painted surfaces

- Black powder canisters will get small balls of debris in the container and on the prints. It's caused by debris and humidity; you don't want that in the print detail.

Dragons Blood

- Made from rattan palm resin, red in color
- Can be used on light/dark surfaces
- Good for
  - Paper
  - High polished stainless steel
  - Bloody prints

Luminescent Powders

Fluorescent Powder

- Available in red, yellow, green, orange, black
- Application with feather brush HIGHLY RECOMMENDED to prevent over saturation
- Charge brush with minimal powder—a charged brush works many, many times
- 1 brush per color, don't mix brushes, clean off excess powder for better contrast
- Works good on leather purses, seats/car seats, dashboards, small items of evidence rather than large items such as window/door, wooden, or stationary items due to ease of use with lights
- Must be viewed with an ALS and a filter
- Orange and green powder are good for scene use
- Will cover everything with powder—very fine, travels far, coats all
- Does produce great prints with strong detail
- Photograph results or lift results with black fingerprint card or gel lifter
- Often used in offices and homes as results are less visible

Sciluminate Powder

- White powder that reacts with UV light
- Dust with feather brush then the item can be viewed with a shortwave UV light 254 nm
- The results will glow a green hue and are easily photographed
- This powder is more sensitive and less destructive to prints than normal powder
- Single application to feather brush lasts MANY times processing
- Results must be photographed

- Works good on guns, cartridge cases, magazines
- Works on porous items like dashboards, child car seats, steering wheels, and tool handles
- Works on bloody footwear prints
- Doesn't stick to surrounding area, cleans between ridges better than black powder

Magnetic Powder

- Can be used on porous and non-porous surfaces, less destructive method since there is no brush contact
- It comes in black, silver, white, bi-chromatic, fluorescent
- It is color powder mixed with iron shavings and must be applied with a magnetic brush
- The coverage is heavier than black powder and works better for different surfaces
- Good for treated wood, interior vehicle doors, thick plastics, Styrofoam, paper products, woodwork inside residences, countertops in gas station, pharmacies, banks, paint on interior vehicles
- Can be used on metal—carefully hold brush above surface and avoid contact
- Can be photographed, lifted with tape/flexible casting/gel lifters
- Don't use on cell phones, bank cards, magnetic items
- Doesn't work well upside down, on dome lights and on ceilings
- Magnetic powder adheres thicker than black powder
- Use a feather brush to remove excess background powder between ridges
- Magnetic powder mixtures
    - 2/3 black magnetic powder, 1/3 black powder—darker black magnetic powder
    - 2/3 black magnetic powder, 1/3 bi-chromatic powder—bi-chromatic contrast benefits, easy lifting results
- Tritech magnetic powder—darker coverage, doesn't fully clear off
    - Good for matte vehicle paint, metal
- Evident magnetic powder—lighter coverage, cleans off with brush
    - Good for most items

Silver Powder/White Powder

- Not recommended for use in a fast-food restaurant as it sticks to grease easily, travels in air easily, coats heavy
- Best used when mixed with black for lifting visibility

- Good for
  - chromed metal
  - filing cabinets
  - lacquered surfaces
  - rubber
  - use on dark colored surfaces
  - varnished surfaces
- Will need to be placed on a black fingerprint card or gel lift to be seen

Options

- Mixed with dark powder to increase contrast and lifting visibility
- 7/8 black powder with 1/8 silver powder—adds contrast and gets solid coverage

Specialty Powders

- Galvanized metal powder for vending machines, doors, pipes
- Homemade powders
  - Baby powder
  - Cigarette ashes
  - Cocoa powder
  - Ground charcoal/carbon/ash
  - Makeup powder

Brush Options

- Single-use brush
  - individually packaged single-use brush, DNA free
  - enables DNA collection after latent processing
  - brush can be stored with evidence if needed
- Repetitive-use brushes
  - not sterile, for continued use
  - can be decontaminated in a UV box
- Feather brush
  - main applicator of fluorescent or Sciluminate powder
  - holds powder very well
  - can remove excess powder/dust/debris/pollen
  - feather spine can scratch print
- Fiberglass brush
  - main applicator for black/bi-chromatic/silver powder
  - used in twirling OR brushing motion
  - change out often (when matted) for best results
  - to untangle ends during use—tap handle on hard surface 4–5 times

- Animal-hair brush
  - horsehair/camel hair/squirrel hairbrush
  - used in brushing motion
  - good for fine detail work, cleaning other prints
- Charging the brush/priming the brush (loading it with powder)
  - dip the end of the brush in powder a few times
  - tap or spin brush to remove unwanted powder from the end
  - brush tips need to have powder coating, or it will smudge fresh prints/streak through the ridges
- Magnetic brush (magna brush, magna wand)
  - used in painting motion with slower linear strokes (if you move too fast powder will fly off)
  - the brush will last a long time, and doesn't decrease in efficiency
  - varied sizes available: Larger size for vehicles and smaller size for smaller items/areas
- GLOVE/PAD applicator
  - large overside cotton glove or cotton pad
  - apply powder in minimal amounts and cover large area of time in a quick amount of time
  - gentle application gives continuous and consistent powder development (the side if a pickup truck to include the bed can be covered in approximately 60 seconds).
- Cotton ball—if in a pinch you can use a cotton ball with minimal pressure

Brush Technique

Option: Twirl Motion

- Twirl brush above substrate without touching surface. It gives some detail to know where to enhance without over powdering anything.
- Twirl brush next to surface touching with ends of brush while moving. You can add more powder to brush to darken results.
- Old prints benefit from large powder dump. Clear excess powder gently.

Option: Brush Motion

- Run brush in linear motion with long slow brush strokes as if painting a wall
- Can use to add powder along ridge lines to darken prints or clean excess

Printing Strategies

- The only way to get better is to PRACTICE AGAIN AND AGAIN

- No prints visible? Add more powder and try again. Still no prints? Change powder type on the substrate and try again. Still no prints? Move on.
- Even if a fingerprint is likely the homeowners, collect anyway, you could be wrong
- Pull tape in one long slow motion or it will make lines on your tape
- Ensure tape is warm before lifting fingerprints
- Sometimes magnetic powder will enhance a print left with black powder and vice versa. Try on a smudge with no ridge detail first to ensure it doesn't wipe the print-off.
- Don't forget to clean off your flashlight after fingerprinting because it will get powder build up and decrease light emittance.
- Huffing—softly breathing your hot air onto a fingerprint to add moisture. Allow to dry for 15 seconds, then powder and lift as normal. Works great on older drier prints and skin followed by magnetic powder application.
- To remove excess powder from developed print, try the following:
  - blowing (unless using clean powder)
  - using your card to "fan" over the area causing a rush of air
  - can of pressed air from a distance
  - feather brush
- Often prints can be lifted more than once
  - If you think you might get a better lift, try again
  - Oily surfaces may have better quality on the second lift

Keeping a Test Kit in the Laboratory Recommended
(For Practice and Control Samples, Not All Inclusive List)

- Bottles—beer, soda, medicine, and so on
- Cans—soda, beer, food, paint, storage, and so on
- Cigar pouch, cigarette box
- Lighter
- Plastic wrappers/empty packaging
- Spray paint cans
- Spark plugs
- Tools
- Various tapes
- Various types of paper

Collection Options of Developed Prints Macrophotography

- Capture overall, mid-range, and close-up photographs prior to this point

- Picture settings should be RAW OR TIFF (+JPEG not instead, as many photograph databases don't work with RAW or TIFF)
- Change camera settings—ISO 50–100, RAW+JPEG/TIFF+JPEG, F/11–16 shutter speed of choice
  - Macro lens ideal, 50 mm lens acceptable
  - Hot shoe level on camera
  - ABFO #2 L scale on same plane
  - Black and white photographs after color photographs are a welcome addition but not replacement
- *3D photographs* (have depth)—take with oblique lighting on width **and** length, relies upon shadows, contrast
  - adjust flashlight height based upon shadow results
  - can adjust exposure/lighting and take extra photographs for submission
- *2D photographs* (flat, no depth)—ensure you have a good quality picture, direct overhead lighting
  - if 2D print needs enhancement, can use black powder or Sciluminate
  - often direct lighting helps photographs
  - can adjust exposure/lighting and take additional photographs for submission

Overlapping Series for Hand Marks

- Can overlap to collect series of photographs—overlap 1/3 per photograph
- First photograph—1–4 inches
- Second photograph—3–7 inches
- Third photograph—6–10 inches

Lifts

Lifting Strategies

- Adhere your tape to the surface outside the print, slowly push the tape in diagonal lines avoiding gaps
- OLD ROLL—the tape at the beginning of your tape roll is thicker than the end and will collect prints better. As you get to the end of your roll thin diagonal lines will appear along the tape. Throw away the tape at this point as it will lose tackiness and flexibility beyond this point.
- AIR BUBBLES—tape with large air bubble is still useable: Push down in middle, even when the tape pops back up the print is still on the tape. You can rub over air bubbles to remove using a wine cork, pencil eraser, or small squeegee.

- CURVED SURFACE—begin pressure near/on print and push outward away from print
- COLD TAPE—cold tape is not your friend on scene, it will rip easier and capture less powder
  - In chilly weather, hold a tape roll in your hand for 10–20 seconds to warm it up, or keep it in front of your shirt or a pocket when working until you are ready to lift prints. This will reduce the risk of white lines forming on the tape and help ensure the tape continues to stick to the print.
  - Place tape over lift of choice. The tape will become cold again after touching the cold substrate.
  - Before lifting the print off the surface, place your hand over the tape and surface for another 30 seconds to warm the tape again

Tape

Clear Tape

- 1–4 inch clear fingerprint tape commonly used, tearable individual rolls
- 4 inch good for lifting palm prints but harder to maneuver for smaller hands
- 2–3 inch easiest to work with but can't get full palm on the tape due to width
- 1 inch easy to handle but doesn't cover large surface
- All tearable

Frosted Tape

- Frosted tape available and easy to work with
- Some examiners report it's harder to see print
- Tearable, easy to use

Hinge Tape

- Tape that is already attached to card

Pre-cut Lift Tape

- Can be manufactured in a pad of 50 strips that tear off one piece at a time
- Good for individuals who struggle with tape rolls, or who don't print often

Flexible Tape

- Polyethylene tape
- Good for doorknobs/door handles/curved surfaces

Diff Lift Tape

- Must be cut
- Good for textured and delicate surfaces

Grip Lifters—Sirchie

- Clear mylar with adhesive
- Individual sized lifts

Tape Placement on Card

- Some agencies will allow you to cover a larger surface by overlapping tape and/or cards
- Ensure tape lays flat on card as much as possible, can smooth out small wrinkles
- Date/initial tape when placed on card near arrow

Card Requirements

- Place an arrow on both sides of the card (tape/drawing) that face the same direction
  - If the arrow points down on the tape, it should point down on the drawing. Can be designating north, up/down, front door, cashier side of counter, and so on.
- Sign/date the tape after placed on card along the edge the same as evidence tape

Tape Lift Method

1. Ensure proper tape placement by hovering tape over area in question without laying down
2. Anchor 1 side of the tape by gently pressing the tape down to the substrate so it won't pull off
3. Keeping finger on tape, slowly move in linear fashion side to side pressing tape to substrate
4. Repeat until entire area of interest is covered by tape
5. Gently lift keeping control of the tape roll
6. Attach to card with same movements and tear end
7. Fold end of tape on roll for next lift
8. Place arrow on both sides of the card
9. Front of card information: Case number, date, CSI/ID, orientation information, location/description information

Silicone Casting Lift

Clear

- Good for lifting fingerprints and powder-enhanced blood prints
- Don't need to be reversed before examination

White

- Good for lifting fingerprints, blood prints, hair, fiber, and paint
- Will need to reverse fingerprint image (just like a gel lift)

AccuTrans

- No hand mixing needed, use extruder gun with spreading tip
- AccuTrans sets in about 4 minutes at 68°F/20°C, though colder weather takes longer

AccuTrans Ice

- For use −10°F/−23°C to 10°F/−12°C—sets in 8 minutes

Option: AccuTrans Collection

- Photograph with/without scale prior to this point
- Clear or white recommended
- Use tip spreader or tongue depressor to even out coverage and remove air bubbles
- Start outside print and move inward in linear fashion
- Allow to dry
- Place directional arrow and item # on back before lifting with ink pen, label, or tape
- Take photograph of print with casting material/markings
- Gently remove and package carefully
- Package all lifts separately or adhere to fingerprint card (can distort each other by sticking)

Mikrosil

- Hand mixing required
- At normal conditions it sets in 5 minutes
- Works below freezing but sets in 15 minutes
- Good for
    - rough surfaces such as painted walls
    - safe
    - fruit
    - curved items such as water bottles and cologne bottles

Option: Mikrosil Collection

- Photograph with/without scale prior to this point
- White recommended
- Mix casting materials
- Spread evenly with gentle pressure
- Fill in gaps with wooden tongue depressor, spread evenly like cake icing
- Leave depressor stuck to back when done—won't distort, use as handle/marker
- Allow to dry
- Mark with directional arrow before removing with ball point pen/label/depressor
- Package all lifts separately in envelope OR adhere to fingerprint card and place in envelope

Gel Lifter

- Can lift prints off porous or non-porous surfaces
- Can cover large area with footwear size lift OR smaller prints with smaller lifters
- Can buy pre-cut or cut yourself
- Provides more flexibility from minute texture-like dashboards

Lifter Options

- Black, white, clear
- Footwear size down to small fingerprint size in pre-cut sizing, you can cut your own size with sharp blade

Method

- Attach tape on a short edge from cover to back
- Pull back cover slowly, gently without separating from backing or breaking tape
- Allow gel lifter to rest for several minutes and fall back in shape as it stretches slightly when removing cover
- Anchor side of gel lift in area to be covered and lay flat over area in question
- Rub back of gel lifter slowly in linear pattern to ensure full coverage
- Draw orientation arrow on backside
- Slowly lift and return cover to original position
- Back of gel lifter should contain the following:
  - Case number
  - Date

- CSI/ID
- Item printed
- Drawing of location
- Description/item information

Fingerprinting Chemicals That Are Good for Scene Use

Cyanoacrylate Fuming (Super Glue)

Facts to Consider

- Can be used on the following:
  - Dry surface
  - Glass
  - Metal
  - Mirror
  - Plastic
  - Semi-gloss cardboard
  - Shiny/dull surface
  - Skin (does not hurt skin, does not interfere with DNA)
  - Full or empty containers (suggest room temperature if full)
- Great way to "fix" prints on items (can fume on scene and photograph after transport)
- Can collect DNA after processing with superglue
- Can use with or without dye in glue
- Can have fingerprint powder applied after fuming
- Often can be photographed based upon superglue results alone—try UV light, yellow filter, F/22, 1/1.3, ISO 100
- Will react to temperature of items, ensure they are all room temperature items. Fuming cold items will cause condensation that will interfere with results. If items are cold or outside after sundown, allow them to return to room temperature before fuming.
- Best results with heat AND humidity
  - 70%–80% humidity recommended
  - DIY chambers benefit from cup of hot water inside chamber to add steam
  - Will need aluminum dish to hold liquid glue and place on heater
- You can clean reusable chambers for better visibility—bleach wipes or a bleach solution cleans off buildup to keep chamber viewable
- Can be used in open air on scene (wand), in a vacuum chamber, or airtight container of your design large enough to include bodies, vehicles, and bicycles (can fume exterior/interior vehicle at same time enhancing the chance to get fingerprints)
- Chamber can be created with plastic bags, tarps, plastic sheeting, or glass containers

  - fish tank/top and box/saran wrap/tape
  - bags taped together to create airtight tarp around large item
  - CHAMBER MUST BE AIRTIGHT—tape on seams mandatory
  - fans can help distribute fumes, but not required for use
  - humidity helps fuming process; lack of humidity will lessen results and slow processing time
- Can expose entire object or isolate specific area by taping a plastic bag over area in question

Superglue Processing Options on Scene

Option: Superglue wand

Option: On scene DIY Cotton Balls (Must Be Pre-made)

- Cotton balls/baking soda/liquid superglue
- Good for use on walls or small items that aren't being collected
- Pre-mix: Mix baking soda and water to paste texture, coat cotton balls with paste and allow to dry overnight

Scene Method

1. All nearby parties must wear masks at this point
2. Put 1 pre-mix dried cotton ball inside a cup or jar (not paper/Styrofoam) and hold cup/jar below area to process
3. Place 3–5 drops liquid super glue on cotton ball
4. Will cause chemical reaction that heats cotton balls, creating superglue fumes
5. Hold below area to be treated (doorknob, lock, etc.) for several minutes to allow fumes to cover area
6. Do not discard in trash can, will ignite with paper products

Option: DIY Superglue Chamber

- Create chamber of chosen size (cup to vehicle size) using many items to include a cardboard box and plastic wrap; PVC pipe and plastic trash bags taped on seals; glass fish tank with plastic wrap or trash bags or similar setup
- Can use premade superglue in strips, can be purchased and work well or metal sample tray with liquid superglue
- Steam/heat will help speed up process and recommended when using pre-made strips but are not necessary (can use steaming cup of water)
- Steam/heat are necessary if using liquid superglue (aluminum dishes and small heater required)
- Fan can help speed up process, not necessary

Iodine Fuming

Facts to Consider

- Iodine vapor applied over surface by wand or chamber and develops latent prints
- Reacts with lipids/fats
- Results must be photographed as soon as possible, will begin to fade
- If it is used on scene it should be used outdoors with crowd moved away
- Monitor development closely, stop when latent developed
- Not for use with metal due to chemical reaction
- Great for
  - paper
  - thermal paper
  - cardboard
- Prints will dissipate in minutes to hours, enabling you to fingerprint documents and return without removing them from the scene

Ninhydrin

Facts to Consider

- Color developed is called Ruhemanns purple
- Great results on older fingerprints, paper/cardboard products
- Not recommended for scene use unless items are un-collectable, results are permanent
- If used on scene recommend immersion method for small items and spray for walls and large items
- It can take up to several days to develop with no steam added so you would need to hold the scene in that case
- If using steam, use home iron vertically expelling steam, or horizontal with a hand towel or several paper towels between the item and iron with steam
- Reacts with amino acids and proteins (most body fluids and vegetable oils)
- Not recommended for recently applied fingerprints, leather products, or currency

Steam Options for Scene Use

- IRON—use iron on steam setting

Option: Hang Paper/Keep Item Vertical

- Hold iron next to item without direct contact

- Apply steam to paper in a slow-moving sweeping motion for several minutes during development, don't sit motionless

Option: Lay Paper/Item Horizontal

- Lay paper towel/thin towel on top of paper
- Set iron to steam setting and lay on top of towel (not directly on item)
- Circular movements for 10–15 seconds

Sticky Side Powder

- Good for:
  - All tape, sticky side of tape
  - Stickers, double sided tape, adhesive posters (sticky side)
  - Window posters, sticky side

Method

- Paint on surface with camel-hair brush
- Let sit 10–15 seconds
- Rinse with tap water

SPR—Small Particle Reagent

Facts to Consider

- Adheres to fatty acids and lipids
- Can have black or white
- Can be used on wet or dry surfaces
- Good for
  - construction tools, power tools
  - greasy food trays/bags
  - iron fences/gates/bars
  - light poles
  - metal carts/dollies/ratchet straps
  - PVC piping
  - semi-smooth to smooth concrete
  - soot-covered glass/metal products
  - sticky beverage cans/Styrofoam cups
  - window weather stripping/trim

Processing Options

- If lifting white spray use black glossy fingerprint card/if lifting black spray use white glossy fingerprint card

- SPR can be lifted with fingerprint tape or photographed with macrophotography

Option: Wet Surface Method

- Spray SPR on wet surface in a sweeping motion and rinse to clear background area
- Apply tape to the wet surface; use a squeegee to remove excess water. Apply tape to a card and squeegee water out again.

Option: Dry Surface Method

- Spray SPR on dry surface in a sweeping motion and rinse multiple times to clear background area
- Allow to dry and lift

Smoke Processing

- Smoke created by burning camphor wood, camphor crystals, pine wood, or a wad of rolled up masking tape

Option: Smoking

- Ignite a smoke source as listed above
- Slowly pass items to be printed through stream of black smoke
- Results will be immediate, continue until developed
- Gently brush off excess soot with fingerprint brush or run under water
- Can photograph results or lift
- Good for warm or cold metals

Chemicals for Bloody Fingerprints on Scene

- POWDER is an option if no chemicals are available for use, and the item cannot be collected. It will still enhance some of the missing areas and light spots.

Amido Black—Water-Based Formula

- Good for
  - enhancement of bloody fingerprints or footwear prints
  - retaining ridge details
  - vertical surfaces
- Scene friendly, easy to use, safe on many surfaces, doesn't eat paint
- Can be used a second time to darken results
- Rinse is optional, can be rinsed with water to reduce background staining

Application

- Spray/dip/squirt/rinse
- Apply
  - Set for 3–5 minutes
  - Rinse
  - Repeat until satisfied

Amido Black—Methanol-Based Formula

- GOOD FOR enhancement of bloody fingerprints or footwear prints
- Can be sprayed or dipped
- Requires acetic acid rinse
- Don't use on painted/stained items
- Must use on DRY blood
- DON'T use with cyanoacrylate fuming
- Caution: Use on scene with caution due to formula

Application

- Dip/spray/rinse
- Caution when using on painted surfaces
- Apply
  - Set for 30–60 seconds
  - Rinse
  - Repeat until satisfied

Gentian Violet

- Results must be photographed, not lifted
- Can be sprayed or dipped
- Good for
  - sticky sides of tape
  - good for electrical tape
  - non-sticky sides of tape
  - bloody fingerprints and footwear prints

Leuco Crystal Violet—LCV

- Results must be photographed, not lifted
- Good for
  - enhancing bloody footwear prints (use a mist for footwear print application)
  - sticky surfaces (tape)
  - horizontal surfaces
- Will develop with sunlight even if no blood is present so use cautiously in sun

- Caution: Mixture is peroxide based, it can begin to "eat" blood once applied
- Caution: Can stain permanently

Application Options for Gentian Violet/LCV

Option: Fine Mist Spray

- Use finest mist possible
- Hold back approximately 6 inch
- Apply directly over stain spraying gently/evenly in sweeping motion
- Let set for 30 seconds
- Blot excess with paper towel corner
- Results must be photographed

Option: Paper Towel Barrier

- Lay dry paper towel over area to be developed
- Spray paper towel with LCV gently/evenly in sweeping motion
- Let liquid set 10–15 seconds
- Remove paper towel
- Can blot excess with paper towel corner

Cases to Consider Regarding Fingerprinting

- 2014: During the scene processing of victim Cassy Farrington, no fingerprint processing was completed because it was believed the scene had been cleaned up. This idea was refuted during trial, creating doubt in the scene processing.
- 2002: Murder of Brenda Robinson—suspect left fingerprints on broken glass from the front door of the scene and exterior doorknob of a neighbor's house.
- 2001: Juvenile A. Flores was kidnapped/murdered. A palm print was developed from plastic bag that also survived a subsequent fire.
- 1992: Murder of Laurie Houts—suspect left fingerprints on the vehicle during her strangulation. Over 80 fingerprints lifted from vehicle interior and exterior with footprints visible on interior windshield.
- 1987: Murder of Susan Woods, suspect left palm prints on the side of the bathtub, bathroom mirror, beer can.
- 1986: Murder of Sandra Martin, suspect duct taped her face, wrists, ankles. A fingerprint developed on duct tape belonged to suspect.
- 1986: Serial rapist Tommie Lee Andrews left a fingerprint on a window screen.
- 1978: Murder of Caroll Bonnet—suspect left palm prints on bottles and a handwritten note.

- 1969: Murder of Diane Maxwell Jackson—suspect left fingerprint on exterior driver door window.
- Richard Ramirez left behind fingerprints on a vehicle and a window screen.

Notes

1 Radford, Michael. "Latent Prints Visualized by Dew." *Journal of Forensic Identification*, vol. 74, no. 3, 2024, pp. 320–323.
2 Roberts, Mark, and Tami Adair. "Latent Print Evidence at Fire Scenes." *104th IAI International Educational Conference, International Association for Identification*, 14 Aug. 2019, Peppermill Resort. Conference Presentation.
3 Neureuther, Katharina, et al. "Reduction of PCR-Amplifiable DNA by Ethylene Oxide Treatment of Forensic Consumables." *Forensic Science International: Genetics*, vol. 12, 2014, https://doi.org/10.1016/j.fsigen.2014.06.006.
4 Miller, Allen. "Choosing the Best Fingerprint Powder for Your Scene." *Evidence Technology Magazine*, Sept. Oct. 2013.

Impression Evidence Collection 23

Impression evidence is delicate and often overlooked at crime scenes due to its elusive nature. This type of evidence includes friction ridge impressions (such as fingerprints and footprints), shoe impressions, bite mark impressions, tire mark impressions, and tool mark impressions. Some impression evidence will be collected for comparison purposes, while other types will be documented to establish direction of travel or sequence of events. The evidentiary value may derive from the shape left by the impression or from trace evidence found within it, such as paint transfers, soil samples, saliva DNA, or fibers. As with all types of evidence, context is crucial, and the significance varies accordingly. This chapter provides guidance on identifying the most effective methods for documenting impression evidence at the scene for further investigation.

Ear Prints

- Often found in crime scenes on doors and windows
- Do not contain ridges
- Cannot be used for identification of individuals
- Can be used for exclusion based on visual comparison of shape/type
- Likely contains DNA
- Fingerprints often found around ear/lip prints

Processing Options

Option: Swab for DNA without further development
Option: Powder for enhancement for photographs/lifting
Option: Clean lift

- Apply clean powder with clean brush
- Lift with clean tape
- DNA can be obtained from lift later at the lab

Lip Prints

- Often found on vehicle windows, mirrors, cups, cigarette butts
- Cannot be used for identification of individuals
- Can be compared for lipstick type/color/brand
- Likely contains DNA

 DOI: 10.4324/9781003503897-24

Processing Options

Option: Swab for DNA
Option: Swab for lipstick/chapstick content sample to compare to a known sample
Option: Tape lift of prints for later processing—no powder
Option: Powder for enhancement with black powder

Dog Nose Prints

- The nose print of a dog is as unique and individual as the human fingerprint
- Dog and cattle nose prints are often used for proof of identification
- Likely contain DNA, if swabbed can be matched to an animal or item

Processing Options

Option: Swab for DNA comparison to known animal
Option: Powdered and lifted from scene deposit

- Use black powder and tape as a fingerprint lift

Comparison Sample Option: Inked Prints for Dog Nose

- Apply food coloring to dog nose instead of black ink when possible due to toxicity/cleanliness
- Press paper/card against nose creating inked print
- Washes off easily, less toxic than black ink or fingerprint powder

Bite Marks

- Animals and humans both leave distinct marks when they bite
- Cannot always get good examination photograph if living person/animal
- ABFO #2 scale recommended for injury photographs
- Items that contain a bite mark can be collected entirely and preserved for analysis in a controlled environment such as gum, wax, and soft foods
- Comparison sample teeth molds not done during scene processing. Consult forensic odontologist for further instruction

Processing Options

Option: Saliva DNA Collection from Impression

- Use swab/cotton/gauze/filter paper of choice
- Begin collecting outside teeth marks working toward center in spiral motion

- Consider using wet/dry method for collection (first wet swab, THEN dry swab over same area)
- Collect buccal swab from receiver of bite for elimination

Option: Photograph of Bite Mark for Comparison

- Collection of saliva DNA from bite mark prior to this point
- Change camera settings—ISO 50–100, RAW+JPEG or TIFF+JPEG, F-stop/shutter speed of choice
- Use macro lens/macro lens attachment for cell phones, hot shoe level
- Affix camera to tripod/camera stand/beanbag—90°, adjust for inclines/angles
- Remove detachable flash from hot shoe
- Lighting—block sun to have better lighting control if applicable
- Detached flash/flashlight at 10–45° angles best approximately 5 feet away, move until desired shadows achieved
- 2–4 angles, consider bracketing
- Label with case information visible in 1 photograph
  - Case number/date/item number/Initials/ID, orientation arrow (nearest body joint for reference point or UP)

Option: Silicone Casting *of Bite Mark for Comparison*

Cast Marks *in Fruit*

- Can be done in laboratory rather than on scene
- Casting options: Formalin solution, AccuTrans, Mikrosil

Cast Marks *on Skin* (Live or Deceased)

AccuTrans—No Hand Mixing, Use Extruder Gun with Spreading Tip

- AccuTrans—sets in about 4 minutes at 68°, colder weather takes longer
- AccuTrans Ice—for use −10°F/−23°C to +10°F/−12°C, sets in 8 minutes

AccuTrans Procedure—Brown/White Recommended

- Photograph with/without scale prior to this point
- Use tip spreader or tongue depressor to even out coverage, use gentle pressure to remove air bubbles
- Allow to air dry
- Place directional arrow and item # on back before lifting (wrist/neck/knee/etc.)
- Take photographs of casting in place

- Gently remove casting and package all lifts separately or adhere individually to a fingerprint card
- Photograph results upon return to laboratory setting

Mikrosil—Hand Mixing Is Required

- Normal conditions set in 5 minutes, below freezing sets in 15 minutes

Mikrosil Procedure—Brown/White Recommended

- Photograph with/without scale prior to this point
- Mix casting materials—even length lines of both materials approximately 4 inch length each
- Spread evenly with gentle pressure using wooden tongue depressor
- Leave depressor stuck to back when done spreading
- Mark with directional arrow before removing using ball point pen/label/depressor
- Package all lifts separately in envelope OR adhere to fingerprint card and place in envelope
- Photograph results upon return to laboratory setting

Glove Marks/Fabric Marks

Glove marks are often left behind by suspects and victims during a crime, but not often seen until fingerprint processing has begun as they are also enhanced by fingerprint powder

Processing Options

Options: Enhance with Black Powder and Fiberglass Brush, Photograph, or Lift

Tool Mark Impressions

Search for Tool Marks

- Wood/metal
  - Doors, door frames, safes, and so on
  - Machinery/tools
  - Broken tools, hand tools
  - Saw blades, knife blades
  - Cut cords/hoses
- Tape—cut ends
- Body—bone/cartilage

Trace Evidence in Tool Marks (Fibers, Paint, Blood, Hair)

Option: Cut around tool mark and take as whole item, remove trace evidence in lab

Option: Silicone casting to remove trace evidence with cast on scene, place in glassine envelope

Processing Options

Option: Photograph *of Tool Mark for Comparison*

- Overall/mid-range/close-up series should be taken PRIOR to collection
- Change camera settings—ISO 50–100, RAW+JPEG/TIFF+JPEG, F-stop/shutter speed of choice
- Macro lens/macro lens attachment for cell phones, hot shoe level
- Affix camera to tripod/camera stand—90°, adjust for inclines/angles
- Remove detachable flash from hot shoe
- Label with case information visible in 1 photograph—case number/date/item number/Initials, orientation arrow (up/north)
- Scale—ABFO #2 L scale, if possible, keep circle in view for distortion adjustment
- Lighting—block sun to have better lighting control if applicable
- Flash/flashlight at 10–45° angles best approximately 5 feet away, move until desired shadows achieved
- 2–4 angles, consider bracketing
- Polarizer filters can add depth

Option: Whole Tool Mark *Collection*

- Photo damages with ABFO #2 L scale prior to cutting
- Add item #/orientation arrow with marker/label prior to removing
- Cut substrate, leaving sufficient gap around the marks
  - If tool marks on door lock, collect whole locking mechanism
  - If tool marks in door frame, cut out section of door frame
  - If tool marks in drywall, cut around defect and cut out section of wall
- Cut shallow, be mindful of wiring in walls

Option: Silicone Casting *of Tool Mark for Comparison/Trace Evidence*

AccuTrans—No Hand Mixing, Use Extruder Gun with Spreading Tip

- AccuTrans—sets in about 4 minutes at 68°, colder weather takes longer

- AccuTrans Ice—for use −10°F/−23°C to +10°F/−12°C, sets in 8 minutes

AccuTrans Procedure—Brown/White Recommended

- Photograph with/without scale prior to this point
- Use tip spreader or tongue depressor to even out coverage; use gentle pressure to remove air bubbles.
- Allow to air dry sufficiently prior to removing from sample
- Place directional arrow and item # on back before lifting (wrist/neck/knee/etc.)
- Take photograph of casting in place
- Gently remove casting and package all lifts separately or adhere individually to a fingerprint card
- Photograph results upon return to laboratory setting

Mikrosil—Hand Mixing Is Required

- Normal conditions set in 5 minutes, below freezing sets in 15 minutes

Mikrosil Procedure—Brown/White Recommended

- Photograph with/without scale prior to this point
- Mix casting materials—lay out even length lines of both materials approximately 4 inch each
- Spread evenly with gentle pressure using wooden tongue depressor, leave depressor stuck to back when done spreading
- Mark with directional arrow after dry before removing using ball point pen/label/depressor
- Package all lifts separately in envelope OR tape to fingerprint card and place in envelope

Footwear Prints/Tire Tracks

Types/Locations

- Footwear/tire impression—3D print in soft object
- Footwear/tire imprint/print—2D print in dust or on hard surface with minimal depth
  - Footwear prints include all foot covering prints
  - Footprints left from bare feet can be collected and compared to an individual
- Tire tracks and footwear prints are found in the same forms and collected in the same manner; both need comparison prints for elimination/confirmation
- Visible prints—can be seen with naked eye (dirt prints left on floor, bloody prints, paint/oil prints on floor)

- Latent prints—need enhancement to see—flashlight, powder, chemicals
- Magnetic powder or black powder to search for prints on doors with forced entry
- Plastic prints—3D print left in soft surface (on gum/food product)

Searching for Footwear Prints/Tire Tracks

Exterior Scene

- Path of travel through scene
- Entry/exits
- Under windows
- In front of doors
- Search 7–15 feet from tire mark for other side of vehicle tire path
- Search 2–7 feet from tire mark for other side of cart, dolly, equipment
- When tire prints from each side of vehicle are present, document width from interior tire to interior tire
- When footprints from left and right foot are present, document distance from left heel to right heel to obtain stride length

Interior Scene

- Body—bruise pattern, dirt/oil deposit on skin
- Counters/cabinets touched when jumping over
- Doors/walls from kicking
- Filing cabinets from overhead entry in business/bank
- Flooring from path of travel through scene
  - Carpet (can use static lift to obtain on carpet and fabric)
  - Wood
  - Linoleum
  - Tile
  - Floor in front of cashier/teller
  - Kitchens and bathrooms walked through
- Windowsills

Tire Standard Collection

- Comparison tracks are needed from vehicles for exclusion/comparison, keep variables similar if possible
- Standards best collected while tires remain on vehicle in question
- Tire standards should be collected from all 4 tires for comparison as they can be rotated/changed/mis-matched

Tire Preparation Options

Option: Black Shoe Polish

- Wipe tires down with DRY rag to remove loose dirt/grease
- Raise vehicle off the ground or apply while rolling forward/backward slowly
- Apply shoe polish to tread of tire with gloved hand or sponge
- Cover entire exterior tire tread
- Lower vehicle to the ground with butcher paper placed beneath each tire
- Mark paper and tire with arrow or starting point
- Roll (in neutral) tire full rotation over paper
- Mark line on tire sidewall/paper at same time with letter/number segments for each quarter turn

Option: Vaseline/Magnetic Powder

- Wipe tires down with rag to remove loose dirt/grease
- Raise vehicle off the ground or apply while rolling forward/backward slowly
- Apply **thin** layer Vaseline/lotion to tread of tire with gloved hand or paper towel
- Lower vehicle to the ground with butcher paper/drafting film on cardboard[1] placed beneath each tire
- Mark paper/tire with arrow or starting point
- Roll (in neutral) tire full rotation over paper
- Mark line on tire sidewall/paper at same time with letter/number segments for each quarter turn
- Remove paper from vehicle
- Apply red or black magnetic powder to Vaseline print to enhance with gloved hand or rag—don't use fiberglass/hair/feather brush
- Photograph results with macrophotography

Option: Cooking Spray/Black Powder

- Wipe tires down with rag to remove loose dirt/grease
- Raise vehicle off the ground or apply while rolling forward/backward slowly
- Spray tire tread with cooking spray
- Wipe tire with gloved hand, ensure full coverage
- Make pile of black fingerprint powder in hands, wipe on tires
- Lower vehicle to the ground with butcher paper placed beneath each tire
- Mark paper and tire with arrow or starting point

- Roll (in neutral) tire full rotation over paper
- Mark line on tire sidewall/paper at same time with letter/number segments for each quarter turn

Footwear Standard Collection

- Consider standards from LEFT AND RIGHT foot

Collection Options

Option: Photographs

- Use cover page with name for each subject
- Photograph of front side of subject to include face
- Photograph bottom of shoe with and without 300 mm L scale (knee on chair easiest/safest position)
- Use normal 50 mm lens, RAW+JPEG/TIFF+JPEG (if possible), ISO 100–400, F11

Option: Foam Collection Pad

- Have each subject step in collection foam box
- Mark box appropriately with name/DOB

Option: Black Powder

- Wipe bottom of shoes with rag to remove loose dirt/debris
- Apply black powder with fiberglass brush to bottom of shoes
- Have subject walk across butcher paper OR step on butcher paper/adhesive paper

Option: Black Shoe Polish

- Wipe bottom of shoes with rag to remove loose dirt/debris
- Apply black shoe polish with sponge to bottom of shoes
- Have subject walk across butcher paper OR step on butcher paper/adhesive paper

Option: Vaseline/Magnetic Powder

- Wipe bottom of shoes with rag to remove all remaining loose dirt/debris
- Apply Vaseline to bottom of shoes in THIN layer
- Step on butcher paper or drafting film adhered to cardboard[2]/NOT adhesive paper
- Apply red or black magnetic powder to prints to enhance

Option: Scene Collection Sheet

- Lay roll of butcher paper down, large enough to accommodate several officers
- Place footwear prints from each officer on scene before they leave, write their name/badge by their footwear prints, and take needed photographs according to policy. Consider having them initial the paper next to their prints. Keep samples together and transport them to laboratory for individual photographs. This will be a quick and efficient plan for multiple officers on scene.

Scene Collection of Unknown Samples

3D Tracks without Individual Detail

- Still valuable—grass, loose sand, loose dirt, water
- Can still tell you direction of travel, number of travelers, path of travel
- Photographs of overall/mid-range prints sufficient, don't need comparative quality when no fine details are present

Macrophotography

- Overall/mid-range/close-up series taken PRIOR to this point
- Can use plastic arrows for overall/mid-range photographs with placards showing directionality
- Change camera settings—ISO 50–100, RAW+JPEG/TIFF+JPEG, F/11–16 shutter speed of choice
  - 35 mm lens ideal, 20–50 mm lens acceptable
  - Hot shoe level or angle finder recommended
  - 300 mm L scale on same plane
  - Can capture black and white photographs after color captured
- *3D photographs* (have depth)—take with oblique lighting on width **and** length, relies upon shadows, contrast
  - adjust flashlight height based upon shadow results
  - can adjust exposure/lighting and take extra photographs for submission
- *2D photographs* (flat, no depth)—ensure you have a good quality picture, direct overhead lighting
  - if 2D print needs enhancement, can use black powder or Sciluminate
  - often direct lighting helps photographs
  - can adjust exposure/lighting and take additional photographs for submission

- Bloody footwear print/tire track
  - enhance with Amido Black, LCV or Sciluminate powder after initial photograph
  - blue star reaction will give overall placement, not detailed photograph for comparison

Option: Snow Highlighting (Spray or Powder)

- Overall, mid-range, close-up of print with no enhancements
- Spray bright colored spray paint 30–45° above print
- Even spray, give light dusting of spray to interior/exterior print
- Reattempt photographs
- Add light dusting as needed
- Block from sun, if possible, paint will absorb light if not specifically made for highlighting
- Forensic Source highlighting spray—highlights detail without adding heat or weight

2D Print Enhancement

- Can use black powder/magnetic powder/silver nitrate for enhancement

Black Powder

- Apply black powder to print to add contrast for photography

Silver Nitrate

- Good on porous surfaces
- Good for salt prints left behind in winter
- Not good for products with waxy coating—water will just bead on top of wax
- Will permanently stain items and hands
- After applied, must be subjected to bright lights for proper development turning silver
- Water based, gentle on items

2D Print Collection Options

Cuttings—Take the Whole Print Back with You

- 2D print on linoleum, fabric, velvet, upholstery, carpet
  1. Take macrophotography first if able
  2. Mark with directional arrow prior to lifting cutting
  3. Cut around print leaving at least 1 inch buffer
  4. Remove entire top layer of substrate (won't need sublayers)

5. Package in envelope or bag
6. Transport with great care

Adhesive Paper (Sticky Paper)

- White
- Black-powder-enhanced prints
- Smooth non-porous surface

Gel Lifters

- Recommended uses: Tire/finger/foot
- Warning: Some ignitable liquids eat gel
- Melts above 104°F/40°C, don't store in vehicle
- Lifter stretches when removed from cover sheet. Allow the gel lifter time to return to original size before lifting pattern evidence.[3]
- Do not fold
- Less tacky/more flexible than adhesive lifter
- Results should be photographed with macrophotography or submitted for analysis as soon as possible
- Gel lift should be stored in bag/envelope/file folder
- Test lift to determine which color is best, if needed—use non-preferred print and adjust method/color
- BLACK GEL LIFTER—dust prints and fluorescent/Sciluminate-enhanced prints
- WHITE GEL LIFTER—black-powder-enhanced prints, prints with residue, bloody prints
- CLEAR GEL LIFTER—prints with residue, black/fluorescent-powder-enhanced prints

Option: Tape Cover to Backing of Lifter

- Place tape on short end attaching cover to backing. Hold to side while collecting sample and return cover to same position once sample is collected.
- Reduces chance of adding more dust/contaminates to the print

Documentation on Gel Lift

Prior to Lifting from Sample

- Mark directional arrow on the back of gel lifter prior to lifting off surface

Prior to Leaving Scene

- Label/back of card information:

- Arrow with notation (up, north, front door, etc.)
- Location (bathroom counter, front porch, etc.)
- Case number
- Date, time
- Initials, badge/ID number
- Diagram (like a fingerprint card)

Casting

2D Prints Using Dental Stone

- Photograph prior to casting and prior to collection—mid-range and close-up with markings
- Can be used to lift 2d impressions—mud, blood, tire residue on concrete, tile, linoleum

Application Procedure

1. Make frame around the print to hold mixture, mix thicker than for 3D cast. You can use metal frames, sticks, folded venetian blinds, mound of dirt, moat in dirt, and so on.
2. Lay popsicle stick/tongue depressor on ground next to impression to use as a leverage when dry
3. Pour on secondary item or off to the side and allow to run onto impression and depressor
4. Mark with directional arrow prior to removal
5. Lift when dry, tongue depressor may help release attachment
6. Casts should be allowed to dry 48 hours prior to storage
7. Package in breathable container

3D Prints

- If you didn't mix enough material, cover the bottom of the print with first batch to keep bottom layer continuous, then add a second batch on top.
- Warm the water in the sunlight if possible, unless using in snow, as it can assist with mixing smoothly
- Photograph prior to casting with macrophotography (casting is not 100%) AND cast material on ground prior to collection (showing development and placement in scene)
- DON'T clean debris off bottom of cast, retain in evidence after lifting
- NOT great for use in snow—gives off heat during curing
- Frames should be cleaned after each use—frame options: Metal frame, wooden stick frame, mound of dirt frame, and so on

- Dental stone most common casting material. Plaster of Paris is an alternative. HOWEVER, it does not hold shape or resist damage the same, much more fragile. Modeling plaster not recommended.
- Adding reinforcement to cast—when casting is filled 1/2 inch +, add layer of sticks/mesh then continue filling impression

Packaging

- Transport in box or paper bag with strong bottom support, no plastic
- Allow to air dry at least 48 hours prior to storage or mail[4]
- Don't clean debris off cast prior to laboratory submission

Dental Stone

Option: Traxtone

1. Mix as instructed (approximately 1 minute)
2. Pour casting material onto secondary item height no greater than 3 inch, such as stick/gloved hand/stir stick and allow to run INTO impression (reduces pressure from pour, can make further impressions ruining the match)
3. Drying time approximately 30–90 minutes

Option: Pre-packaged Dental Stone

- 1 package = 1 footwear print, mix according to instructions

Option: Mix Your Own Dental Stone

- 1 lb. stone to 6 oz water AND 1 GALLON freezer bag/zip lock bag for mixing
- 2 lb. to 10–12 oz water AND 2 GALLON freezer bag/zip lock bag

Dental Stone Application Procedure

1. Photograph with scale prior to this point
2. Place rectangle or oval frame around print, allowing 1–2 inch space between print and frame, minimally pressing into ground to ensure it makes a barrier and prevents leakage of mixture
3. *Gently and quickly* massage bag 3–5 minutes reaching pancake batter/milkshake consistency (not waffle batter, too runny). Mixture will settle in the corners of bag, try to keep clumps small during first minute. If large clumps begin to form while mixing and you can't break them up within 4–5 minutes, discard and try again. Likely you mixed too long. Don't stop mixing too early, mix at least 3 minutes no longer than 5 minutes. If mixing large quantity in bucket mix at least 5 minutes.

4. Pour casting material onto secondary item such as stick/gloved hand/ stir stick and allow to run INTO impression (reduces pressure from pour, can make further impressions ruining the match)
5. Pour casting material until entire print covered and small edge forms around print—should be approximately 3/4–1 inch thick to prevent breakage
6. Allow to dry approximately 30 minutes—longer to set in colder weather
7. Can remove any small debris that falls into top of cast while wet but don't remove debris from bottom
8. Carve directional arrow in casting material when hard but not fully set, using a small stick, toothpick, or pencil OR write on top with marker OR apply label to top of cast
9. Take photograph of cast in place with arrow with mid-range photographs, showing the print in relation to the scene
10. Don't remove debris from bottom of print, set print in butcher paper, secure inside a box

Labeling

- When dry write on back with Sharpie
- Arrow, case, marker #, collector
- Mark directional arrow prior to collection (north, front door, etc.)
- If using labels, affix to back while still wet
- Dry label to dry cast will not stick

Tire Tracks

- Average need 7–8 lbs. of dental stone
- Bucket good size for larger batch, stir 3–5 minutes stir slowly and continuously
- Cast segments of 3 feet for structural integrity

Plaster of Paris

Footwear Print

- 5 lbs. of Plaster of Paris with 15 ounces water = footwear size print[5]
- 2lb coffee can good for mixing (don't shake)
- Tap sides to release air bubbles in mixture

Pouring Casting Material

1. Place rectangle or oval frame around print, allowing 1–2 inch space between print and frame

2. Minimally press frame into substrate to prevent leakage of dental stone
3. Pour casting material NEXT to impression not INTO impression from height of approximately 2 inches, will overflow down into impression. Can diffuse flow with gloved hand, clipboard (with paper over it to minimize mess), stick, and so on.

Option: Add Frame Materials for Stability

- Fill print halfway with casting materials
- Lay reinforcement material along top of cast in strips (sticks, wire, popsicle sticks, pencils, etc.)
- Continue pouring dental stone until impression is complete

Casting Suggestions

Option: Print Is in Standing Water/Blood

- Can be either water filled print or under shallow water
    1. Make dam around print or place frame around print and try to remove as much liquid as possible
    2. Sprinkle dental stone powder on base of print and allow to cover area, try for 1 inch thick
    3. Mix casting material at this time
    4. Add thick mixture, at least 2-inch depth, can place by scooping rather than pouring. If pouring, pour outside the print and allow to slowly move into print, displacing water from the print.[6]
    5. Allow to set in place 1–2 hours

Option: Water/Wet Blood in Print

1. Pipette out excess moisture if possible
2. Sprinkle casting powder on moisture
3. Cast print as normal
4. Allow to dry 1 hour

Option: Print in Wet Soil/Mud

1. Sprinkle small bit of casting material into print covering wet areas
2. Cast as normal
3. Let dry 45 minutes

Option: Print on Dry Soil

1. Can spray hair spray above print
2. Cast as normal
3. Let dry for 20 minutes

Casting in Sand

- Casting in sand is extremely transient
- Wind and stepping near print can change shape

Option: Harden Sand

1. Spray HAIR SPRAY/HAIR LACQUER/ACRYLIC SAND HARDENER directly across the top of the print before casting
2. Spray across NOT directly down in several short bursts of spray
3. Helps reduce volatility of top layer of sand
4. Can be used with plaster, silicone, dental stone

Option: Increase Contrast

1. Spray SPRAY PAINT in a direction across the top of print not down
2. Hold can at 45°
3. Several short bursts of spray until contrast is sufficient
4. Photograph with macrophotography

Casting in Snow

Option: Dental Stone Cold

1. Use as normal but keep mixture cold
2. Can sprinkle light dusting of powder casting into snow impression
3. Mix cold powder and cold water
4. Pour casting mix as normal

Option: Snow Print Plaster

- Casting mix for use in snow

Option: Snow Print Wax

- Stabilizes snow movement for application of dental stone. Used before casting material—not instead of.
- Will not stop snow from melting with warm water
  1. Spray impression with snow print wax or sprinkle with talcum powder[7]
  2. Add snow to water to lower temperature of casting material
  3. Mix and pour cast as normal

Option: Sulfur Cast

- This method should be practiced prior to scene work
- Sulfur melted and poured in print, hardens with snow contact

- Can pour dental stone on top of sulfur cast to thicken/stabilize print[8]
- Cast can be removed like dental stone in dirt
- Photograph prior to casting and prior to collection
- Does not work on snow with hard top crust (soft snow only)

Option: Loose Snow Inside Print

- Use canned air to remove loose snow on top of print crust
- Leaf blower can be used for tire tracks/footwear prints (Adach)
- Good with dry/powder snow, bad with heavy wet snow

Option: Increase Contrast

- Spray SPRAY PAINT in a direction across the top of print not down
- Hold can obliquely from distance of 8–12 inches/20.32–31 cm[9]
- Several short bursts of spray can be helpful
- Photograph with macrophotography aided by increased contrast of spray paint

Static Lift

- Lift 2D dust prints/light dirt prints with mylar—charge will hold up to approximately 72 hours
- Results should be photographed within 24 hours with macrophotography then compared to known samples
- Results should be photographed prior to submitting to the property room
- Static lifts should be included in sketch measurements and placement
- Can be completed using kit that deploys a charge, or single-use mylar sheets that charge with static electricity and do not require a machine source
- Each lift requires a sketch/directional arrow/location information like a fingerprint card and gel lift
- Does not impact any other form of processing, can be lifted/processed/photographed after static lift use

Uses—Areas

- Dust prints, light dirt prints
- Entryway/exit
- Floor in front of register
- Floor in front of safe
- Great with tile/laminate flooring

Uses—Surfaces

Do Use On

- Porous and non-porous surfaces
- Countertops, flooring, window ledges, walls, floors, doors, metal cabinets
- Textiles (hoodies, blankets, couches)
- Deceased bodies
- Blind lifts in scene when you can't turn down lights—banks, 7–11, grocery store, and so on
- Metal surfaces
  - MUST BE GROUNDED FIRST (USE GROUNDING PLATE)
  - Release charge before touching
  - Refer to manufacturer instructions in packaging
- DON'T use on wet/previously wet prints

Mylar

- Mylar is re-useable for training only, NOT FOR SCENE USE—can wipe dust off back side until clean, will work 4–5 times losing more static each time.
- Can use mylar that is self-charging and does not require a machine

Dangers

- Don't touch mylar or unit while applying charge
- Don't use on wet prints/impressions
- Always ground unit with metal surfaces

Storage/Packaging

- Discard or store mylar based upon agency requirements, static hold will dissipate quickly
- Use clean file folder or shallow box. Can roll film with shiny side on exterior. Never reuse static lift packaging.[10]
- Tape/tack unused corner to secure mylar
- Plastic bags/sheet protectors not recommended—they contain static
- Pizza boxes and other low-quality cardboard not recommended—they likely contain static

Cases to Consider regarding Impression Evidence

- Richard Ramirez, the Night Stalker, had multiple cases linked to him due to footwear prints left on scene.
- The Unabomber wore shoes with smaller soles attached to the bottom to ensure he did not leave accurate footwear prints.

- 2015: Brittney Gargol was murdered by her friend Antoine, who strangled her with his belt leaving distinct marks in the dust on the exterior vehicle and impressions on Gargol's neck. Antoine and Gargol took a selfie and uploaded it to Facebook right before the murder, and Antoine can be seen wearing the belt in the photograph, which was collected from the crime scene.
- 2011: Margaret Purk was exhumed and still maintained a belt impression on the back of her neck and rope impressions across her chest from her death in 1985. The original autopsy concluded suicide and did not mention the marks, though her second autopsy ruled homicide, and her husband was found guilty in 2015 of her murder.
- 2000: Christina Sanoubane murder—footprints left on scene were compared and matched to a barefoot suspect.

Notes

1 "Documentation of Shoe and Tire Impression Evidence." *California Department of Justice: Bureau of Forensic Services*, oag.ca.gov/bfs.

2 "Documentation of Shoe and Tire Impression Evidence." *California Department of Justice: Bureau of Forensic Services*, oag.ca.gov/bfs.

3 ANSI/ASB (2020) *049—Best Practice Recommendation for Lifting of Footwear and Tire Impressions.*

4 ANSI/ASB (2020) *049—Best Practice Recommendation for Lifting of Footwear and Tire Impressions.*

5 Hilderband, Dwayne S. *Footwear, the Missed Evidence.* Staggs Publishing, 2007.

6 "Best Practice Recommendation for Casting Footwear and Tire Impression Evidenced at the Crime Scene." *ANSI/ASB Best Practice Recommendation 126*, 2022.

7 Hilderband, Dwayne S. *Footwear, the Missed Evidence.* Staggs Publishing, 2007.

8 "Best Practice Recommendation for Casting Footwear and Tire Impression Evidenced at the Crime Scene." *ANSI/ASB Best Practice Recommendation 126*, 2022.

9 "Best Practice Recommendation for Lifting of Footwear and Tire Impressions." *ANSI/ASB Best Practice Recommendation 049*, 2020.

10 ANSI/ASB (2020) *049—Best Practice Recommendation for Lifting of Footwear and Tire Impressions.*

Bloodstain Evidence 24

Blood evidence appears in crime scenes in various forms for numerous reasons, each holding unique value depending on the case. It is crucial for the Crime Scene Investigator (CSI) to recognize the significance of blood evidence on-site and take appropriate steps to collect or preserve it. If the scene requires later reconstruction, the CSI must provide detailed and accurate documentation to support future analysis. Both visible and non-visible blood should be located and assessed, as even diluted blood retains significant evidentiary value. There are ways the bloodstain evidence can be documented so that it can be analyzed later by someone who specializes in bloodstain pattern analysis.

The use of blood enhancement chemicals should not be avoided. Modern advancements have made these chemicals less destructive, with studies showing that reliable DNA profiles can still be obtained after enhancement and washing. White cotton fabrics consistently yield the best results. Additionally, both fresh and older blood samples can contribute meaningfully to an investigation, so older samples should not be disregarded.[1] A 2019 study by CSIs examined blood-stained items, including the soil beneath them, that had been exposed to outdoor conditions and rainfall for 5 months. Phenolphthalein testing conducted after this period produced some confirmatory results showing that even after months of exposure to the elements including rain, obtaining blood from the soil was probable.[2]

Searching for Bloodshed Patterns/Locations in Scene

Locations

- Search walls, floors, ceilings, furniture, pillows/lamps
- Inside of drawers/doors/window wells/vents
- Behind desks/tables/dressers/doors
- Behind wall outlets, baseboards, wall decorations
- Thrown documents
- Sinks/handles and edges
- Garbage cans and underside of lid
- Laundry rooms and inside of appliances
- Floors/drain traps/baseboards/grout lines

DOI: 10.4324/9781003503897-25

Appearance Can Be Confused with Household Stains from

- Coffee (grounds and liquid stains)
- Tobacco/drug products that create dark water
- Food residue, sauces
- Fecal matter
- Rust
- Paint/stain/pigment

Crime Specific

- Bludgeon incident
  - Fine misting of blood
  - Elongated droplets
  - Pattern often does not include bone/hair/tissue
  - Suspect likely has same pattern on lower part of clothing/shoes
- Shoe contact
  - Victim head swinging with force can create small arc with swing
  - Stomping—pattern found on bottom of shoe by arc and on opposite pant leg of suspect
  - Kicking—pattern on toe of shoe and shin area same pant leg of suspect

Photograph Suggestions

- No direct flash recommended—from built-in or detached flash

Label Information

- Number/letter designator assigned
- Directional arrow (up, north, front door, etc.)
- Case number/date
- Photographer/ID
- Consider placing metric side of scale by item and place scale along edge of frame

Blood spatter Marks on Clothing/Bedding/Pillows

- Can be done on scene or back at lab
  - Easier to photograph in controlled environment
  - Wrap/roll in butcher paper to preserve blood patterns during transport
- Can photograph wet or dry
  - Hard to lay flat once dry as fabric may bunch/pull
  - Easier to see stains when dry

- Any measuring/labeling should be done when dry if analysis is performed
- Lay item on clean butcher paper/clean paper bag on driveway/roadway, hospital floor, hood of vehicle

- Add scale and markers after initial photographs taken
  - Be mindful of black clothing difficulties
  - Gray scale may help focus/lighting issues
  - Can include circle, arrow, and scale markers
- Sketching marks on clothing, beds, and so on
  - 2 measurements needed (height/width)
  - Measurements on clothing, bedding, and so on required when doing reconstruction
  - Can measure shirts—up from bottom/across from side
  - Can measure pants—down from waist band/across from side OR up from leg hem/across from side
  - Can be documented with hand-drawn sketch

Blood Spatter Documentation

Consider

- Not all patterns of bloodstains will provide enough information to justify detailed mapping photography. Sometimes overall, mid-range, and scaled close-up photographs are sufficient for what is present on scene.
- Not all bloodstains will have enough detail to even be classified into organized patterns.[3] They may lack details, overlap details with other stains, or have been altered in some manner.
- Complete ALL macrophotography prior to any chemical enhancement
- All blood collected from scene should be tested, so collect with the expectation to process—you need to know if it is victim or suspect's blood
- Include tested/swabbed areas on sketch
- Document all locations of first aid provided inside the scene and any suspected blood travel based upon first aid (trail from gurney, stepped in spillage, etc.)
- Photograph all blood stains and area surrounding the stain to ensure none are missed
- For linear or arcing stains, ensure the ends of all are located and photographed
- Consider digital scanning and video documentation IN ADDITION TO PHOTOGRAPHS for scenes with heavy blood activity, multiple victims and areas of origin, and multiple types of spatter.

- Can scan in black/white to increase contrast
- Small drops will show up in scan and have all measurements recorded
- Don't forget to get reference measurements before leaving scene
- Scan can be viewed by bloodstain analyst at a later time

Angle of Travel

- Droplet(s)' shape is only reliable within 4–5 feet of travel for angle prediction. After that the terminal velocity has been reached and the diameter of the blood spot is no longer a reliable predictor.
- 90° angle droplet creates circular shape drop but edges may be irregular due to surface landing (common with ceilings, textured walls, carpeting)
- Smaller angle of travel—stain is longer with elliptical shape

Angle of Impact

- SINE = Width/length
- Width is the shorter axis/length is the longer axis

Area of Convergence

- Shown on 2D drawing/diagram
- Draw straight lines through the long axis of the bloodstains
- Extend lines out
- The area the lines meet represents possible blood source location

Area of Origin

- Shown in 3D, on scene, in vehicle—re-enactment with lasers/stringing
- Use identified angle of impact

Stringing

- Visual representation for area of origin—hanging of strings for each determined path to find intersection
- Used for short distances

Process

1. Identify pattern and bloodstains to be used, origin will be determined for each pattern separately
2. Collect all DNA from stains if applicable

3. Complete any enhancements needed
4. Identify angles of impact for all chosen stains (W/L). String several stains for each pattern.
5. Adhere strings to surface blood is on using push pins, sticky hooks, tripods, and so on. Can be horizontal or vertical surface, keep strings taut regardless.
6. Follow angle of impact and attach string to fixed object (tripod, yardstick, wall, etc.)
7. Repeat for each string in pattern and affix to same stationary placement showing the estimated origin using the already identified angle of impact for all chosen stains.
   a. **OPTION**: Use different color for each pattern for ease of visibility
8. Results will provide approximate area of origin for bloodletting
   b. Area of origin will continue to move until it accommodates all chosen stains of SAME PATTERN, wait until you are finished to determine the origin.
9. Photograph overall results from multiple angles.

Minimum Mapping Documentation (Yellow Scale Sticks, Yard Sticks, Spatter Sticks, Tape Measure)

1. Complete the following prior to beginning:
   a. Remove all barriers from view in immediate area—don't move the items being photographed
   b. Photograph section with overall/mid-range/close-ups without scales
2. Apply scale along 2 borders of section in "L" shape or "+" shape—photograph anything that will be covered by tape in advance if it is of value
   a. Place measuring sticks along horizontal AND vertical axis (spatter sticks, measuring tape, ruler tape)
   b. Can be affixed to surface or handheld (small bits of wax/dental wax can help stick)
   c. Sections 2 × 2 feet for larger areas, sections 6 × 6 inches for smaller areas
3. Capture overall and mid-range photographs of area with sticks visible and aligned with camera frame

Detailed Mapping Documentation (Metric Scale Preferred)

1. Complete the following prior to beginning:
   a. Remove all barriers from view in immediate area—don't move the items being photographed

   b. Photograph section with overall/mid-range/close-ups without scales
   c. Ensure item is photographed rather than collected
   d. Place camera on tripod and adjust camera settings, lens, and flash needs
   e. Adjust level to ensure 90°
   f. Ensure camera is in level with grid in viewfinder, camera level or plumb bob
   g. Use remote or timer
2. Apply scale along 2 borders of section in "L" shape or "+" shape—photograph anything that is covered by tape in advance if it is of value
   a. Can use painters tape, scale tape, ruler tape, paper scales, hand drawn with Sharpie, yard sticks, scale sticks, trajectory rods (keep as thin as needed)
   b. Begin at fixed intersection (wall/floor)
   c. Sections 2 × 2 feet for larger areas, sections 6 × 6 inches for smaller areas
   d. Use line level or plumb bob to ensure straight direction
3. Identify each section, pattern, and individual stain of interest and assign letter or number
   a. Can use subsequent lettering for pattern distinction (section A, pattern 1, stain 1)
   b. Apply labels and scales
   c. Place orientation arrow on scale or substrate, can use plumb bob or line level for true "up"
4. Take overall and mid-range photographs of area once labeled to show relationship to scene
5. Take close-up photographs of any stains needing analysis or DNA collection
   a. Align scale to frame of picture
   b. Remain perpendicular (90°)
   c. Adjust lighting/exposure as needed, consider bracketing
   d. Identify a minimum of 9 stains for larger areas[4]
6. Record needed measurements for samples to include height/depth of each section, pattern, and individual stain
7. Collect needed DNA samples

Documentation Needed for Off-Scene Analysis

Minimum information needed for Bloodstain Analyst to follow up:

- Victim wound information if known
- Weapons used if known

- Location information—dimensions of scene/room/item with blood present
- Locations with no blood activity present documented
- Description of the substrate the blood has landed on—sample collected for later reference if needed
  - Fixed/moveable
  - Porous/non-porous
  - Smooth/textured/thin/curved/flat
- Patterns involved—types, location, repeating patterns
- Overall size (metric preferred)[5]
  - Spatter—width in mm
  - Non spatter—overall dimensions and location in scene
- Overall direction—tail generally points in direction of force
- Shape of individual stains
  - Circular, elliptical, irregular, linear or curvilinear, intact/broken
  - Edges—shape, condition
  - Debris among stain—hair, bone, defects, biological matter, GSR, and so on
- Traits of stains
  - Wet/dry/flaking/solid
  - Diluted appearance?
  - Clotted/thin smears
  - Flow/spatter
- Altered/impressions
  - Patterns/stains documented with scale
  - Overall/mid-range photographs with scale in place helps with orientation
  - Up arrow placard visible in mid-range photographs beneficial
  - Close-ups needed for analysis
  - Use horizontal and vertical scales
  - Keep photograph 90° to avoid distortion
  - Use L scale with circle in corner for angle correction
  - Visible debris/blood/bone/hair/GSR/so on
- Rough sketch of area being examined with placement of spatter stains
  - Complete 1 wall at a time
  - Include measurements of chosen stains

Non-Visible Blood—Detection

- Chemicals react with old/cleaned blood to identify areas of interest
- Photographs of enhancement reaction highly recommended but not required

Where to Use

- Textiles/porous/non-porous
- Soil/plants
- Vehicles/joints/metals/carpets/seats/glass
- Where baseboard meets floor/wall
- Where couch meets wall
- Outlet covers/light switches
- BlueStar is safe to use on human skin AND pets' fur/feet

Chemical Controls

- Always use positive/negative controls BEFORE USE in scene/on evidence
- Photographs of controls optional but recommended

Positive Control

- Swab a known blood card, apply chemical to blood swab
- Chemical should have appropriate color reaction, if not don't use chemical

Negative Control

- Apply chemical to clean swab with no blood, should have no color reaction

Chemical Options

Luminol

- CAN collect DNA for several hours after application
- Don't oversaturate when applying, will dilute
- Chemiluminescence results
- Reacts with iron in hemoglobin found in old bloodstains
- Found to be one of most effective enhancements

Results

- Almost immediate
- Fade within minutes
- Must be viewed in complete darkness
- Can be photographed easily—ISO 400, F/8, 2-minute exposure a good start, adjust from there—bounce flash off ceiling or roof of vehicle

Good for

- Diluted and/or cleaned blood
- Dark/multi-colored surfaces
- Recommended for footwear/tire/pattern marks
- Not recommended for fingerprint processing due to poor ridge clarity
- Blood that is just hard to see because of placement
    - Cracks of baseboards, doorways, between floorboards
    - Carpet backings, car seat padding, mattress covers

Application

- Set up photo equipment first, tripod and all
- Apply chemicals after camera is set up
- After mixing pour into spray bottle
- Shelf life of mixture, several hours
- Fine spray bottle with mist setting recommended
- Set up photo equipment first, tripod and all
- Darken room as much as possible
- Spray in sweeping motion. If spraying while shutter is open on camera wear black gloves and remove watch.
- Photograph results immediately
- Singular application if possible as an excess of solution will water down DNA

Reaction

- Positive reaction—blue/white chemiluminescence
- False positives—copper salts, brass, bronze, cobalt (locks, doorknobs, etc.), some paint/varnish, some fibrous fruits, and vegetables such as beets, turnips, green beans, and banana
- Enhancement of Luminol reaction—180–280 nm with ALS

Options: F3.5, ISO 400–800[6]

- The higher the ISO the shorter the film exposure time
- Tripod, cable release needed
- 15 or 30 second exposure, 45, 60 second
- Quick flash of light at beginning of exposure can lighten up view
- Manual focus (Autofocus light can mess up light metering)

Option: F2.8 or Lowest, ISO 400[7]

- Bulb shutter speed setting—40–80 second exposure time
- Move to F16 and fire flash unit once
- Release shutter

Option: F8, 2 minute, ISO 300
Option: F5.6, 30 seconds, ISO 400
Option: Black and white photographs AFTER color photographs

- Enhances visible results
- Recommend color as well as black and white (not instead)

Bluestar

- CAN collect DNA sample from results for several hours after application
- Training formula will impact DNA, ensure right formula and NOT expired
- Can be applied after Luminol and have positive reactions
- Results must be photographed
- Will work on blood dating back hundreds of years

Results

- Almost immediate
- Fade within minutes
- Must be viewed in complete darkness
- Can be photographed easily

Good for

- Diluted cleaned blood on dark/multi-colored surfaces
- Recommended for footwear/tire/pattern marks
- Not recommended for fingerprint processing due to poor ridge clarity
- Viewing blood that has been cleaned up
- Blood that is just hard to see because of placement
  - Cracks of baseboards, floorboards, doorways
  - Carpet backings, car seat padding, mattress covers

Reaction

- Blue glow that lasts for several minutes
- Best reaction in low light to total darkness
- False positives
  - Bleach—reaction for bleach is often quicker and fades immediately
  - Detergents, chlorine
  - Paints/varnishes
  - Copper, manganese
  - Lichens/thyme/some moss
  - Turnips, banana, radish, ginger, carrot

Camera Setting Options

Option: F2.8, ISO 800[8]

- Partially darkened room
- Tripod and cable release
- Bulb setting or timed at 15, 30, 45 seconds—check at each time interval, adjust if needed

Option: Other Settings Options, Adjust Accordingly

- 45 second shutter release with F8, ISO 400
- 30 second shutter release with F5.6, ISO 600

Application

- When mixing—swirl don't shake
- Apply with mist applicator, don't oversaturate
- Ensure your applicator is empty from the last use, pump several times to ensure empty
- Set up photo equipment prior to application—tripod and all. Consider starting a timed exposure and spraying while the shutter is open to capture reaction. Wear black gloves and remove watch.
- Spray top layer prior to moving anything, if no reaction move items layer by layer checking each time.

Practice Option

- Find glowsticks with blue liquid (blue optimal, any color works)
- Open and sprinkle accordingly in a "scene"
- Photograph with Bluestar settings
- Good for photography/video/labeling practice

Fluorescein

Results

- Allow to air-dry before photographs
- Must be viewed with ALS—445 nm, orange goggles/filter

Good for

- Horizontal surfaces
- Multi-colored/dark surfaces, flooring
- Impressions needing higher contrast

Reaction

- Positive reaction—fluorescent impression visible with ALS

Application

- Spray working solution on item/area
- Spray hydrogen peroxide solution on item/area
- Does not contain fixative so excessive spraying will cause stain to run

Visible Blood—Enhancement with Chemicals

Controls

- Always use positive/negative controls before using
- Photographs of controls recommended

Positive Control

- Swab a known blood sample and apply chemical to sample
- Should have appropriate color reaction (dark blue/black)

Negative Control

- Apply chemical to swab with no blood
- Should have no color reaction

Amido Black

- Collect needed DNA prior to use
- Messier than LCV due to rinse process
- Can be used before ninhydrin
- Can be methanol or water based
- Working solution shelf life: 1–2 years—cost-efficient
- Solution works best if made ahead of time (2 days ideal)
- Useable on porous and non-porous
- Dilute solution down for porous surfaces
- Rinse will clear background stain
- Results must be photographed—ISO 100, F/8–22, tripod

Good for

- Fingerprints retain fine details and ridges
- Footwear prints
- Porous and non-porous surfaces
- Can be used on deceased bodies—cleans off skin with 10% bleach solution

Not Good for

- Presumptive testing because of false positives
- Non-visible blood detection (other fluids have proteins)

Reaction

- Immediate results often seen, allow to develop 30–60 seconds
- Positive result is black/deep purple coloring
- Reacts to proteins in blood
- Permanent color stain
- Rinse with tap water OR a rinse solution then tap water

Formula Options

Option: Methanol Formula (Good for Evidence Processing)

- Strong, but toxic
- Requires rinse
- Provides finer detail after rinse

Option: Water Formula (Preferred for Scene Use)

- Better for use on scenes
- Less damaging to tape and other substrates
- Prepared use mix does not need rinse (fixer in formula already)

Application

- Spray or squirt bottle
- Allow to air-dry
- Can allow to develop up to 5 minutes before rinsing

Option: Spray/Squirt Stain Directly

- Hold back approximately 6 inch
- Spray above area of interest
- Allow liquid to run down covering area
- Spray gently, evenly
- Let sit 3–5 minutes
- Tap water rinse if necessary
- Rinse not always necessary

Option: Spray Towel Over Stain

- Lay paper towel over area of interest
- Hold spray approximately 6 inch

- Spray/squirt area of interest, soaking paper towel
- Allow to sit 30 seconds to 5 minutes in place
- Gently remove towel from stains
- Rinse with tap water if needed

Option: Dip

- Fully submerge item in tray
- Let sit 1–3 minutes
- Dip in rinse and agitate gently

Ninhydrin

- Should be used with fume hood and humidity source
- Not recommended for use on scene

Good for

- Charred (lightly) documents—can remove soot leaving original content visible
- Bloody prints on porous, non-glossy surfaces

Results

- Dark purple color
- Must be photographed

Application

- Dipping, brushing, spraying
- Once applied, allow to air-dry
- Apply heat/humidity to item
  - Chamber 60%–80%
  - Iron—set to steam setting. Works best vertically—be mindful of water drips. Horizontal application—place thin towel between item and iron.

LCV—Leuco Crystal Violet

- Contains hydrogen peroxide—DNA collection could be compromised

Good for

- Fire scenes with blood on floor
  - Bloodstains can get covered with soot and not be seen
  - Will wash off soot covering leaving blood enhanced

Reaction

- Reacts to hemoglobin in blood
- Violet or purple coloring results
- Loses fine details
- Must be photographed immediately
- Over days will all turn purple
- Reacts with UV light

Application Options

Option: Spray Towel on Top of Stain

- Affix paper towel over area of stain print
- Spray area of interest, soaking paper towel
- LCV will soak through paper towel evenly

Option: Spray Stain Directly

- Use aerosol/fine mister application
- Works well for footwear prints
- May affect fine details with fingerprints

Option: Dip

- Fully submerge item in tray
- Let sit 30 seconds (some tape can sit 1–2 minutes)
- Rinse with tap water
- Allow to dry
- Photograph results

Option: ALS to Increase Contrast

- Process with LCV
- Allow to dry 24 hours (not in direct sunlight)
- View with ALS
- Red goggles at wavelengths of 525, 530, 570 nm
- Orange goggles at wavelengths of 485, 450 nm

Hungarian Red Spray

- Water-based formula
- Sensitive, sometimes more than Amido Black
- Safe for field use
- Can still collect DNA after processing

Results

- Deep magenta-colored results
- Can be photographed or lifted with gel lifter but should be done within a couple of hours
- Can use with ALS for enhancement or to eliminate background colors
    - orange/red filter
    - fluoresces with 520–560 nm light[9]

Good for

- Human skin (live/deceased), blood stains on non-porous surfaces and flooring (linoleum, tile, wood), latent fingerprints and footprints, most surfaces

Not Good for

- Handwriting samples, inks, hairs, or fluids, paper, clothing/bedding

Application

- Test background first to ensure suitable
- If entire background reacts, do not use this method
- Methods: Dip or spray

Spray

- Cover area in question with paper towel
- Spray fixative over area soaking paper towel, remove paper towel
- Cover entire area to be processed, ensure fully saturated
- Allow to process 1 minute
- Rinse with tap water
- Air-dry completely
- Lift results with gel lifter or collect examination quality photographs

Non-Chemical Options—*Don't Have Any Chemicals?*

Collect Whole Item

- Photographs with marker/scale prior to collection
- Collect entire item of interest
- Can wrap in butcher paper if needed
- Transport to laboratory for further processing

Cutting of Item

If Smaller Area on Cuttable Item: Wall/Couch/Laminate Flooring

1. Photograph with and without marker identification/scale
2. Mark orientation arrow in corner of area to cut
3. Cut out area of interest leaving considerable space around suspected area needing enhancement
4. Place in box or can depending on size/item, can wrap in butcher paper for conservation
5. Transport to laboratory for further processing

Tape Lift of Stain

If Smooth Non-porous Surface

1. Cover pattern area with fingerprint tape having slight overlap of tape ensuring full coverage
2. Mark with orientation arrow prior to removing, lift slowly and evenly
3. Place in clear sheet protector or plastic bag
4. Transport to laboratory for further processing: View with ALS, UVIR, process with LCV or Amido Black

POWDER—Black powder and Sciluminate powder have been known to enhance bloody prints. They may be photographable or liftable depending upon stain and surface

Bloodstain Facts

- Human body contains 5–6 liters of blood
- 40% volume of blood loss will cause death
- Blood is 55% plasma and plasma will separate from the blood pool over time
- When bloodstains dry and are disturbed the middle will often dislodge leaving a ring around the stain

Common Stain Names/Causes

Bloodstain

- A deposit of blood on a surface

Skeletonized Bloodstain

- Exterior ring of dried bloodstain after center flakes/wipes away
- Shape of original stain with only outer edge remaining

Spatter Stain

- A bloodstain that has been dispersed through the air due to force

Splashed Bloodstain

- Is a quantity of blood more than 1.0 ml?
- Contact from minor force or free fall to surface

Patterns of Bloodstain

Impact Pattern

- Bloodstain pattern resulting from an object striking liquid blood

Expiration Pattern—(Bubble Ring, Breath Ring)

- Circle shape in bloodstain from air bubble
- Airflow from mouth/nose/wound pushing blood away from body
- Can be misinterpreted when there's a lack of air bubbles

Cast Off Pattern

- Bloody object moving in arc flinging blood along path
- Counting is only approximate number of blows, not exact
- First strike may not leave cast off since no blood is on the item to cast
- If victim keeps moving, several blows can have no blood response
- If victim was already bloody from different impact, first blunt force hit may leave an arc

Arterial Spray

- Spurt of blood released when damage to major artery
- Spray ejected with heart pumping pressure/regular pattern
- Be mindful it can hit 2 walls in same path
- Creates linear pattern of blood with heart pump

Arcing Patterns

- Result of swinging motion
- Normally circular at start, elongated in flight path

Active Bloodstaining—Projected Spatter

- Back spatter
  - Blood traveling opposite direction as force
  - Blood leaving entrance wound
  - Typically, larger/fewer stains than forward spatter

- Forward spatter
  - Traveling in same direction as force
  - Blood leaving exit wound
  - Typically, a fine mist
- High-velocity spatter
  - Fine misting of blood with small blood spots
  - Often found high on wall/ceiling
  - Pattern can include hair/tissue/bone pieces with blood
- Size of droplets directly related to speed of travel
  - Smaller droplets travel faster
  - Larger droplets travel farther
- Voids
  - Spot missing blood in an area where continuous blood flow would be expected
  - Shape can show what items were removed—person, chair, door opened
  - Always look for voids when blood spatter present

Passive Bloodstaining

- Caused by gravity only—flow patterns, dripping stains, pooling, drip trail, drip from hand/weapon
- Surface blood lands on determines final shape of stains
  - Non-porous provides circular smooth shape
  - Porous substrate provides rougher edges
- Blood trail
  - Drops of blood falling on ground from injury, often linear or semi-linear pattern
  - Blood trail is often delayed as blood needs to bleed through clothing/hoodie/coat, so look beyond area of casings to find start of blood trail
  - Follow trail to find pool/additional victims/and so on
  - Photograph end of trail to include location/address/identifiers
- Pooled blood
  - Often pooled at end of blood trail, not at location of shooting (unless fatal shot) because it takes time to pool, victim needs to be stationary for some time
  - Check sides for straight or specific shaped edges (voids, what was removed)

Transfer Patterns—Swipe, Wipe, Impression Patterns

- Swipe—bloody object moves across area leaving blood behind
- Wipe—object moves through blood leaving blood on object

- Impression pattern
  - Shoe prints, tire marks, tool marks, weapon marks
  - Footprints, fingerprints
- Insect stain (fly spots)
  - Resemble high-velocity blood spatter
  - Often comma shape rather than circular
  - Look for repetition of tails in spots
  - Tails appear randomly placed, no repetitive directionality
  - If located near skeletonized remains would have DNA value
- Fly feces
  - Will test positive for blood with presumptive tests
  - Can contain DNA value
- Fly vomit
  - Likely will not test positive with presumptive tests
  - Likely will not have DNA value

Practice Option with Bloody Prints

- Create your own bloody prints to practice processing and photography so you won't be rusty when you process real evidence
- Make your own handprints with silicone lifter of choice (AccuTrans works well), dip in blood (real, synthetic, animal), and print away. Process as needed, can use wet or dry.
- Use to practice your blood enhancement as well

Cases to Consider regarding Bloodstain Evidence

- David Camm was a former Indiana State Trooper who was tried 3 times for the murder of his wife and children, being exonerated on the third trial. Some issues from trial included blood evidence being overlooked during scene processing and mis-identified during later examination. Because the items in question were collected and secured in property, they were available for later testing and examination, which shows the value of evidence collection rather than photograph and leave.
- Kathleen Peterson was found deceased by her husband Michael in 2001 at the bottom of their staircase inside their home with a large amount of blood on the floor and surrounding walls. There was a great deal of speculation as to how she died and who committed the murder. Neither scene processing nor evidence processing included chemical enhancement or ALS.
- Upon return to the crime scene 2 weeks after the death of juveniles James M. Moore, Steven Branch, and Christopher Byers, Luminol was utilized to search the surrounding area resulting in a footwear

print discovery. Minimal visible blood was located at the original scene even though one child suffered from mutilation and was a great setting for Luminol use.

Blood Enhancement Chemicals Can Be Useful But Are Not without Issue

- 2007: Scene processing of Meredith Kercher—Luminol produced a positive result; however, a later test with tetramethylbenzidine provided negatives results causing strain during the investigation.
- 1986: Scene processing of Lindy Chamberlain scene—confirmatory tests showed the presence of blood in her vehicle from Orthotolidine; however, the laboratory consumed the entire sample, and no further testing could be done.

Notes

1 Hartley, Gabrielle and Claire Glynn. "A Comparative Analysis of Protein and Peroxidase Blood." *Journal of Forensic Research and Analysis*, 2017, pp. 1–5.
2 Pope, Lisa. "Chemical Testing for Presumptive Blood on Items and the Ground below Them during Months of Exposure to Sun, Rain, Rust." *Journal of Forensic Identification*, 2020, pp. 416–425.
3 Organization of Scientific Area Committees for Forensic Science (OSAC) *2022-S-0030-Standard for Methodology in Bloodstain Pattern Analysis.*
4 Maloney, Michael S., and Donald G. Housman. *Crime Scene Investigation Procedural Guide*. CRC Press, 2014.
5 OSAC 2022-S-0030.
6 https://www.bluestar-forensic.com/.
7 Miller, Larry. *Police Photography*, 5th ed. Anderson Publishing, 2006.
8 https://www.bluestar-forensic.com/.
9 Penven, Don. "Latent Blood Prints—Methods for Chemical Enhancement." *Crime Scene Investigator Network*, 1 Mar. 2013.

25 Firearms Evidence Collection

Firearms evidence is found and collected for many reasons. Aside from the possibility of being matched to shooting they can provide additional evidentiary value such as DNA, fingerprints, fibers, hair, oil residue, or pattern imprints. Processing firearms on first contact increases chances of gathering additional trace evidence and reduces the chances of contamination. While it is widely known that obtaining fingerprints off firearms is difficult, it is not impossible, and many great products have been created for this purpose. Firearms carry a large amount of DNA, but that DNA should, as a standard, be collected prior to the firearm being widely handled. It is important that if someone is being charged with possession of a firearm that it is processed to identify the correct owner. While there is a benefit to swabbing firearm evidence for blood or touch DNA on scene, if items are transported with care, fingerprinting can be accomplished afterward in the laboratory environment with stronger results than scene processing.

In the last decade, there have been several studies completed on how to successfully recover DNA and fingerprints off cartridge cases and firearms and the odds of retrieval are better than ever and recommended that all casings be processed. A study done in Raleigh NC concluded that it is more beneficial to collect contact DNA from cartridge cases than attempting to get latent prints. The DNA results they were getting were beneficial, whereas the latent prints they were able to develop were not useful.[1] San Diego has been getting usable DNA off approximately 30% of their cartridge cases since about 2019[2] and a new study found usable profiles from cartridge cases with 67% success rate.[3]

On-scene References

- Headstamp codes—Cartridgecollectors.org
- Headstamp guide with pictures—AFTE.org—(The Association of Firearm and Tool Mark Examiners)
- Police Officer Guide to Recovered Firearms—ATF—Bureau of Alcohol, Tobacco, Firearms and Explosives
- Online firearm and accessory guide with visuals and names—PICA Identification guide (Illinois.gov)

DOI: 10.4324/9781003503897-26

Facts to Consider

- Alternative cartridge cases exist—discuss with the local ATF any trends they have observed
- Cell phone/tablet/e-cigarette hit with a projectile can cause ignition of lithium battery and have flash fire that will burn through flesh, wallets, clothing, backpacks, and so on—burns quick/intense leaving char residue after fire
- Check tires of all parties leaving the scene of a shooting since cartridge cases often get stuck in tires of first arrivals (witnesses, paramedics, officers)
- DNA is widely found on firearms evidence, handle with caution, wear clean gloves for each firearm
- Search for all projectiles on scene to include third-party damages, surrounding homes/vehicles
- Serial numbers were required on firearms AFTER 1968. Obliterated SN—removal of SN, engraving is not readable. Altered serial number—partially removed/damaged/changed—partially readable.
- Prior to rendering firearms safe: Photograph in place (even if it was reported moved prior to your arrival), visually inspect for blood/biological evidence with flashlight, ensure you are comfortable with firearms or get assistance
- Consider orange zip ties or red rope for rendering firearms safe—wipe off with bleach wipe or alcohol wipe prior to placing inside firearm

Types of Firearms Evidence

- After firearms are rendered safe, consider viewing/photographing the barrel for recent activity (presence of cobwebs may indicate it was not fired recently, presence of blood may indicate otherwise)
- Projectiles from long guns and handguns may contain markings valuable for a comparison to a firearm

Handguns

- Single shot, revolver, semi-automatic, automatic
- Caliber measurement of bore in hundredths of inch
- 45 caliber bore is 45/100-inch diameter
- Revolvers can be marked for placement of ammunition with a wax pen, or they can all be placed individually in coin envelopes with marking on the envelopes

Suppressors

- Sound suppressor (silencer) or flash suppressor—attached to muzzle of firearm to reduce noise and flash. Can be store bought or homemade (potatoes, bread)—look for soot marks/holes on pillows, blankets

Switches

- Small devices placed on guns that change them from semi-automatic to automatic weapons (may be factory manufactured or 3D printed)

Long Guns

- Rifles and shotguns
- Electrochemical etching another way to rifle barrels (faster, cheaper): The barrel is drilled out, surface coated, and voltage applied to etch grooves

Shotgun

- Most barrels are not rifled
- Shoots pellets (lead, salt), slugs (rifled or not), shot (bird, buck, snake)
- Slug gun—shotgun with rifled barrel, shoots large metal projectile
- Types: Single or double barreled, pump action, lever action, top break, bolt action, semi-automatic

Gauge *(Shotguns)*

- Measurement of load (smaller gauge = larger diameter)
- 12 gauge emits equivalent to lead slug 1/12 pound

Zip Guns

- Homemade guns, multiple styles
- Check with ATF for trends in your area

Non-lethal Firearms

- Bean bag guns
- Pepper ball guns
- Tear gas guns
- Tasers, taser guns

Ammunition

Bullet Fragment—*Metal Fragments*

- Jacket OR lead piece—not an intact projectile
- High-velocity bullets fragment more than low velocity
- Bullet core—lead/metal piece
- Bullet jacket—copper jacket pieces or polymer jacket

- Small pieces of metal placed in shotshell can be examined such as Bird shot, Buck shot, Snake shot, and BB shot

Projectile

- Lead OR lead with jacket (copper or polymer)
- Called fired ammunition, fired bullet, bullet
- Some projectiles may contain a head stamp and should be photographed if present
- Projectiles should be examined for trace evidence to include DNA, fibers, and glass damage[4]
- Federal Syntech Total Synthetic Jacket (TSJ) bullets retain their polymer coating when fired and the projectile will appear red on the exterior. This can resemble red plastic pieces on a scene, especially at night.

Cartridge

- Also, it may be referred to as live bullet, live round, rounds, ammunition
- Can be examined/compared for markings from ejection port, extractor, and firing pin (if firearm was jammed or racked prior to firing)
- They should be treated and packaged the same as a fired cartridge case
- May still contain DNA/fingerprints

Cartridge Case

- Also, it may be referred to as casing, case, brass, fired casing
- Have been known to begin rusting while on scene in certain weather
- Check cartridge cases for fingerprints, they are sometimes touched after being discharged from weapons
- More likely to get DNA than fingerprints on fired casings
- Casings made for revolvers do not have extractor groove
- Some calibers are interchangeable

Headstamp Information

- Imprinted information on end of cartridge OR cartridge case
- Words/shapes/numbers or mixture
- +P has been loaded to produce a higher internal pressure when fired than is standard for ammunition of its caliber
- Cartridge cases can be either metric (e.g., 7.62 × 39) or standard (40S&W)

Hollow Point

- Holes are often larger than non-hollow point
- Depression in nose of bullet with lines
- Expands in flower petal shape

Misfired Cartridge

- Unfired cartridge with defect in primer (can be compared to firearm)

Shotshell

- Unfired shotgun shell

Shotshell Case

- Casing from fired shotshell

Shotgun Slug

- Metal projectile larger to fit shotgun

Shotshell Components

- Shot cup, wadding, cups, wrapper
- Interior shotshell components hold the shot and don't travel far when guns are fired

Subsonic Cartridge

- Travels slower than speed of sound
- Made to fire quieter, NOT silent—when paired with silencer becomes very quiet
- Projectiles are heavier and made to travel slower
- .45ACP inherently subsonic due to heavy projectile

Supersonic Cartridge

- Travels faster than speed of sound
- Loud cracking noise when fired
- Majority of cartridges fall into this category
- Higher velocity, better range, flatter trajectory

Non-lethal Firearms/Weapons

Tasers

- Discharge barbs with prongs and AFIDS when deployed

AFIDS

- Anti-Felon IDentification
- Small circular paper discs that contain the SN of taser: 20–30 discs discharged when taser is deployed
- Collection will tell you which taser was deployed—a sample of each area of taser AFIDS should be collected

- If only 1 taser is deployed, consider collecting a sample of AFIDS anyway as it can confirm or refute

BARBS/Hooks

- Do not cut wires if on scene
- Collect taser/wire/barbs as 1 item if connected
- Collect from hospital when applicable
- Inspect for blood if found disconnected from source
- If in clothing collect intertwined, don't remove on scene

Taser Injuries

- Take photographs of barb injuries: Small circular punctures
- Can cause subject loss of movement control, resulting in secondary injuries/fall
- Can cause seizures

Stun Guns

- Discharge electrical shock with direct contact

Non-lethal Ammunition

- Bean bag rounds
- Rubber rounds
- Pepper spray capsules
- Can be collected and compared to source

Defects/Damages—*Projectile Impact Patterns*

- 1 bullet can leave holes, ricochets, swipes, and so on

Bullet Wipes

- Soot marks from bullet travel
- Ring around bullet hole
- Dark linear mark from bullet travel along substrate

Elongated Bullet Holes—*Keyhole*

- Caused from bullet traveling sideways after hitting a surface and tumbling
- Holes are not relative to size of projectile

Penetrating Defect

- Enters item and does not exit

Perforating Defect

- Goes through item, enters and leaves

Ricochet Marks

- Linear marks—bullet hitting item then deflecting off
- Can leave depression and markings and provide direction of bullet travel

Substrates

Drywall Bullet Holes

- Holes are relative to size of projectile

Hard Plastic Bullet Holes

- Often consistent with size of ammunition used

Metal Bullet Holes

- Entrance is mostly true to size with 90° angle

Rubber Bullet Holes

- Vehicle tires—hole size is greatly reduced due to stretching, often there is light colored ring around entrance
- Window trim/door trim—hole size is often larger than the projectile

Textiles/Clothing Bullet Holes

- Projectiles can go through multiple layers as traveling
- Can stop in the middle or stretch fabric
- Holes are not commonly true to size of ammunition used (larger, smaller, linear, etc.)

Wood Bullet Holes

- Holes are typically smaller than projectile
- Can deviate trajectory greatly with knots and grains

Distance

Contact Defects

- Weapon was touching the substrate when fired
- Outline of muzzle on skin
- Powder burns cover a smaller area than close range

Close Range Defects

- Skin—irregular/stellate tearing

- Clothing—melting/singeing possible
- Soot/stippling likely on any surface

Medium-Range Defects

- Powder particles likely
- Bullet wipes (rings) likely

Long-Range Defects

- Bullet wipes possible

Presumptive Testing for GSR/Bullet Wipes

Griess Test—*Chemical Methods to Visualize GSR Patterns*

- React to nitrites
- False positives—urine

GSR

- Primarily used to determine distance of shot fired
- Can degrade sample
- Laboratory sample, not immediate result

Lead Test

- Bullet hole testing for lead
- Immediate result
- Many lead-free bullets are currently being used

Copper Test

- Bullet hole testing for copper
- Immediate result

Sodium Rhodizonate Test—*Used to Visualize the Dispersal of Lead in GSR Pattern*

- React to lead in GSR

Presumptive Testing for Explosive Materials

- Multiple testing options; however, you need to contact your local bomb squad or DOJ for further information.
- If you think you have explosive materials on scene, you should have them present to assist you

DNA of Firearms Evidence

Firearm—DNA Collection

- Contact (Touch) DNA from firearms continues to provide great results and gives weight to the value of collecting DNA from all firearms collected
- Follow grooves moving slowly and leave flat surfaces for latent prints if viable
- Avoid getting gun oil on your DNA sample if visible
- Always swab for DNA even if first responders touched item to clear it—you can get multiple profiles, it's okay
- Can use singular swab, singular filter/cloth or two (2) simultaneous swabs depending upon agency protocol for DNA collection

Option Samples from Handguns

- 3 samples, can be singular swab/cloth samples or 2 simultaneous swabs from each gun (magazine separate)
  1. Slide (including muzzle, front sight, frame, rear sight, and grooves on slide)
  2. Grip (including backstrap, grip, front strap, and slowly following texture)
  3. Trigger (trigger and safety if present)
- 1 sample from each gun (magazine separate)
  1. Slide, textured areas and trigger
- Additional samples
  1. Sample from interior barrel if substance present
  2. Sample from exterior chambered round (cartridge)
  3. Sample from exterior magazine (don't forget the bottom) and removed ammunition
  4. Sample from secured area (pocket, holster, magnet, etc.)

Cartridge Cases—DNA Collection

- New technology continues to increase scene processing abilities
- DNA is recommended to be collected from all cartridge cases, prior to NIBIN
- Studies have shown that when it is collected on scene it greatly improves collection results (prior to being placed inside an envelope)
- Methods used in the laboratory are also highly effective—collect your cartridge cases on scene with utmost care to prevent contamination and package individually

- Consider using Nylon flocked swabs, or cotton swabs with a pointed tip to aid in DNA recovery. Suggest using one (1) singular swab rather than two (2) swabs due to item size.
- Determine if you swab individually or by caliber/grouping based upon agency protocol. For example, all 9 mm casings swabbed with the same singular swab, all 40 caliber casings swabbed with the same singular swab.

Method

- Swab individually OR per caliber grouping, dependent upon your agency protocol
- Swab for DNA (with one (1) singular swab or folded filter/paper) around headstamp area, follow grooves/indents. Complete on scene or at laboratory depending upon your protocol.

Collection of Cartridge Cases on Scene

- Pick up casing with swab stick/toothpick/clean gloved hand. Package each casing in individual coin envelopes, not in one bag together (unless emergency situation). Can retain swab for later contamination exclusion if concerns exist.
- Alternative options exist such as FRISC caps[5] to contain the GSR or the IBIS Clear case[6] for increased results depending upon budget size

Bullet Trajectory

- It is never 100%, but it is most likely/reasonable determination
- Can provide information on direction of travel of projectile; sometimes rifling information is present in imprint.
- Bullets travel in an arc path, trajectory is mostly done with a straight path
- 1 bullet can leave multiple holes/dents/ricochets/wipes
- Trajectory impacted by weather to include wind, humidity, and temperature

Angle of Impact

- Width divided by length
- Width is always the shorter side, and length is always the longer side
- Can use ruler or calipers or template to measure
- Bullet holes 90° generally circular
- Bullet holes less than 90° generally oval

- Bullet holes projectile shaped were tumbling after hitting something else
- Don't use greatly distorted holes to determine angles

Finding Angle from Ricochet Marks on Metal Vehicles[7]

- First 1/3 of mark shows angle entered
- Last 1/3 of mark shows angle left
- When following path of projectile remember it will deflect off anything and change course of travel. Use your judgment and account for bullet deflection. Document directionality if known, don't feel the need to always know the answer.

Laser

- Can be handheld or tripod mounted
- Can point directly to the direction of origin
- If it's a large reconstruction scene use tripod mounted laser, no one is in that good of shape
- If only using it to find location of projectile and not official reconstruction, it can be handheld
- If photographing a laser, you can use baby powder or chalk dust to see better along path
- Can place solid color tarp/screen behind laser to see better along path

Plumb Bob

- Hang weight (plumb bob) from defect, it will hang straight down due to weight giving true "up"
- Can mark arrow/line

Probes

- Can be placed in hole to prevent damage and hold rod in place
- Results should always be photographed
- Good for glass and drywall

Trajectory Rods

- Shows approximate angle not exact
- Accounts for mostly straight path
- Collect needed blood/trace prior to inserting rods
- Needs 2 angles, x and y axes
- Place protractor under rod/next to rod for angle

Templates

- Bullet hole templates reference for angle
- Hold template up to hole and will give approximate angle of impact

Option: Photograph template overlaying hole

Scanning—Leica/Faro/Digital Scanning

- Great for reconstruction at a later time
- Don't forget your control measurement on scene

Trajectory Kit Options

- Angle finder/angle locator/digital angle finder
- Centering cones, rod connectors, rings
- Masking tape/painters' tape
- String (colored, not white)/string hooks/string clips
- Plumb bob on string
- Lasers/stand
- LEICA DISTO or another laser measuring device
- Level (not hot shoe level)
- Protractor/half protractor, laser mount optional (forensic protractor has "zero edge" for accuracy)
- Rods—wooden/plastic/metal/fiberglass dowel rods, multiple of diameter options, or cones to accommodate size change (can be forensic rods or home made from hardware store)
- Template sheet for hole size/angle
- Tips (pointed and for string attachment)
- Tripod or monopod with laser/camera mounts
- Spray fog
- Sharpie markers
- Scale labels/ruler tape

Phone App Options for Scene Use

- Angle finder
- Plumb bob
- Calipers
- Level
- Compass

Trajectory Documentation

- Photograph trajectory results if needed or per agency requirements
- Hole measurement: Width/length = angle of impact

1. Photograph defects with scale prior to this point, include arrow and marker #
2. If large area—section area with scale tape to include a horizontal and vertical measurement. Section off similar to grid, assigning letter/number to each section.
3. Known sequential defects should be marked as such (1A, 1B, 1C)
4. Complete presumptive testing if applicable (lead, copper, etc.) and photograph test results
5. Record measurements in scene to include height/depth
6. Record width/length of defect individually
7. Deploy trajectory rods with level and protractor, photograph results (glass defects can be done with cones/rods, lasers, or string)
8. Record angle/photograph protractor
9. Hang plumb bob next to defect and make line for true up or north with arrow
10. Take overall/mid-range photographs of grid as a whole showing placement of all markers
11. Take close-up photographs of each defect to include scale (ABFO, 6 inch gray scale, ruler, sticker)
12. Overhead photograph and sideview photograph with protractor placed accordingly to show angle

Projectile Recovery

- You can use metal detectors to find projectiles. Some detectors find lead and have high tones for lead. Some projectiles have steel.
- Chances of getting a useable projectile are high; many projectiles are useable and mostly intact even after passing through vehicles and bone.
- All reasonable efforts should be made to document and collect ALL projectiles
- Make all attempts to collect the projectiles without additional markings/damages
- Don't use metal plyers or forceps to remove projectiles since it can damage markings on projectiles

Photographs

- Close-ups of projectile in place should occur prior to recovery
- If you can't photograph in place prior to collection

1. Photograph where it landed, in place
2. Photograph holding in front of source location if known
3. Photograph damages with scale after projectile recovery
4. Explain in notes what happened and where it was recovered

Recovery Options

Projectile That Needs DNA Collection

- Swab exterior of projectile prior to packaging
- Collect all present hair/fiber/blood
- Any projectiles suspected of having passed through someone should be swabbed

Projectile in Dirt

- Place knife in dirt 2 inch from projectile
- Push projectile out of soil from the bottom without touching
- Knock off excess soil

Projectile in Drywall

- Cut wall around bullet hole for hole collection if applicable
- Cut shallow, be wary of wiring in wall
- Projectiles are often found in studs OR on ground directly below impact
- Remove by cutting around holes first
- If bullet continues into insulation, check to see if it goes through wall behind
- If bullet does not continue into insulation look/feel for hole in nearest stud
- Cut hole at bottom of drywall directly below

Option: Drywall Cutting of Bullet Defect

- Mark wall with UP arrow and identification number/letter prior to removing from wall
- Cut square around defect, approximately 4 × 4 inches (be wary of wiring)
- Mark front or backside with additional information: Case #, Date, Collector
- Package in envelope individually

Option: Wall Cutting to See Trajectory Markings

- Cut sizeable hole in drywall
- View wall behind hold to gauge trajectory

- Discard cutting with no bullet holes

Projectile in Floor

- Cut top layer around bullet hole (carpet, linoleum, tile, etc.)
- Check sublayer—often found in sublayer, concrete/padding
- Continue until projectile is reached

Projectile in Small Item—*Section of Tire, Chair Leg, Doorknob, and so on*

- Submit entire item with projectile intact, it can be removed in a controlled environment

Projectile in Tire Rubber

- Use knife to cut rubber around projectile and free from tire if loose
- If not loose: Cut square around embedded projectile, submit whole piece

OPTION: CUT SQUARE AROUND PROJECTILE IN RUBBER

- Submit entire square
- Projectile can be removed in controlled environment instead

Projectile in Thick Blood Pool

- Gently press down along length/width of blood pool, be systematic, cover all areas to ensure it is not hidden in a blood clot or depression in the substrate
- Check all pooled blood along victim's path
- Remove excess blood clots from projectile to assist drying

Projectile in Wood/Concrete

- Use wood chisel to cut around projectile, do not push/pry projectile with chisel
- Remove wood/concrete until projectile is recoverable
- Collect entire wood item if wood is small and projectile deep

Projectile in Vehicle Door

- Remove door panel with arm rest and cloth covering (remove screws and bolts)
- Remove plastic covering if present
- Projectile/metal fragments often at bottom of door in open area
- Endoscope or mirror on wand help search

- Collection: Suck out with shop vac hose, collect with grabbing tool, reach arm into area
- Can often see contents with endoscope prior to recovery attempts

Cases to Consider regarding Firearms Evidence

- After the collection of multiple cartridge cases from a shooting scene 1 was found to have a usable fingerprint. The print came back to a witness on scene, who then admitted to handling several items prior to officer arrival.
- 2001: Pamela Shelley was ruled to have committed suicide with a gun to the head; however, the coroner and sheriff did not agree. Her injuries were later re-examined and determined to be impossible to be self-inflicted based upon the angle. In 2013 the suspect confessed to her murder and received 22 years in prison.

Notes

1 Johnson, Stacey. "Examining the Effectiveness of Processing Fired Cartridge Cases for Latent Evidence." *Journal of Forensic Identification*, 2019, pp. 27–34.
2 Givens, Ann. "A New Method of DNA Testing Could Solve More Shootings: Criminologists thought It Was Impossible to Get DNA Off Shell Casings, But a Technique Pioneered in the Netherlands Is Having Notable Results." *Police1*, 8 Apr. 2019.
3 Bille, Todd, et al. "An Improved Process for the Collection and DNA Analysis of Fired Cartridge Cases." *Forensic Science International: Genetics*, vol. 46, 2020, https://doi.org/10.1016/j.fsigen.2020.102238.
4 Graff, Gary, and Iris Dalley Graff. "Advanced Crime Scene Documentation." *Tritech Forensics*, 17 Sept. 2018, Houston. Lecture/training.
5 "Signature Science's FRISC Service Enables DNA Recovery from Spent Shell Casings." *Signature Science*, 4 Oct. 2019, www.signaturescience.com/press/signature-sciences-frisc-service-enables-dna-recovery-from-spent-shell-casings/.
6 "IBIS ClearCase." *Leads Online*, leadsonline.com/clearcase.
7 Rynearson, J. *Tips and Tricks*. National Crime Investigation and Training, n.d., http://ncit.com/Tips___Tricks/tips___tricks.html.

26 Document, Printer, Ink Evidence

Documents are collected from various scenes for diverse purposes, each possessing distinct evidentiary value depending on the context. They may be gathered for their written content, such as names, numbers, or photographs. In some instances, documents are retrieved because they were used to start a fire that did not burn as intended and may lack accelerants or DNA evidence. Additionally, documents may hold significance due to their association with a known or unknown author. While the scope of analysis on these documents can be extensive, this chapter will provide guidance on effectively transferring the evidence from the scene to the laboratory for further examination.

Common Document-Related Items of Evidence to Be Collected

- Common office equipment: Staplers, paper clips, envelopes, tape, glue
- Driver's license, passports, currency, other templates for printing
- Inks and toners for machines
- Inks and pens for handwriting
- Labels
- Laminators
- Notepads
- Postage machines
- Receipts, receipt pads
- Stamps and embossing equipment—paper, rubber, wooden, metal
- Sticky notes
- Tags
- Typed/handwritten documents

Comparison Sample Examples—*Can Be Collected from Scene for Later Comparison*

Contemporaneous Writing Samples

- Notes taken while on phone, in meeting, during a conversation
- Collect similar writing instruments/papers from scene (you can have the subject write a sample later in a different location)

Handwritten Dated Document with Name

- Sticky notes, to do lists, journals, business documents, checks, receipts, ID cards with signatures

DOI: 10.4324/9781003503897-27

Machine Collection

Document and Photograph the Following

- Make/model
- Serial number
- Information about toner supplies/components
- Machine repair/service history
- If possible, remove ink cartridges *after* processing and *before* storage. Store them separately.

Typewriters

- Do not remove ribbon or keys on scene or until being analyzed
- Contact DNA and fingerprints can be collected from exterior surfaces

Accessories

- Collect power cords for all machines if possible

Enhancement Options for Indented Writing

ALS Search for Inks/Indented Writing

- Helps visualize indented writing on scene—first glance often appears as just flat paper
- ENHANCEMENTS ARE TO READ CONTENTS ONLY, not handwriting analysis. That should be done in a controlled environment, not on scene.
- Different ink reflects different wavelengths of light

Option: Light

- Dim light—best with oblique lighting source
- Older yellow streetlights can show differences in ink
- White light (flashlight, overhead room lights)—deep indentions can be seen with overhead lights
- Yellow filter helps show indented writing, some ink discrepancies
- IR wavelength 700–1100 nm good for inks

Option: Toner/Magnet

- Sprinkle particles of powdered toner ink over document
- Cover document with plastic sheet protector
- Move electrostatic wand above plastic sheet protector
- Toner will gather in indented areas

Option: Tracing Paper

- Lay tracing paper over top of document
- Run wooden pencil sideways across questioned areas
- Indented writing should appear on paper

Packaging for Document Evidence

- Package with least amount of movement while enroute
- Paper bag laid on side
- Box
- Plastic zip lock bag
- Stiff envelopes to prevent folding/edge rolling

Document Collection/Preservation from Scene

Charred Documents

- Photograph documents *first as discovered, second prior to packaging, third after removal from packaging*

Option: Collection for Document Content

- Don't separate on scene, transport as 1 item
- Slide rigid item underneath pile/documents, lift carefully (file folder, cardboard, box lid)
- Transport in box—can use fabric padding to reduce damage
- Don't fold to put in arson can
- Hand carry box/don't stack

Option: Collection for Accelerant Testing

- Place immediately in arson can, metal fireproof box—can fold to fit
- Seal can (with rubber mallet) fully at time of collection
- Mark with appropriate information on can/lid and photograph writing—Case #/date, collector/ID, item #/description, time of collection

Documents in Pieces

- Photograph documents *first as discovered, second prior to packaging, third after removal from packaging*
- Collect all pieces

Documents with Suspected Indented Writing

- Do not separate pages on scene
- Use oblique lighting to visualize

- Padded packaging should be considered—write on packaging PRIOR to placing documents inside
- Do not stack packages
- Processing and analysis done in LAB

Document on Fixed Substrate—Writing on Wall/Floor/Window with Paint/Marker

Option: Take Cutting of Writing

- Cut section of drywall/wood panel, package, and transport

Option: Photograph Writing for Documentation

- Overall/mid-range/close-ups
- 90° angle, with and without scale, good lighting
- OPTION: Consider digital scan/video in addition to photos
- OPTION: Consider paint sample if not cutting writing out

Document on Non-fixed Substrate

Option: Smaller in Size (A Photograph or Poster)

- Collect entirely when possible
- Do not fold/bend/write on, place sticker on
- Place in envelope, paper bag, box—plastic bag may impact later DNA collection

Option: Larger in Size—Door/Chair/Pillow

- Wrap with butcher/craft paper
- Can wrap door/chair/cushion

Shredded Documents

- Collect with minimal disturbance
- Take whole bag or shred bin from scene
- Don't combine locations of shredded paper
- If shredder is present, collect shredder equipment
- Collect paper left between shredder blades, don't allow to fall out during collection

Wet Documents (with No Accelerant)

- Do not separate on scene, collect as 1 item
- Slide rigid item underneath pile/documents, lift carefully (file folder, cardboard, box lid)

- Transport in box, bag, or arson can—can use fabric padding to reduce damage
- Hand carry box/don't stack

Drying Option: Air-Dry Prior to Separation in Controlled Environment

- Lay absorbent items on top/below (paper towel/butcher paper) with air flow
- Once dry, move to breathable container
- Retain/book butcher paper/paper towels

Wet Documents (with Accelerants)

- Place immediately in arson can, metal fireproof box—can fold to fit
- Seal can (with rubber mallet) fully at time of collection

Entomology Evidence Collection

27

In many crime scenes, various insects and other animal activities can be observed. The relevance of insects to your investigation will depend on the specific factors of your scene. Insects involved in decomposition, as well as bird and mammal scavengers, can influence your understanding of the decomposition processes, blood evidence, or even the scene's location. It is crucial to document this information promptly, as there will not be another opportunity to do so. Decomposers and scavengers present on land and in aquatic environments provide different types of clues; therefore, it is important to accurately preserve and record these findings when they are encountered. This chapter will guide you in selecting the appropriate solutions and methods for packaging evidence, as well as where to collect soil and temperature samples.

When dealing with burials, skeletons, or decomposing bodies at a scene, it is crucial to consider entomological samples. The presence of insects in unexpected locations—such as an abundance of flies in a window, maggots in a wound, or maggots within a residence—should also be carefully noted. It is advisable to prepare in advance with a few supplies and consult an entomologist when in doubt. This preparation will ensure that all relevant evidence is identified and not overlooked due to its uncommon nature. The data obtained from entomological samples can provide significant detail; however, caution must be exercised when attempting to determine the time elapsed since death, or postmortem interval (PMI). Such interpretations should be made by an entomology expert and include consideration of all pertinent variables.

Entomology Tool Kit Supply Options

- ☐ Agency SOP (laminated or inside zip lock bag) and all note paperwork/forms
- ☐ Bleach wipes
- ☐ Boxes for item transportation
- ☐ Butterfly net/fish net—suggest 18 inch diameter with 3-foot handle
- ☐ Cooler packs (refreeze able or gel) and Styrofoam cooler for sample transport
- ☐ Cotton balls
- ☐ Dawn dish soap/wash tub/water supply
- ☐ Disposable spoons (for maggot collection)
- ☐ Ethanol (70%–95%)

DOI: 10.4324/9781003503897-28

- ☐ Fine paint brush/camel-hair brush (for egg collection)
- ☐ Flashlight
- ☐ Forceps/tweezers
- ☐ Graphite pencil or waterproof pen AND regular ink pens
- ☐ Hand shovel/trowel
- ☐ Headlamp (for hands-free light)
- ☐ Labels for exterior packaging (adhesive labels) and heavy cotton paper labels for interior packaging
- ☐ Paper towels/tissue paper
- ☐ Pipette for aquatic sample
- ☐ Plastic freezer bags/zip lock bags/paper bags
- ☐ PPE
- ☐ Vials, containers, and sealant materials (neoprene stoppers or screw top closure)
- ☐ Ruler or scale
- ☐ Shovel (large and hand shovel)
- ☐ Solutions—premade—consider KAA for a quick maggot killing on-scene solution
- ☐ Thermometers (ambient air, probe, and laser or IR) and humidity gauge
- ☐ Thermos/hot water container
- ☐ Sticky paper strips/tape/pads

Land Activity

- Flies, beetles, ants, and wasps are all valuable to the investigation for timeline and location. Body lice, head lice, mites, and scabies may be beneficial to document living conditions of living or deceased subjects.
- Insect activity in wounds of live subjects can be indicative of neglect/abuse—known as myiasis
- Blow flies are the most common insect on scene—seeks wounds and orifices first. Wasps feed on maggots, bees feed on body liquids, ants feed on maggots and dead flies, butterflies feed on body liquids, and fly larvae feed on flesh.
- Lack of flies in mouth but presence elsewhere could indicate poison was ingested: They are finding a better source of food while avoiding the poison.
- Activity dependent upon the environment/exposure to fresh air. Open door/window = greater insect activity/cold air source = lower insect activity.
- Temperature readings help with entomological information
- Live and dead samples are both recommended (i.e., adults flies to pin; maggots to preserve or rear out for ID)

- Consider approaching the body with a video camera to capture initial insect activity you will miss with a regular camera due to the change in insect numbers as you approach
- If insect activity is present on the hands/feet, place bags accordingly and make attempts to contain activity inside the bags
- Search: Backside of blinds/curtains/shades, windowsills, window ledges, floors, ground, under furniture, under body for insect activity
- Be mindful that insects can leave transfer patterns when traveling through wet blood; they also can deposit feces on surfaces that resemble blood spatter (e.g., insect artifacts).
- Samples should be turned over to an entomologist or preserved for storage. Contact your area entomologist upon return from scene for instructions, or have your supervisor call for you while you are out processing. They will tell you what they want done with the samples and how they want them preserved.

Beetles

- Flesh-eating beetles can clean a skull in 2 days with the right variables
- Beetles can be present at all stages of decomposition as carrion beetles prefer fresh decay, predatory beetles will prey upon maggots, and dermestid beetles come through once the flesh has dried out consuming hair, skin, and dry flesh
- Dermestid beetles feces can provide DNA and toxin information as the feces are well preserved naturally[1]
- Beetle larvae will eat fly larvae skewing the estimation of fly activity

Blow Fly (Lives 15–30 Days)

- Fly activity on decedent begins within minutes to hours after death, and adults begin to lay eggs within 24 hours. Eggs hatch 18–21 hours after laid, depending upon temperature.
- Adult appearance: Metallic green, blue, bronze, gold, black 6–14 mm in size
- Maggot appearance: White/cream colored with mouth hooks
- Larval development (maggots)—3–4 days, feed on flesh during this stage. After maturing, begin to move from deceased to pupate.

Flesh Flies

- Adult appearance: Gray and black stripes; checkerboard pattern on abdomen. Do not have metallic appearance of blow flies, 2–14 mm in size.

- Females hatch their own eggs, then lay their instars on a food source, or body (develops for approximately 5 days)
- In the SE United States, this is the primary fly found on bodies, indoors, during summer.[2] Arrive with or slightly after blow flies, often found indoors but do not mind bad weather.

Maggots (Live/Eat 5–7 Days, Larval Stage)

- Jump up to 3 feet/1 m (approximately)—travel across rooms/yards, up on counters/tables/beds—they move quickly and far (approximately 20–30 feet away)
- Once body is disturbed, they will begin to wiggle quickly and hide
- Maggots will leave body and burrow down in dirt approximately 1 inch/2.54cm—6 feet/1.8 m for pupal stage
- Their contents (when examined) will show you what and who they have been eating; DNA can still be intact and poison contents are often still intact.
- Development is impacted by narcotics = accelerated after consuming cocaine and decreased after consuming barbiturates[3]

Pupae Stage (8–12 days)

- Check dirt under body for collection
- Appearance: Thicker than eggs/maggots/adults, can be confused with rodent feces
- Larvae hatch as new baby flies

Insect Artifacts (Fly Spots)

- Deposits of fly vomit/feces with remnants of blood
- Large deposits change shape of blood pools
- Feces will fluoresce with an ALS (465 nm with orange filter), insect vomit will not

Appearance

- Resemble high-velocity blood spatter
- Often comma shape rather than circular
- No directionality with tails, appear random

DNA Value

- If located near skeletonized remains would have DNA value
- Feces will test positive for blood with presumptive tests

Scorpion Fly

- Often present for the first 1.5 days of decomposition

Notes/Documentation Needed[4]

- Method of collection
- Approximate number of specimens collected
- Death stage at time of collection
- Locations collected from and locations found
- Temperature readings
- Thermostat settings if indoors
- Insect access to body (inside with windows/doors open, holes in roof, outside covered in leaves/mattress)
- Presence of decaying food/garbage/animal waste
- Any changes scene personnel made to the scene such as open/close doors/windows, turn on fans/AC/heating systems/lights

Onset Delay Variables—For Flies and Beetles

- Extreme temperature/direct sun decrease activity
- Time of day—flies less active at night, more active during warm hours
- Barriers to accessing body—bag, closed trunk, closed doors delay activity
- Fire ants and beetle larvae—eat fly larvae quickly, reducing fly numbers and skewing time estimate

Photographs Should Also Be Captured of the Following

- Fly spots, insect feces
- Larvae shedding
- Dead adults
- Samples collected
- Ground directly beneath body after removal

Temperature Collection Location Options *(For Body Dumps and Entomology Samples)*

Timing

- Hourly temperature reading during scene processing from area near body
- If average is needed for entomologist
  - Readings 4–5 times per day/4–6 days in length
  - Same locations/times
  - Collect GPS coordinates from location of readings

Locations

- Ambient air above victim: 1 foot/above and 4 feet above
- Ground surface, near body
- Maggot masses
- Ground surface, under body (between body and ground)
- Ground surface, after body is removed, where the body used to be
  - Ground level
  - 4 inch (10 cm) deep
  - 8 inch (20 cm) deep
- 3–6 feet away from body
  - Ground level
  - 4 inch (10 cm) deep
  - 8 inch (20 cm) deep

Order of Insect Sample Locations

First—Insects AROUND body—Often sit on plants 10–20 feet/3–6.1 m from body

Second—Insects ON body

- Only insects in plain view, don't open/manipulate body/clothing
- Start with eyes, nose, mouth ears, trauma sites, genitals, neck, hairline, body folds

Third—Insects FLEEING FROM body

- It can be in carpet/textiles/clothing/sheets/and so on
- Travel, distance of 2 m
- Found under appliances, furniture
- Many species try to burrow—check soil/carpet/and so on

Fourth—Insect UNDER body

- In soil—depth of 10 cm/distance of 2 m[5]
- Buried and wrapped bodies should include a search of the surrounding soil
- Wrapped bodies may drop evidence as unwrapped

Fifth—Insects from autopsy

- Recommend HIGHLY using NEW body bag for bodies with insect activity

Collection Steps

1. Record weather, temperature, thermostat settings if indoor, sun activity if outdoor, and time of day started processing
2. Prepare water, containers, labels, food, and packaging
3. Consider taking video at this time (full 360) or using IR photography
4. Take photographs of surrounding area and body without touching anything (move slowly and quietly)
5. Take photographs of any insect activity with/without scale, on and around body, and throughout scene
6. Collect insects from exterior body/surrounding area up to 25 feet from body (10–20 feet common distance). Look for flying and crawling, on plants and ground, in/under furniture, behind curtains.
7. Collect any soil samples or temperature readings from surrounding area. Consider sifting topsoil through screen.
8. Collect temperature from center of maggot mass on body, then collect maggot from area
9. Collect insects from on top of body (don't open clothing)
10. Collect insects fleeing from body at this time
11. Remove body from scene as soon as possible, as insects will remain inside the body bag for later collection
12. Collect temperature samples, soil samples, and insects under body after body removal
13. Screen soil below/around body for additional evidence
14. While on scene store collected samples out of direct sun, ideally in paper bag in shade

Sample Size Suggestions

- Ideal—50+ insects/maggots of largest and smallest—up to several hundred acceptable
- If fewer are present, attempt for 25+ insects/maggots
- Can mix sizes/stages

Sample Labels/Containers

- FILL OUT LABELS—graphite pencil first choice, ballpoint pen second choice, liquid ink *not recommended*
- 1 ON vial, 1 IN vial
- Time of collection, date, case #, item #, location, ethanol concentration used (if suspended in a liquid)

Collection Method Options—*Don't Forget Temperature Readings*

Fly Net

- Using butterfly net/fish net/craft net—catch as many as possible

- Move net in the shape of a number 8 (or inifinity symbol) over the body or area in question for 6–10 passes
- Gently fold net to contain flies and place in secure container

Grab with Hand

- Using gloved hand without pressure, pick up sample

Screen

- Sift ground cover/soil beneath body
- Use 1/4 inch screen (6 mm), then sift with 1.4 mm screen

Shovel

- Hand shovel recommended for top layers

Sticky Traps *(Sticky Tape/Pads/Strips)*

- Place traps near body upon arrival
- Collect traps at end of scene processing
- Place whole trap in plastic bag/glassine envelope
- Avoid damage, don't crush

Solution Suggestions for Land Insects

- Ethyl alcohol = ethanol, grain alcohol
- Ethyl Alcohol—70%–95%—good for killing and preservation of adults, preserving larvae
- Dilution of—95% diluted to 80%—80 parts ethyl alcohol/15 parts water
- Isopropyl alcohol can interfere with DNA testing
- Isopropyl alcohol and ethyl alcohol interfere with toxicological testing of sample
- Samples collected in a net can be placed in a jar with the net to help reduce loss
- Can use commercially made or homemade "kill jar"

Kill Jar, Home Made[6]

- Wide mouth glass jar with screw lid
- Place 1 inch/2.54 cm of wet Plaster of Paris in bottom of jar and allow to dry completely
- Saturate Plaster of Paris with ethyl acetate and pour off excess liquid. Jar is now ready to use.
- Place insect in jar for several minutes. Remove after deceased and place in preservation solution of choice.

- Place and retain lid on jar when not in use, re-using until rendered useless. Add more ethyl acetate to the jar and begin again.

Solutions[7]

Ethyl Alcohol *(Ethanol) 75%–80% Solution—Killing and Preserving Adults and Preserving Larvae after Fixing with K.A.A or Kahle's Solution—Use Amount Needed Per Scene*

K.A.A—killing of larvae only
80–100 ml—95% ethyl alcohol
20 ml—glacial acetic acid
10 ml—kerosene
Upon death of sample, remove from solution and preserve within 12 hours with ethyl alcohol 75–80%

Kahle's Solution—*Killing and Preservation of Adults, Preservation of Larvae*

30 ml—95% ethyl alcohol
12 ml—formaldehyde
4 ml—glacial acetic acid
60 ml—water

Samples Transported Dead

- Preservation should be done on scene if possible
- If not preserved within hours, it will mold and lose all value

Boil Option: Found Alive/Transported Dead[8]

- Place in boiling water 176° or higher for 60 seconds. Bring thermos of hot water or a car cup heater for hot water.
- Strain water, remove sample
- Place sample directly in container of 70% ethyl alcohol

Option: Found Alive/Transported Dead

- Place adults directly in container of 70%–80% ethyl alcohol[9]
- 70%–95% ethyl alcohol acceptable

Option: Found Alive/Transported Dead

- Place directly glass vial with cotton balls soaked in ethyl acetate
- Let sit for 5 minutes—will die in this time
- Once dead, transfer to vial with 75% ethyl alcohol or pin to dry board
- Label on scene

Option: Found Dead/Still Dead

- Place sample in clean glass or plastic vial, no liquids
- Transport to laboratory for further packaging
- Remove from container within hours to prevent moisture damage

Samples Transported Alive

- Live samples can be stored on scene and transported in a cooler with gel pack or refreeze able ice (NOT ice made with water)

Option: Found Alive/Transported Alive

- Place sample in plastic zip lock bag with moist paper towel
- Make pin holes for air
- Place in secondary plastic bag, seal top
- Upon return from scene, place in freezer

Option: Found Alive/Transported Alive

- Fold new aluminum foil into shape of cup
- Fill with sample
- Fold over top and seal
- Place foil cup in plastic cup with 1 inch sand in bottom
- Upon return from scene place in freezer

Option: Found Alive/Transported Alive

- Need temperature-controlled container to keep alive
- Place in vial with food—raw chicken liver/cat food—60 maggots can eat 3 inch liver
- Beetle larvae can eat fly eggs for food; carrion beetles will eat flesh; dermestids will eat dry flesh and bones.
- Transport to lab/mail as needed
- Kill sample or prepare for long-term storage at lab

Option: Eggs/Larvae

- Place in clean glass/plastic container with/without moist paper towel or soil collected from
- No liquids, no food, or alcohol
- Transport to the laboratory in airtight container for further packaging or until hatches

Aquatic Activity

Facts to Consider for Aquatic Insects and Wildlife

- Collect LIVE and DEAD samples if collecting samples
- Aquatic insects don't always feed on body, often use for habitat which can still give indication of timeline, locations body traveled, location of dump, and so on
- Sea snakes, jellyfish, and Man-o-war can be found with bodies in ocean water. They can make marks resembling trauma to the body. Blood worms can appear as fibers or hair.
- Larvae can be found on body underneath the algae and residue left on skin after removal from water

Alligator

- More likely to take to den and eat later
- Often found in pieces

Dermestid Beetles

- Clean skeletons
- Can give estimate of time of death in months with activity

Crustaceans

- Crayfish, lobsters, crabs, shrimp
- Shallow warm water
- Can clean a skeleton in a week's time
- Begin with wounds first/face second

Fish

- Juveniles will eat off bodies, adults rarely will

Maggots

- Fly eggs won't get laid under water. If a body surfaces with eggs on it, it was out of the water at some point.
- Fly eggs will hatch in 24 hours
- Pupa—maggot in brown hard shell—1 week stage depending upon conditions
- Growth will continue until placed in preservation liquid or freezer

Screw Fly

- Mostly seen in Europe
- Can deposit eggs deep in body before submersion and eggs will be intact upon resurfacing. Must have been exposed to air at some point if eggs present.

Sea Lice

- Large group of crustaceans found together, they will clean a body quickly

Collection Options for Aquatic Insects

Water Sample

- Collect as soon as possible from surrounding water even if using a solution on scene for preservation
- Try not to kick up dirt from bottom first
- Plastic/glass container with good lid
- Fill container to top to reduce movement
- Keep in Styrofoam cooler during scene processing/transport—NOT in direct sunlight or closed vehicle

Solution Options for Aquatic Insects[10,11]

Ethyl Alcohol—90%–95%—preservation of eggs/larvae/pupae
Ethyl Alcohol—75%–80%—preservation of adults

Original Water—*Live Immature or Soft Bodied Adult Aquatic Insects*

- Fill container with the water the sample was found in, fill to the top to prevent jarring movement. Secure the top.

Carnoy Fluid—*Killing and Preservation of Most Soft Bodied Aquatic Insects*

30 ml—Chloroform
60 ml—Ethyl alcohol (95% concentration)
10 ml—Glacial acetic acid

K.A.A—*Killing of Larvae Only*

80–100 ml—95% ethyl alcohol
20 ml—glacial acetic acid
10 ml—kerosene
Upon death of sample, remove from solution and preserve within 12 hours with ethyl alcohol 75%–80%

Kahle's Solution—*Killing and Preservation Adults, Preservation of Larvae*

30 ml—95% ethyl alcohol
12 ml—formaldehyde

4 ml—glacial acetic acid
60 ml—water

Pampel's Solution

10 ml—formalin
30 ml—95% ethyl alcohol
7 ml—glacial acetic acid
53 ml—water

Sea Lice and Maggot Preservation

85%–90% alcohol
10%–15% formalin
5% glycerin

Cases to Consider for Entomology Factors

- 2017: Kirstin Lobato's 2006 murder conviction was overturned after a new trial and examination of entomology evidence challenged time of death for the victim.
- 2006: Jonathan Blackwell's remains were located and due to entomological evidence, it was determined his body had been moved from his original location.
- 2003: Joanie Harper, Ernestine Harper, and Joanie's three children were found murdered in their home. Detectives used the insect content on Joanie's husband's radiator to challenge his alibi and place him near the victim rather than his reported location.
- 1958: Lynn Harper's body contained entomological evidence that cleared her convicted friend, Steven Truscott.
- 1935: Isbella Ruxton and Mary Jane Rogerson were murdered and dismembered. Entomology was used to identify a time of death based upon the entomology evidence.

Notes

1 Bauer, Erin, Larry Barksdale, Emma Sidel, and Justine La Violette. "Death Scene Insect Succession in Nebraska: A Guidebook." Faculty Publications: Department of Entomology, 2022. 983, https://digitalcommons.unl.edu/entomologyfacpub/983.
2 "Forensically Important Flies." Forensic Entomology, University of Nebraska, Lincoln, 2025.
3 Bauer, Erin, Larry Barksdale, Emma Sidel, and Justine LaViolette. "Death Scene Insect Succession in Nebraska: A Guidebook." Faculty Publications: Department of Entomology, 2022, 983, https://digitalcommons.unl.edu/entomologyfacpub/983.

4 Crime Scene Investigation and Reconstruction Subcommittee Scene Examination Scientific Area Committee, Organization of Scientific Area Committees (OSAC) for Forensic Science 2022-N-0039, Collecting and Preserving Entomological Evidence from a Terrestrial Environment.
5 Crime Scene Investigation and Reconstruction Subcommittee Scene Examination Scientific Area Committee, Organization of Scientific Area Committees (OSAC) for Forensic Science 2022-N-0039, Collecting and Preserving Entomological Evidence from a Terrestrial Environment.
6 Bauer, Erin, Larry Barksdale, Emma Sidel, and Justine LaViolette. "Death Scene Insect Succession in Nebraska: A Guidebook." *Faculty Publications: Department of Entomology*, 2022, 983, https://digitalcommons.unl.edu/entomologyfacpub/983.
7 Byrd, Jason, and James Castner. *Forensic Entomology, the Utility of Arthropods in Legal Investigations*. CRC Press, 2001.
8 Crime Scene Investigation and Reconstruction Subcommittee Scene Examination Scientific Area Committee, Organization of Scientific Area Committees (OSAC) for Forensic Science 2022-N-0039, Collecting and Preserving Entomological Evidence from a Terrestrial Environment.
9 Byrd, Jason, and James Castner. Forensic Entomology, the Utility of Arthropods in Legal Investigations. CRC Press, 2001.
10 Geberth, Vernon. *Practical Homicide Investigation: Tactics, Procedures and Forensic Techniques*. CRC Press, 1996.
11 Byrd, Jason, and James Castner. *Forensic Entomology, the Utility of Arthropods in Legal Investigations*. CRC Press, 2001.

Digital Evidence 28

Electronic evidence comes in many forms and is constantly evolving. As technology has advanced, understanding its evidentiary value can be challenging, especially for those who didn't grow up in the digital age. While most electronic devices share similar surfaces that are excellent for collecting contact DNA or fingerprints, their true value often lies in the data they hold. This chapter is not exhaustive of listed items that are beneficial to collect but aims to equip you with the knowledge needed to navigate the next scenario effectively. Appropriate collection is vital to the preservation of digital evidence and can benefit you down the road.

Common Types/Locations of Digital Data

- Cellphones
- Computer hard drive, laptop/desktop
- Electronic meters on utilities
- File servers, databases, modems
- Medical equipment and logs such as BiPap machines, pacemakers, and CPAP. Some keep logs of time and activities. Gather machine information and submit to doctor or laboratory such as Regional Computer Forensics Laboratory.[1]
- Smartwatches, fitness watches, fitness rings
- Smart home devices and home automation and it's digital history—lights, cameras, outlets, alarms, thermostats, appliance power, and so on
- Tablets
- Traffickcam—Public access database with photographs of hotel rooms for comparison
- Vehicles
- Video footage from ATM machines
- Video footage from traffic cameras, toll booth cameras
- Video gaming systems (Xbox, PlayStation, etc.)
- Wi-Fi, Bluetooth, or smart device

Cell Phone Data Available

- GPS locations
- Photographs/videos

DOI: 10.4324/9781003503897-29

- Social network information
- Contacts
- Text messages/emails
- Phone calls
- Internet history

Vehicle Data Available

- Connected vehicle service information provided from vehicle manufacturers such as OnStar and Ituran
- Vehicle data is downloaded from vehicles with programs such as Berla
- Speed, engine parameters, other data
- Vehicle tracker from rental agency, insurance agency
- Wi-Fi providers based upon vehicle type
- Phone calls, contacts, texts, emails
- Black box/Vehicle Event Data Recorder
    - Owner or lessee owner of information
    - No location information
    - Braking status, speed, steering, and so on
    - Door opening/closing, gear shifts, odometer readings, speed logs
    - National Highway Traffic Safety Administration can help download
- Vehicle digital forensics—infotainment
    - Vehicle performance
    - Connected devices and all data calls, texts, contacts
    - Location information
    - Event information (start, stop, etc.)
- Vehicle video recording systems
    - Can be aftermarket cameras
    - Can be motion activated
    - Can record even when vehicle is unattended
    - Often have 360° exterior/interior view

Video Gaming System Data Available—Not an Exhaustive List

- Collect controller and power cord with all gaming systems

Microsoft Xbox 360 Detachable Hard Drive Contains

- Xbox live content
- Social network information
- Contacts
- Text messages, emails, chat logs

- Internet history (has full access)
- Downloaded content
- Modified and unmodified appearance is the same

Move and Kinect

- Upgrades to Sony and Xbox in 2010
- Uses cameras and motion tracking to record motions of users
- Port only found on older models

Nintendo DS/DSI/3DS

- Contains SD card reader

Nintendo WII

- Can be used the same as a PC
- Web browser, bookmarks
- Daily log of system usage
- Contact list
- Photos/images sent over player messaging system

Pictochat—Often Used by Child Predators

- Contains camera/image storage

Sony PlayStation Portable (PSP)

- Can access internet
- Search/download history

Sony PlayStation 3 Contains Same as Xbox 360 as well as

- Full internet browsing without modification
- Search/download history
- Can install third-party operating system

Digital Evidence Collection Options

DVR Collection

Option: Download DVR Footage, Leave DVR Unit on Scene

- Take photographs needed at time of collection
  - Front/back of DVR being downloaded
  - Model/SN
  - Screen images if any
  - Time/date on screen—verify accuracy before unplugging machine (look at your watch)

- Download in universal format
  - AVI—audio video interleave
  - MVW—windows media video
  - MP4—moving pictures group 4

Option: DVR Unit Collected Entirely, No Digital Downloading

- Take needed photographs—overall, mid-range with item in place, front and back to include label
  - Cable configuration
  - Close-ups on model and SN
  - Screen images if applicable
  - Close-ups of surrounding items being collected
  - Time/date on screen—verify accuracy before unplugging machine (look at your watch)
- Collect unit with power cables attached, label wires if large needed
- Unplug from wall prior to unplugging from each other
- Package each system/cable as 1 item in bag or box (preferred)
- Prevent accidental contact with magnets/2-way radios
- Look for items of interest around DVR/screen area—memory sticks, hard drives, DVDs, documents with computer data

Remote Controls

- Collect remotes from individuals on scene as soon as possible
- Consider placing it in faraday bag

Satellites on Structures

- Check roof for satellites/devices, unplug as soon as possible if able

Underwater Electronics

Option 1

- Collect still submerged in water found in Tupperware/plastic zip lock bag/bucket
- Transport to the laboratory in water

Option 2

- Remove from water
- Place immediately in plastic bag AND SEAL to retain moisture inside bag, squeezing out extra air
- Transport to laboratory for immediate examination

Video Game Consoles/CPU Collection

- Photograph complete set-up front/back with cords/labels
- Unplug from wall
- Collect whole item with power cords attached and controller
- Don't remove CDs, USB, cartridges

Remote Wiping Prevention

- Multiple types of digital evidence can be remotely wiped while on scene or in storage
- Static bags do not stop remote transmissions, they stop static electricity build-up

Option: Place in Airplane Mode

- Prevents transmissions to/from item
- You cannot "look around" in phone on your way to doing so

Option: Place in Faraday Bag (Not Static Bag)

- Faraday bag is ideal because it blocks transmissions
- If you have an unused faraday bag, you can collect DNA/fingerprints later

Option: Wrap item or packaging in 8–10 layers of overlapping aluminum foil

Cases to Consider with Digital Evidence

- 2022: When Connie Dabate was murdered by her husband, her Fitbit she was wearing ruined his alibi.
- 2022: When Michael Logsdon died it was determined his BiPap machine had been tampered with, resulting in his death. Records were obtained from the maker of the machine that provided needed details.
- 2016: State of Ohio used pacemaker information to debunk the alibi of Ross Compton and place him at the scene of a fire; however, Compton died while waiting for his trial.
- 2015: James Bates was charged with the murder of a friend found deceased at his home. Digital evidence was obtained from his "Alexa" device as well as water usage from a smart water meter.
- Amazon refused to turn over information until consent was obtained.
- The Alexa information has not been publicly shared, though all charges were dropped in 2017.

- 2012: After Katrina Smith was murdered, her husband successfully removed the tracker from beneath her vehicle prior to it being searched by crime scene personnel. However, a search of his laptop provided all tracker and route information including her body disposal, which he did not delete.

Note

1 Regional Computer Forensics Laboratory, an FBI digital forensics lab in the United States, https://www.rcfl.gov/.

29 Mental Health

CSIs will encounter some disconcerting crime scenes including mass casualty incidents or violent acts that could be considered emotionally traumatic and we have found that no one exposed to trauma or violence comes away from it untouched. Long-term stress is cumulative and can overwhelm the ability to cope. Small doses of daily stress are not bad, but long-term or cumulative stress *is* unhealthy. Under long-term stress you can become forgetful, it's harder to concentrate, thinking may slow down, and it's difficult to think in long complicated thoughts. When people are acutely stressed, they tend to use more emotional thinking rather than rational, logical thought and they tend to act automatically.

Stress is common and it often serves as a precursor to anxiety, depression, and PTSD. Stress, anxiety, and depression are significantly more likely to occur in jobs that handle the dead, and this is exacerbated when there is a death of a child, or children. Workers whose job frequently exposes them to traumatic events can trigger mental health issues that need to be addressed. PTSD is also severe, characterized by intrusive memories, flashbacks, and significant emotional distress following a traumatic experience.

> It is important for those of us who work disasters and have responsibility for others to understand the consequences of our assignments.
>
> —**Sandy Ramsey**[1]

Burnout

"Physical, emotional or mental exhaustion, accompanied by decreased motivation, lowered performance and negative attitudes towards oneself and others."[2] Burnout is best described as a state of complete mental, physical, and emotional exhaustion caused by prolonged or excessive stress.

- Exhaustion from being in a constant, long-term state of stress or ongoing situations
- Work/home life become out of sync and not compatible, you are depleting

Contributors

- Working long hours and revolving work hours, irregular hours, shift work hours

DOI: 10.4324/9781003503897-30

- Regular overtime shifts to fill staffing voids
- Poor sleep length and/or quality of sleep
- Management expectations/new expectations
- Expectations at home that you are unable to fulfill
- Not having someone to regularly discuss the long-term emotional impact of being a CSI

Warning Signs

- Idealism and optimism become cynicism, negativity, or pessimism
- Decrease in work performance/small tasks are overwhelming/daunting
- Depression/anxiety, decision paralysis, negative thoughts, decreased motivation
- Strong feelings of apathy/dissatisfaction, hard to bring yourself out of "funk"
- Physical symptoms: Regular headaches, regular cold/flu-type symptoms, high blood pressure, muscle tenseness, fatigue, insomnia, body pain, clumsiness, and disorganization
- Vacation
    - IS rejuvenating, relaxing
    - Return refreshed
    - Gives needed time to re-connect and relax

Depression

"Negative affective state, ranging from unhappiness and discontent to an extreme feeling of sadness, pessimism, and despondency, that interferes with daily life."[3] Depression is a persistent feeling of sadness. You have no energy, and you lose interest in activities you once loved. Some people with depression think about hurting themselves. Anxiety involves fear or worry that you can't control. Both depression and anxiety are common and can often occur together. While it's normal to feel anxious or down sometimes, severe or ongoing feelings of anxiety and depression should be addressed.

- Depression can occur if burnout is not addressed
- Depression doesn't always have a specific beginning

Contributors

- Burnout that does not get addressed
- Stressful prolonged work and family situations, prolonged grief
- Not having an emotional or intellectual outlet to discuss work stress

- Ongoing feelings of powerlessness or helplessness, at home or work
- Worry about your ability to be able to continue the work in the future

Warning Signs

- Severe levels, not daily fluctuations
- Physical symptoms: Sleep disruption, stomach pain, elevated heart rate, changes in appetite/weight loss or gain, trembling, shakiness, easily startled, increased clumsiness
- Losing interest in hobbies/activities/fun stuff that was once enjoyable
- Increased and long-term anger, irritability, pessimism, and lack of objectivity in normal conversations
- Not mentally present when spending time with friends/spouse/children/family
- Decrease in work performance and attendance
- Vacation
  - NOT rejuvenating, relaxing
  - NEVER feel refreshed
  - Does not lead to a positive mood shift or decrease in stress

PTSD (Post-traumatic Stress Disorder)

Exposure to death and dead bodies, especially those of children, has repeatedly been identified as a major stressor and a major risk factor for PTSD. The profound sensory stimulation associated with the dead, identification of those who have died, and volatile contacts with the families and loved ones of those who have died are all significant stressors.

Contributors

- Unaddressed stress burnout
- Unaddressed depression and anxiety
- Not feeling safe at work to talk
- Not taking time away from work when needed
- Not being debriefed after a particularly traumatic scene (can be from one exposure)

Warning Signs

- Intrusive reexperiencing (terrifying memories, nightmares, or flashbacks)
- Extreme attempts to avoid disturbing memories (such as through substance use)
- Extreme emotional numbing (completely unable to feel emotion, as if empty)

- Being easily startled
- Feeling tense, on guard, or on edge
- Having difficulty concentrating
- Insomnia
- Using alcohol or drugs excessively to self-medicate
- Feeling irritable and having angry or aggressive outbursts
- Engaging in risky, reckless, or destructive behavior
- Hyperarousal (panic attacks, rage, extreme irritability, intense agitation)
- Severe anxiety (paralyzing worry, extreme helplessness, compulsions, or obsessions)
- Severe depression (complete loss of hope, self-worth, motivation, or purpose in life)

Facts to Consider

- National Suicide Prevention Lifeline, 1-800-273-TALK (8255)
- Police officers and firefighters are more likely to commit suicide than be injured in the line of duty
- EMS personnel more likely to commit suicide than members of the public
- 80% of veterinarians suffer from clinical depression during their career, and are 5 times more likely to die by suicide than the general public
- 20% of physicians in the United States suffer from depression
- 24% of dispatchers in the United States report suffering from PTSD
- Healthcare support workers are at higher risk of suicide than the general public

What to Do About It—CSI

Do

- Practice aggressive personal time management and retain ownership of your time (don't blur boundaries)
- Leave work at work—keep mental focus off work-related items and be present at home
- Make time for self-care, stress reduction, and things you enjoy (hobbies, exercise, meditation, etc.)
- Monitor yourself regularly and honestly
- Take your vacation/sick days—use that time for health/happiness
- See your friends slipping? Check in with them.
- Take frequent and regular breaks
- Frequent and regular exercise (any kind, just move)

- Follow the schedule YOU set for yourself on your time off
- Be mindful of your own biases and need for resilience work (resilience is created, not born)
- Use mental health resources for debriefing

Don't

- Work more hours, don't *routinely* come in on your days off/stay late/come early
- Withdraw
- Minimize your concerns, the struggle is real
- Try to override your exhaustion and stress with commitment and good intentions, it won't work
- Stay at work when it's time to leave
- Think that constant, long-term stress won't affect you

What to Do About It—Employer

Do

- Have debriefings after OIS or high-stress scenes regularly
- Eliminate barriers to efficient work procedures with overlapping shift change
- Have a clear chain of command structure and defined roles
- Provide updates on cases worked
- Rotate low- and high-stress job duties
- Provide an experienced mental health therapist to debrief as part of your health package
- Allow workers a confidential space so that they can talk about an incident with co-workers
- Provide flexible schedules and time off for staff (minimum of 12 hours between shifts)
- Provide ergonomic work environments when possible
- Ask the workers what their needs are and what resources are required for the job
- Be proactive not reactive with policies/programs
- Keep plants in the office
- Encourage fitness activities during work time/end of shift
- Allow workers to take sick days without shaming them
- Therapy dogs can be helpful, ask in advance
- Make your workers feel safe

Don't

- Neglect standard procedures OR have sudden and often shifts in practices

- Shame employees for seeking help or use for discipline
- Create an environment of unrealistic unattainable perfection
- Make false promises of rewards, time off, recognition, or new procedures
- Assume employees need to speak to you about their feelings or that everyone exposed to trauma needs help

Notes

1 Ramsey, Sandy. "Aftermath of Disaster: Effects on Mental Health Professionals." Annals of American Psychotherapy, no. Fall, 2009, pp. 71–73.
2 American Psychological Association, 19 Apr. 2018, dictionary.apa.org.
3 American Psychological Association, 19 Apr. 2018, dictionary.apa.org.

Tips and Resources 30

There are a lot of directions for how to do the work; these are suggestions to help the CSI. Here is some information that will make your job easier. This chapter includes suggestions to help make your work environment more comfortable as well as general information regarding the forensic field and all those involved. It is going to be imperative for your resilience and longevity in the field to find ways that work best for you and find ways to make your job easier and take steps out of your day. If you can keep many of your habits routine, you can focus your active thoughts on the scene you are processing and provide a better outcome.

Online On-scene Electronic Resources

1. Ameslab.gov—online pictures/video of bloodletting for reference
2. Assault Weapon Identification Guide—Illinois State Government—online firearm and accessory guide with visuals and names
3. Chesapeake Bay Division International Association for Identification. www.cbdiai.org/—Latent Fingerprint Processing Techniques Selection and Sequencing Guide—online reference for fingerprinting techniques and sequential questions
4. Forensic Pocket guide.com—online digital scene processing and evidence processing guide
5. International Association of Arson Investigators—downloadable arson evidence guide—www.iaaievidenceguide.com
6. Headstamp Codes—International Ammunition Association—cartridgecollectors.org
7. Headstamp Guide—The Association of Firearm and Tool Mark Examiners—AFTE.org
8. National Crime Investigation and Training—downloadable guide—NCIT.COM—Evidence and Crime Scene Reconstruction guidebook
9. NIST—Trace materials crime scene investigation guide,—downloadable—www.nist.gov
10. NIJ National Institute of Justice—Databases of comparison information to include paint, footwear prints, vehicle tires, etc.—www.nij.gov/journals/258/forensic-databases.html

DOI: 10.4324/9781003503897-31

11. OJP—Office of Justice Programs—downloadable guide www.ojp.gov—Electronic Crime Scene Investigation: A Guide for First Responders, Second Edition
12. RCFL.GOV—training and on scene assistance

Measurement References

Distance

- 1 cm = 10 mm
- 1 inch = 2.54 cm
- 1 foot = 12 inches
- 1 yard = 3 feet
- 1 m = 3 feet 3 inches

Dry Measurements

- 1 gram = 0.035 ounces = 1000 mg
- 1 ounce = 0.06 pounds = 28.35 grams
- 1 pound = 16 ounces = 453.6 grams
- 1 kg = 1000 grams

Liquid Measurements

- 1 KL = 1000 L
- 1 L = 1000 ml
- 1 ML = 0.034 fluid oz
- 1 fluid oz = 29.573 ml
- 1 cup = 1/2 pint = 8 fluid oz
- 1 quart = 4 cups = 2 pints = 0.946 liter
- 1 PT = 2 cups = 473.176 ml
- 1 gallon = 4 quarts = 16 cups = 128 fl. oz = 3.79L

Temperatures

- 32°F = 0°C
- Boiling point of water = 212°F/100°C
- Coffee average temperature = 160–200°F/71–93°C
- Normal water heater setting = 120–140 F/49–60°C
- First-degree burns start at 118°F/48°C
- 140°F/60°C takes 3 seconds for severe burns to occur

Bindle Instructions *(Small Hand Folded Envelope, Aka Druggist Fold, Drug Bindle, Paper Bindle)*

- Using any size square piece of paper, fold as directed below

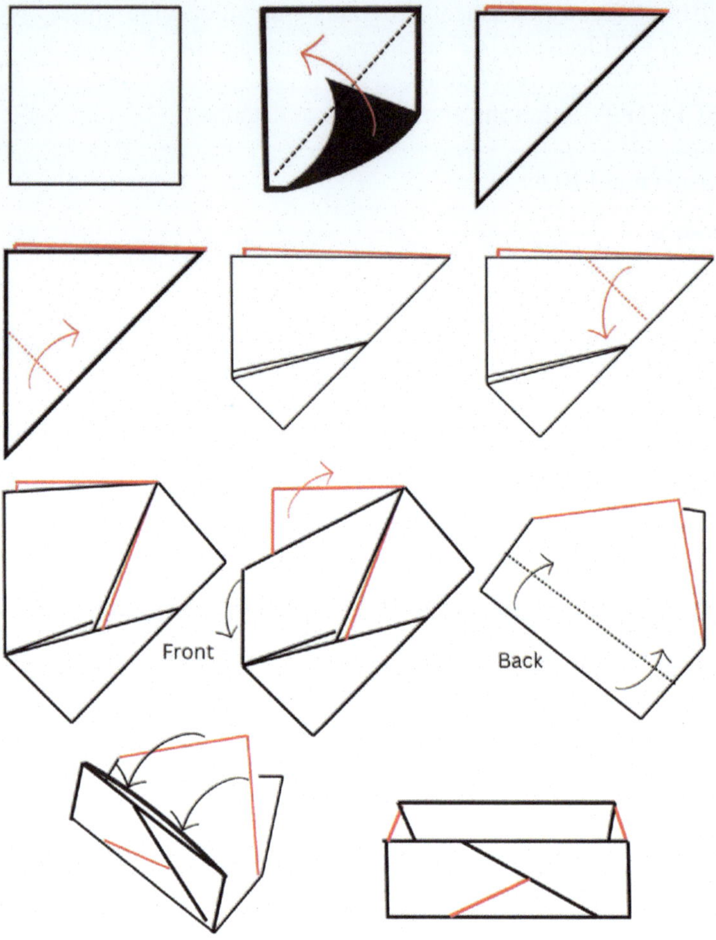

Figure 30.1 Bindle instructions: Depicting the steps needed to fold paper into a bindle.

- Useful for small bits of powders, hairs, fibers, and other small items. It will unfold nicely for the laboratory and not spill contents during transport.

Suggestions for CSIS

- ADAPT AND MOVE ON
- Wear a clean uniform each shift—GREATLY reduce the chance of contamination between scenes. Ideally a clean uniform for each scene; however, few CSIs only respond to one location per day.

- Wear 2 gloves (or a glove liner with gloves) during examination/collection activities. You will need to change gloves frequently and quickly to avoid contamination and still keep a good pace. A glove liner beneath your gloves will absorb sweat and facilitate quick and easy glove changes; however, keep in mind it does leave room to drop press on fingernails on scene.
- A wrist band on the arm below the glove line can absorb sweat dripping from glove as well as wipe sweat from forehead, reducing contamination and uncontrolled dripping.
- Hydration products allow you to stay hydrated while drinking less water and using the toilet less often
- Practice A LOT. Practice everything before you do it on scene.
- Keep your statistics, if possible, even if only an average. You will be asked in court at least once and most agencies do not keep track for their employees.
- Use muscle memory, every time—keep actions repetitive, you will work on autopilot more than you think you do.
  - Keep kits organized the same way
  - Keep order of processing the same
  - Same trash pocket (yes, you need one)
  - Same drawer in the vehicle for same supplies
  - Same clean/dirty hands (left dirty, right clean, or vice versa) on every scene
  - Same abbreviations/symbols in notes
- *Cold on scene?*
  - Take off coat for 5 minutes and put back on
  - Double glove
  - Wear cloth gloves under nitrile/latex gloves—glove liners
  - Handwarmers (hands/feet)—rechargeable/single use
  - Flashlight with handwarmer
  - Portable heater
- *Overheating on scene?*
  - Pour cold water over head/neck
  - Use cooling rag on back of neck
  - Use portable neck fan/vest fan
  - Remove bullet proof vest over 100°F/37°C
  - Wear wrist/head sweat bands to absorb sweat so it does not drip on evidence
  - Heatstroke symptoms: Dizziness, shallow rapid breathing, confusion, disorientation, slurred speech, nausea/vomiting, muscle weakness

- *Smelling bad from decomposition/fire scene?*
  - Febreze on clothing/shoes (wash hair twice when you get home)
  - Spray clothing with 90% isopropyl alcohol to deodorize
  - Coffee grounds absorb foul odors from decomp or fire—mark container accordingly so you don't accidentally brew it for your boss
  - Place small box of ground coffee (unbrewed) in vehicle to absorb odor driving back to lab
  - Place shoes/hat in small box of ground coffee (unbrewed) and let sit 24–48 hours
  - Can dispose of coffee grounds in trash or leave in office under desk until fully absorbed
- *Nightshift?*
  - Place reflective tape on your gear to find it quickly
  - Allow yourself sufficient time to adjust schedules
  - Place red dome light in vehicle to reduce night vision adjustments for safety and eye strain
  - Use headlamps, have clip on lighting, extra flashlights, and so on

Common on Scene Dangers

Airborne Dangers

- Aerosolized fecal matter and *E. coli*
- Ammonia (hoarding/boarded up structures)
- Chicken pox
- Covid, cold, influenza
- Dried body fluid flaked particles
- Fungus and Anthrax spores
- Hanta virus (rat/mouse urine/saliva/feces)
- Toxic fumes can be inhaled or absorbed through skin—containing heavy metals and PAH—Polycyclic Aromatic Hydrocarbons, common at fire scenes
- Measles, mumps, diphtheria, meningitis
- Mold
- Parasites
- San Joaquin valley fever (mold in soil)
- Tuberculosis

Bodily Fluid Pathogen

- Hepatitis A, B, C
- HIV/AIDS
- Malaria

- MRSA/staph infection
- Syphilis
- Wet body fluids

Bites That Can Carry Disease

- Fleas, ticks, bed bugs, rodents, mosquitoes, spiders, snakes
- Lyme disease—tick bites
- Plague—flea bites
- Rocky Mountain Spotted fever—tick/fleas/lice/mites

Bug Bite Prevention

- Have mask handy even if you don't think you need it
- Wipe down/shake equipment when you leave
- Bug repellant—spray before/after entry to scene
- Consider fly net hat
- Have fire ant spray—they will get in your pants/socks
- OPTION: SCENE PREVENTION—tape bottom of pants to top of boots to ensure no insects crawl inside pants
  1. Kneel on ground at your vehicle, put non-weight bearing leg in front of you (this length will allow for flexibility during evidence collection)
  2. Tape bottom of pants to tops of boots, go around a couple of times to ensure there is no gap in the barrier. This should prevent anything from crawling up inside your pant legs.
  3. Switch, repeat legs
  4. Optional: Tape sleeves to gloves if needed.

Contagious Skin-to-Skin or Skin-to-Item Contact

- Bacterial skin infections
- Fungal infections
- Impetigo
- Meningitis
- MRSA/staph infection
- Poison oak, poison ivy—can take up to 48 hours after contact
- Rabies—infection from animal licking or biting—yes, licking is enough to get you sick
- Ringworm
- Scabies/mites

Biohazard Identifiers

- Red bags, red containers, orange labels, or orange-red labels should be used to identify biohazards[1]

Decontamination on Scene

- Bleach spray (homemade)—10% bleach (1 part bleach/10 parts water = 1 oz. bleach/10 oz. water)
  - Date bottle, spray as needed
  - May discolor uniform/top of boot (haven't seen it happen but theoretically possible)—sole of boot will not discolor

Spray down

- Bottoms of shoes
- Feet of equipment and tripod
- Wheels of equipment

Wipe down

- Camera/lens
- Phone
- Bottom side of posse box
- Flashlight

Liquid Blood Spill Cleanup—Small Spills

- Put on PPE, goggles if you are a splashy cleaner
- Cover area of spill with paper towels
- Spray area with disinfectant on top of paper towels, ensuring fully doused
- Let sit for 10 minutes to fully saturate dried edges of stain
- Gather all materials moving from the outside in with dustpan/broom or forceps, not your hands even if gloved to prevent accidental puncture
- Using new towels or pads, wipe up any drips or remaining liquid
- Spray area with bleach solution and air-dry 15 minutes,[2] do not wipe
- Discard all materials in biohazard receptacle

Small Blood Drips, Scene Waste/Processing Waste

- Hydrogen peroxide application, water rinse optional
- Small amounts of blood can be put in trash receptacles (bloody gloves/bloody butcher paper), and large amounts of blood (pooled) must go in biohazard receptacle depending on the risk of contamination to others
- Per OSHA, regulated waste (waste that must go in biohazard bag) is liquid or semi-liquid blood, items contaminated with liquid or semi-liquid blood if compressed, items caked with dried blood[3] that would disperse when agitated.

Valuable Resource Agencies

ANSI—American National Standards Institute

ASCLD—American Society of Crime Laboratory Directors

ASTEE—American Society of Trace Evidence Examiners

ASTM—American Society for Testing and Materials—ASTM standards lay out scene/evidence standards. Refer to ASTM E1188 AND E1459.

ATF—Basic Post Blast Investigative Techniques training course—40-hour training course that provides instruction in explosives identification and applications, explosives effects, IED component recognition, and evidence collection

Berla—https://berla.co—vehicle forensics to include software

Bureau of Justice Assistance—Bja.ojp.gov, grant information

Delta Forensics—forensic consultation and training, www.delta-forensics.com/

FEMA—Federal Emergency Management Agency, training, and education

GAP Science.com—training and training materials

Gulf Coast Forensic Solutions—training, scene assistance, consultation

IABPAI—International Association for Bloodstain Pattern Analysts

IAI—International Association for Identification

IAAI—International Association of Arson Investigations

IAATI—International Association of Auto Theft Investigators

Interfire.org—Field guide for arson scene processing/collection

International Organization for Standardization—www.iso.org

Lynn Peavey Company—standard and individualized forensic gear, lynnpeavey.com

Microtrace LLC—forensic analysis and consulting

NAMUS—National Missing and Unidentified Persons System, https://namus.nij.ojp.gov/

National Criminal Justice Training Center

Necro Search International—volunteer multidisciplinary team of specialists dedicated to assisting law enforcement with locating clandestine graves

National Fire Protection Association—NFPA 921 contains good reference materials

NICB.ORG—National Insurance Crime Bureau—www.nicb.org/law-enforcement

NIST—National Institute of Standards and Technology—www.nist.gov

North American Export Committee—export of stolen vehicles

OSAC—Organization of Scientific Area Committees for Forensic Science

OTHRAM—DNA solves.com—DNA and genealogy, often used for cold cases

Regional Computer Forensics Lab—assists law enforcement with a multitude of services such as cell phones, electronic evidence, consultation, etc.

TEEX Texas A&M engineering extension service—CSI training classes

Texas EquuSearch—volunteer search and recovery organization used across the US

The Innocence Project.org

Notes

1 United States, Code of Federal Regulations, 1910.1030 (2024).

2 "Biological Spill Kit and Cleanup Job Aid." Center for Disease Control, reach.cdc.gov/sites/default/files/job-aids-resources/Bloodborne%20Pathogens%20Spill%20Kit%20and%20Cleanup%20Job%20Aid_508.pdf.

3 https://www.osha.gov.

Bibliography/Resources

Standards

1. American National Standards Institute ANSI/ASB (2021) *050—First Edition Best Practice Recommendation for Photographic Documentation of Footwear and Tire Impression Evidence.*
2. American National Standards Institute ANSI/ASB (2022) *126—Best Practice Recommendation for Casting Footwear and Tire Impression Evidenced at the Crime Scene.*
3. American National Standards Institute ANSI/ASB (2020) *049—Best Practice Recommendation for Lifting of Footwear and Tire Impressions.*
4. American Society for Testing & Materials (2003) *ASTM C1256-93—Standard Practice for Interpreting Glass Fracture Surface Features.*
5. American Society for Testing & Materials (2023) *ASTM E1188-11 (2017)—Standard Practice for Collection and Preservation of Information and Physical Items by a Technical Investigator.*
6. American Society for Testing & Materials (2018) *ASTM E1610-18—Standard Guide for Forensic Paint Analysis and Comparison.*
7. American Society for Testing & Materials (2023) *ASTM E1610-18—Standard Guide for Forensic Paint Analysis and Comparison.*
8. American Society for Testing & Materials (2019) *ASTM E3272-23—Standard Guide for Collection of Soils and Other Geological Evidence for Criminal Forensic Applications.*
9. American Society for Testing & Materials (2009) *ASTM F444-88—Standard Consumer Safety Specification for Scald-Prevention Devices and Systems in Bathing Areas.*
10. Organization of Scientific Area Committees for Forensic Science (OSAC) (2020) *Trace Materials Crime Scene Investigation Guide* (NIST.GOV).
11. Organization of Scientific Area Committees for Forensic Science (OSAC) (2020) *Standard Guide for Crime Scene Photography.*
12. Organization of Scientific Area Committees for Forensic Science (OSAC) (2020) *Guiding Principles for Crime Scene Investigation and Reconstruction.*
13. Organization of Scientific Area Committees for Forensic Science (OSAC) (2023) *S-0006—Standard Guide for Photographing Scars, Marks, and Tattoos.*
14. Organization of Scientific Area Committees for Forensic Science (OSAC) (2021) *N-0015—Guiding Principles for Crime Scene Investigation and Reconstruction: Transparency and Ethics Proposed Standard.*
15. Organization of Scientific Area Committees for Forensic Science (OSAC) (2021) *N-0016—Standard for Initial Response at Scenes by Law Enforcement—Proposed Standard.*

16. Organization of Scientific Area Committees for Forensic Science (OSAC) (2021) *N-0019—Standard Practice for the Documentation and Processing of Shooting Scenes.*
17. Organization of Scientific Area Committees for Forensic Science (OSAC) (2023) *N-0020—Standard for the On-Scene Collection and Preservation of Friction Ridge Impressions.*
18. Organization of Scientific Area Committees for Forensic Science (OSAC) (2022) *N-025—Standard for Scene Response: Initial Response by Scene Investigators.*
19. Organization of Scientific Area Committees for Forensic Science (OSAC) (2022) *S-0030—Standard for Methodology in Bloodstain Pattern Analysis.*
20. Organization of Scientific Area Committees for Forensic Science (OSAC) (2022) *N-0033—Standard for Processing Evidence for the Detection of Friction Ridge Impressions.*
21. Organization of Scientific Area Committees for Forensic Science (OSAC) (2022) *N-0035—Standard for on Scene Collection and Preservation of Document Evidence.*
22. Organization of Scientific Area Committees for Forensic Science (OSAC) (2022) *N-0039—Collecting and Preserving Entomological Evidence from a Terrestrial Environment.*
23. Scientific Working Group for Shoeprint and Tire Tread Evidence (SWGTREAD) (2008) *Guide for the Chemical Enhancement of Bloody Impression Evidence.*
24. Scientific Working Group on Materials Analysis (SWGMAT) (2002) *Forensic Human Hair Examination Guidelines.*
25. Scientific Working Group on Materials Analysis (SWGMAT) (1998) *Trace Evidence Recovery Guidelines.*
26. Scientific Working Group on Materials Analysis (SWGMAT) (2004) *Glass Fractures.*
27. Scientific Working Group on Materials Analysis (SWGMAT) (2004) *Introduction to Forensic Glass Examination.*
28. Scientific Working Group on Materials Analysis (SWGMAT) (2004) *Collection, Handling, and Identification of Glass.*
29. United States, Code of Federal Regulations, 1910.1030 (2024).

Sources

30. Adach, Edward. "Recovering Buried Footwear and Tire Impressions in Snow: A Simple and Easy Method." *Journal of Forensic Identification*, 2021, pp. 197–204.
31. *American Psychological Association*, 19 Apr. 2018, dictionary.apa.org.
32. Newman, Russ. "The Road to Resilience." *American Psychological Association*, 1 Jan. 2002.
33. Anderson, Elizabeth. "Transfer of Latent Prints on Duct Tape." *Journal of Forensic Identification*, 2023, pp. 143–168.
34. Anderson, Gail. "How the Absence of Blow Flies Overturned a Wrongful Conviction." *www.phys.org*, 1 Oct. 2008, phys.org/news/2018-12-absence-flies-overturned-wrongful-conviction.html.

35. Archer, Emily, et al. "12. Validation of a Dual Cycle Ethylene Oxide Treatment Technique to Remove DNA from Consumables Used in Forensic Laboratories." *Forensic Science International: Genetics*, vol. 4, no. 4, 2010, pp. 239–243, https://doi.org/10.1016/j.fsigen.2009.10.004.
36. "Dog-Fighting DNA Database Breaks New Ground in Crackdown on Animal Cruelty." *ASPCA*, 15 Jun. 2010, www.aspca.org.
37. Ballesteros, Michael F., et al. "CDC Guidance for Communities Assessing, Investigating and Responding to Suicide Clusters, United States, 2024." *Morbidity and Mortality Weekly Report*, vol. 73, no. 2, 2024.
38. Ballou, S., et al. "The Biological Evidence Preservation Handbook: Best Practices for Evidence Handlers," *NIST Interagency/Internal Report (NISTIR), National Institute of Standards and Technology*, Gaithersburg, MD, 2013, https://doi.org/10.6028/NIST.IR.7928.
39. Bandyopadhyay, Samir Kumar, and Goutam Roy Chowdhury. "Analysis of Bloodstain Patterns at the Crime Scene Due to Arterial Bleeding." *International Journal of Development Research*, vol. 7, no. 1, 2016.
40. Bauer, Erin, Larry Barksdale, Emma Sidel, and Justine LaViolette. "Death Scene Insect Succession in Nebraska: A Guidebook." *Faculty Publications: Department of Entomology*, 2022, 983, https://digitalcommons.unl.edu/entomologyfacpub/983.
41. Beggin, Riley. "Questions Arise over Police Searches of Car Data Systems." *The Detroit News*, 1 Jan. 2022.
42. Bevel, Tom, and R. M. Gardner. Bloodstain Pattern Analysis with an Introduction to Crime Scene Reconstruction. CRC Press, 2008.
43. Bille, Todd, et al. "An Improved Process for the Collection and DNA Analysis of Fired Cartridge Cases." *Forensic Science International: Genetics*, vol. 46, 2020, https://doi.org/10.1016/j.fsigen.2020.102238.
44. Biography.com, editors. "Harold Shipman British Serial Killer Harold Shipman, Who Worked in England as a Medical Doctor, Killed over 200 of His Patients before His Arrest in 1998." *Biography*, 3 Oct. 2023, www.biography.com/crime/harold-shipman.
45. "Biological Spill Kit and Cleanup Job Aid." *Center for Disease Control*, reach.cdc.gov/sites/default/files/job-aids-resources/Bloodborne%20Pathogens%20Spill%20Kit%20and%20Cleanup%20Job%20Aid_508.pdf.
46. Blanco, Juan I., and Susan Wilson. "Dr. Buck RUXTON." *Murderpedia*, murderpedia.org.
47. "Bluestar, the Miracle Product That Solves Many Criminal Investigations." *Bluestar Forensic*, 1 Apr. 2019, www.bluestar-forensic.com/.
48. Bodziak, William J., and Lesley Hammer. "An Evaluation of Dental Stone, Traxtone, and Crime-Cast." *Journal of Forensic Identification*, vol. 56, no. 5, 2006, pp. 769–787.
49. Borgeson, Kevin, and Kristen Kuehnle. Serial Offenders Theory and Practice. Jones & Bartlett Learning, 2012.
50. Breuer, Howard. "Sons of Anarchy Actor Johnny Lewis Kills Woman, Dies in a Fall: Cops." *People*, 27 Sept. 2012.
51. Brooks Brownlie, H. W., and R. Munro. "The Veterinary Forensic Necropsy: A Review of Procedures and Protocols." *Veterinary Pathology*, vol. 53, no. 5, 2016, https://doi.org/10.1177/0300985816655851.

52. Brown, Jalessa, and Susan Clutter. "Fingerprinting Different Food Sources at Crime Scenes." *Journal of Forensic Identification*, vol. 69, no. 3, 2019, pp. 271–279.
53. Brown, Jerry. "Murder of Mary Yoder by Her Son's Ex-Girlfriend, Kaitlyn Conley, Examined on a Time to Kill." *Daily Crime*, 23 Aug. 2021, www.dailycrime.com/murder-of-mary-yoder-by-her-sons-ex-girlfriend-kaitlyn-conley-examined-on-a-time-to-kill/.
54. "Burn Exposure Chart." *ANTISCALD.COM*, antiscald.com/index.php?route=information/information&information_id=15.
55. Byrd, Jason, and James Castner. Forensic Entomology, the Utility of Arthropods in Legal Investigations. CRC Press, 2001.
56. Canadian Kennel Club. www.ckc.ca/en/
57. "Cara Knott Family Seeks Public Help to Block Parole of CHP Officer Craig Peyer, Convicted of SDSU Student's Murder." *East County Magazine*, 1 Dec. 2011.
58. Carson, Leslie M., et al. "An Analysis of Suicides among First Responders-Findings from the National Violent Death Reporting System, 2015–2017." *Journal of Safety Research*, vol. 85, Jun. 2023, pp. 361–370, https://doi.org/10.1016/j.jsr.2023.04.003.
59. Casali, F., et al. "Validation of Presumptive Tests for Non-Human Blood Using Kastle Meyer and Hemastix Reagents." *Science & Justice: Journal of the Forensic Science Society*, vol. 60, no. 1, 2020, pp. 30–35, https://doi.org/10.1016/j.scijus.2019.10.003.
60. Castello Ponce, Ana, et al. "Bloodstains on Leather Examination of False Negatives in Presumptive Test and Human Hemoglobin Test." *Journal of Forensic Sciences*, vol. 62, no. 5, 2017, pp. 1308–1313.
61. Choi, Hyeong In, et al. "Study on the Viability of Canine Nose Pattern as a Unique Biometric Marker." *Animals: An Open Access Journal from MDPI*, vol. 11, no. 12, 25 Nov. 2021, p. 3372, https://doi.org/10.3390/ani11123372.
62. "Contamination Controls: Scene of Crime (Accessible)." *Forensic Science Regulator*, 2023, www.gov.uk/government/publications/crime-scene-dna-anti-contamination-guidance/contamination-controls-scene-of-crime-accessible.
63. Committee on Identifying the Needs of the Forensic Sciences Community, National Research Council. Strengthening Forensic Science in the United States: A Path Forward. National Academies Press, 2009.
64. Compitus, Katherine. "Silent Suffering: The High Rate of Suicide in Veterinarians, High Stressors in Veterinary Medicine Often Have Fatal Consequences." *Psychology Today*, 17 Nov. 2023.
65. Coren, Stanley. "Are Dogs' Nose Prints Really Unique and Unchanging? Are Dogs' Nose Prints Distinctive Enough to Be Used for Identification?" *Psychology Today*, 2021, https://doi.org/doi.org/10.1177/1365712720930600.
66. Technical Working Group on Crime Scene Investigation. Crime Scene Investigation: A Guide for Law Enforcement. National Forensic Science Technology Center, 2013.
67. "Crime Scene Response Technical Procedures." *Phoenix Police Department Crime Lab*, 1 Jan. 2019, crimelab.phoenix.gov/QTDocuments/1697.PDF.
68. US Department of Justice. Death Investigation: A Guide for the Scene Investigator. US Department of Justice, 1999.

69. Dehaan, J. D. Kirk's Fire Investigation, 6th ed. Pearson Education Inc., 2007.
70. "Deputies Used DNA Sample from Urine Left at Scene to Arrest Suspect Who Burglarized Magnolia Park Church in 2021." *KPRC*, 28 Feb. 2023, www.click2houston.com/news/local/2023/03/01/deputies-used-dna-sample-from-urine-left-at-scene-to-arrest-suspect-who-burglarized-magnolia-park-church-in-2021/.
71. National Institute of Justice. "DNA Evidence: What Law Enforcement Officers Should Know." *NIJ Journal*, no. 249, Jul. 2003.
72. Dobkin, Rachel. "Inside the Tetris Murders and Chilling Clue the Russian Mafia Was behind Deaths of Vladimir Pokhilko, His Wife and Son." *The US Sun*, 5 Dec. 2022.
73. "Documentation of Shoe and Tire Impression Evidence." *California Department of Justice; Bureau of Forensic Services*, oag.ca.gov/bfs.
74. Dolinak, David, et al. Forensic Pathology, Principles and Practice. Elsevier Academic Press, 2005.
75. Ducharme, Jamie. "Investigators Collected the Suspected Golden State Killer's DNA While He Shopped at Hobby Lobby." *Time*, 2 Jun. 2018.
76. Duncan, Christopher. Advanced Crime Scene Photography, 2nd ed. CRC Press, 2023.
77. Duke, Alan. "Sons of Anarchy Actor Dead in Hollywood Murder Mystery." *CNN*, 28 Sept. 2012, www.cnn.com/2012/09/27/showbiz/hollywood-murder-mystery/index.html.
78. Edds, Kimberly. "Ex Glendale Adventist Worker Pleads Guilty to 'Angel of Death' Murders." *Metropolitan News Enterprise*, 13 Mar. 2002.
79. Edwards, Brad. "Chicago Tylenol Murders: Who Did It? No One Has Ever Been Charged, But Questions Still Surround James Lewis." *CBS News*, 30 Sept. 2022, www.cbsnews.com/chicago/news/painkiller-1982-tylenol-murders-questions-james-lewis/.
80. Elamroussi, Aya. "Minnesota Family of 7, Including 3 Children, Died of Apparent Accidental Carbon Monoxide Poisoning, Police Say." *ABC12 News*, 28 Jan. 2024, www.abc12.com/news/national/minnesota-family-of-7-including-3-children-died-of-apparent-accidental-carbon-monoxide-poisoning-police/article_017c800b-0702-5ead-8aae-518d472d2b8e.html.
81. Elayas, Malak, et al. "Using Silver Nitrate and Ultraviolet Light to Enhance Footwear Impressions Containing Salt Residue." *Journal of Forensic Identification*, 2022, pp. 200–224.
82. US Department of Justice. Electronic Crime Scene Investigation: A Guide for First Responders, 2nd ed. US Department of Justice, 2008.
83. Ellison, Garret. "Poisoning the Pecks: New Book Details Infamous 1916 Grand Rapids Murder Case." *MLIVE*, 30 Oct. 2014.
84. Elmarije, K., et al. "The Interpretation of Forensic Conclusions by Criminal Justice Professionals: The Same Evidence Interpreted Differently." *Forensic Science International*, vol. 313, 2020, p. 110331, ISSN 0379-0738, https://doi.org/10.1016/j.forsciint.2020.110331.
85. "Emergency Response Tools." *EPA.GOV*, 20 Nov. 2024, www.epa.gov/emergency-response/response-tools.
86. Fang, T. "Physical Characteristics of Spatter Stains on Textiles: Influence of Impact Surface Texture, Blood Drop Volume and Blood Drop Velocity." *OJP.GOV*, www.ojp.gov/ncjrs/virtual-library/abstracts/physical-characteristics-spatter-stains-textiles-influence-impact.

87. Federal Bureau of Investigation. FBI Handbook of Crime Scene Forensics. Skyhorse Publishing, 2008.
88. Fenster, Jordan. "Homicide Scene Missteps: How Not to Investigate a Murder." *Westchester Journal News*, 20 Jul. 2017.
89. Fisher, Barry. Techniques of Crime Scene Investigation, 7th ed. CRC Press, 2004.
90. US Department of Justice. Firearms Identification and Tracing Procedures. US Department of Justice, 1998.
91. "Forensic Recovery of Identification from Shell Casings." *Signature Science*, www.signaturescience.com.
92. Frégeau, C. J., Germain, O., and Fourney, R. M. "Fingerprint Enhancement Revisited and the Effects of Blood Enhancement Chemicals on Subsequent Profiler Plus Fluorescent Short Tandem Repeat DNA Analysis of Fresh and Aged Bloody Fingerprints." *Journal of Forensic Sciences*, vol. 45, no. 2, Mar. 2000, pp. 354–380, PMID: 10782955.
93. Friedman, Bob. "Michael Peterson: 'What Happened in That Trial Could Not Happen Today'." *Attorney at Law Magazine*, 31 Aug. 2023.
94. KOLN. "Gage County Sheriff's Office Files to Take Ownership of Horses in Livestock Neglect Investigation." 1011 NOW.Com, 5 Sept. 2023.
95. Gardner, Ross. Practical Crime Scene Processing and Investigation. CRC Press, 2005.
96. Gardner, R. Practical Crime Scene Processing, 3rd ed. CRC Press, 2018.
97. Garner, Marcus K. "Guilty Plea from Rockdale Twin Accused in Mother's Death." *The Atlanta Journal-Constitution*, 8 Apr. 2016.
98. Garrison, Robert. "Teen Mom Suffocates Newborn by Shoving Rock down Child's Throat, Denver Police Say." *Denver7*, 8 Nov. 2017.
99. Geberth, Vernon. Practical Homicide Investigation Checklist and Field Guide, 2nd ed. CRC Press, 2014.
100. Geberth, Vernon. Practical Homicide Investigation: Tactics, Procedures and Forensic Techniques. CRC Press, 1996.
101. Geberth, Vernon. "Missteps at the Homicide Crime Scene." *PI Magazine: Journal of Professional Investigators*, vol. 22, no. 3, 2008.
102. Gehl, Rod, and Darryl Plecas. Introduction to Criminal Investigation: Processes, Practices and Thinking. Justice Institute of British Columbia, 2016.
103. Genge, N. E. The Forensic Casebook: The Science of Crime Scene Investigation. Ballantine Books, 2002.
104. George, Chris. "Photography Cheat Sheet: Color Temperature & the Kelvin Scale." *Digital Camera World*, 2 Aug. 2024, www.digitalcameraworld.com.
105. Gilmartin, Kevin. Emotional Survival for Law Enforcement. E-S Press, 2002.
106. Givens, Ann. "A New Method of DNA Testing Could Solve More Shootings: Criminologists Thought It Was Impossible to Get DNA off Shell Casings, But a Technique Pioneered in the Netherlands Is Having Notable Results." *Police1*, 2018.
107. Glaub, Gina. "The Ultimate Betrayal: The Coleman Family Murders." *The Midwest Crime Files*, 10 Nov. 2021.
108. Goldfarb, Kara. "The Alleged Crimes of the West Memphis Three—and Why the Accused 'Satanic' Killers Were Set Free." *All That's Interesting*, 8 Sept. 2024, allthatsinteresting.com/west-Memphis-three.

109. Gootman, Elissa. "Defendant Pleads Guilty to Role in '79 Killing of Suffolk Boy." *The New York Times*, 20 Jun. 2003.
110. Graff, Gary, and Iris Dalley Graff. "Advanced Crime Scene Documentation." *Tritech Forensics*, 17 Sept. 2018, Houston. Lecture/training.
111. Gross, A. M., et al. "The Effect of Luminol on Presumptive Tests and DNA Analysis Using the Polymerase Chain Reaction." *Journal of Forensic Science*, vol. 44, no. 4, 1999, pp. 837–840.
112. "Guidelines for Investigating Deaths in Custody." *International Committee of the Red Cross*, 1 Oct. 2013, www.icrc.org.
113. Hayden, M. E. "The Strange Rise and Violent Fall of Long Island's Dirtiest Police Chief." *Vice*, 14 Mar. 2016, www.vice.com.
114. Hagerty, Jim. "Todd Smith's Latest Attempt at New Trial Hits Roadblock: Smith Was Convicted in 2017 of Beathing His Wife to Death with a Baseball Bat." *WIFR*, 16 May 2023.
115. Hamilton, Charles. "7-Year Sentence for Gargol Killer Incase with Facebook Selfie Evidence." *CBC News*, 15 Jan. 2018, www.cbc.ca/news/canada/saskatoon/women-pleads-guilty-in-brittney-gargol-murder-1.4487758.
116. Hanzlick, Randy. Death Investigation Systems and Procedures. CRC Press, 2007.
117. Harris, Chris. "Receptionist Sentenced for Fatally Poisoning Ex Boyfriend's Mom, Who Was Also Her Boss." *People*, 12 Jan. 2018.
118. Hartley, Gabrielle, and Claire Glynn. "A Comparative Analysis of Protein and Peroxidase Blood." *Journal of Forensic Research and Analysis*, 2016, pp. 1–5.
119. Hartnett, Stephen. "The Death Penalty: An American History." *Journal of American History*, vol. 90, no. 3, 2003, pp. 983–984, https://doi.org/10.2307/3660892.
120. Haskell, Neal, and Elmer Catts. Entomology and Death: A Procedural Guide. Joyce's Print Shop, 1990.
121. Hawthorne, M. R. First Unit Responder: A Guide to Physical Evidence Collection for Patrol Officers. CRC Press, 1999.
122. Helsel, Phil. "4 Adults, 3 Kids Found in Minnesota Home Died of Carbon Monoxide Poisoning Most of the Victims Were in Their Beds Saturday Night in Moorhead, Near Fargo, N.D., after Family Members Could Not Reach Them." *NBC News*, 22 Dec. 2021, www.nbcnews.com/news/us-news/4-adults-3-kids-found-minnesota-home-died-carbon-monoxide-poisoning-rcna9733.
123. Herbst, Diane. "South Carolina Woman Sentenced to 25 Years for Fatally Poisoning Husband with Eye Drops." *People*, 16 Jan. 2020.
124. Hilderband, Dwayne S. Footwear, the Missed Evidence. Staggs Publishing, 2007.
125. Houck, Max M. Forensic Pathology. Elsevier, 2016.
126. Hueske, Edward. Practical Analysis and Reconstruction of Shooting Incidents, 2nd ed. CRC Press, 2021.
127. Hulsey, Steven. "Forensic Light Sources for the Detective of Biological Evidence in Crime Scene Investigation: A Review." *Malaysian Journal of Forensic Sciences*, vol. 1, no. 1, 2010.
128. "IBIS ClearCase." *Leads Online*, leadsonline.com/clearcase.
129. Inman, Keith, and Norah Rudin. Principles and Practices of Criminalistics: The Profession of Forensic Science. CRC Press, 2001.

130. "Instagram Influencer's Birthday Party Ends with 3 Dead after Dry Ice Stunt Went Wrong." *Today Online*, 1 Mar. 2020, www.todayonline.com/world/instagram-influencers-birthday-party-ends-3-dead-after-dry-ice-stunt-went-wrong.
131. "Investigation of Officer-Involved Shootings and Other Serious Incidents." *The International Association of Chiefs of Police*, 1 Apr. 2019, www.theiacp.org/.
132. "Introduction to Forensic Fiber Examination." *Forensic Science Communications*, vol. 1, no. 1, 1999, https://archives.fbi.gov.
133. Innes, Brian. The Body in Question: Exploring the Cutting Edge in Forensic Science. Sterling Publishing Co, 2005.
134. Jacobs, Becky. "A Woman Was Groped at the University of Utah: Skin Cells on Her Clothing Helped Investigators Catch Her Attacker: The Use of Touch DNA in That 'Groundbreaking' Case Changed the Way Evidence Is Collected: Now a BYU Researcher Is Sharing This Method with Others." *The Salt Lake Tribune*, 25 May 2021.
135. James, S. H., et al. Principles of Bloodstain Pattern Analysis Theory and Practice. CRC Press, 2005.
136. Jansson, Linda, et al. "Factors Affecting DNA Recovery from Cartridge Cases." *Forensic Science International: Genetics*, vol. 48, 2019.
137. Jason, Alexander. "Collecting, Transporting and Processing DNA on Fired Cartridge Casings." *Forensic Magazine*, 11 Oct. 2024.
138. Jenkins, John Philip. "Harold Shipman." *Encyclopedia Britannica*, 31 Jan. 2025, www.britannica.com/biography/Harold-Shipman.
139. Johnson, Stacey. "Examining the Effectiveness of Processing Fired Cartridge Cases for Latent Evidence." *Journal of Forensic Identification*, vol. 69, no. 1, 2019, pp. 27–34.
140. Kail, Tony. "Ritualistic Crimes and Religious Extremism." *Tritech Forensics*, 12 Jun. 2023, Pasadena. Lecture/training.
141. Kail, Tony M. Magico-Religious Groups and Ritualistic Activities: A Guide for First Responders. CRC Press, 2008.
142. Kail, Tony. "Ritual Homicide Special Report: Cultural and Forensic Aspects of Nigeria's Badoo Cult." *Symbol Intelligence Group*, www.symbolintelligence.com.
143. Kaplan, N., et al. "Calculation of Likelihood Ratios for Gunshot Residue Evidence—Statistical Aspects." *Law, Probability and Risk*, vol. 15, no. 2, 2016, pp. 107–125, https://doi.org/doi.org/10.1093/lpr/mgw001.
144. Kollar, Mark. Best Practices for Investigating an Officer Invovled Critical Incident. Ohio Attorney General's Bureau of Criminal Investigation, 2021.
145. *Latent Fingerprint Processing Techniques Selection and Sequencing Guide*. Chesapeake Bay Division International Association for Identification, www.cbdiai.org/.
146. Lee, Henry, et al. Henry Lee's Crime Scene Handbook. Academic Press, 2007.
147. Levenson, Michael. "James W. Lewis, Suspect in the 1982 Tylenol Murders, Dies at 76." *The New York Times*, 10 Jul. 2023.
148. Levine, Alaina. "Conventional Forensic Theory on Order of Bugs That Feast on Corpses Upended." *Scientific American*, 2012.
149. "Lindy Chamberlain: The True Story of What Happened to Baby Azaria." *News.Com*, 28 Sept. 2020.

150. Maloney, Michael S., and Donald G. Housman. Crime Scene Investigation Procedural Guide. CRC Press, 2014.
151. Markowitz, Mollie, and Michael Ruiz. "Judge Dumbfounded by Error in Ellen Greenberg 'Suicide' Probe—after Teacher Was Found Stabbed 20 Times." *New York Post*, 22 Dec. 2024.
152. Maras, M. H., and Adam S. Wandt. "State of Ohio V. Ross Compton: Internet-Enabled Medical Device Data Introduced as Evidence of Arson and Insurance Fraud." *The International Journal of Evidence & Proof*, vol. 24, no. 3, 2020, pp. 321–328, https://doi.org/10.1177/1365712720930600.
153. Martinez, Edecio. "Ex-Marine Chris Coleman Found Guilty of Murdering Wife, Kids, on Second Anniversary of Ill. Killings." *CBS News*, 6 May 2011, www.cbsnews.com/news/ex-marine-chris-coleman-found-guilty-of-murdering-wife-kids-on-second-anniversay-of-ill-killings/.
154. Maxwell, Virginia, and Martha Smith-Blackmore. Investigating Animal Abuse Crime Scenes: A Field Guide. CRC Press, 2023.
155. Melinek, J., et al. "National Association of Medical Examiners Position Paper: Medical Examiner, Coroner, and Forensic Pathologist Independence." *Academic Forensic Pathology*, vol. 3, no. 1, 2013, pp. 93–98, https://doi.org/10.23907/2013.013.
156. McCall, Keenan, et al. "Detecting Blood in an Outdoor Environment with the Bluestar Reagent and DNA Analysis." *Journal of Forensic Identification*, 2021, pp. 309–338.
157. Miller, Allen. "Choosing the Best Fingerprint Powder for Your Scene." *Evidence Technology Magazine*, Sept./Oct. 2013, pp. 20–23.
158. Miller, David, and Jason Hodges. "Validation of Abacus SALIgAE Test for the Forensic Identification of Saliva." *West Virginia State Police Forensic Laboratory*, 7 Oct. 2005, archive.gfjc.fiu.edu/workshops/resources/literature.
159. Miller, Larry. Police Photography, 5th ed. Anderson Publishing, 2006.
160. Mitchell, Roger, et al. "National Association of Medical Examiners Position Paper: Recommendations for the Definition, Investigation, Postmortem Examination, and Reporting of Deaths in Custody." *Academy of Forensic Pathology*, vol. 7, no. 4, 2017, pp. 604–618.
161. Moorhouse, Drusilla. "A Cop Who Killed a San Diego College Student in 1986 Gave 'Safety Tips' in a TV News Ride-Along Days Later." *Huffpost*, 27 Dec. 2023.
162. Morgan-Besecker, Terrie. "A Regretful Wolsieffer Is Released/The Ex-Dentist Is Back in the Area after 13 Years in Prison for Killing His Wife in 1986." *Time Leader*, 10 May 2005, www.timesleader.com/archive/1079810/a-regretful-wolsieffer-is-released-the-ex-dentist-is-back-in-the-area-after13-years-in-prison-for-killing-his-wife-in-1986.
163. Morrissey, Angela. "Location of Clandestine Graves—Clues from Plants." *Forensics for Writers*, 21 Jun. 2013, forensicsforwriters.blogspot.com/2013/06/location-of-clandestine-graves-clues.html.
164. Mullenneaux, Lisa. "Choose Your Poison: The Curious Case of Dr. Waite." *Hektoen International, a Journal of Medical Humanities*, vol. 9, no. 1, Winter 2017.
165. Murder Accountability Project. "Murder Accountability Project." *Murder Data*, www.murderdata.org.

166. Neureuther, Katharina, et al. "Reduction of PCR-Amplifiable DNA by Ethylene Oxide Treatment of Forensic Consumables." *Forensic Science International: Genetics*, vol. 12, 2014, https://doi.org/10.1016/j.fsigen.2014.06.006.
167. Noam, Gonen, et al. "Using an Alternate Light Source to Recover Sticker Marks from a Vehicle." *Journal of Forensic Identification*, 2022, pp. 313–319.
168. Noon, Randall K. Scientific Method, Applications in Failure Investigation and Forensic Science. CRC Press, 2009.
169. International Association of Chiefs of Police. Officer-Involved Shootings: A Guide for Law Enforcement Leaders. International Association of Chiefs of Police, 2015.
170. Olsen, Robert. Scott's Fingerprint Mechanics. Thomas Publishing, 1978.
171. Park, Madison, et al. "DNA, Shoe Leather Help Arizona Police Identify Killer of 6." *CNN*, www.cnn.com/2018/06/04/us/arizona-killings-timeline/index.html.
172. Parsons, Mckenzy. "Gage County Horse Owner Won't Face Criminal Charges, Surviving Horses to Be Auctioned off." *KETV7*, Mar. 2024.
173. Pelisek, Christine, and Gregb Hanlon. "The 'Grim Sleeper' Serial Killer: 7 Things to Know after Lonnie Franklin's Death: Lonnie Franklin, the Serial Killer Known as the 'Grim Sleeper', Died in His Prison Cell on March 28, 2020." *People*, 15 Oct. 2022.
174. Penven, Don. "Latent Blood Prints—Methods for Chemical Enhancement." *Crime Scene Investigator Network*, 1 Mar. 2013.
175. Pfefferli, Peter. Forensic Evidence Field Guide: A Collection of Best Practices. Academic Press, 2015.
176. Phatak, Darshan R., and Jeffrey Walterscheid. "Huffing Air Conditioner Fluid: A Cool Way to Die?" *The American Journal of Forensic Medicine and Pathology* vol. 33, no. 1, 2012, pp. 64–67, https://doi.org/10.1097/paf.0b013e3181dd5b5e.
177. Phillips, Kristine, and Keith McMillan. "Suspect in Six Arizona Killings Fatally Shoots Himself in Hotel Room as Officers Close in, Police Say." *The Salt Lake Tribune*, 5 Jun. 2018.
178. "Physical Evidence Bulletin." *California Department of Justice*, 1 Jan. 1998, oag.ca.gov/bfs/peb.
179. Platt, Richard. Crime Scene: The Ultimate Guide to Forensic Science. DK Publishing, 2003.
180. Pope, Lisa. "Chemical Testing for Presumptive Blood on Items and the Ground below Them during Months of Exposure to Sun, Rain, Rust." *Journal of Forensic Identification*, vol. 70, no. 4, 2020, p. 416.
181. Possley, Maurice. "National Registry of Exonerations." *University of Michigan Law School*, 4 Jan. 2018, www.law.umich.edu/special/exoneration.
182. Potter, Tim. "Science Crucial to Cracking BTK Case." The Wichita Eagle, 8 Aug. 2014.
183. "Psychological First Aid: Field Operations Guide." *National Child Traumatic Stress Network and National Center for PTSD*, 2005.
184. Radford, Michael. "Latent Prints Visualized by Dew." *Journal of Forensic Identification*, vol. 74, no. 3, 2024, pp. 320–323.
185. Ramsey, Sandy. "Aftermath of Disaster: Effects on Mental Health Professionals." *Annals of American Psychotherapy*, no. Fall, 2009, pp. 71–73.

186. "Remembering 90'S R&B Group Hi-Five: Love & Tragedy." *Black Doctor*, blackdoctor.org/remembering-90s-rb-group-singer-tony-thompson/.
187. Reyes, Ronny. "Suicide Ruling Upheld for Philly Teacher Found with 20 Stab Wounds But Judges Slam 'Deeply Flawed' Investigation." *New York Post*, 14 Sept. 2023.
188. Reza, H. G. "Prosecutors Outline Evidence They Say Ties Peyer to Slaying of Knott." *LA Times*, 20 Jan. 1988.
189. Roberts, Mark, and Tami Adair. "Latent Print Evidence at Fire Scenes." *104th IAI International Educational Conference, International Association for Identification*, 14 Aug. 2019, Peppermill Resort. Conference Presentation.
190. Robinson, Edward. Crime Scene Photography, 2nd ed. Academic Press, 2007.
191. Ruslander, H. W. "Using Small Particle Reagent to Obtain Latent Fingerprints from the Adhesive Side of Clear Plastic Tape." *Crime Scene Investigator Network*, www.crime-scene-investigator.net/SPRonTape.html.
192. Rynearson, Joe. "Tips and Tricks." *National Crime Investigation and Training*, ncit.com.
193. Rynearson, Joseph M. Evidence and Crime Scene Reconstruction, 7th ed. Anderson Publishing, 2015.
194. "Sample Collection." *US Davis Veterinary Genetics Laboratory*, vgl.ucdavis.edu/sample-collection.
195. Scientific Working Group on Bloodstain Pattern Analysis. "Scientific Working Group on Bloodstain Pattern Analysis, Recommended Terminology." *Forensic Science Communications*, vol. 11, no. 2, 2009.
196. Schilke, Rachel. "Half of US Homicides Go Unsolved, Ranking Last among Western Nations." *Washington Examiner*, 6 Mar. 2023. www.washingtonexaminer.com/news/2576215/half-of-us-homicides-go-unsolved-ranking-last-among-western-nations/.
197. Sciluminate, www.sciluminate.com/.
198. Sederstrom, Jill. "Young Nurse Found Dead in Her Overflowing Bathtub—Who Would Murder Her: Cassy Farrington Was Found Floating Face down in Her Scrubs in a Bathtub of Her Home, But the Investigation Would Be Stalled by Missteps." *Oxygen True Crime*, 6 Oct. 2021, www.oxygen.com/dateline-secrets-uncovered/crime-news/cassy-farrington-nurse-found-murdered-in-bathtub.
199. Shapiro, Emily. "DJ Admits to Cold Case Murder after Being Linked through Novel DNA Technique, Apologizes to Victim's Family in Court. Christy Mirack, 25, Was Murdered at Her Pennsylvania Home in 1992." *ABC News*, 8 Jan. 2019.
200. Shaw, Kirsty, et al. "Comparison of the Effects of Sterilization Techniques on Subsequent DNA Profiling." *International Journal of Legal Medicine*, vol. 122, 2008, pp. 29–33.
201. Shedge, Rutwik, et al. Posmortem Changes. Treasure Island: StatPearls Publishing, 2023.
202. Shrivastava, Priya, V. K. Jain, and Suman Nagpal. "Gunshot Residue Detection Technologies-a Review." *Egyptian Journal of Forensic Sciences*, vol. 11, no. 1, 2021, p. 14.
203. "Signature Science's FRISC Service Enables DNA Recovery from Spent Shell Casings." *Signature Science*, 4 Oct. 2019, www.signaturescience.com/press/signature-sciences-frisc-service-enables-dna-recovery-from-spent-shell-casings/.

204. Smith, Jordan M. "The Scientist Using Bugs to Help Solve Murders: At Crime Scenes around the World, the Forensic Entomologist Paola Magni Is Taking Her Field into Uncharted Waters." *Smithsonian Magazine*, Jan/Feb. 2024.
205. Spawn, Mark A. "Effects of Fire on Fingerprint Evidence." *Spawngroup.Com*, spawngroup.com/media/EFFECTS_OF_FIRE_ON_FINGERPRINTS.pdf.
206. Spitz, W. U., et al., Spitz and Fisher's Medicolegal Investigation of Death, Guidelines for the Application of Pathology to Crime Investigation, 3rd ed. Charles C. Thomas Publisher, 1993.
207. Staff. "Tony Thompson Death Caused by Freon Huffing." *The St. Louis American*, 5 Jul. 2007.
208. Staff. "Twin Sisters Confess to Brutal Murder of Mother: The Twins Describe What Really Happened the Morning of Their Mother's Murder 10 Years Ago." *11ALIVE*, 19 Dec. 2019, www.11alive.com/article/news/investigations/twisted-twins-jasmiyah-tasmiyah-whitehead-confess-to-killing-mother.
209. Stauffer, Eric, and Monica Bonfanti. Forensic Investigation of Stolen-Recovered and Other Crime-Related Vehicles. Academic Press, 2006.
210. Steel, Fiona. "The West Memphis Three." *Crime Library*, crimelibrary.org/.
211. Steele, Christine. "Former Cop Found Guilty of First-Degree Murder." Silver City Daily Press, 17 Aug. 2018.
212. Story, Justin. "Mother, Daughter Suspected in Barren Man's Death Return to Court." *Bowling Green Daily News*, 3 May 2024.
213. Sturelle, V., et al. "The Use of Camphor in the Development of Latent Prints on Unfired Cartridge Casings." *Journal of Forensic Identification*, vol. 56, 2006, pp. 694–705.
214. Tabachnick, Cara. "How Animal DNA Puts Killers behind Bars." *A&E*, 21 May 2018, www.aetv.com/real-crime/animal-dna-crimes-csi-forensics-murder-kidnapping.
215. Teather, Robert G. Encyclopedia of Underwater Investigations. Best Publishing Company, 1994.
216. "The Chicago Tylenol Murders." *Chicago History.Org*, 28 Sept. 2022, www.chicagohistory.org/tylenol-murders/.
217. "The Murder Accountability Project; Uniform Crime Report for Homicides: 1965–2023." *Project Cold Case*, 27 Sept. 2024, projectcoldcase.org/cold-case-homicide-stats/.
218. The Stanford Criminal Justice Center. "Use of Tasers by Law Enforcement Agencies: Guidelines and Recommendations." *Prepared for the City of Mountain View Human Relations Commission*, 2005, www.law.stanford.edu/academic/programs/criminaljustice.
219. Thompson, Desire. "Georgia Twins Sentenced to 30 Years in Jail after Confessing to Killing Their Mother." *News One*, 15 Mar. 2015, news-one.com/3101682/georgia-twins-sentenced-30-years-jail-confess-killing-mother.
220. "Three Die in Dry-Ice Incident at Moscow Pool Party." *BBC*, 29 Feb. 2020, www.bbc.com/news/world-europe-51680049.
221. "Tips for Managing and Preventing Stress: A Guide for Emergency Response and Public Safety Workers." *Substance Abuse and Mental Health Services Administration Center for Mental Health Services*, 2007, www.samhsa.gov.

222. Tobe, et al. "Evaluation of Six Presumptive Tests for Blood, Their Specificity, Sensitivity, and Effect on High Molecular-Weight DNA." *Journal of Forensic Science*, vol. 52, no. 1, 2007, pp. 102–109, https://doi.org/10.1111/j.1556-4029.2006.00324.x.
223. Touroo, R., and A. Fitch. "Identification, Collection, and Preservation of Veterinary Forensic Evidence: On Scene and During the Postmortem Examination." *Veterinary Pathology*, vol. 53, no. 5, 2016, pp. 880–887, https://doi.org/10.1177/0300985816641175.
224. Trapecar, Matej, and Mojca K. Vinkovic. "Techniques for Fingerprint Recovery on Vegetable and Fruit Surfaces Used in Slovenia—a Preliminary Study." *Science & Justice*, vol. 48, no. 4, 2008, pp. 192–195, https://doi.org/10.1016/j.scijus.2008.05.003.
225. Trimpe, Michael. "The Current Status of GSR Examinations." *FBI Law Enforcement Bulletin*, 1 May 2011.
226. "Unabomber Evidence Reveals New Insights." *CBS News*, 29 Nov. 2006, www.cbsnews.com/news/unabomber-evidence-reveals-new-insights.
227. U.S. Department of Homeland Security. WMD Response Guidebook. U.S. Department of Homeland Security, 2009.
228. Vallee, Andrew. "Connected Cars for Law Enforcement." Https://Ncjtc-static.Fvtc.Edu/Resources/RS01753995.Pdf. Webinar.
229. Valiente, Alexa, et al. "DC Mansion Murders: A Look at the Evidence That Helped Convict the Killer." *ABC News*, 26 Oct. 2018, abcnews.go.com/US/dc-mansion-murders-evidence-helped-convict-killer/story?id=58775381.
230. Vander Hayden, Aly. "Decomposition 'Pig' Test Suggests Body of Potential 'Smiley Face' Victim Todd Geib Was Not in Water Since Day He Went Missing 'Based on Our Study, [It Is] Unlikely That His Clothing and His Body Had Been in for 21 Days,' Said Dr. M. Eric Benbow." *Oxygen True Crime*, 23 Feb. 2019, www.oxygen.com/smiley-face-killers-the-hunt-for-justice/crime-time/todd-geib-decomposition-test.
231. Van Zandt, Clint. "Real CSI May Have Solved Imette's Murder." *NBC News*, 13 Mar. 2006, abcnews.go.com/US/dc-mansion-murders-evidence-helped-convict-killer/story?id=58775381.
232. Warden, Rob. "Illinois Death Penalty Reform: How It Happened, What It Promises." *The Journal of Criminal Law and Criminology*, vol. 95, no. 2, 2005, pp. 381–426.
233. Warsmith, Stephanie, and Paula Schleis. "How an Exhumation Solved the Murder of a Pregnant Akron Woman, Decades Later." *Akron Beacon Journal*, 16 Dec. 2020.
234. Watkins, M. D., and King C. Brown. "'A Comparison of Visual Enhancement Chemicals for the Recovery of Possible Blood Stains at the Crime Scene' Luminol vs. BlueStar." *Bluestar-Forensic*, www.bluestar-forensic.com/wp-content/uploads/2020/09/watkins_brown_luminol_bs.pdf.
235. Watson, Christopher, and Shari Forbes. "An Investigation of the Vegetation Association with Grave Sites in Southern Ontario." *Canadian Society of Forensic Science Journal*, vol. 41, no. 4, 2008.
236. Westervelt, Eric. "More People Are Getting away with Murder: Unsolved Killings Reach a Record High." *NPR*, 30 Apr. 2023, www.npr.org/2023/04/29/1172775448/people-murder-unsolved-killings-record-high.

237. Whitaker, Barbara. "Ex Therapist Makes Deal to Avoid Death Penalty in Hospital Killings." *The New York Times*, 13 Mar. 2002.
238. Wolf, Jody. "Tackling Employee Wellness." Phoenix Police Department. January 2025. Webinar.
239. Yifat, Bitton, and Dayan Hava. "'The Perfect Murder': An Exploratory Study of Staged Murder Scenes and Concealed Femicide." *The British Journal of Criminology*, vol. 59, no. 5, 2019, pp. 1054–1075, https://doi.org/10.1093/bjc/azz015.
240. Yonah, J. B. "Supreme Court Upholds Murder Conviction of First, Third Wife." *The Jerusalem Post*, 2022.
241. Van Sant, Peter. "S.C. Nurse Who Fatally Poisoned Husband with Eye Drops: 'I Just Wanted Him to Suffer'." *CBS News*, 29 Jul. 2023, www.cbsnews.com/news/lana-steve-clayton-eye-drop-poison-suffer-48-hours/.
242. Zeldes, I., and D. Stoner. "Speedometer Examination—an Aid in Accident Investigation." *FBI Law Enforcement Bulletin*, vol. 49, no. 3, 1980, pp. 11–15.

Index

Note: Page numbers in *italics* indicate a figure on the corresponding page.

C

D

E

M

N

O

P

Q

R

U

V